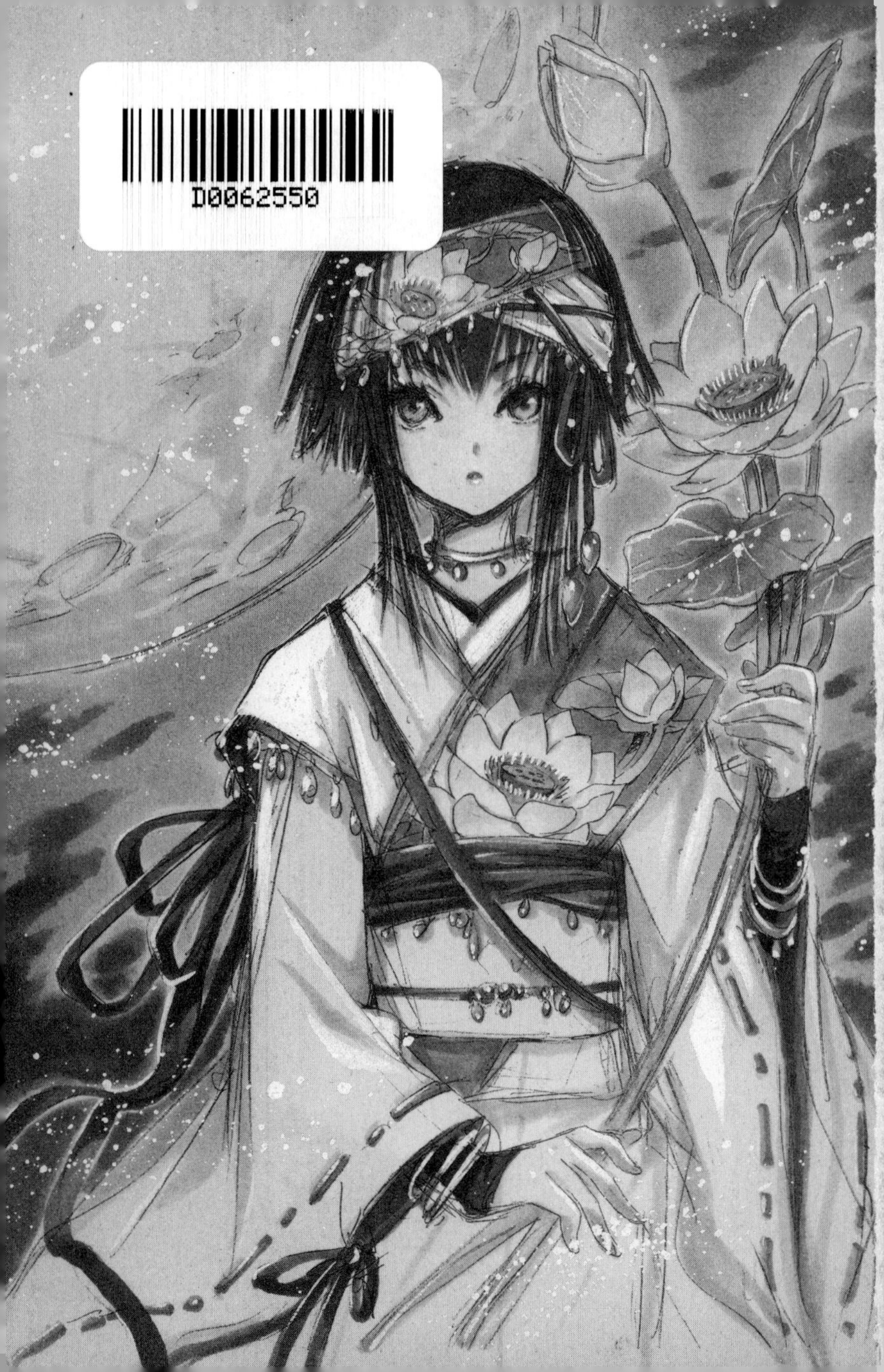

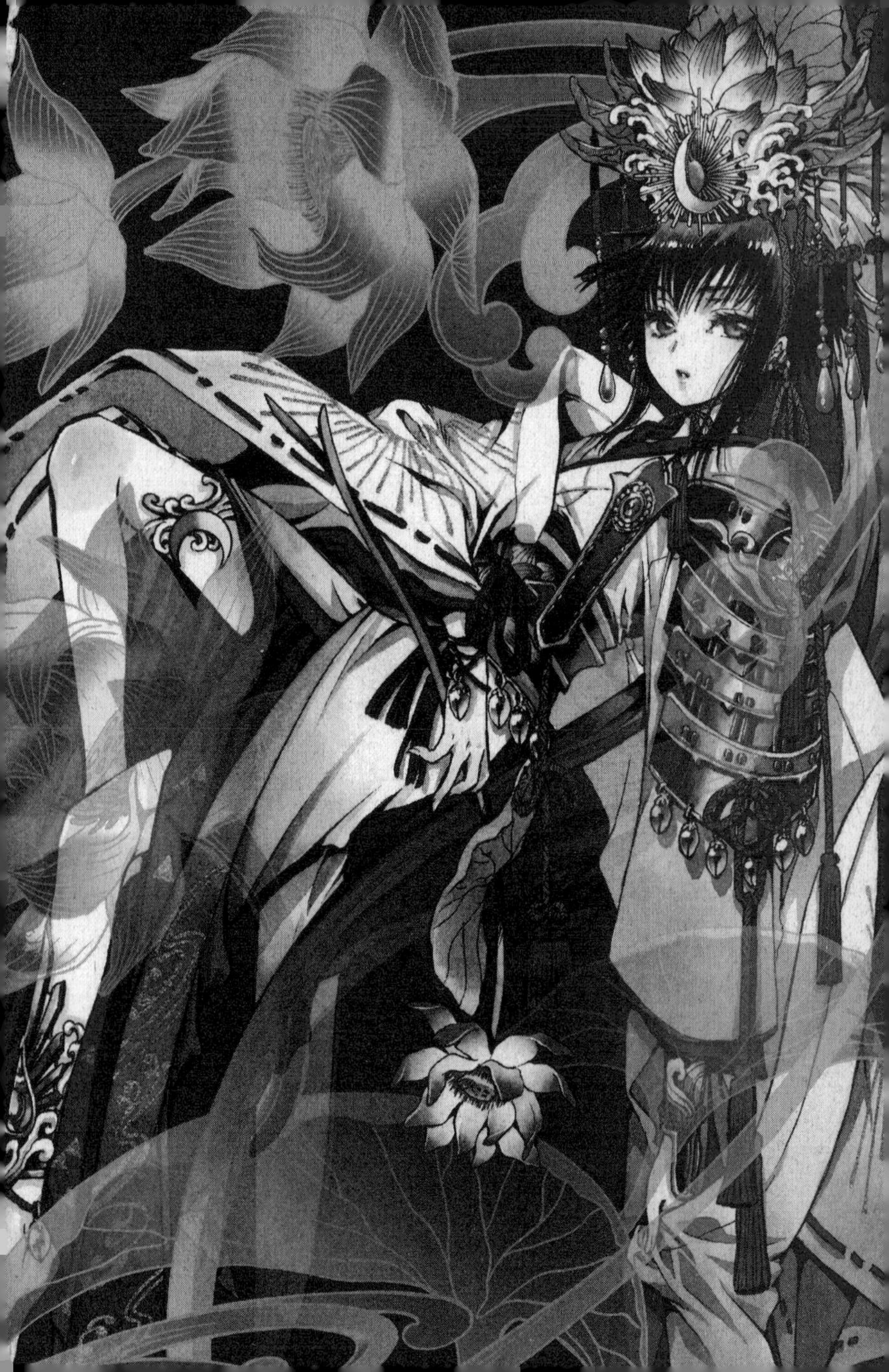

GATE 7 ①

TRANSLATION BY **WILLIAM FLANAGAN**
ENGLISH ADAPTATION BY **WILLIAM FLANAGAN & PHILIP SIMON**
LETTERING BY **STEVE DUTRO**

 CONTENTS

PUBLISHER **MIKE RICHARDSON**

EDITOR **PHILIP SIMON**

ASSISTANT EDITOR **JOHN SCHORK**

COLLECTION DESIGNER **TINA ALESSI**

DIGITAL PRODUCTION **RYAN JORGENSEN**

Special thanks to Michael Gombos, Annie Gullion, Carl Gustav Horn, Chris Horn, and Jeremy Niece.

GATE 7 VOLUME 1

Dark Horse Manga, a division of Dark Horse Comics, Inc.
10956 SE Main Street, Milwaukie, OR 97222
DarkHorse.com

To find a comics shop in your area, call the Comic Shop Locator Service toll-free at 1-888-266-4226.

First edition: October 2011
ISBN 978-1-59582-806-4

10 9 8 7 6 5 4 3 2 1

Printed at Lake Book Manufacturing, Inc., Melrose Park, IL, USA

GATE 7
ゲート セブン

CLAMP

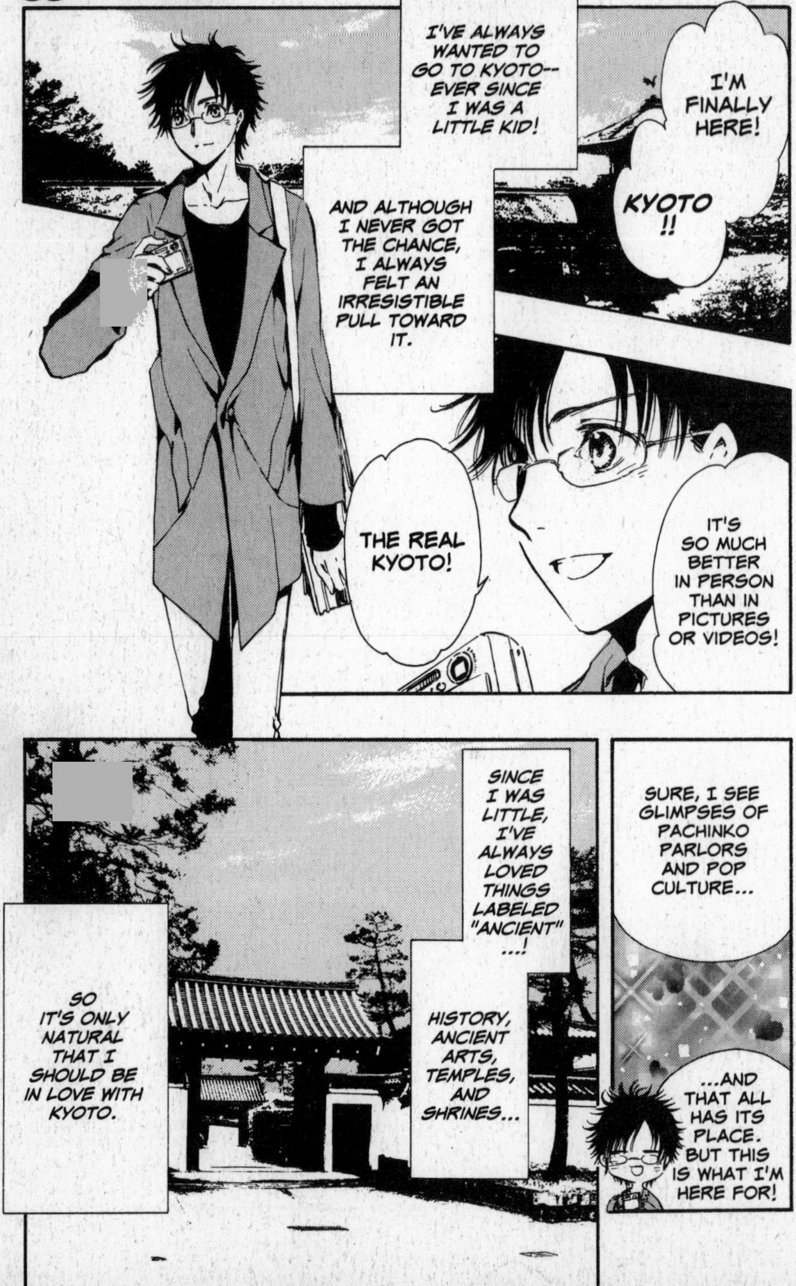
I'M FINALLY HERE!
KYOTO!!
I'VE ALWAYS WANTED TO GO TO KYOTO--EVER SINCE I WAS A LITTLE KID!
AND ALTHOUGH I NEVER GOT THE CHANCE, I ALWAYS FELT AN IRRESISTIBLE PULL TOWARD IT.
IT'S SO MUCH BETTER IN PERSON THAN IN PICTURES OR VIDEOS!
THE REAL KYOTO!
SURE, I SEE GLIMPSES OF PACHINKO PARLORS AND POP CULTURE...
...AND THAT ALL HAS ITS PLACE. BUT THIS IS WHAT I'M HERE FOR!
SINCE I WAS LITTLE, I'VE ALWAYS LOVED THINGS LABELED "ANCIENT"...!
HISTORY, ANCIENT ARTS, TEMPLES, AND SHRINES...
SO IT'S ONLY NATURAL THAT I SHOULD BE IN LOVE WITH KYOTO.

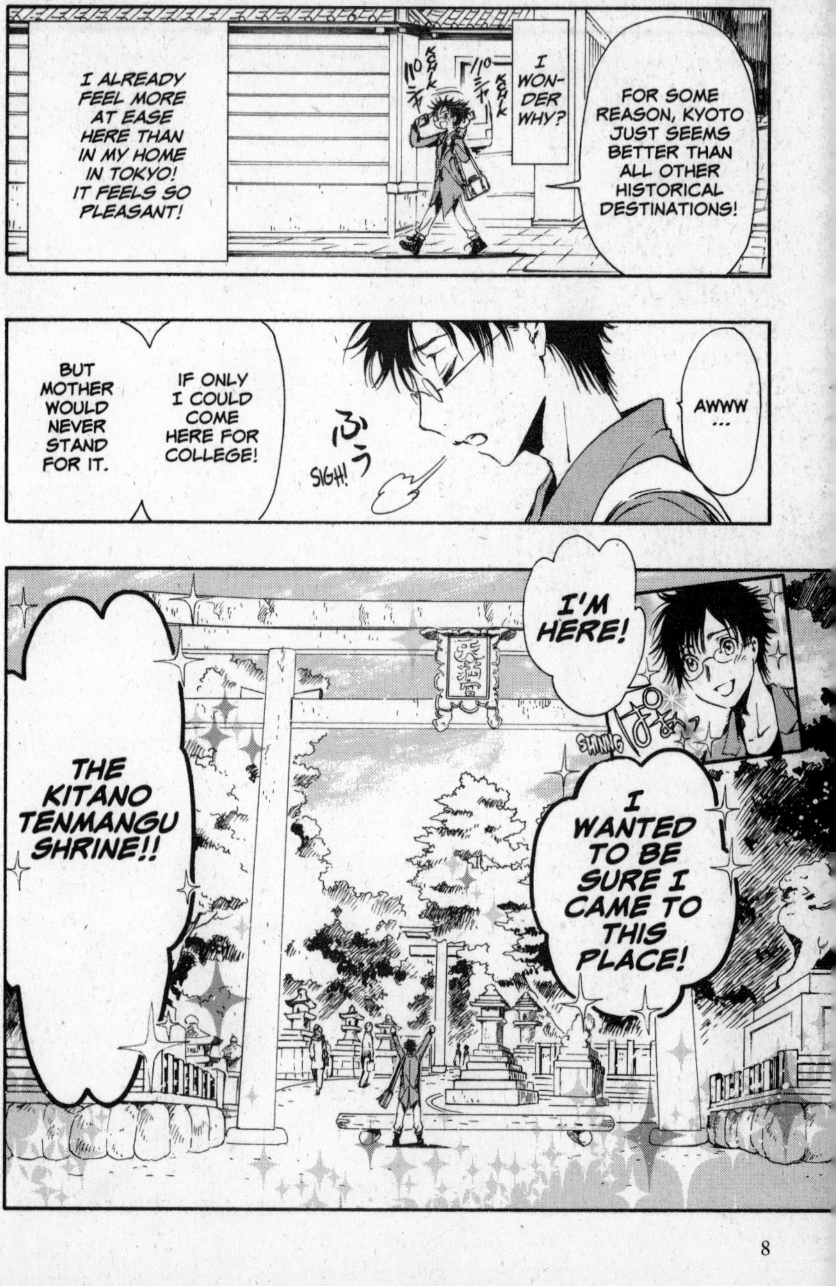
FOR SOME REASON, KYOTO JUST SEEMS BETTER THAN ALL OTHER HISTORICAL DESTINATIONS!
I WONDER WHY?
KCHIK
KCHIK
I ALREADY FEEL MORE AT EASE HERE THAN IN MY HOME IN TOKYO! IT FEELS SO PLEASANT!
AWWW ...
SIGH!
IF ONLY I COULD COME HERE FOR COLLEGE!
BUT MOTHER WOULD NEVER STAND FOR IT.
I'M HERE!
I WANTED TO BE SURE I CAME TO THIS PLACE!
THE KITANO TENMANGU SHRINE!!

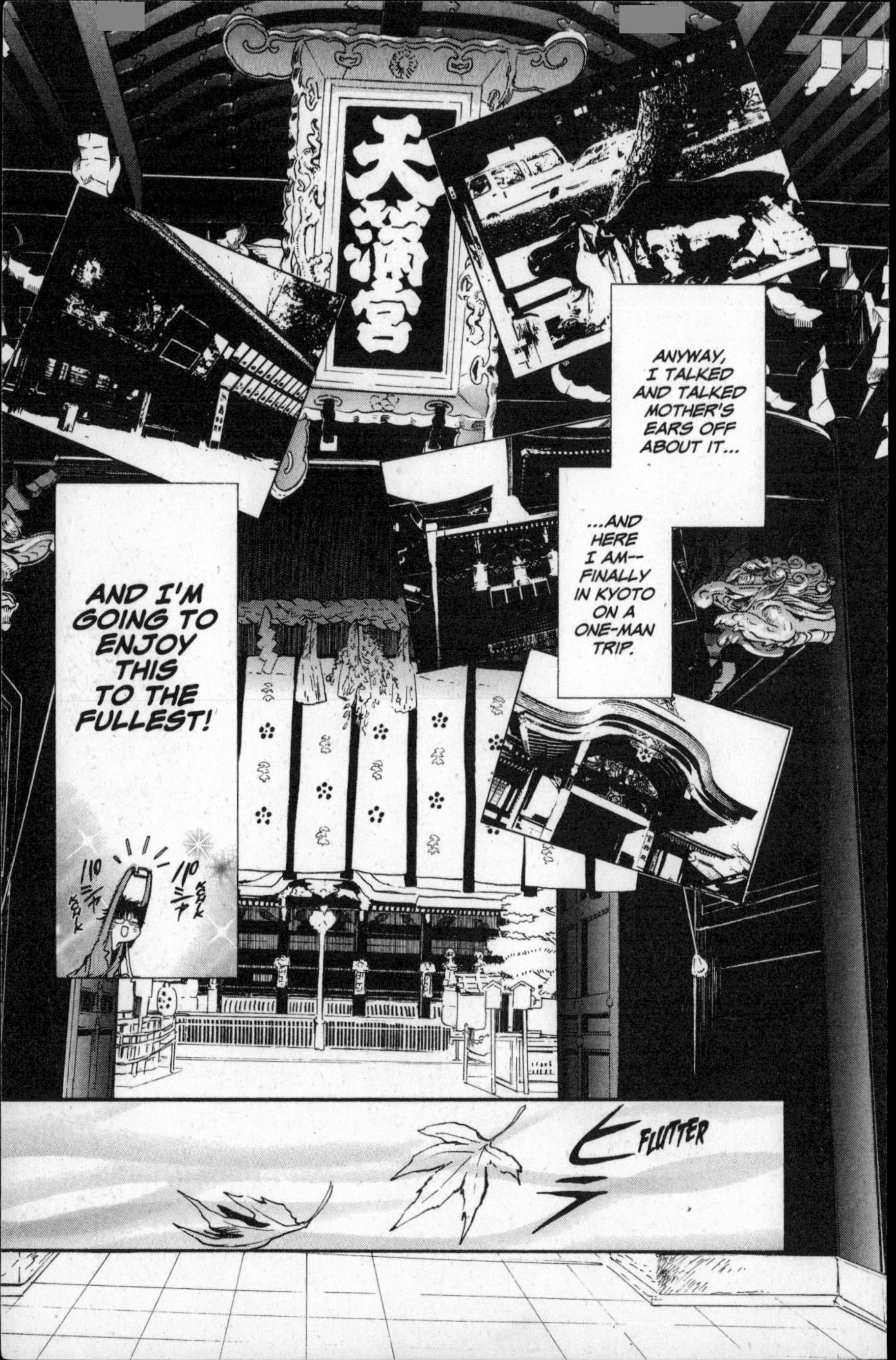
天満宮
ANYWAY, I TALKED AND TALKED MOTHER'S EARS OFF ABOUT IT...
...AND HERE I AM-- FINALLY IN KYOTO ON A ONE-MAN TRIP.
AND I'M GOING TO ENJOY THIS TO THE FULLEST!
KSHK
KSHK
FLUTTER

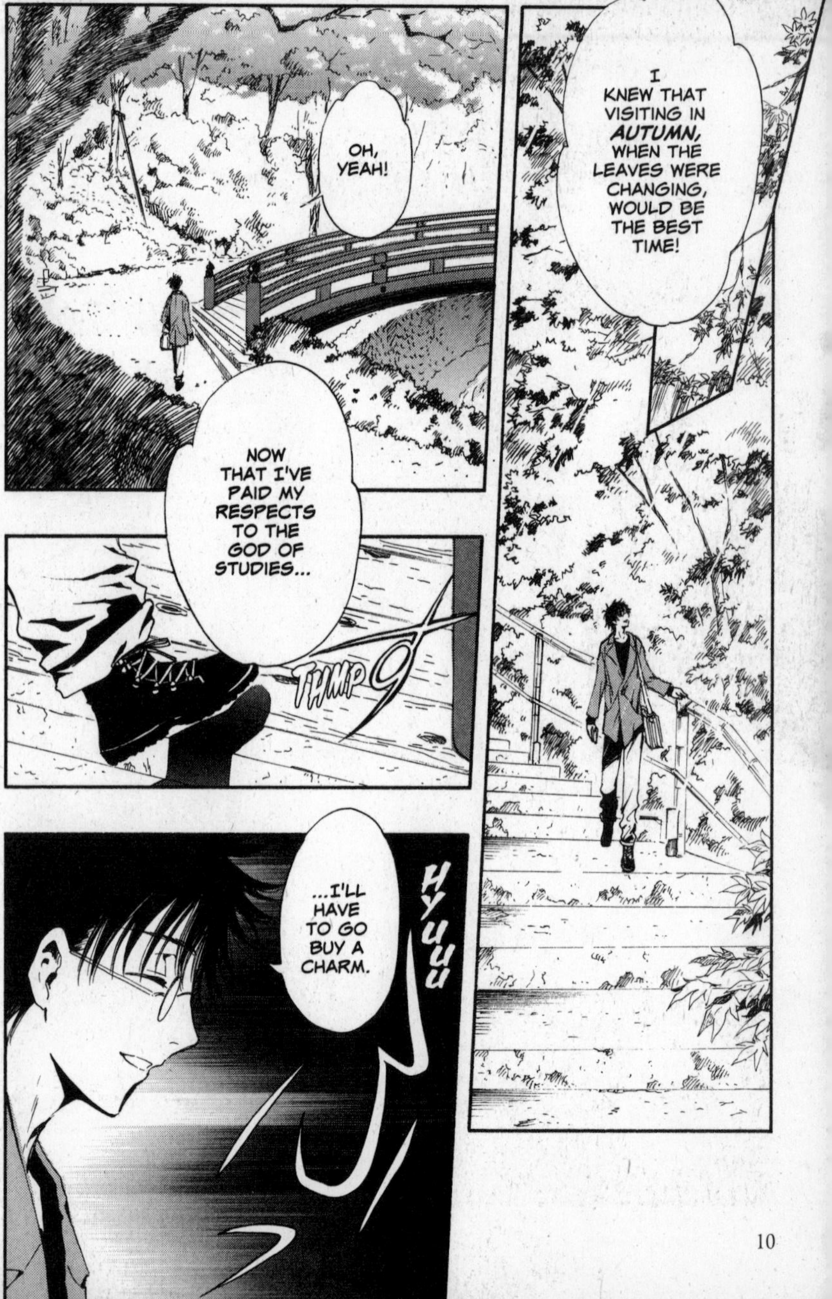

I KNEW THAT VISITING IN AUTUMN, WHEN THE LEAVES WERE CHANGING, WOULD BE THE BEST TIME!
OH, YEAH!
NOW THAT I'VE PAID MY RESPECTS TO THE GOD OF STUDIES...
THMP
...I'LL HAVE TO GO BUY A CHARM.
HYUUU

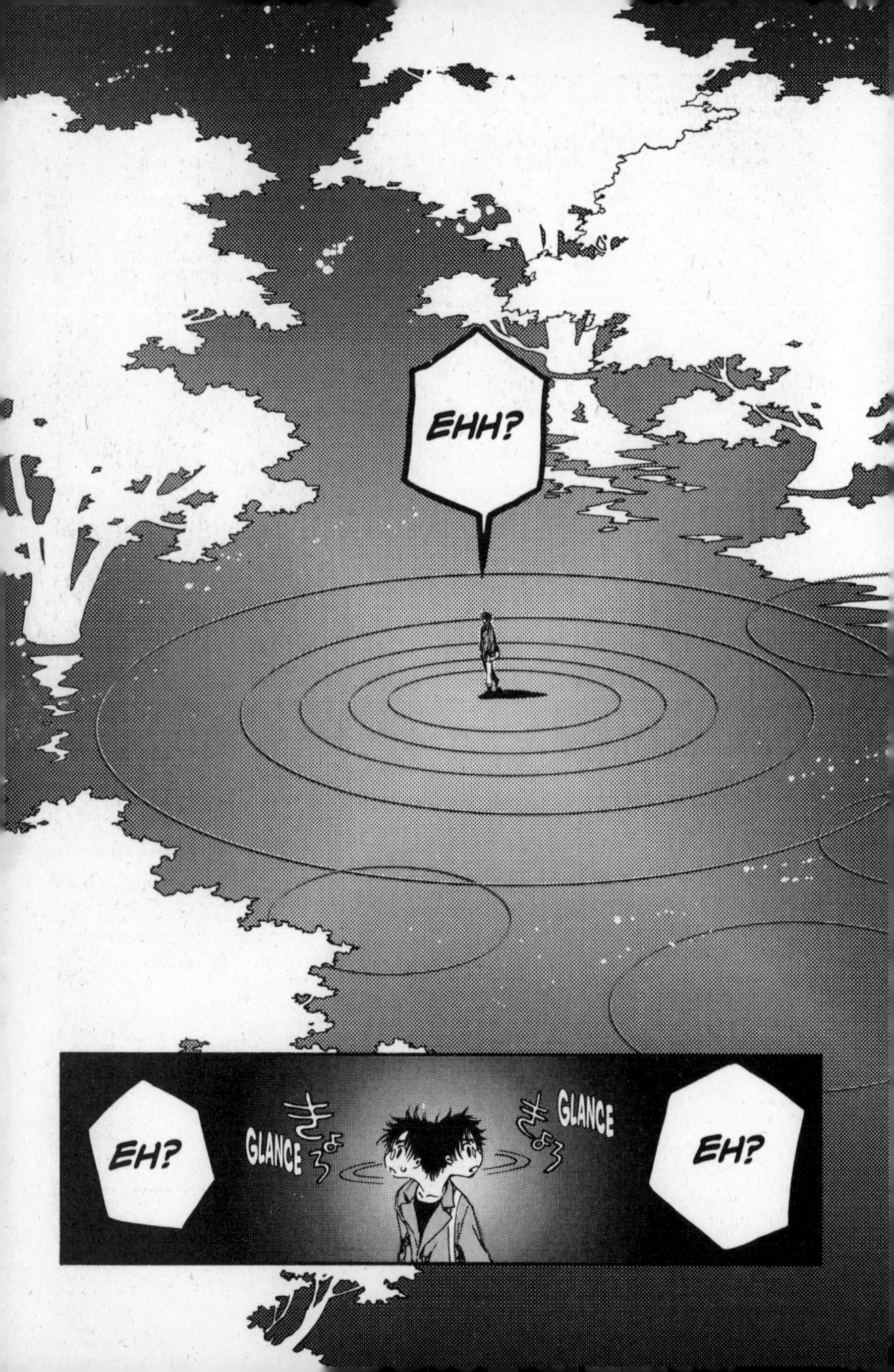
EHH?
EH?
きょろ
GLANCE
きょろ
GLANCE
EH?

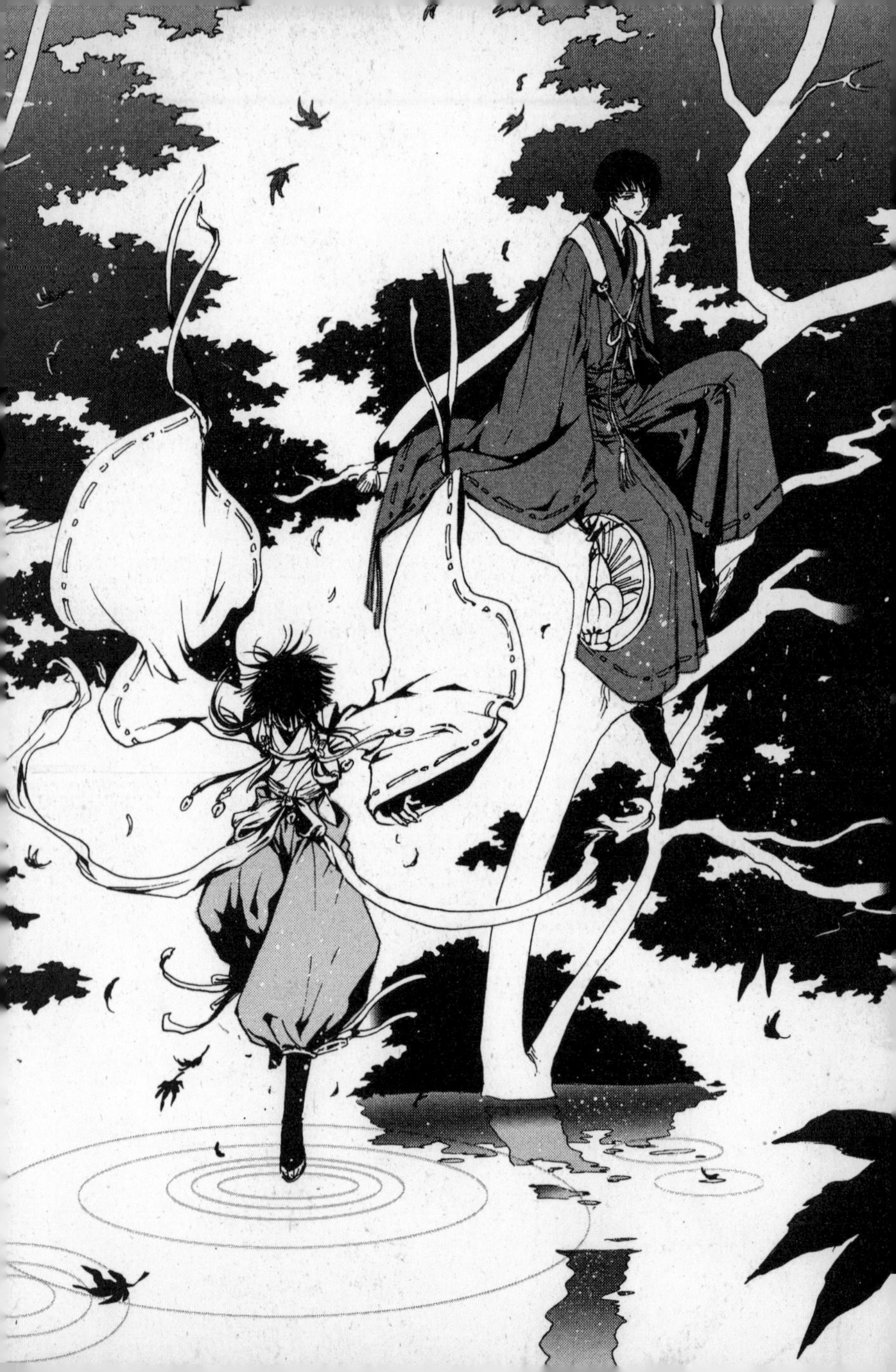

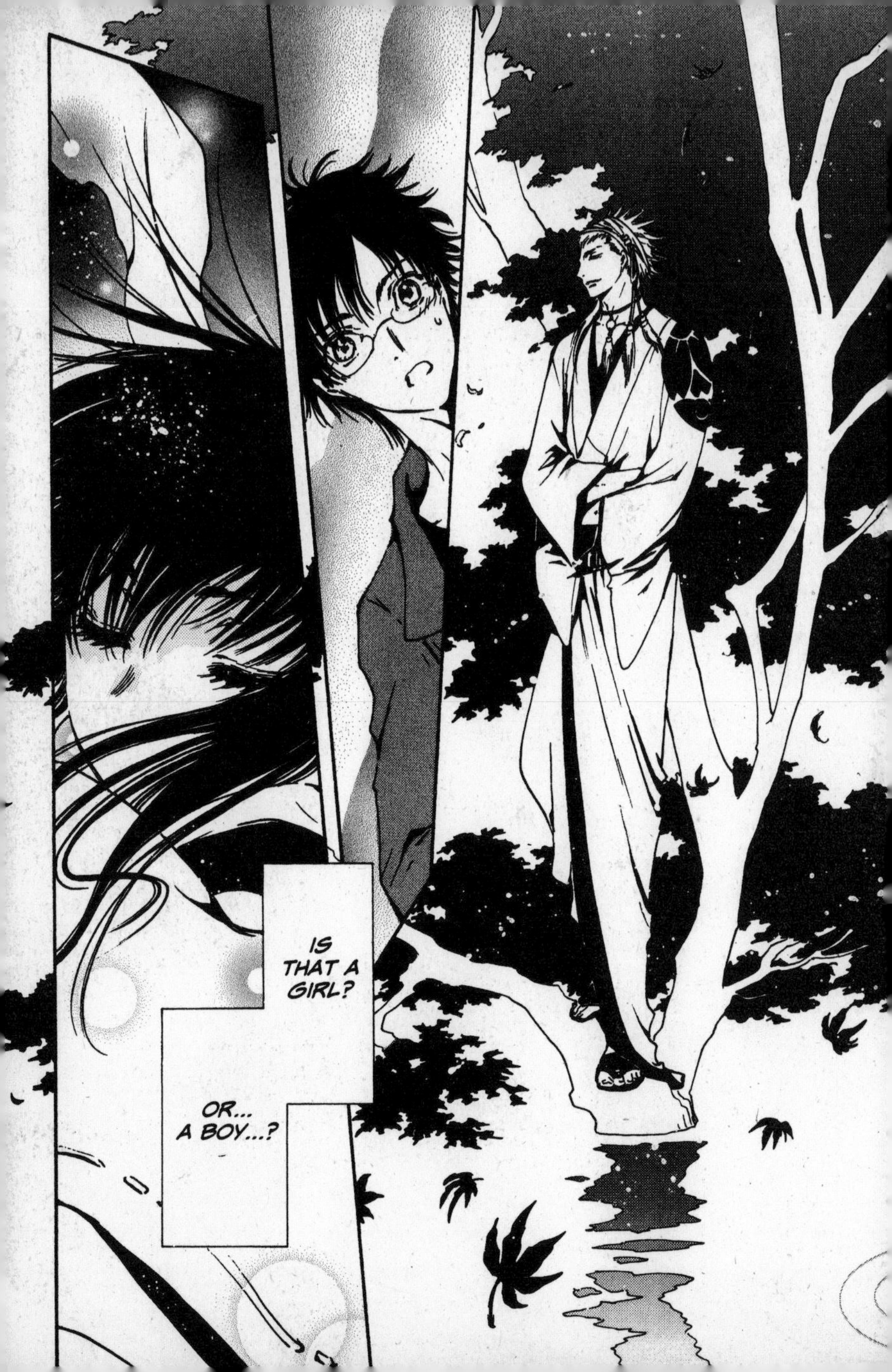
IS THAT A GIRL?
OR... A BOY...?

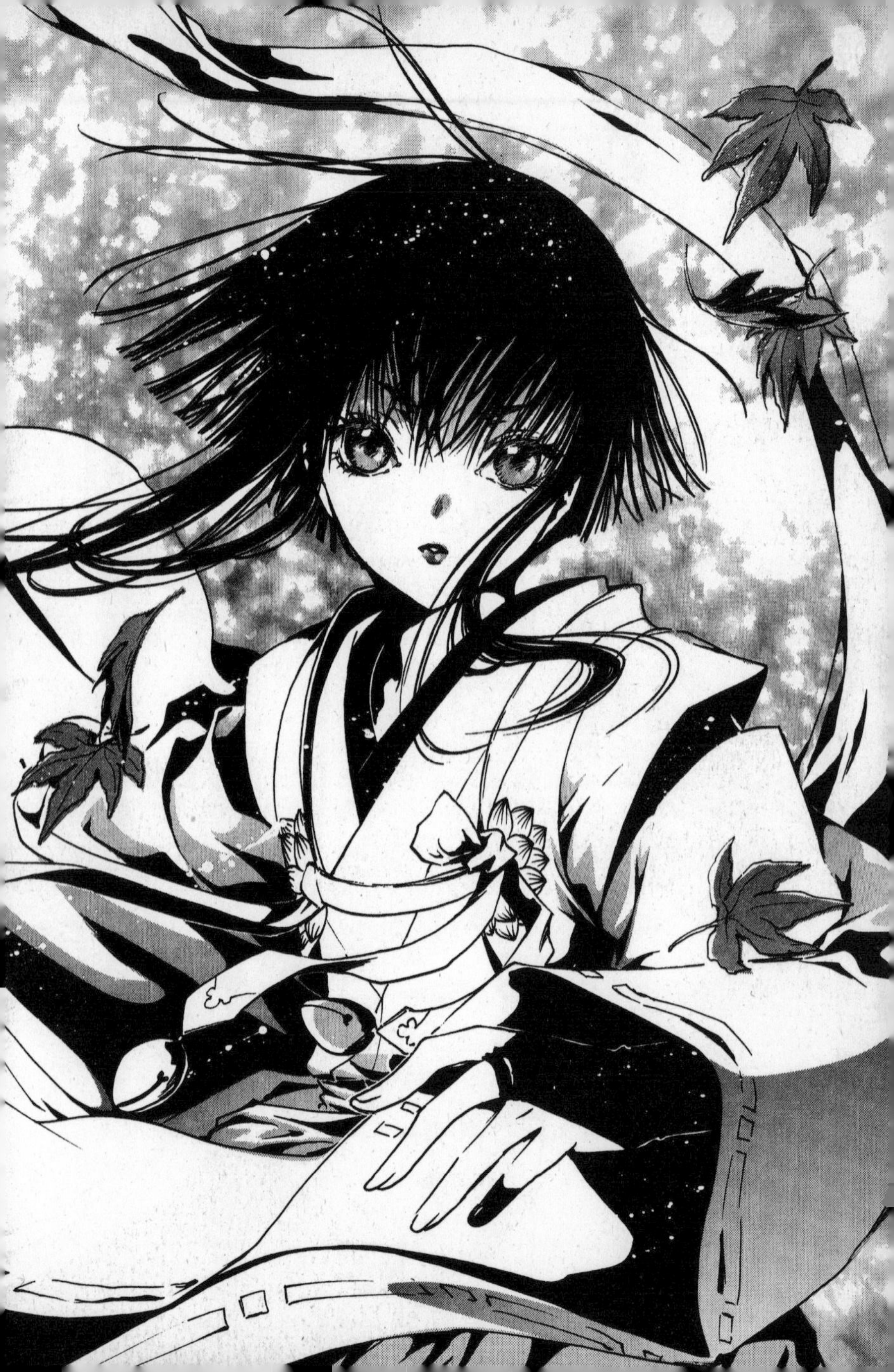

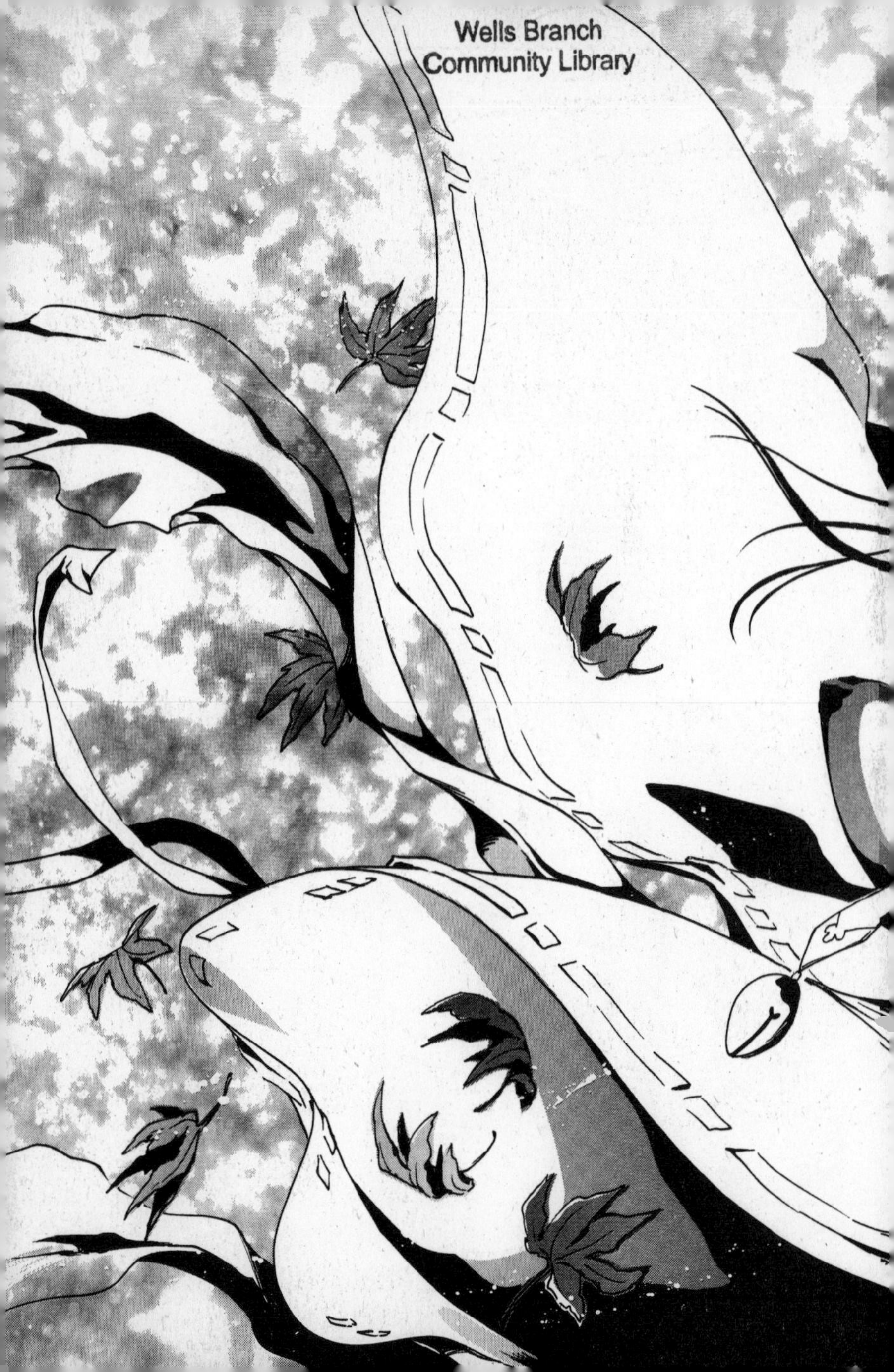

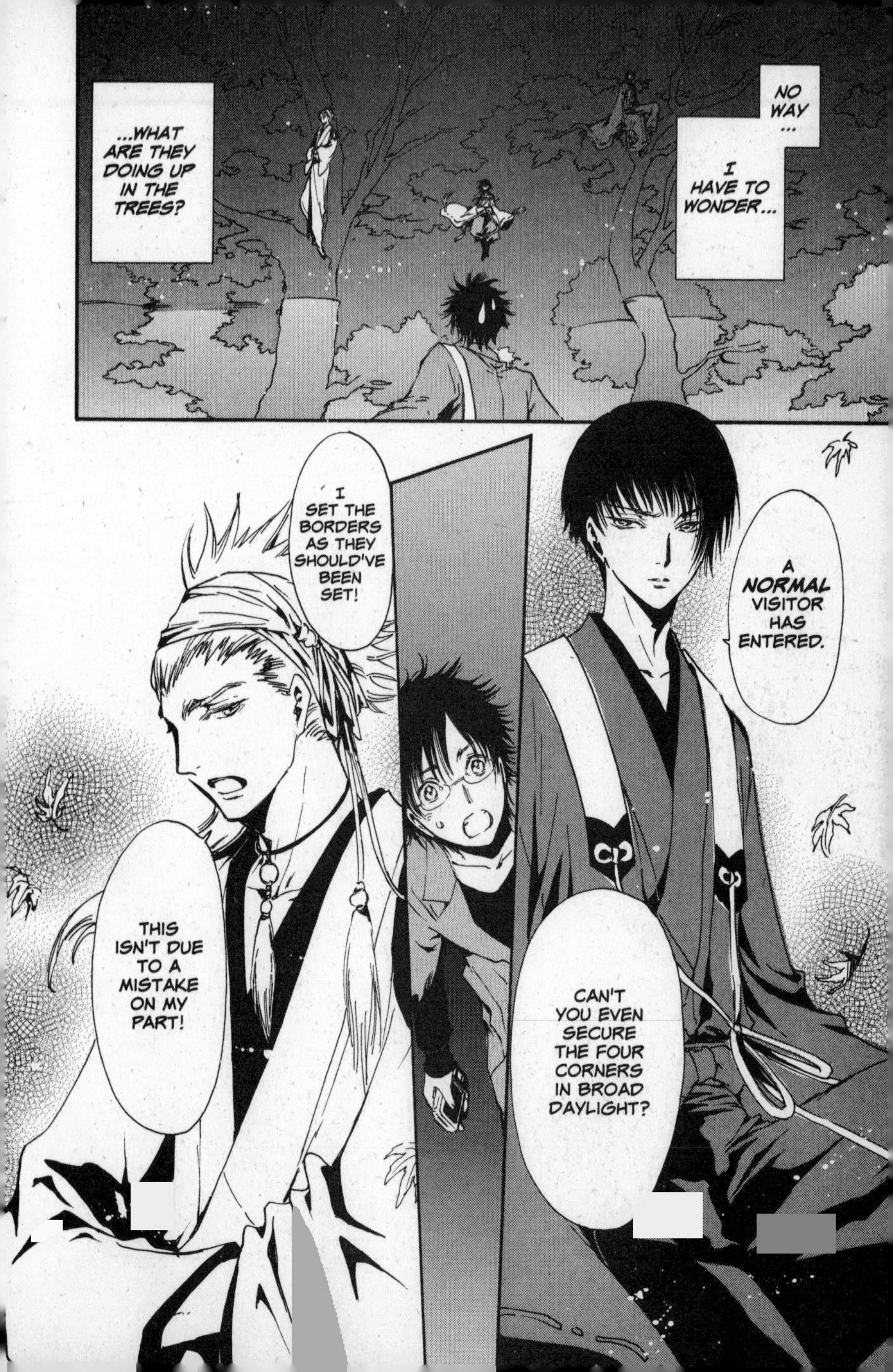
NO WAY...
I HAVE TO WONDER...
...WHAT ARE THEY DOING UP IN THE TREES?
A **NORMAL** VISITOR HAS ENTERED.
CAN'T YOU EVEN SECURE THE FOUR CORNERS IN BROAD DAYLIGHT?
THIS ISN'T DUE TO A MISTAKE ON MY PART!
I SET THE BORDERS AS THEY SHOULD'VE BEEN SET!

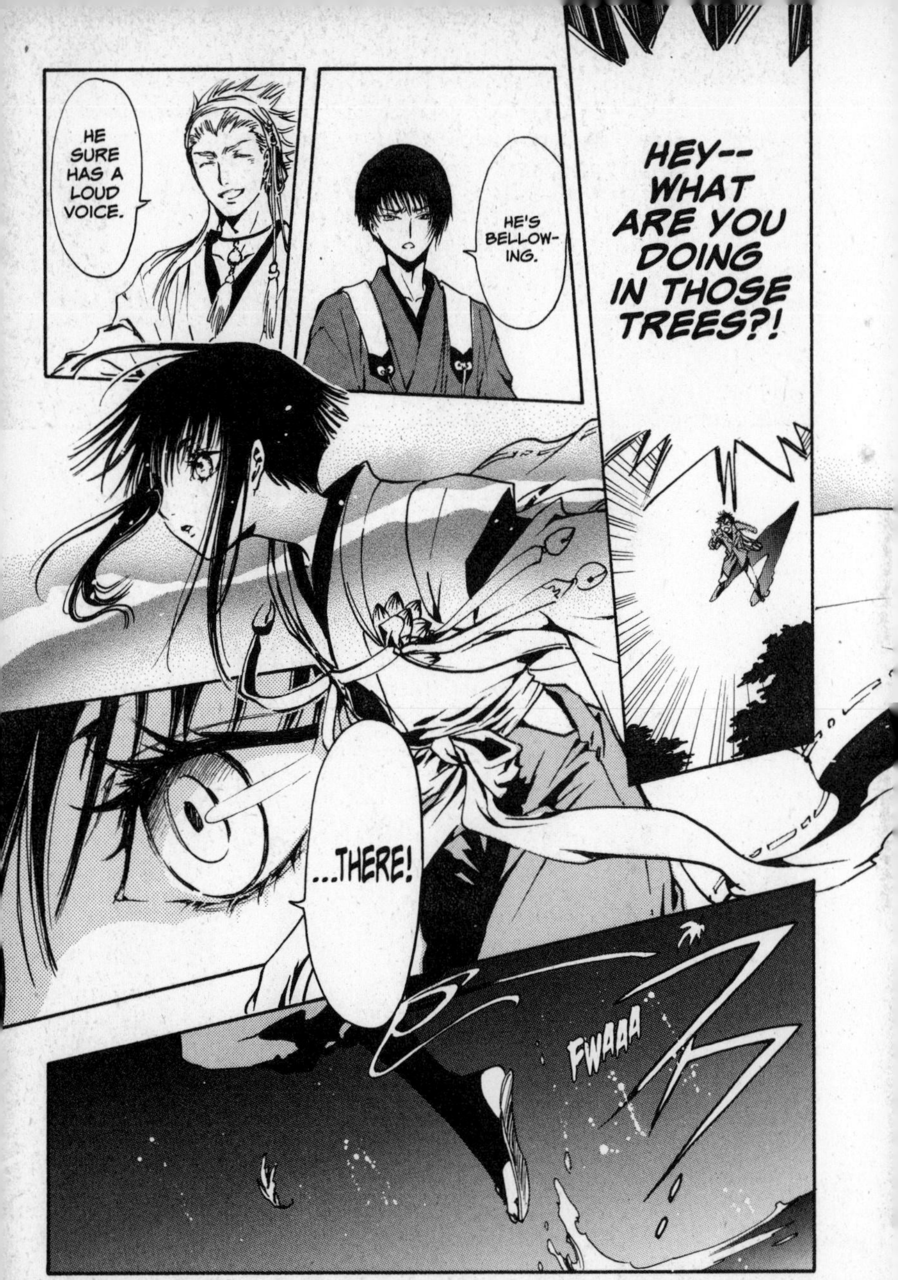
HEY-- WHAT ARE YOU DOING IN THOSE TREES?!
HE'S BELLOW-ING.
HE SURE HAS A LOUD VOICE.
...THERE!
FWAAA

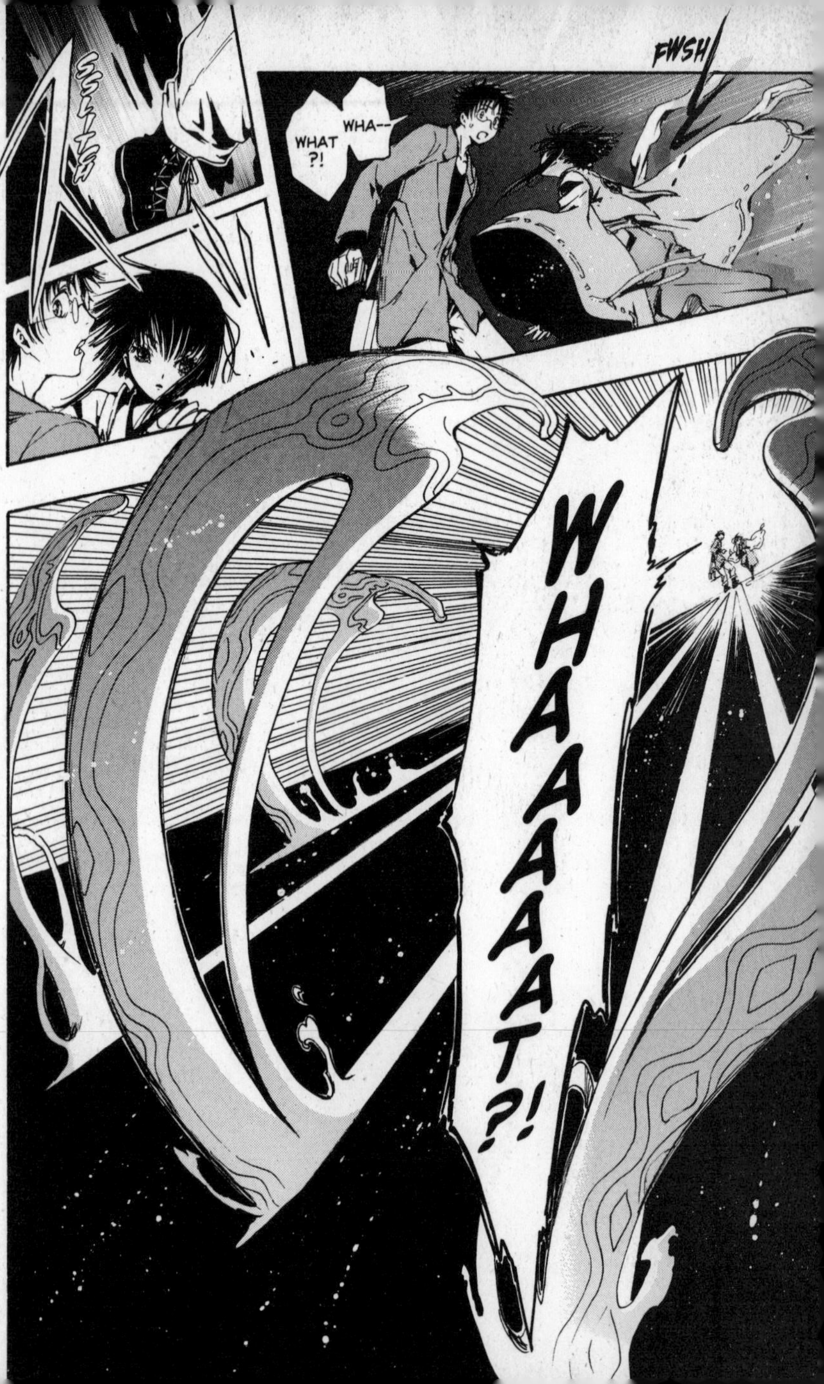
FWSH
WHA--
WHAT ?!
SSLITCH
WHAAAAAT?!

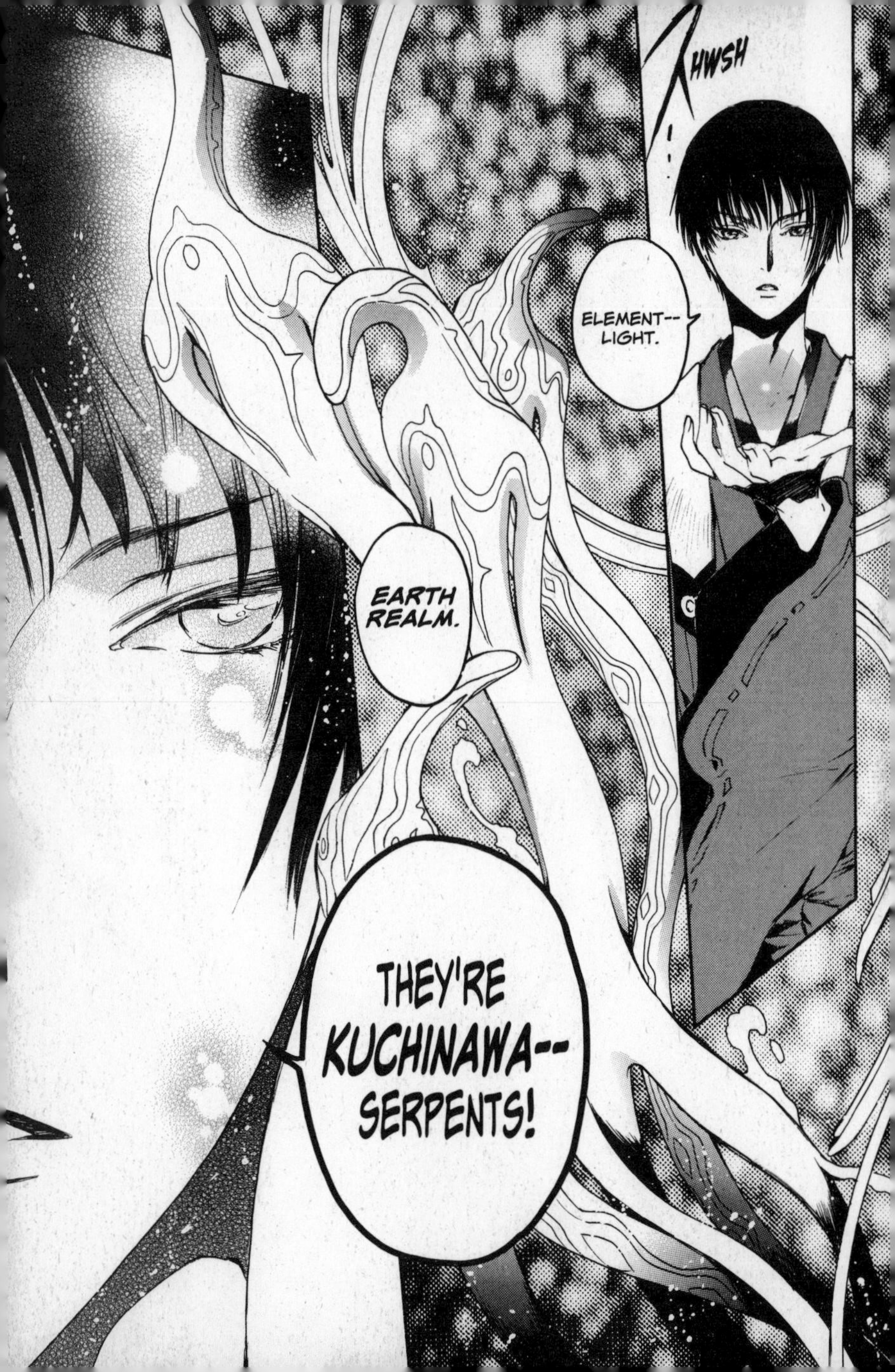
KHWSH
ELEMENT-- LIGHT.
EARTH REALM.
THEY'RE KUCHINAWA-- SERPENTS!

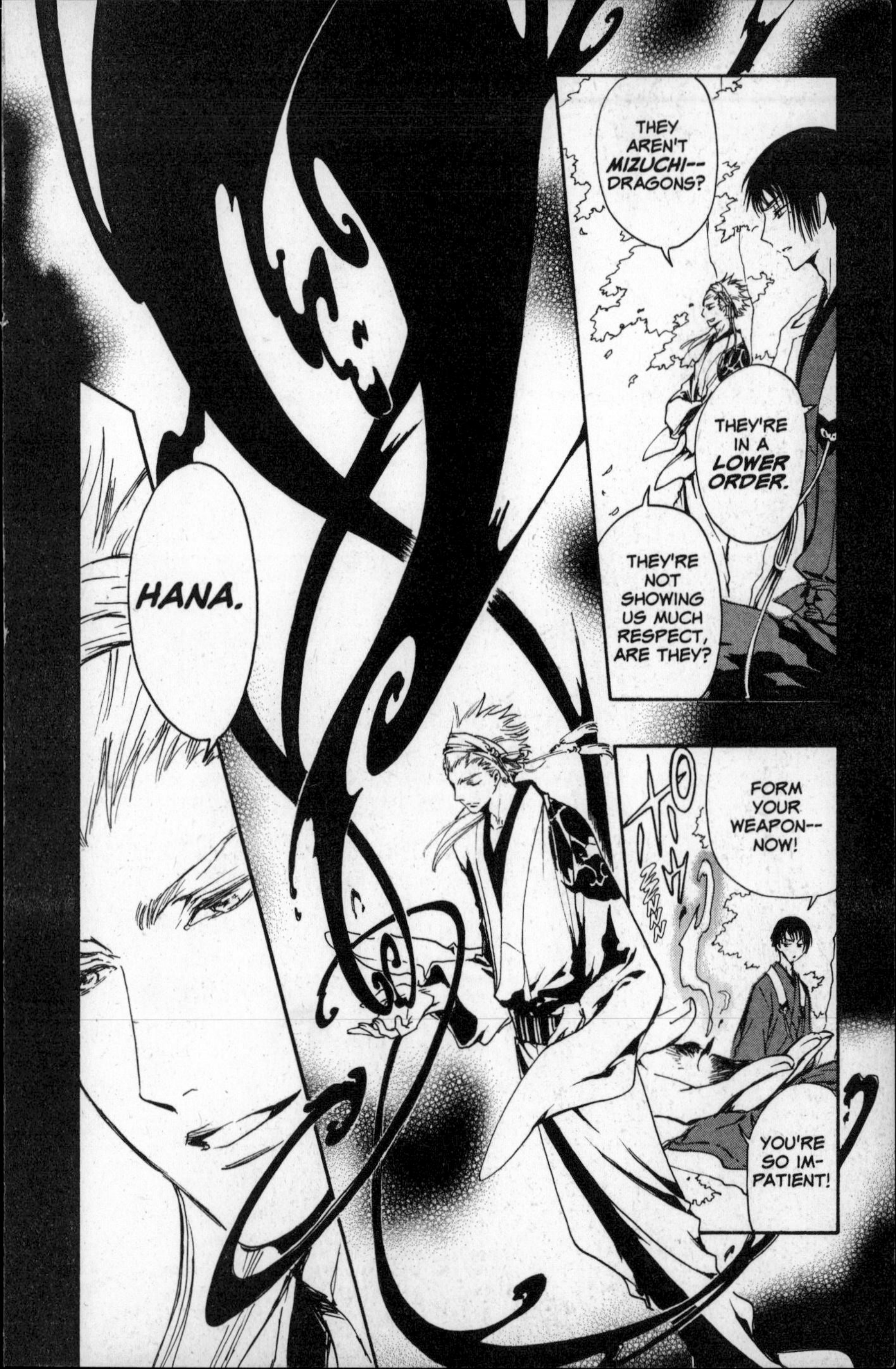
THEY AREN'T MIZUCHI--DRAGONS?
THEY'RE IN A LOWER ORDER.
THEY'RE NOT SHOWING US MUCH RESPECT, ARE THEY?
FORM YOUR WEAPON--NOW!
YOU'RE SO IM-PATIENT!
HANA.

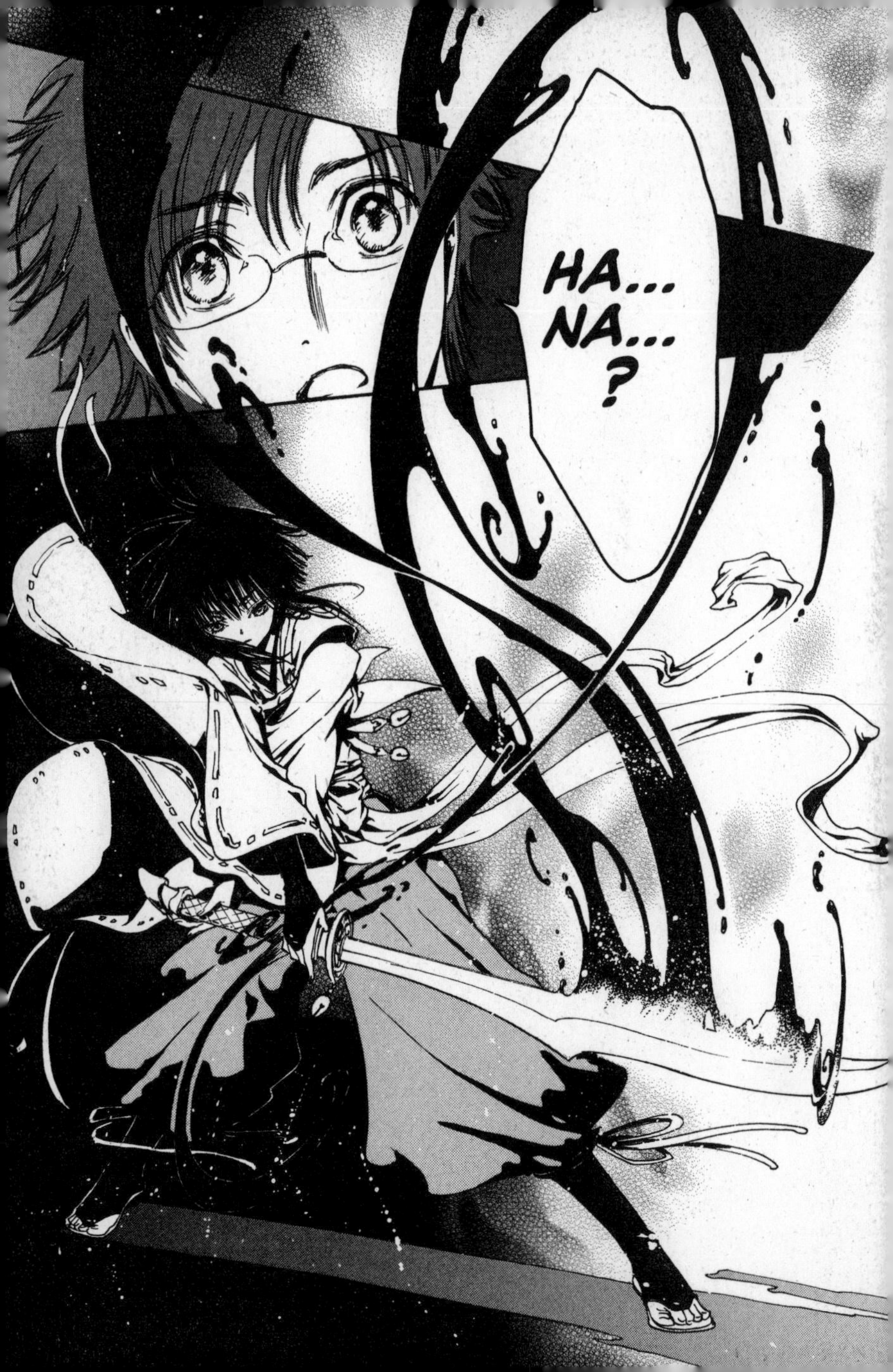
HA... NA... ?

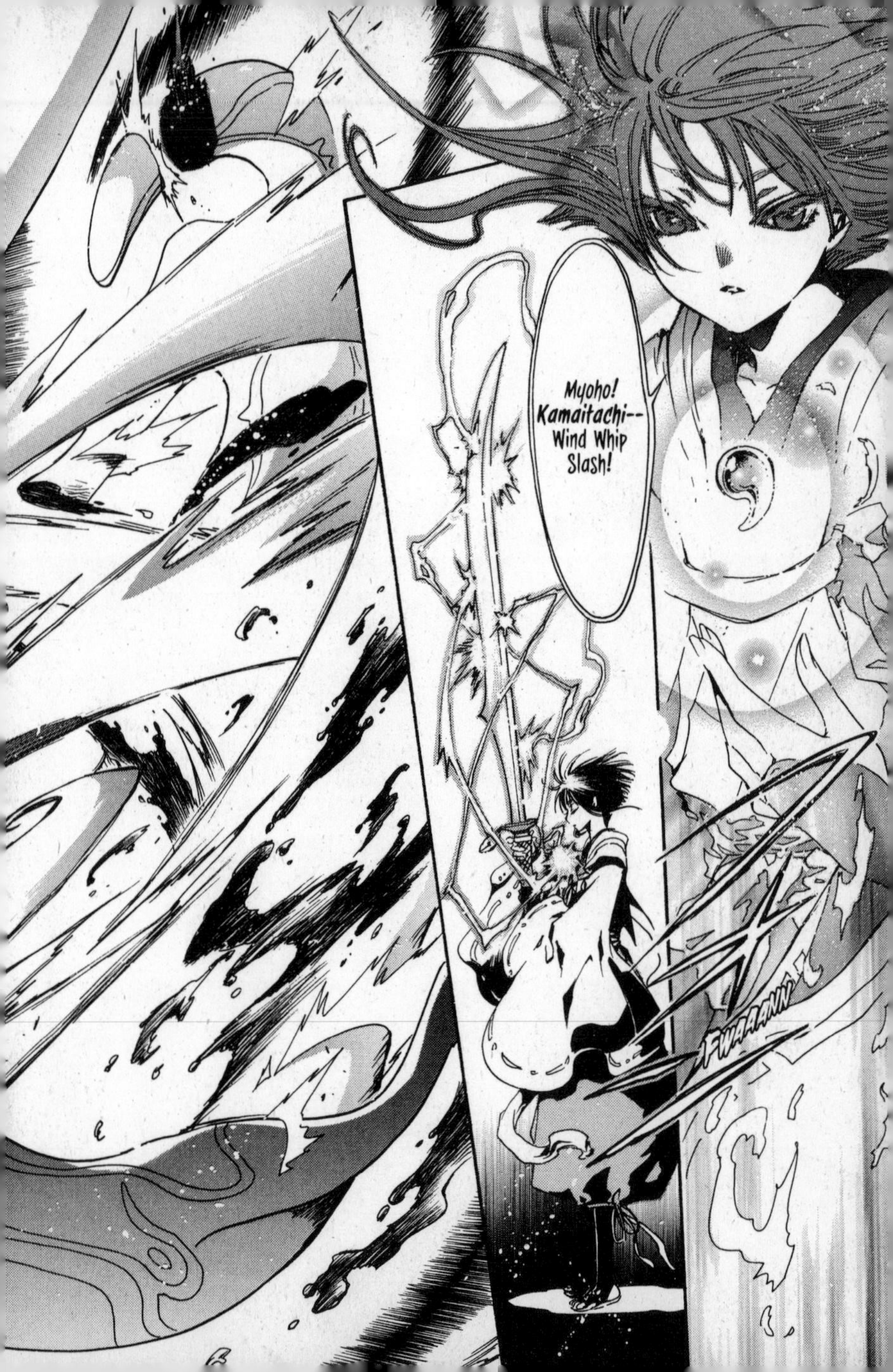
Myoho! Kamaitachi-- Wind Whip Slash!
FWAHANN

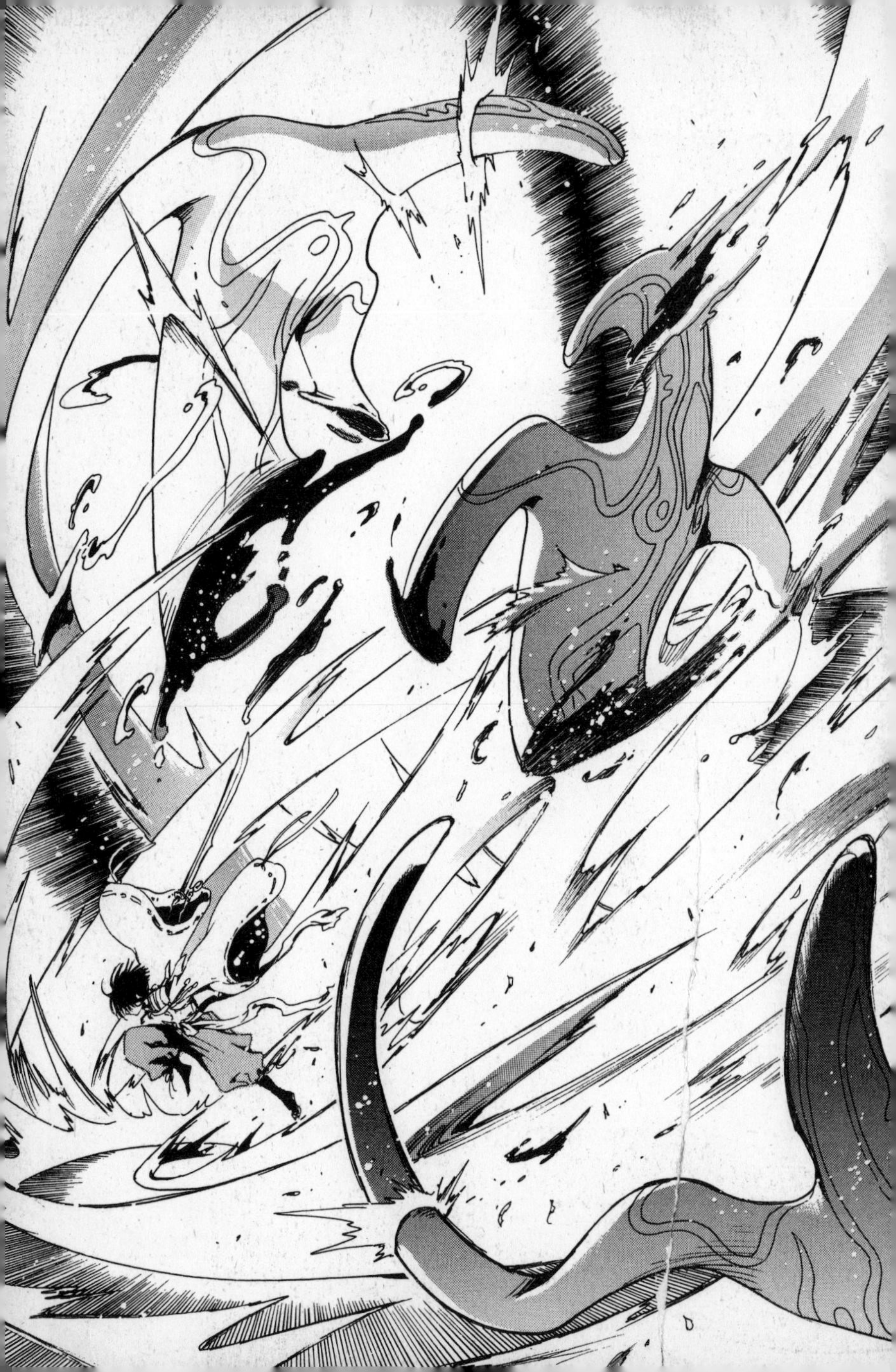

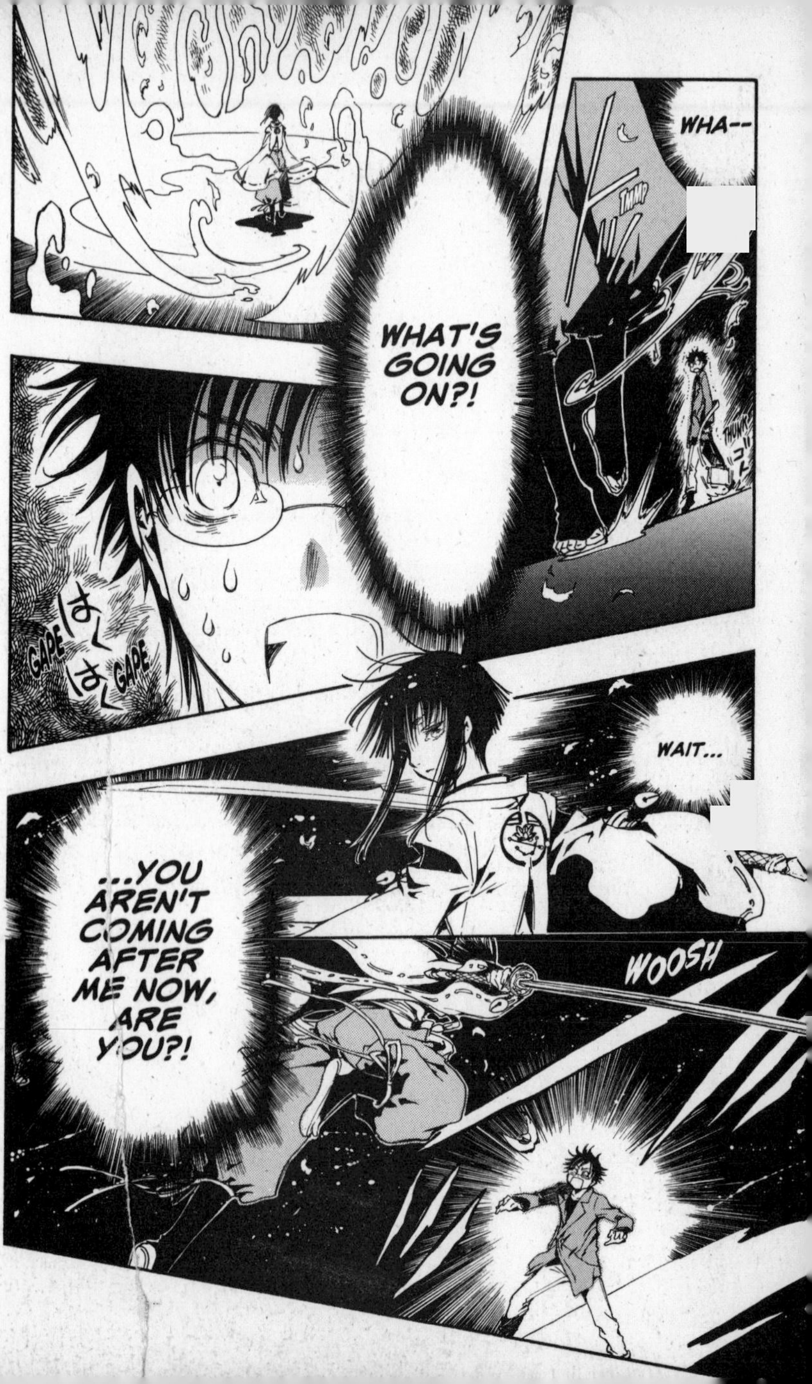
WHA--
TMMP
THUNK
WHAT'S GOING ON?!
GAPE
GAPE
WAIT...
...YOU AREN'T COMING AFTER ME NOW, ARE YOU?!
WOOSH

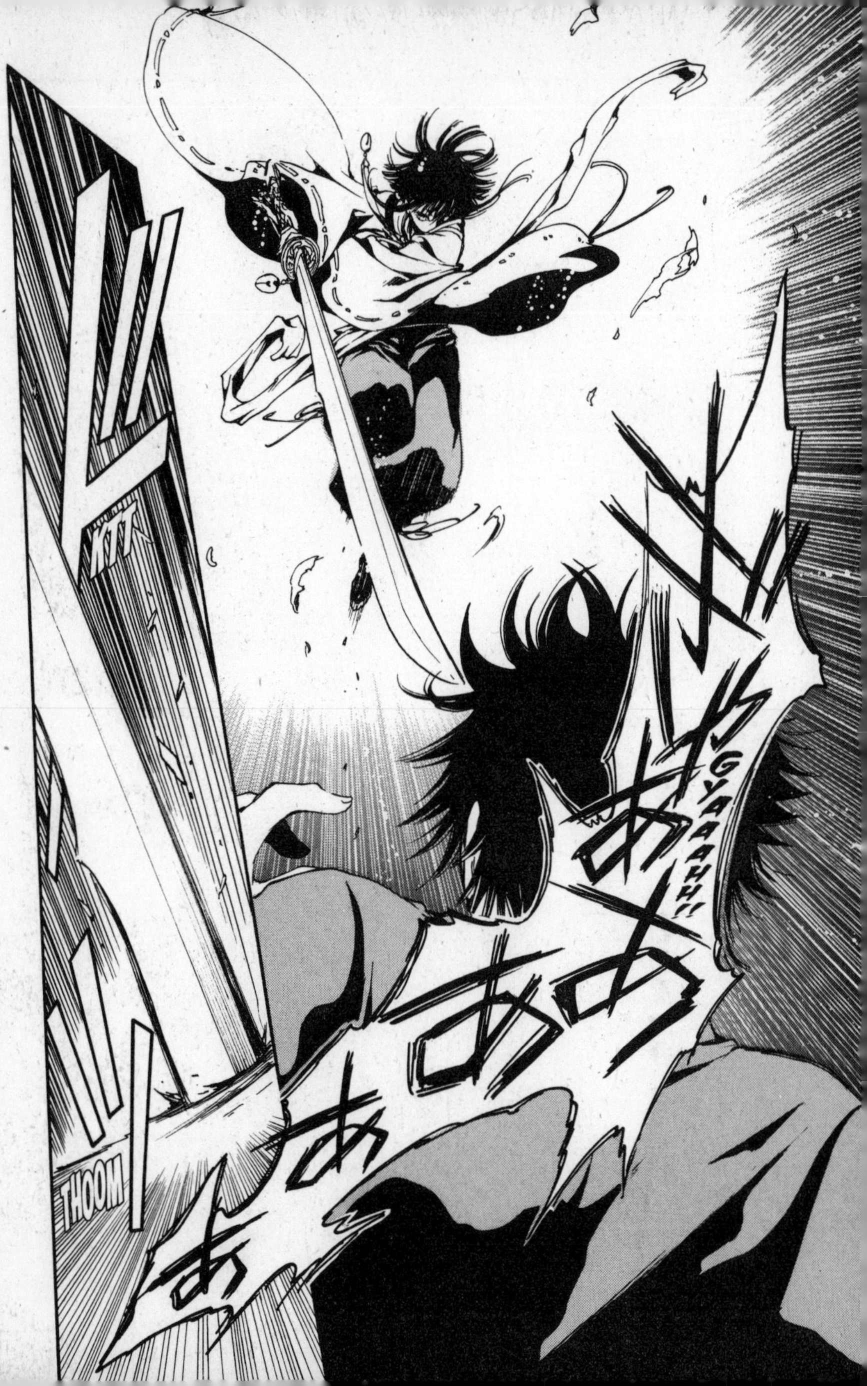
GYAAAAHH!!
KTT
THOOM

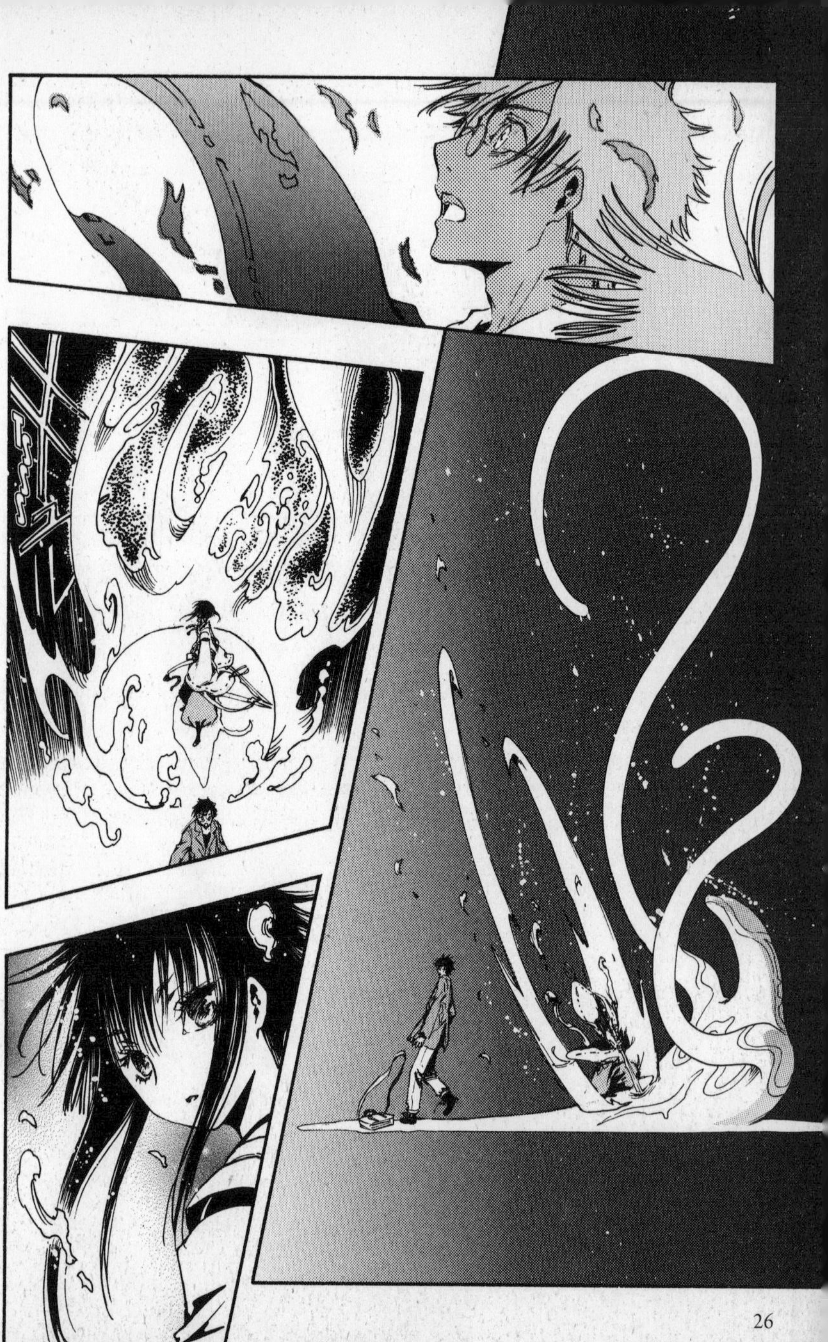
TSSSS

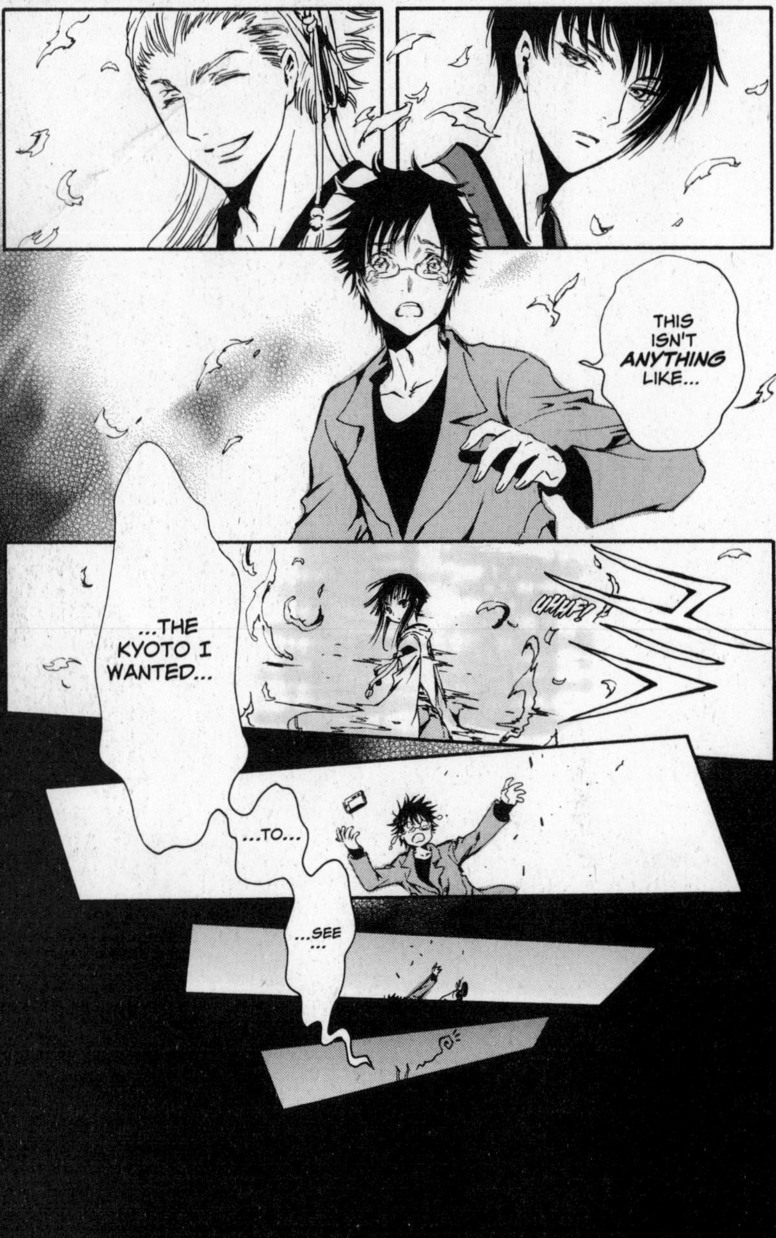
THIS ISN'T ANYTHING LIKE...
...THE KYOTO I WANTED...
...TO...
...SEE ...

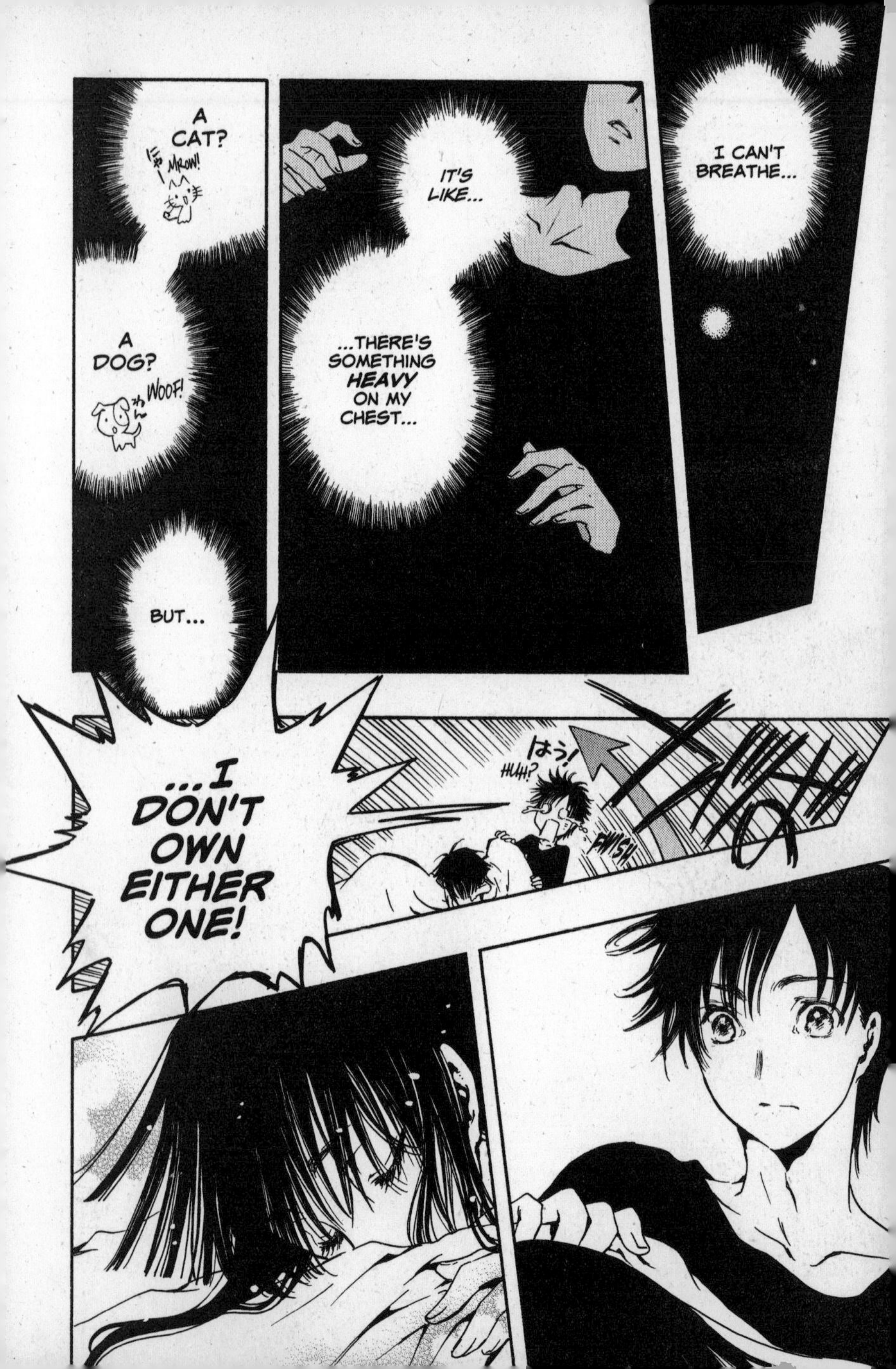
I CAN'T BREATHE...
IT'S LIKE...
...THERE'S SOMETHING HEAVY ON MY CHEST...
A CAT?
MROW!
A DOG?
WOOF!
BUT...
...I DON'T OWN EITHER ONE!
はう!
HUH?
FWISH!

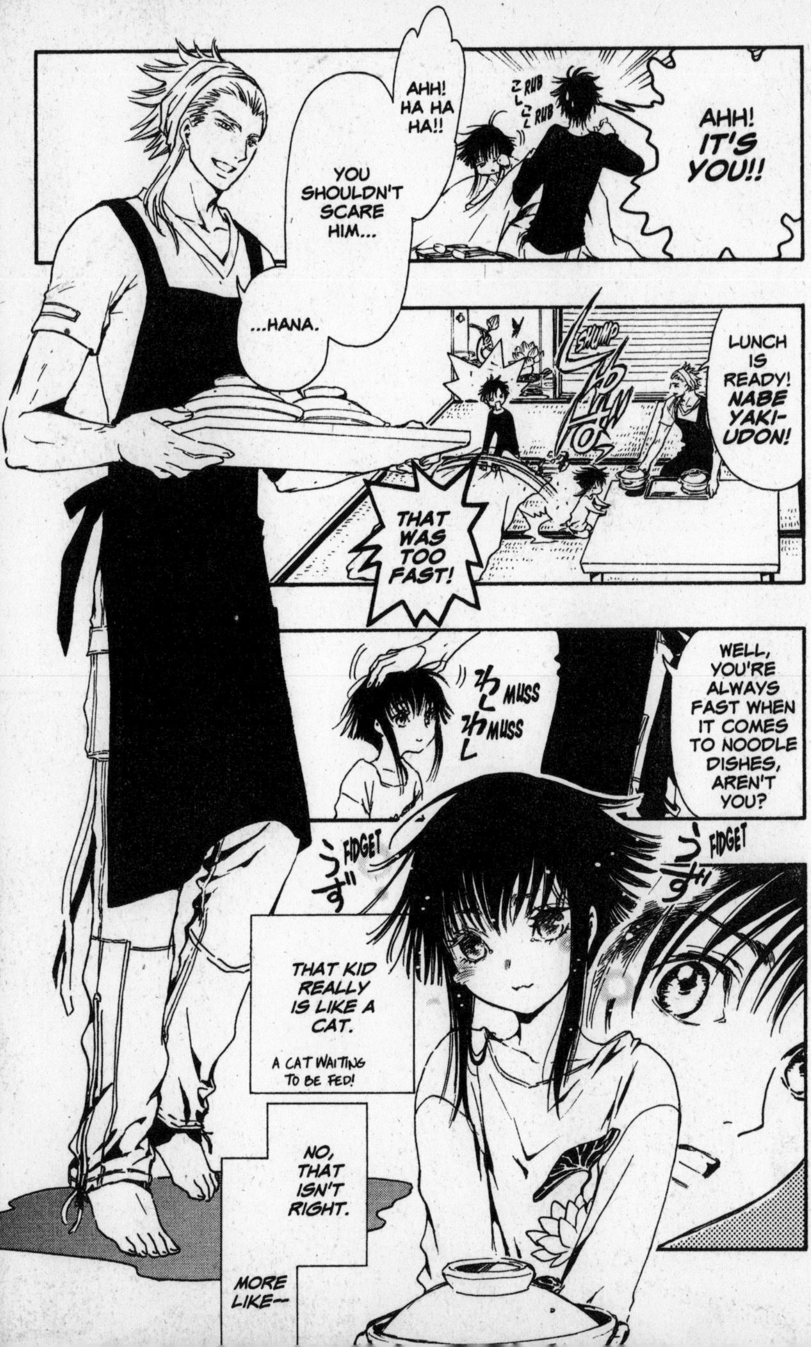
AHH! IT'S YOU!!
RUB RUB
AHH! HA HA HA!!
YOU SHOULDN'T SCARE HIM...
...HANA.
LUNCH IS READY! NABE YAKI-UDON!
SHUMP
THAT WAS TOO FAST!
WELL, YOU'RE ALWAYS FAST WHEN IT COMES TO NOODLE DISHES, AREN'T YOU?
MUSS MUSS
FIDGET
FIDGET
THAT KID REALLY IS LIKE A CAT.
A CAT WAITING TO BE FED!
NO, THAT ISN'T RIGHT.
MORE LIKE--

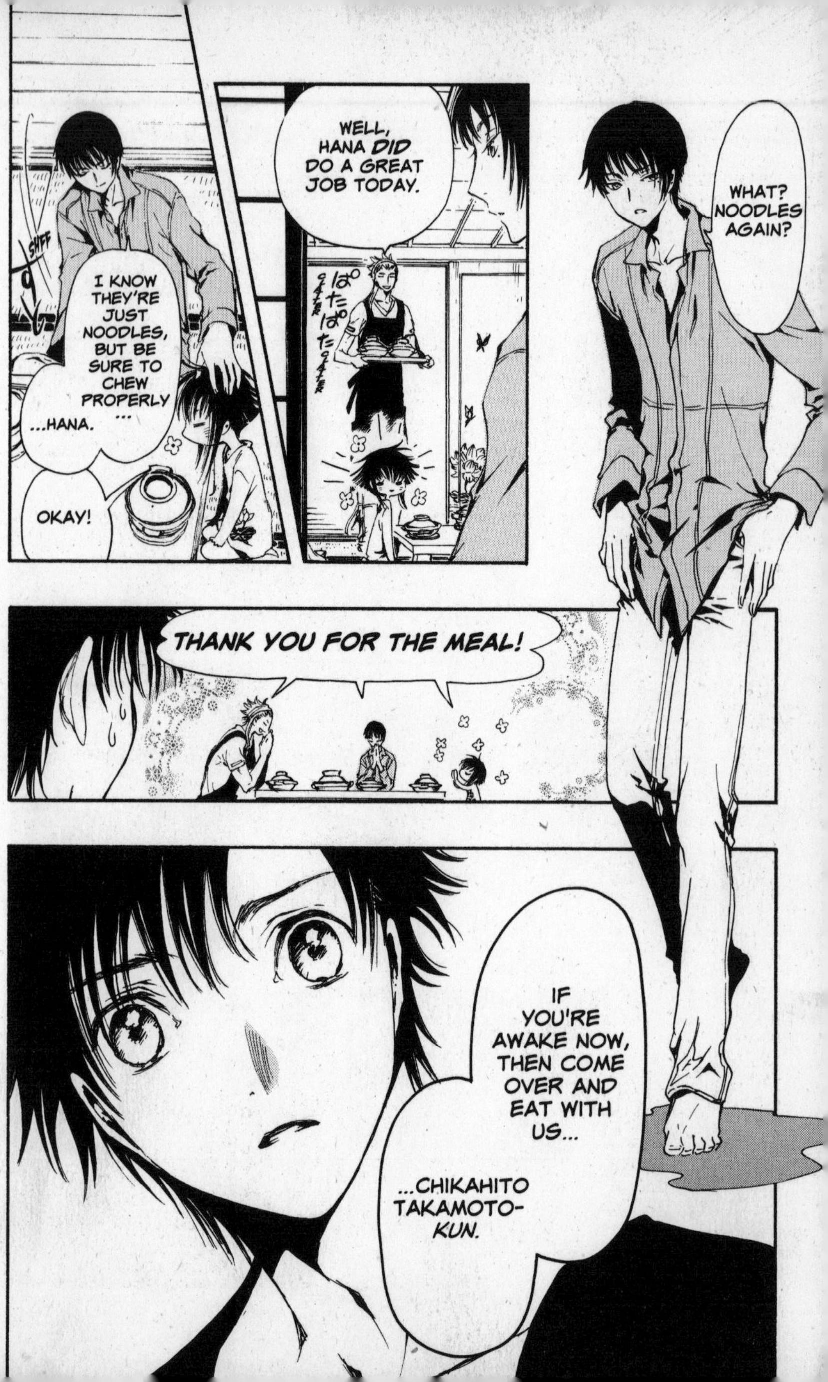
WHAT? NOODLES AGAIN?
WELL, HANA DID DO A GREAT JOB TODAY.
ぱたぱた
CLATTER CLATTER
SHFF
I KNOW THEY'RE JUST NOODLES, BUT BE SURE TO CHEW PROPERLY ...
...HANA.
OKAY!
THANK YOU FOR THE MEAL!
IF YOU'RE AWAKE NOW, THEN COME OVER AND EAT WITH US...
...CHIKAHITO TAKAMOTO-KUN.

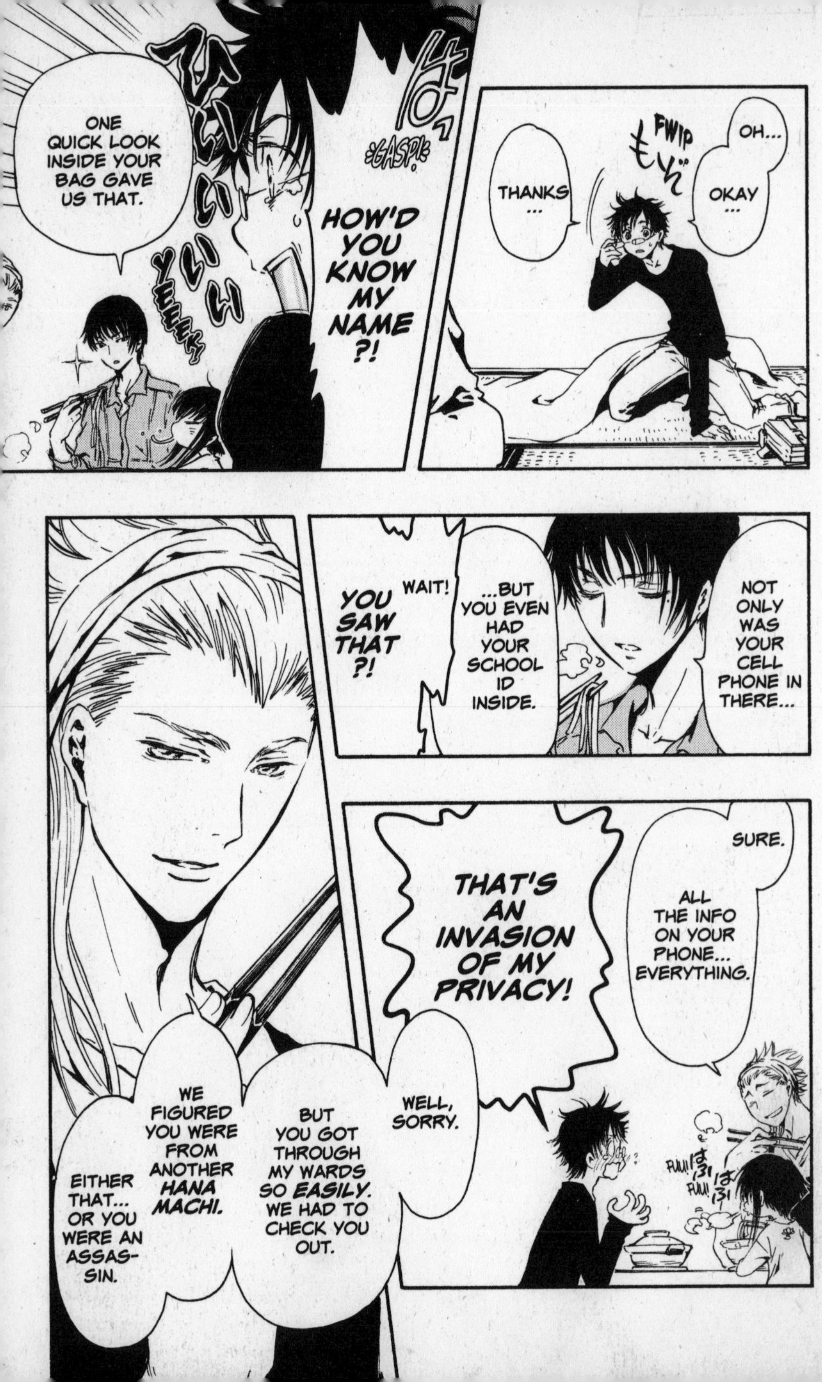
OH... OKAY ...
FWIP
THANKS ...
GASP!
HOW'D YOU KNOW MY NAME ?!
YEEEK
ONE QUICK LOOK INSIDE YOUR BAG GAVE US THAT.
NOT ONLY WAS YOUR CELL PHONE IN THERE...
...BUT YOU EVEN HAD YOUR SCHOOL ID INSIDE.
WAIT!
YOU SAW THAT ?!
SURE.
ALL THE INFO ON YOUR PHONE... EVERYTHING.
THAT'S AN INVASION OF MY PRIVACY!
FUU! FUU!
WELL, SORRY.
BUT YOU GOT THROUGH MY WARDS SO *EASILY*. WE HAD TO CHECK YOU OUT.
WE FIGURED YOU WERE FROM ANOTHER *HANA MACHI*.
EITHER THAT... OR YOU WERE AN ASSAS- SIN.

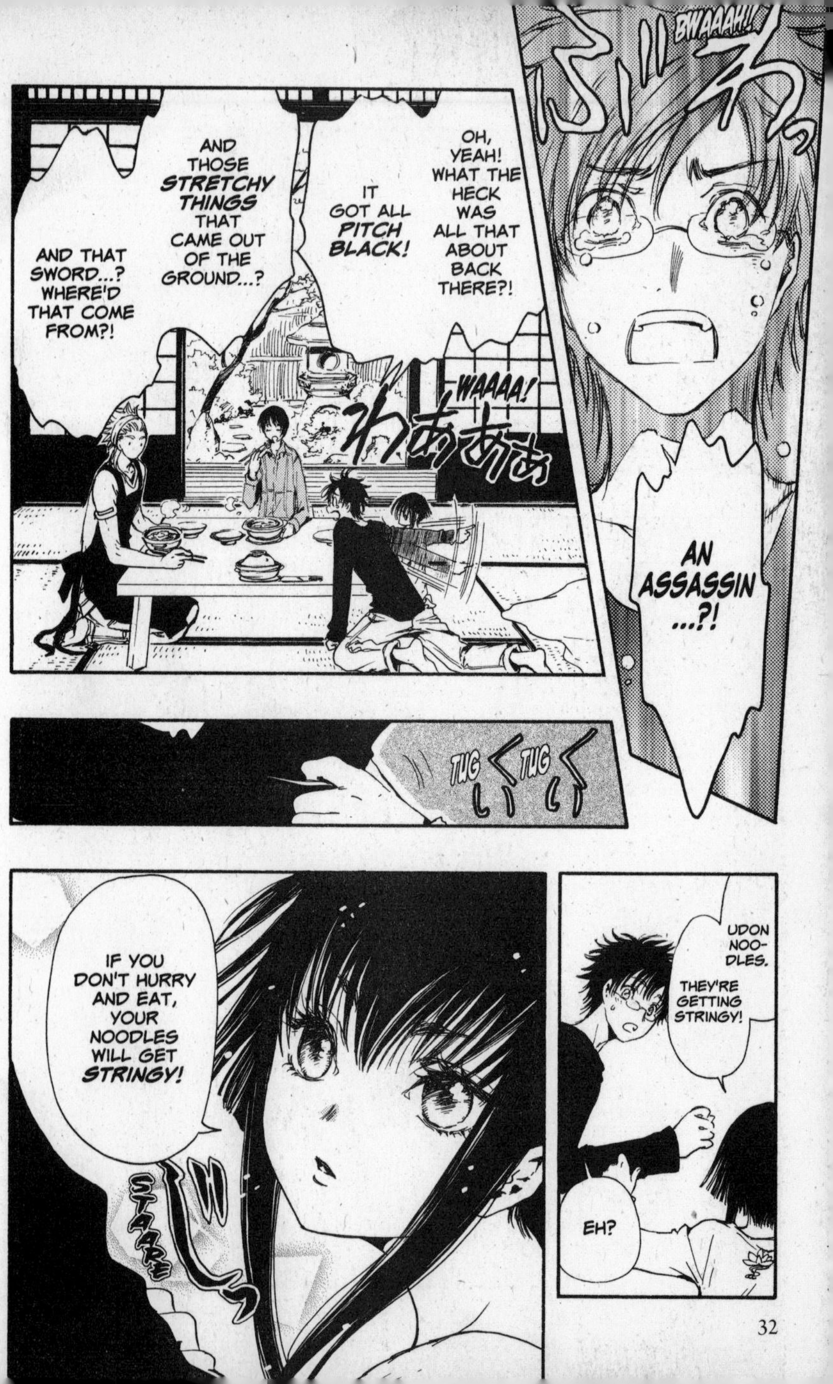

BWAAAH!!
AN ASSASSIN ...?!
OH, YEAH! WHAT THE HECK WAS ALL THAT ABOUT BACK THERE?!
IT GOT ALL PITCH BLACK!
AND THOSE STRETCHY THINGS THAT CAME OUT OF THE GROUND...?
AND THAT SWORD...? WHERE'D THAT COME FROM?!
WAAAA!
TUG TUG
UDON NOODLES.
THEY'RE GETTING STRINGY!
EH?
IF YOU DON'T HURRY AND EAT, YOUR NOODLES WILL GET STRINGY!
STAARE

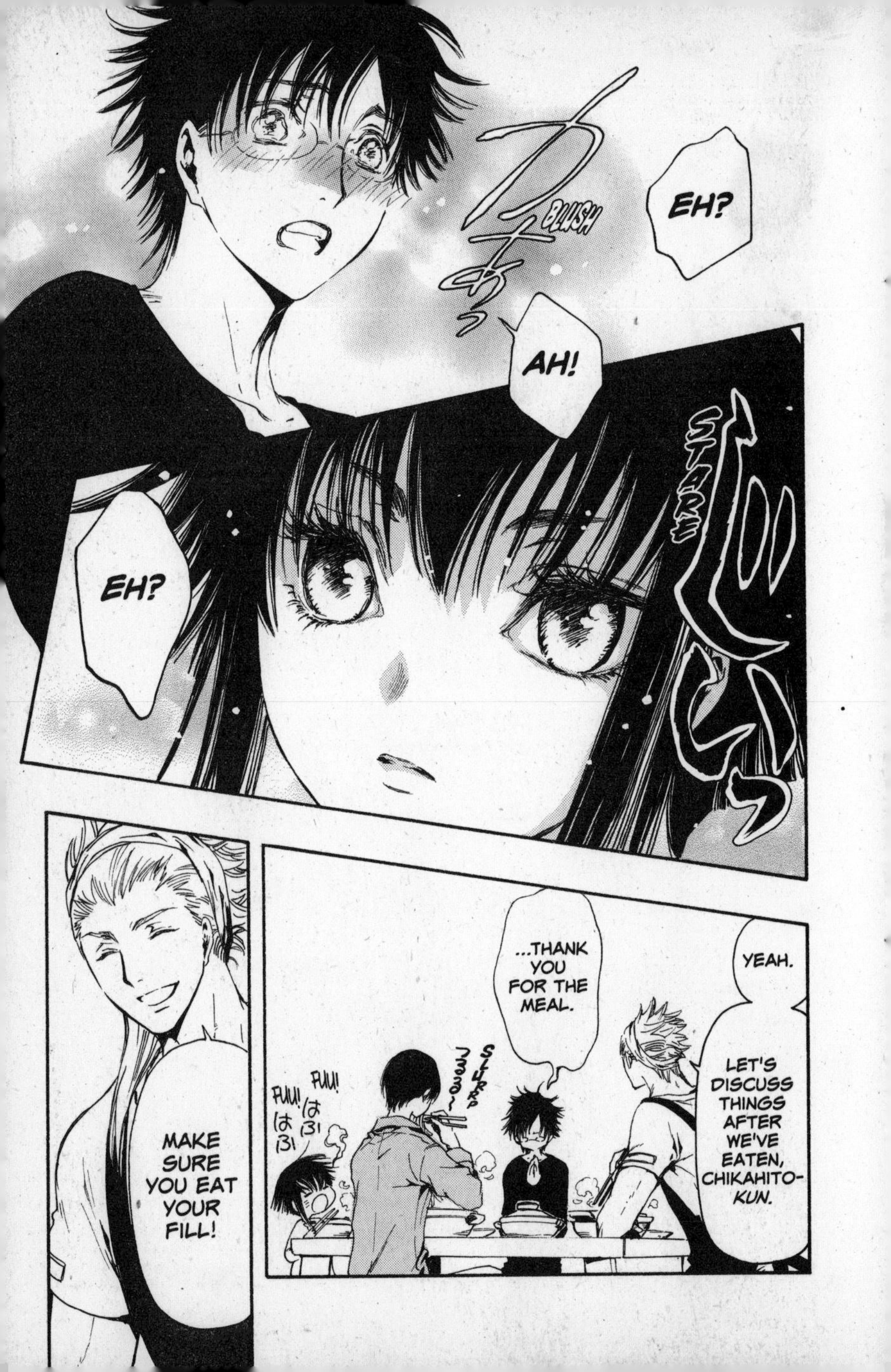
EH?
BLUSH
AH!
STARE
EH?
YEAH.
LET'S DISCUSS THINGS AFTER WE'VE EATEN, CHIKAHITO-KUN.
...THANK YOU FOR THE MEAL.
SLURP
FUU! FUU!
MAKE SURE YOU EAT YOUR FILL!

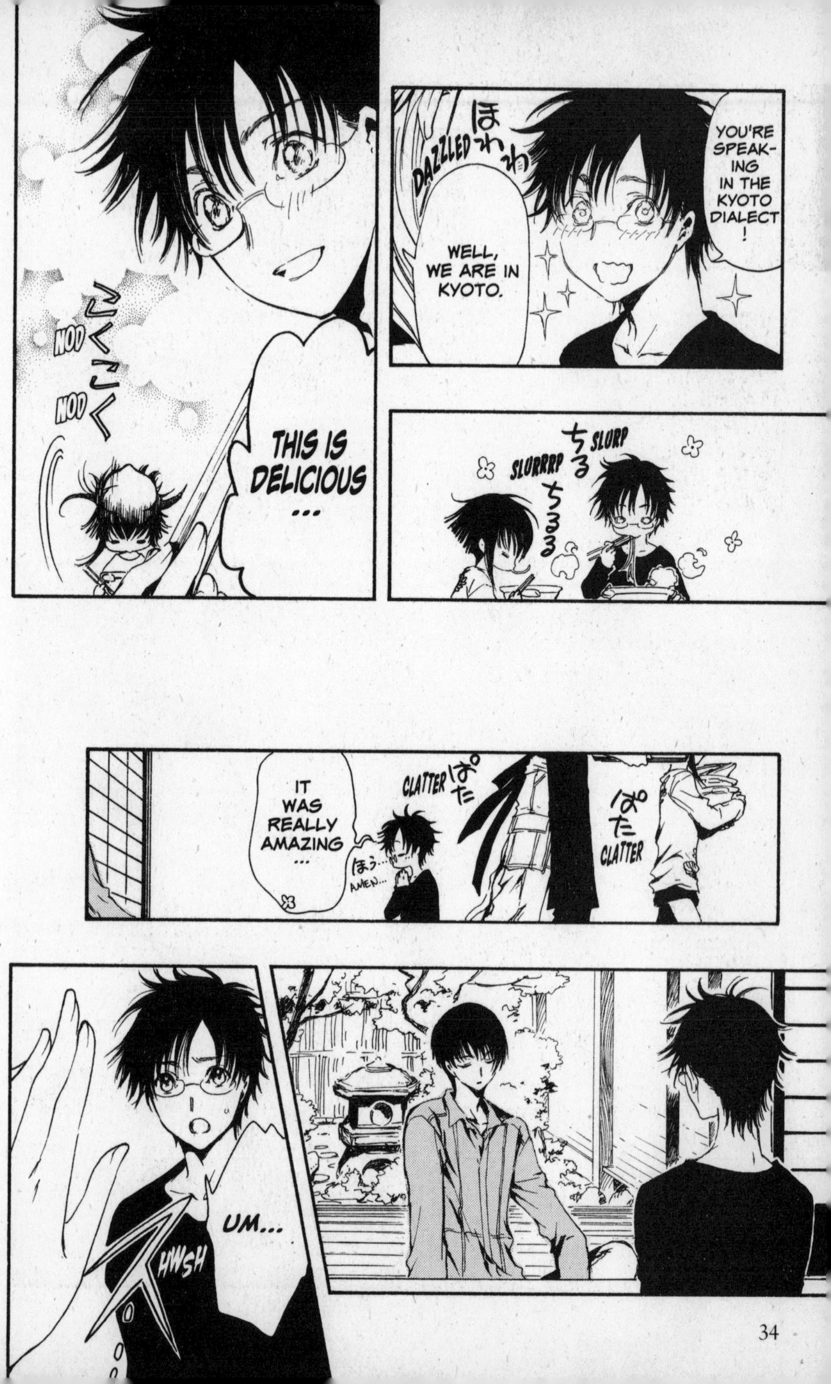
YOU'RE SPEAKING IN THE KYOTO DIALECT!
ほわわ
DAZZLED
WELL, WE ARE IN KYOTO.
ちる
SLURP
SLURRRP
ちるるる
THIS IS DELICIOUS ...
こくこく
NOD
NOD
ぱた
CLATTER
ぱた
CLATTER
IT WAS REALLY AMAZING ...
ほぅ...
AMEN...
UM...
HWSH

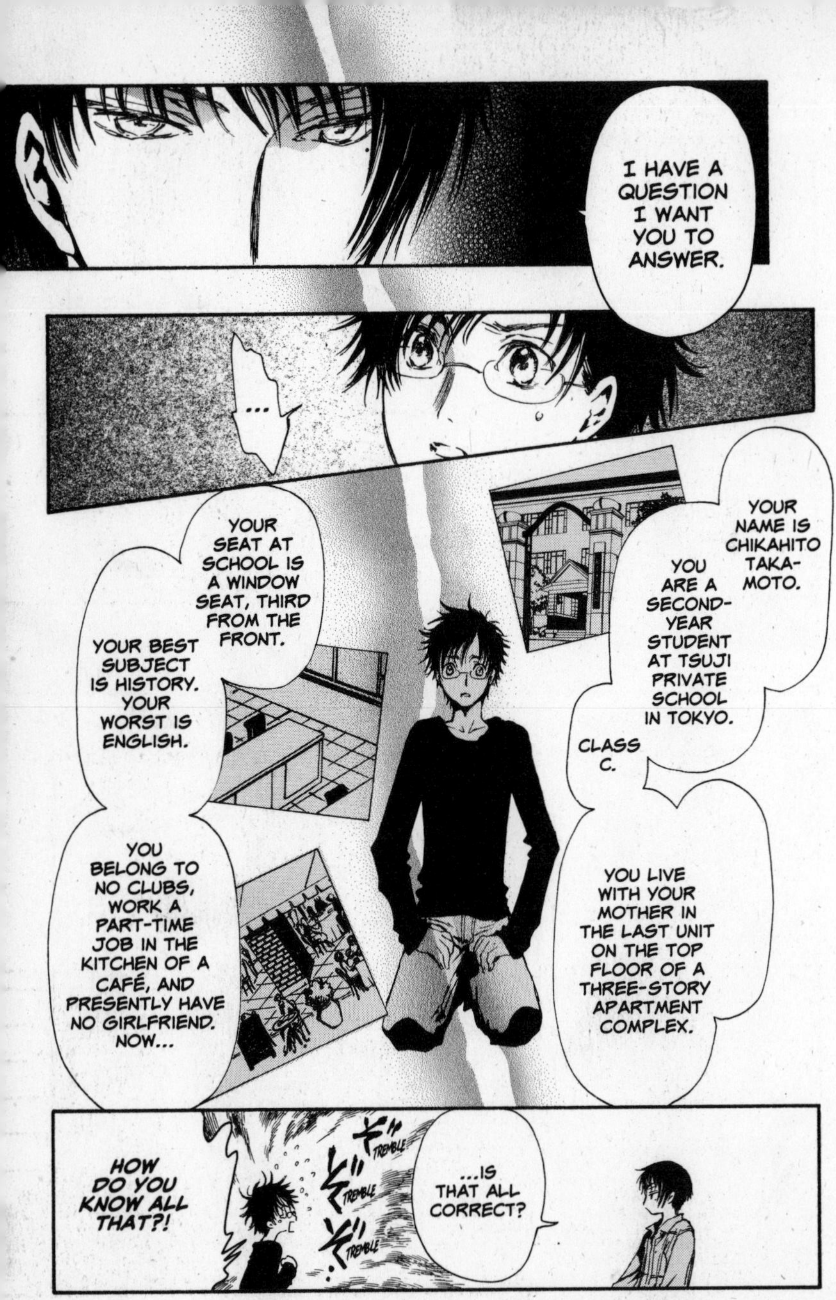
I HAVE A QUESTION I WANT YOU TO ANSWER.
...
YOUR NAME IS CHIKAHITO TAKA-MOTO.
YOU ARE A SECOND-YEAR STUDENT AT TSUJI PRIVATE SCHOOL IN TOKYO.
CLASS C.
YOUR SEAT AT SCHOOL IS A WINDOW SEAT, THIRD FROM THE FRONT.
YOUR BEST SUBJECT IS HISTORY. YOUR WORST IS ENGLISH.
YOU LIVE WITH YOUR MOTHER IN THE LAST UNIT ON THE TOP FLOOR OF A THREE-STORY APARTMENT COMPLEX.
YOU BELONG TO NO CLUBS, WORK A PART-TIME JOB IN THE KITCHEN OF A CAFÉ, AND PRESENTLY HAVE NO GIRLFRIEND. NOW...
...IS THAT ALL CORRECT?
TREMBLE
TREMBLE
TREMBLE
HOW DO YOU KNOW ALL THAT?!

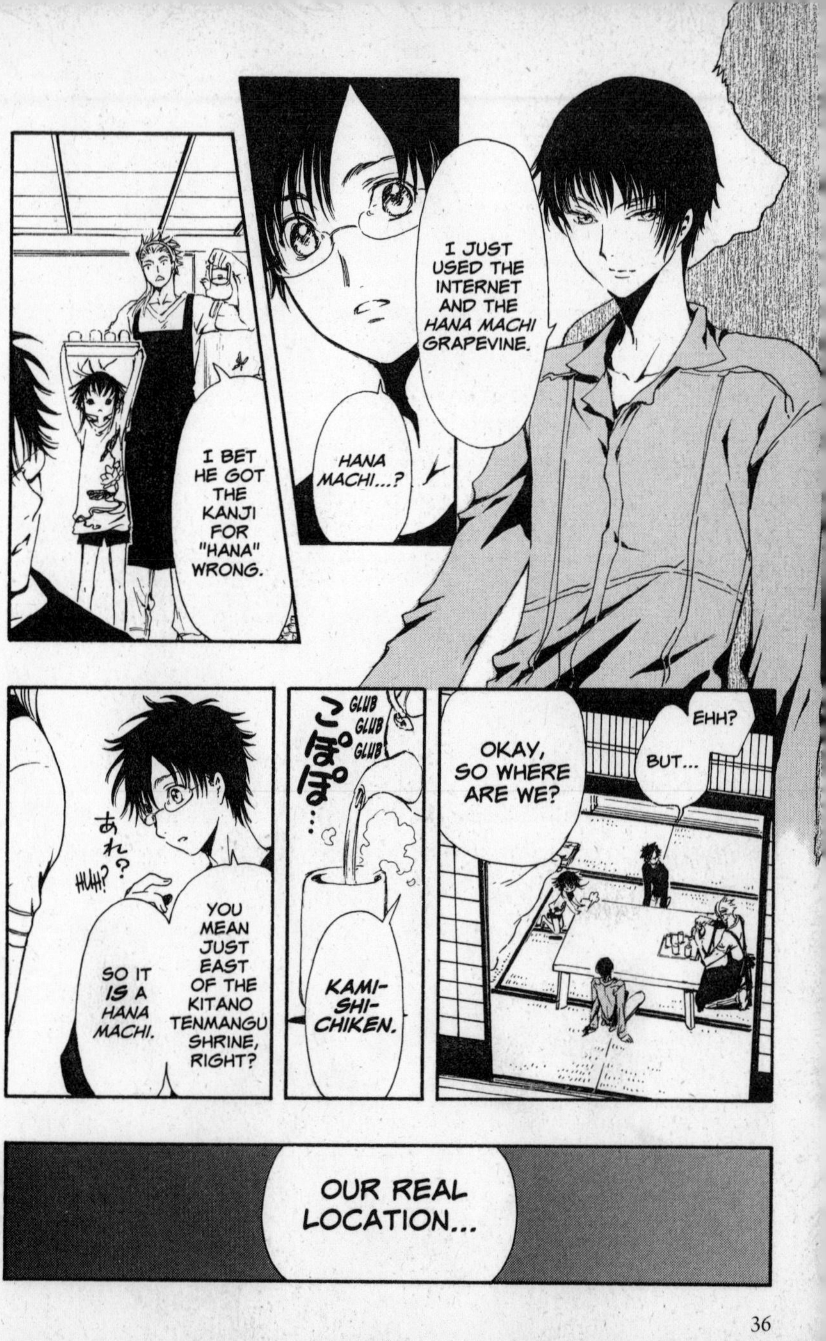
I JUST USED THE INTERNET AND THE HANA MACHI GRAPEVINE.
HANA MACHI...?
I BET HE GOT THE KANJI FOR "HANA" WRONG.
OKAY, SO WHERE ARE WE?
EHH? BUT...
こぽぽ…
GLUB GLUB GLUB
KAMI-SHI-CHIKEN.
YOU MEAN JUST EAST OF THE KITANO TENMANGU SHRINE, RIGHT?
あれ？
HUH?
SO IT IS A HANA MACHI.
OUR REAL LOCATION...

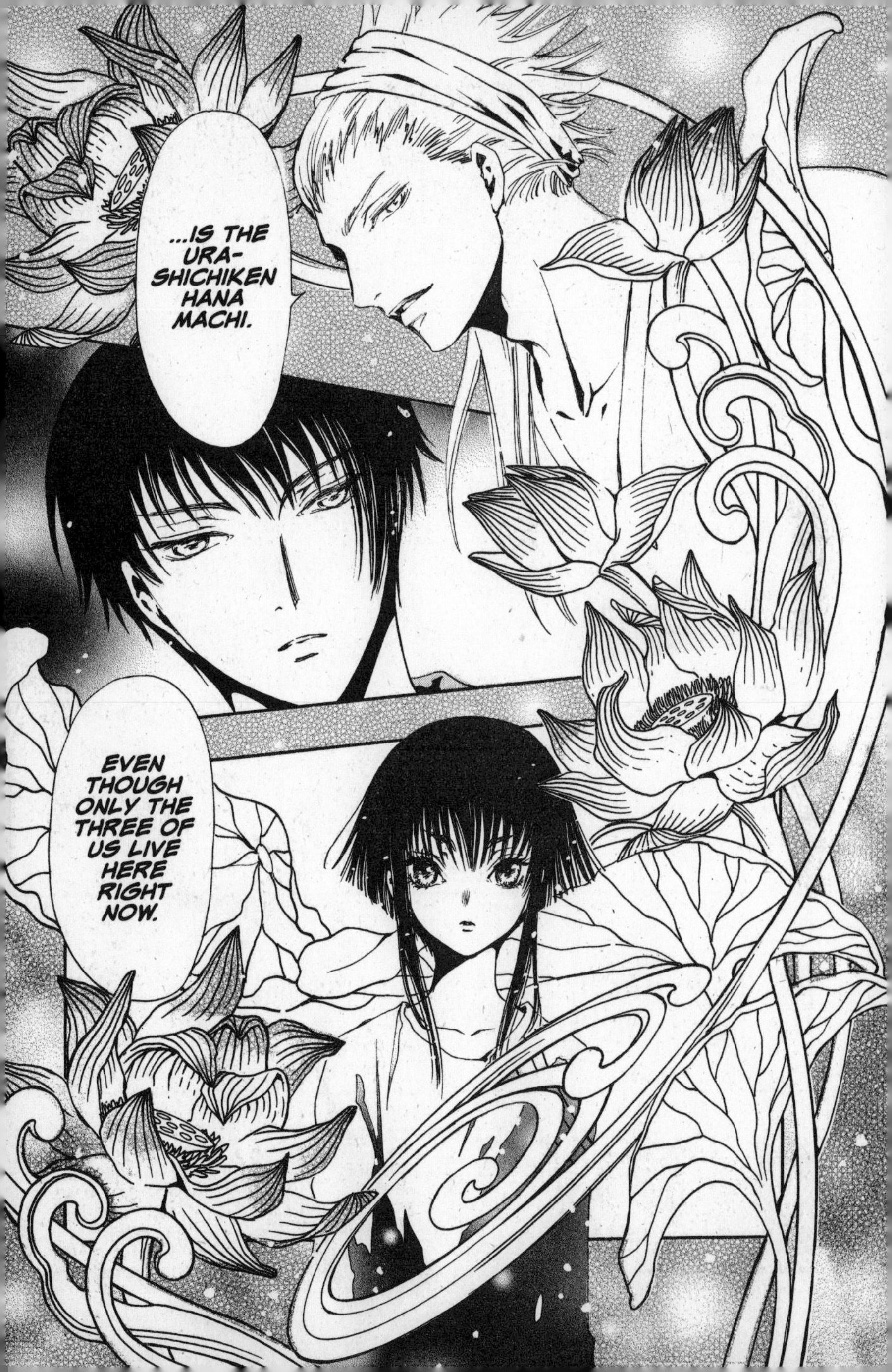
...IS THE URA-SHICHIKEN HANA MACHI.
EVEN THOUGH ONLY THE THREE OF US LIVE HERE RIGHT NOW.

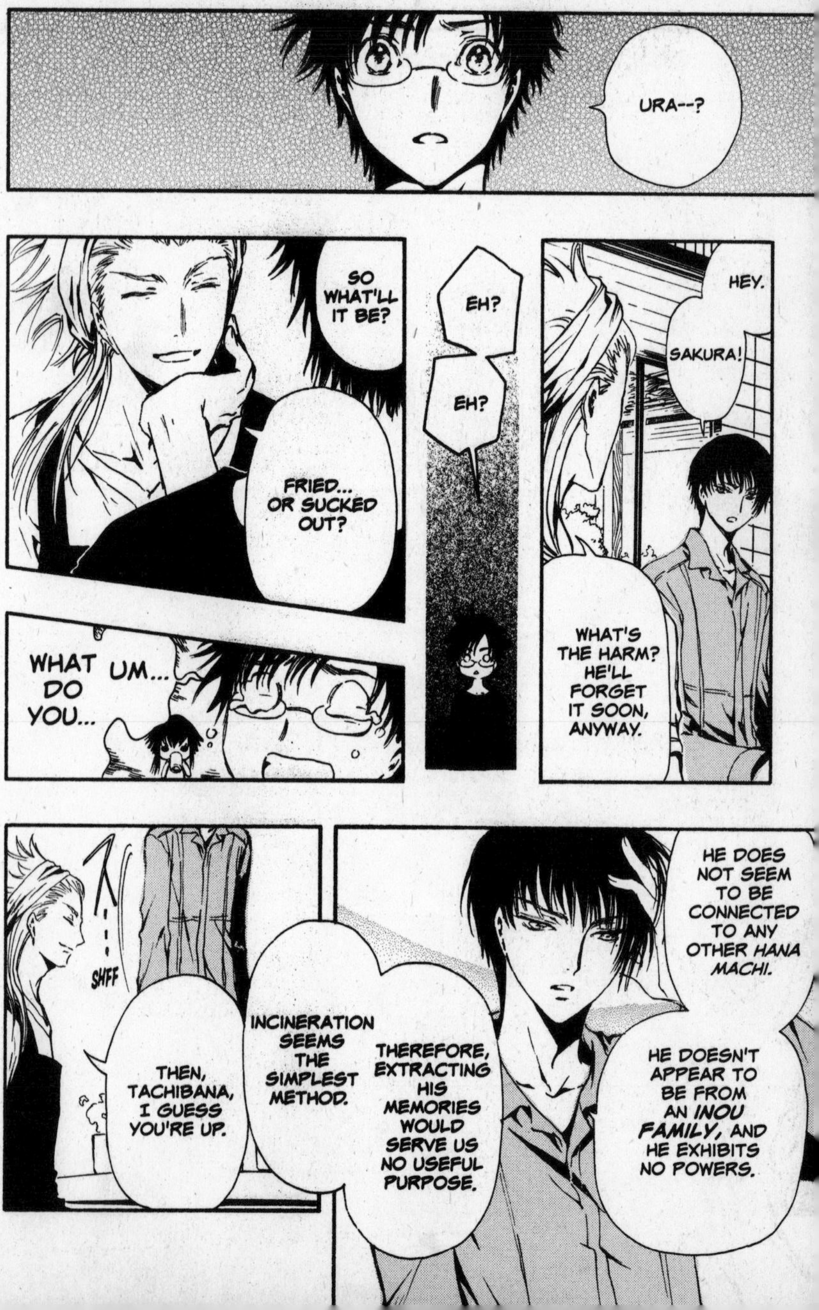
URA--?
HEY.
SAKURA!
WHAT'S THE HARM? HE'LL FORGET IT SOON, ANYWAY.
EH?
EH?
SO WHAT'LL IT BE?
FRIED... OR SUCKED OUT?
UM...
WHAT DO YOU...
HE DOES NOT SEEM TO BE CONNECTED TO ANY OTHER *HANA MACHI.*
HE DOESN'T APPEAR TO BE FROM AN *INOU FAMILY,* AND HE EXHIBITS NO POWERS.
THEREFORE, EXTRACTING HIS MEMORIES WOULD SERVE US NO USEFUL PURPOSE.
INCINERATION SEEMS THE SIMPLEST METHOD.
SHFF
THEN, TACHIBANA, I GUESS YOU'RE UP.

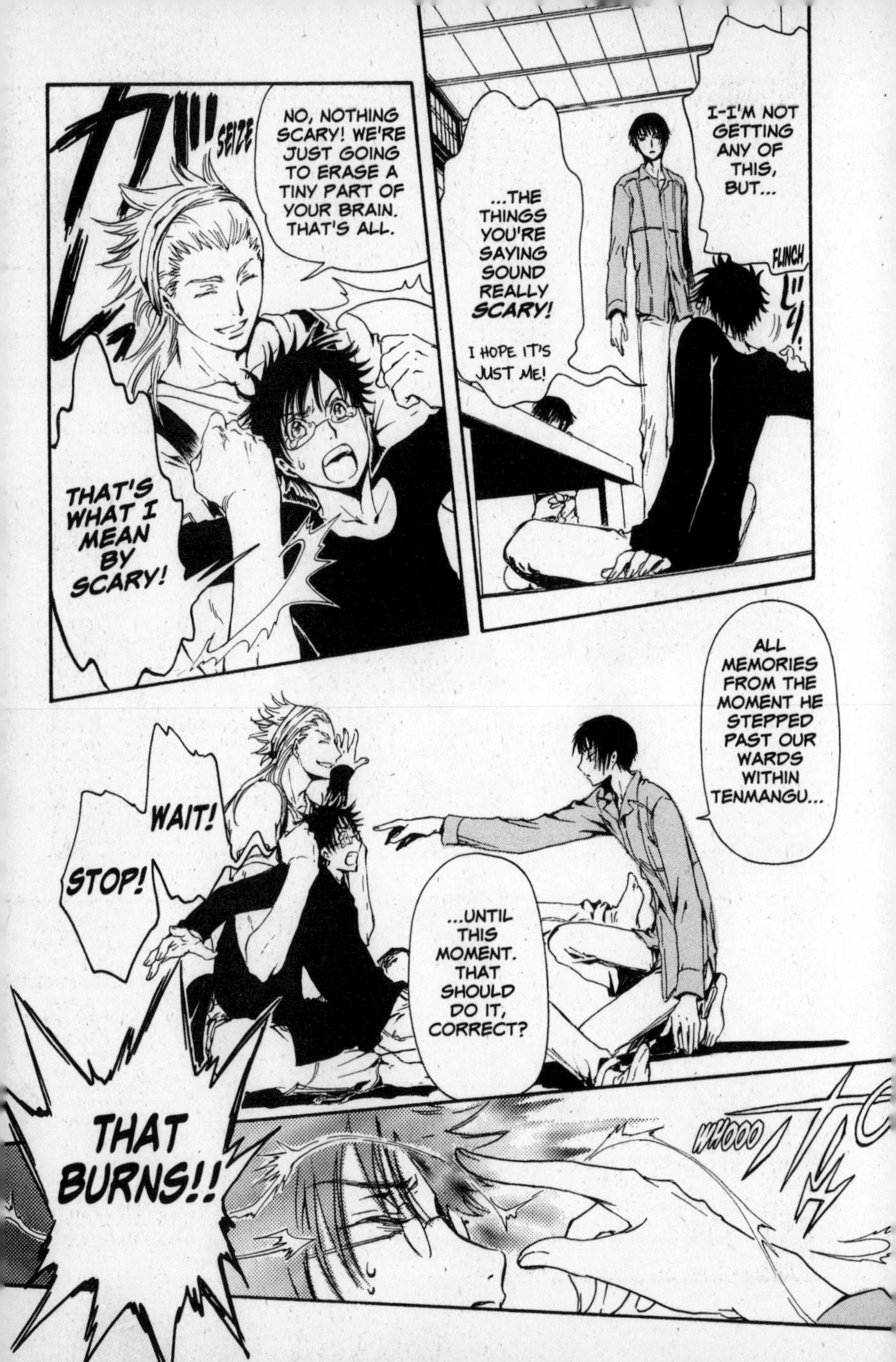
I-I'M NOT GETTING ANY OF THIS, BUT...
...THE THINGS YOU'RE SAYING SOUND REALLY SCARY!
I HOPE IT'S JUST ME!
FLINCH
SEIZE
NO, NOTHING SCARY! WE'RE JUST GOING TO ERASE A TINY PART OF YOUR BRAIN. THAT'S ALL.
THAT'S WHAT I MEAN BY SCARY!
ALL MEMORIES FROM THE MOMENT HE STEPPED PAST OUR WARDS WITHIN TENMANGU...
...UNTIL THIS MOMENT. THAT SHOULD DO IT, CORRECT?
WAIT!
STOP!
WHOOO
THAT BURNS!!

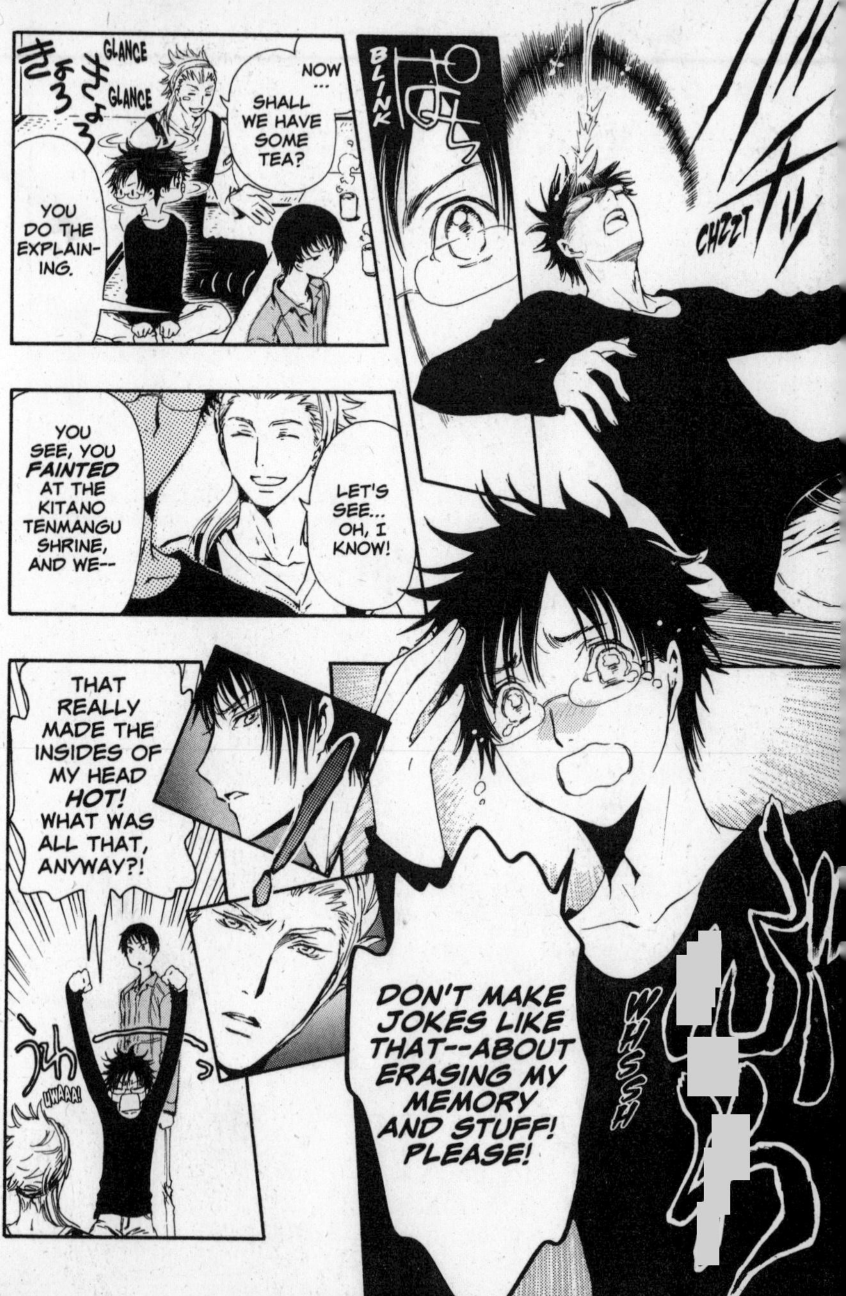
CHZZT
BLINK
WHSSH
DON'T MAKE JOKES LIKE THAT--ABOUT ERASING MY MEMORY AND STUFF! PLEASE!
GLANCE GLANCE
NOW... SHALL WE HAVE SOME TEA?
YOU DO THE EXPLAIN-ING.
LET'S SEE... OH, I KNOW!
YOU SEE, YOU FAINTED AT THE KITANO TENMANGU SHRINE, AND WE--
THAT REALLY MADE THE INSIDES OF MY HEAD HOT! WHAT WAS ALL THAT, ANYWAY?!
UWAAA!

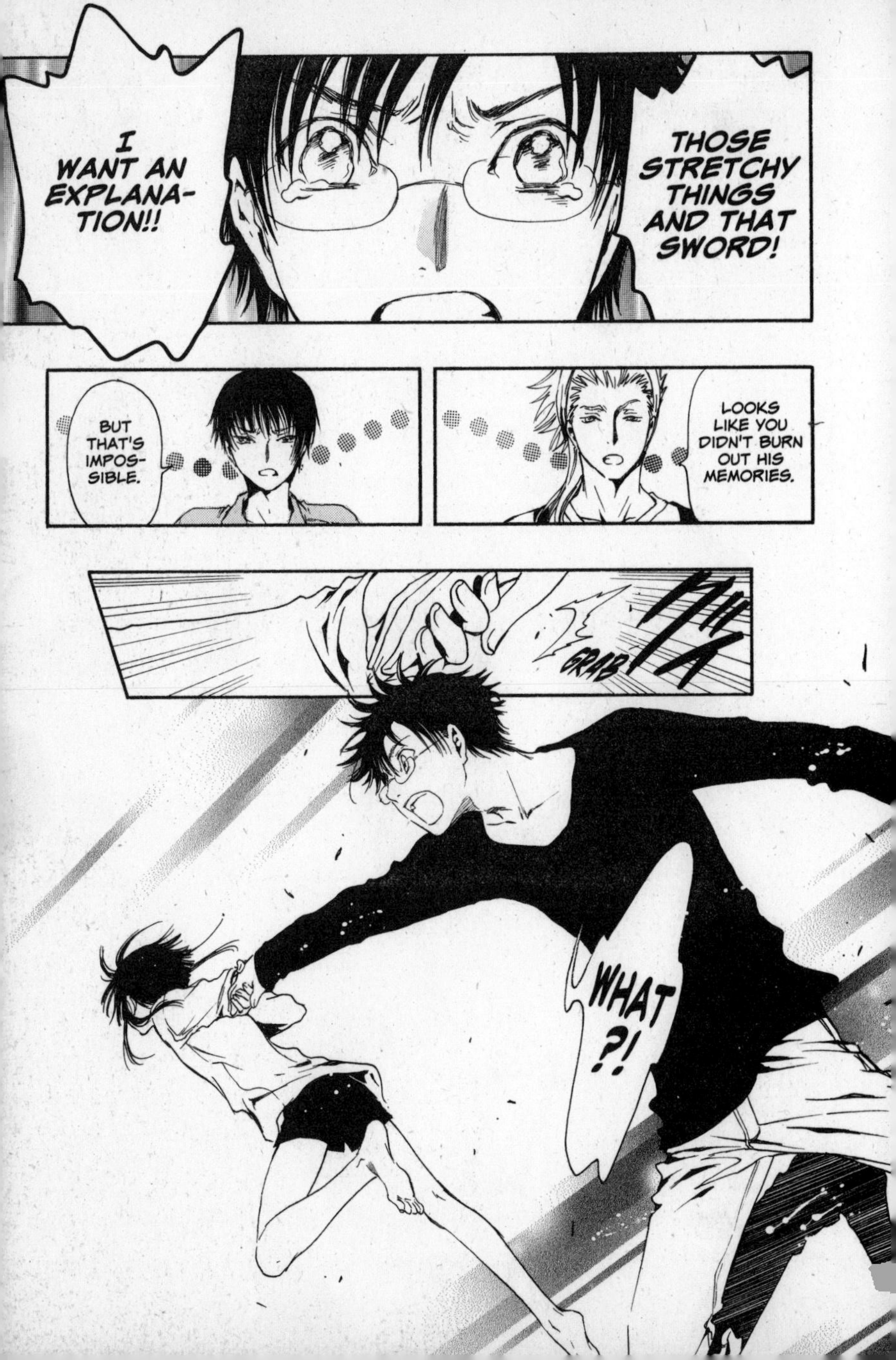

THOSE STRETCHY THINGS AND THAT SWORD!
I WANT AN EXPLANATION!!
LOOKS LIKE YOU DIDN'T BURN OUT HIS MEMORIES.
BUT THAT'S IMPOSSIBLE.
GRAB
WHAT?!

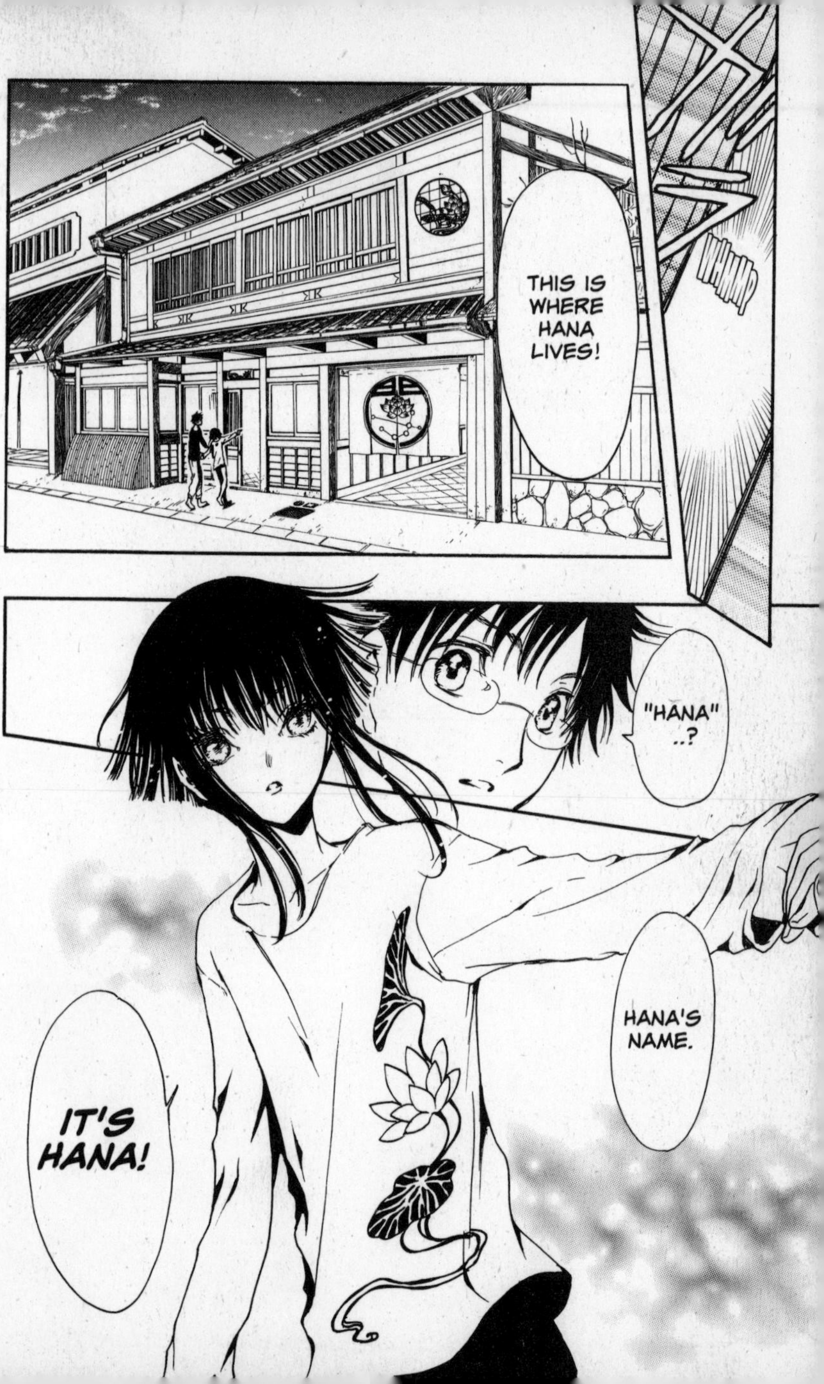
WHAMP
THIS IS WHERE HANA LIVES!
"HANA" ..?
HANA'S NAME.
IT'S HANA!

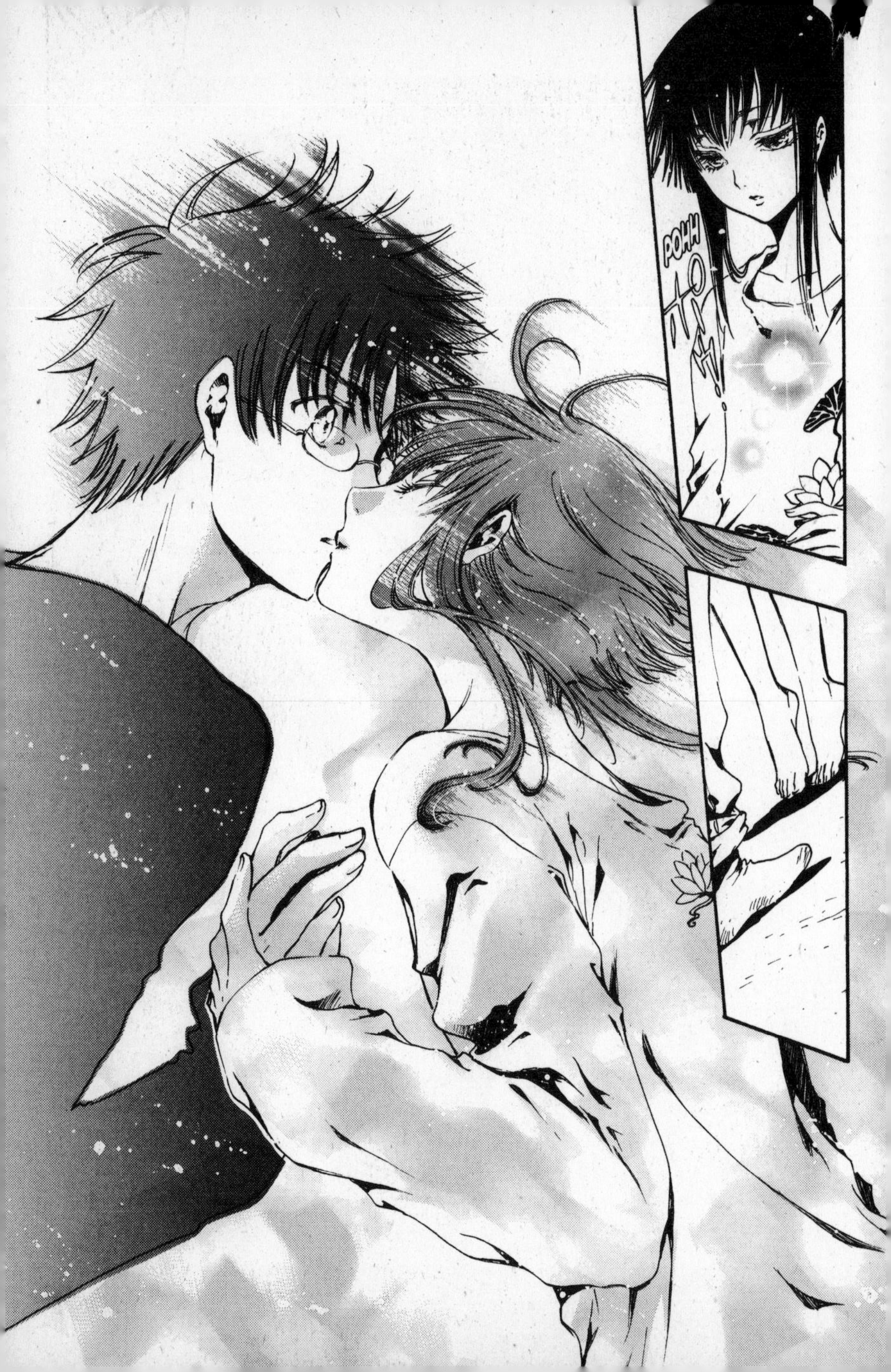
POHH

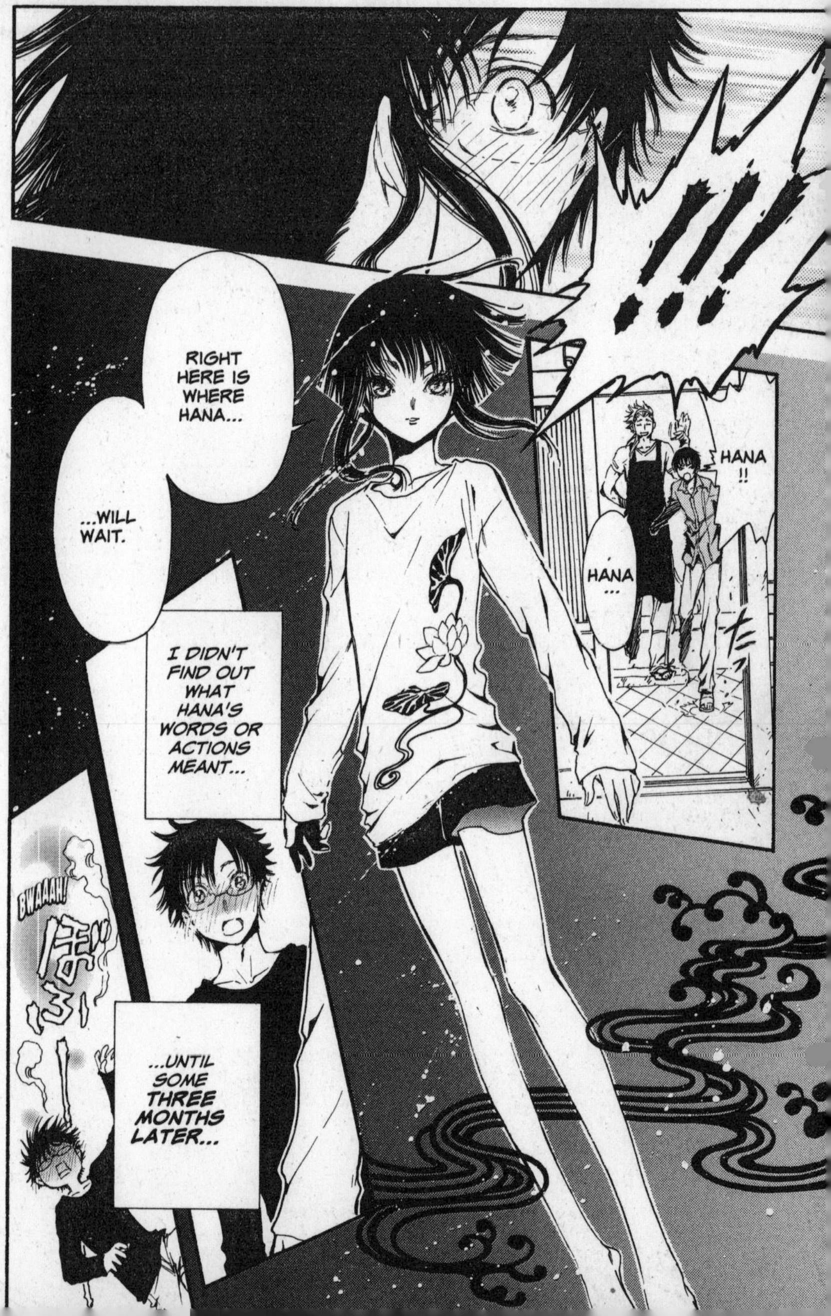
!!!
HANA !!
HANA ...
RIGHT HERE IS WHERE HANA...
...WILL WAIT.
I DIDN'T FIND OUT WHAT HANA'S WORDS OR ACTIONS MEANT...
BWAAAH!
...UNTIL SOME THREE MONTHS LATER...

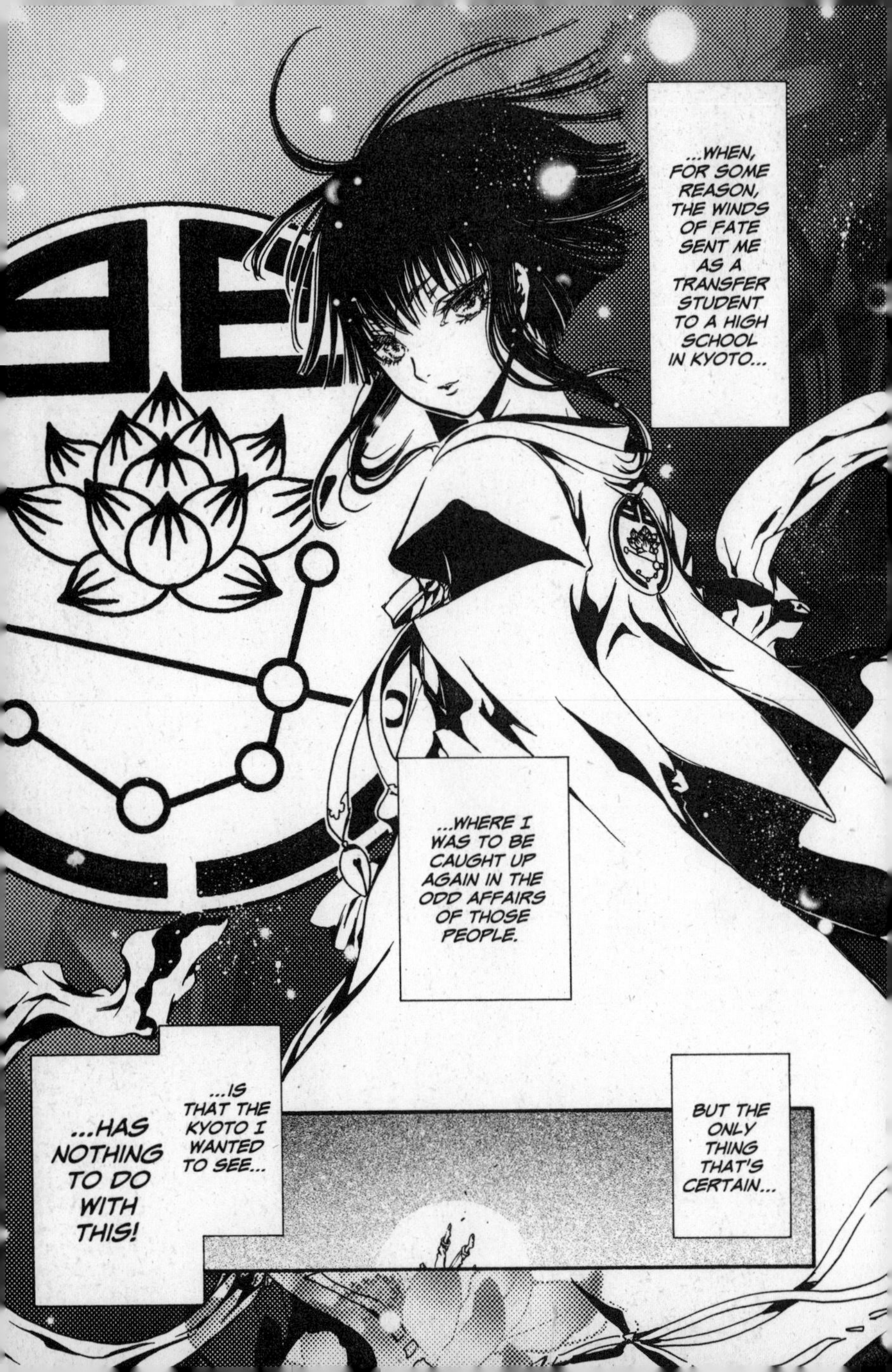
...WHEN, FOR SOME REASON, THE WINDS OF FATE SENT ME AS A TRANSFER STUDENT TO A HIGH SCHOOL IN KYOTO...
...WHERE I WAS TO BE CAUGHT UP AGAIN IN THE ODD AFFAIRS OF THOSE PEOPLE.
BUT THE ONLY THING THAT'S CERTAIN...
...IS THAT THE KYOTO I WANTED TO SEE...
...HAS NOTHING TO DO WITH THIS!

GATE 7
ゲート セブン

CHAPTER ONE: CHIKAHITO AND HANA

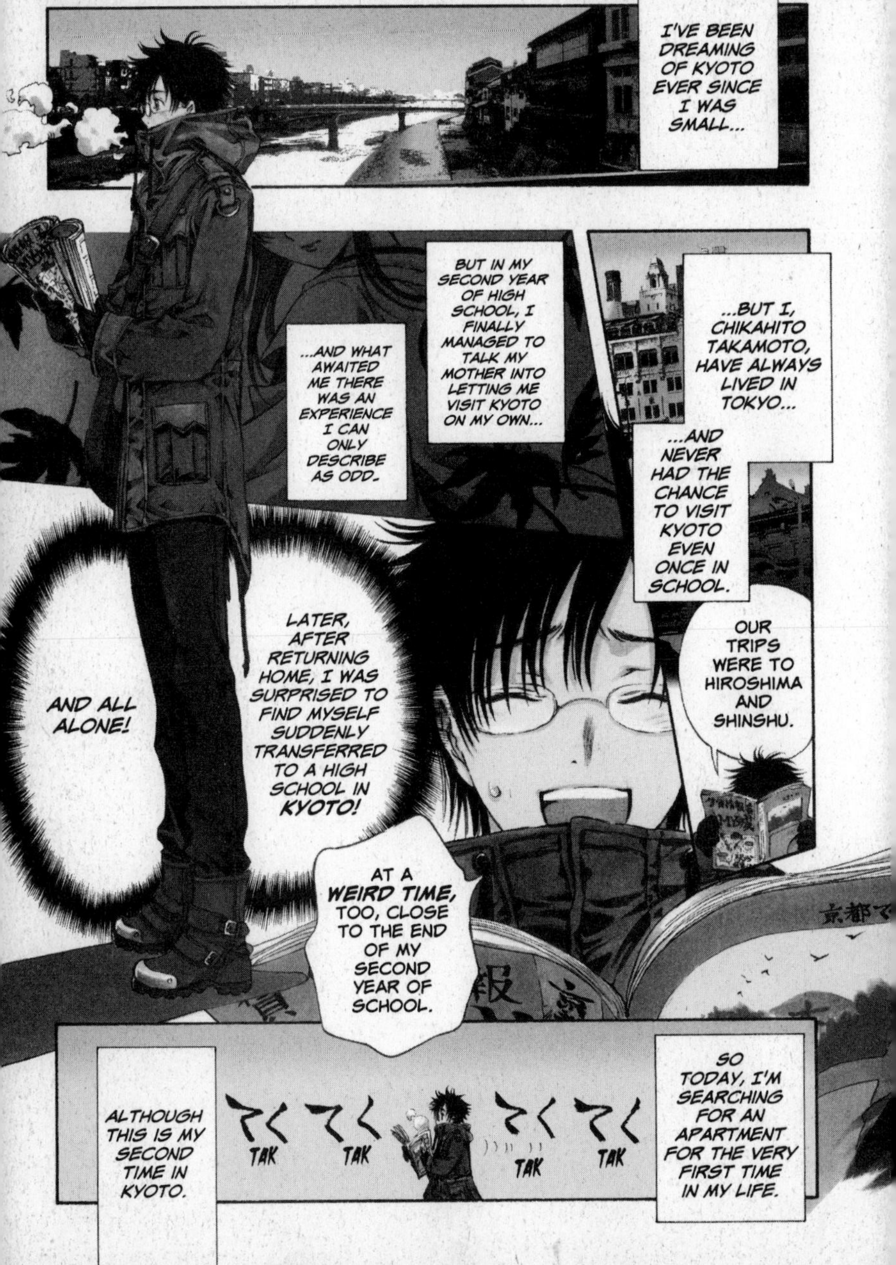

I'VE BEEN DREAMING OF KYOTO EVER SINCE I WAS SMALL...
...BUT I, CHIKAHITO TAKAMOTO, HAVE ALWAYS LIVED IN TOKYO...
...AND NEVER HAD THE CHANCE TO VISIT KYOTO EVEN ONCE IN SCHOOL.
OUR TRIPS WERE TO HIROSHIMA AND SHINSHU.
BUT IN MY SECOND YEAR OF HIGH SCHOOL, I FINALLY MANAGED TO TALK MY MOTHER INTO LETTING ME VISIT KYOTO ON MY OWN...
...AND WHAT AWAITED ME THERE WAS AN EXPERIENCE I CAN ONLY DESCRIBE AS ODD.
LATER, AFTER RETURNING HOME, I WAS SURPRISED TO FIND MYSELF SUDDENLY TRANSFERRED TO A HIGH SCHOOL IN KYOTO!
AND ALL ALONE!
AT A WEIRD TIME, TOO, CLOSE TO THE END OF MY SECOND YEAR OF SCHOOL.
京都で
SO TODAY, I'M SEARCHING FOR AN APARTMENT FOR THE VERY FIRST TIME IN MY LIFE.
てく てく
TAK TAK
てく てく
TAK TAK
ALTHOUGH THIS IS MY SECOND TIME IN KYOTO.

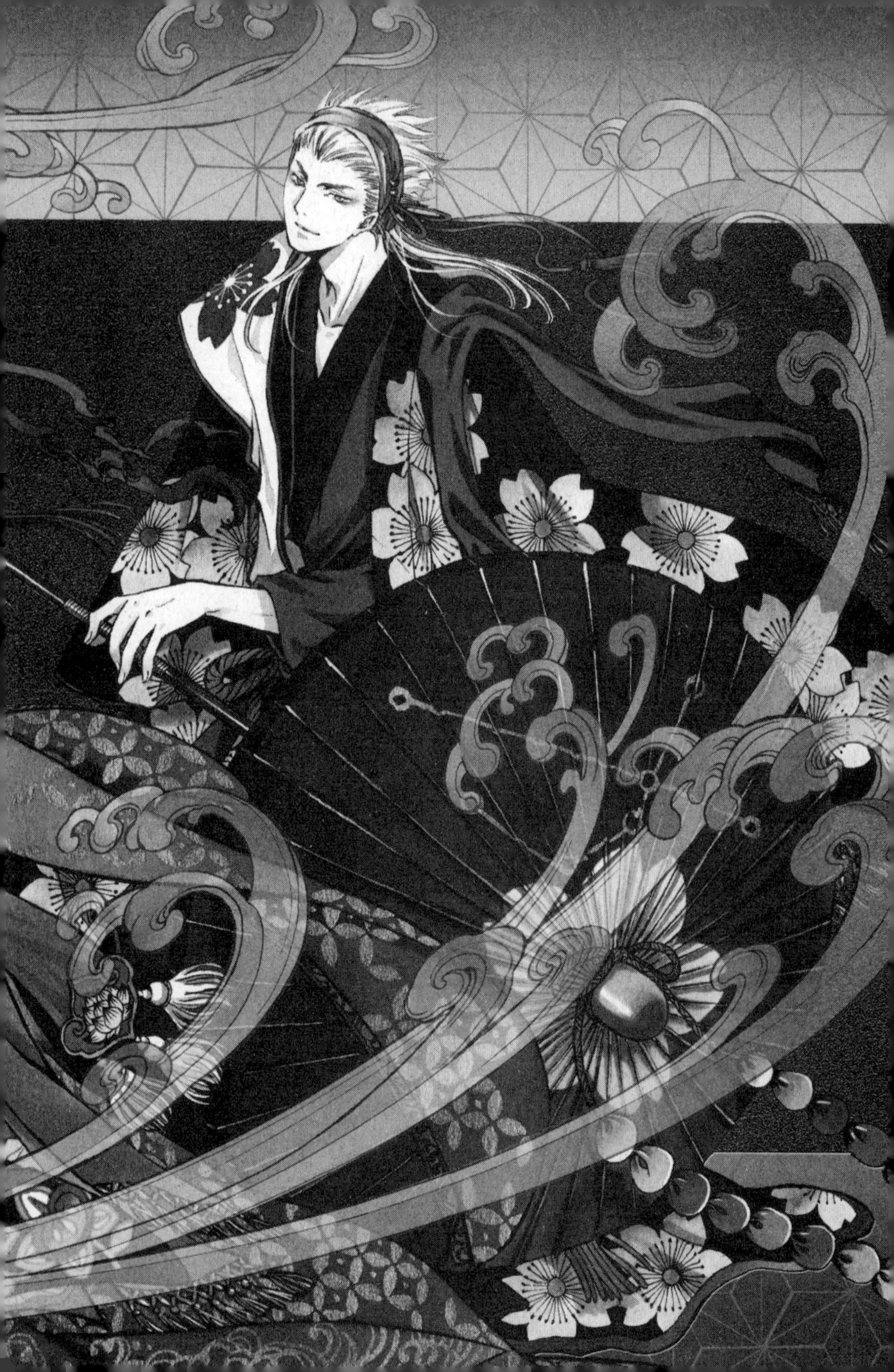

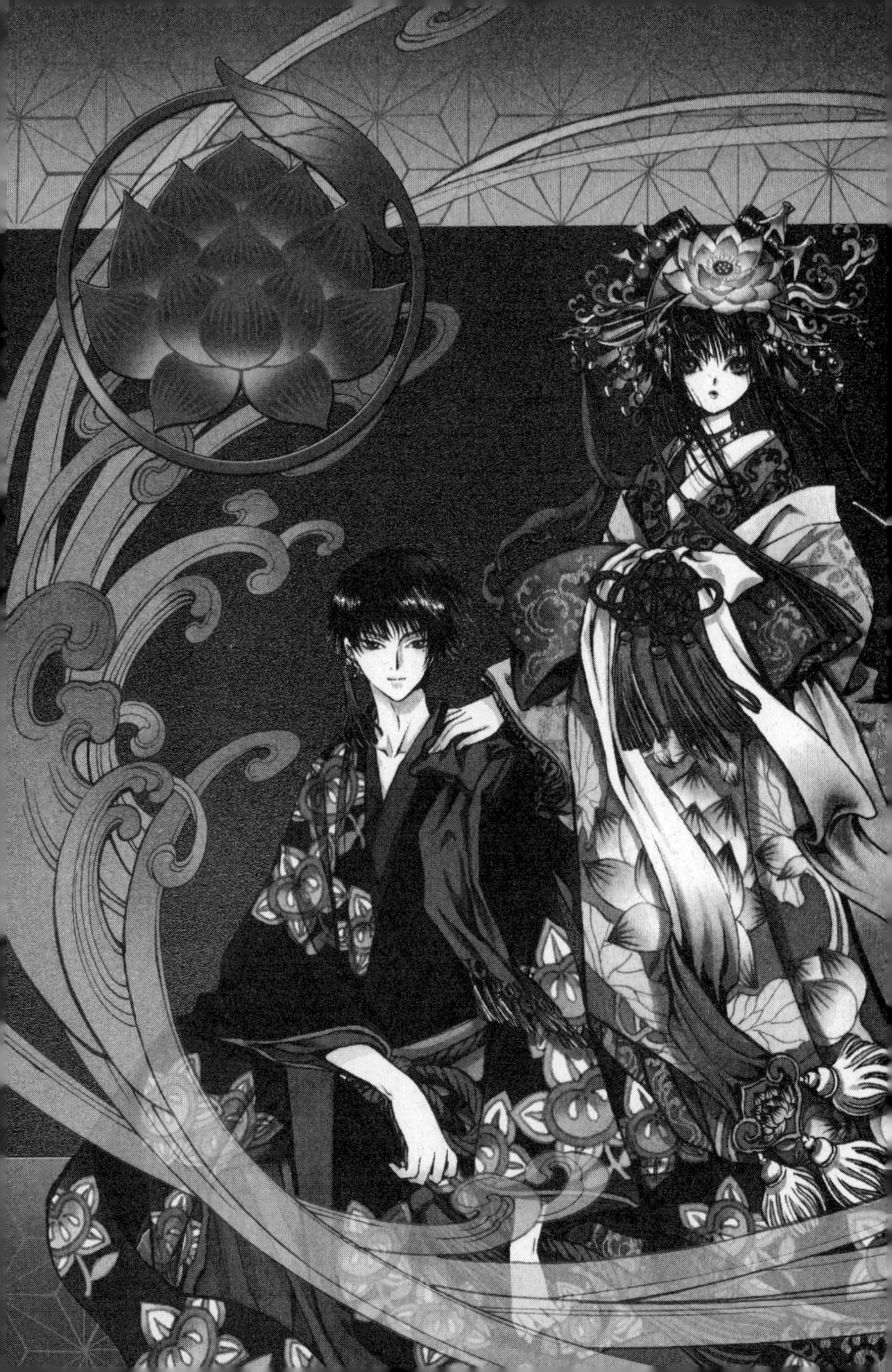

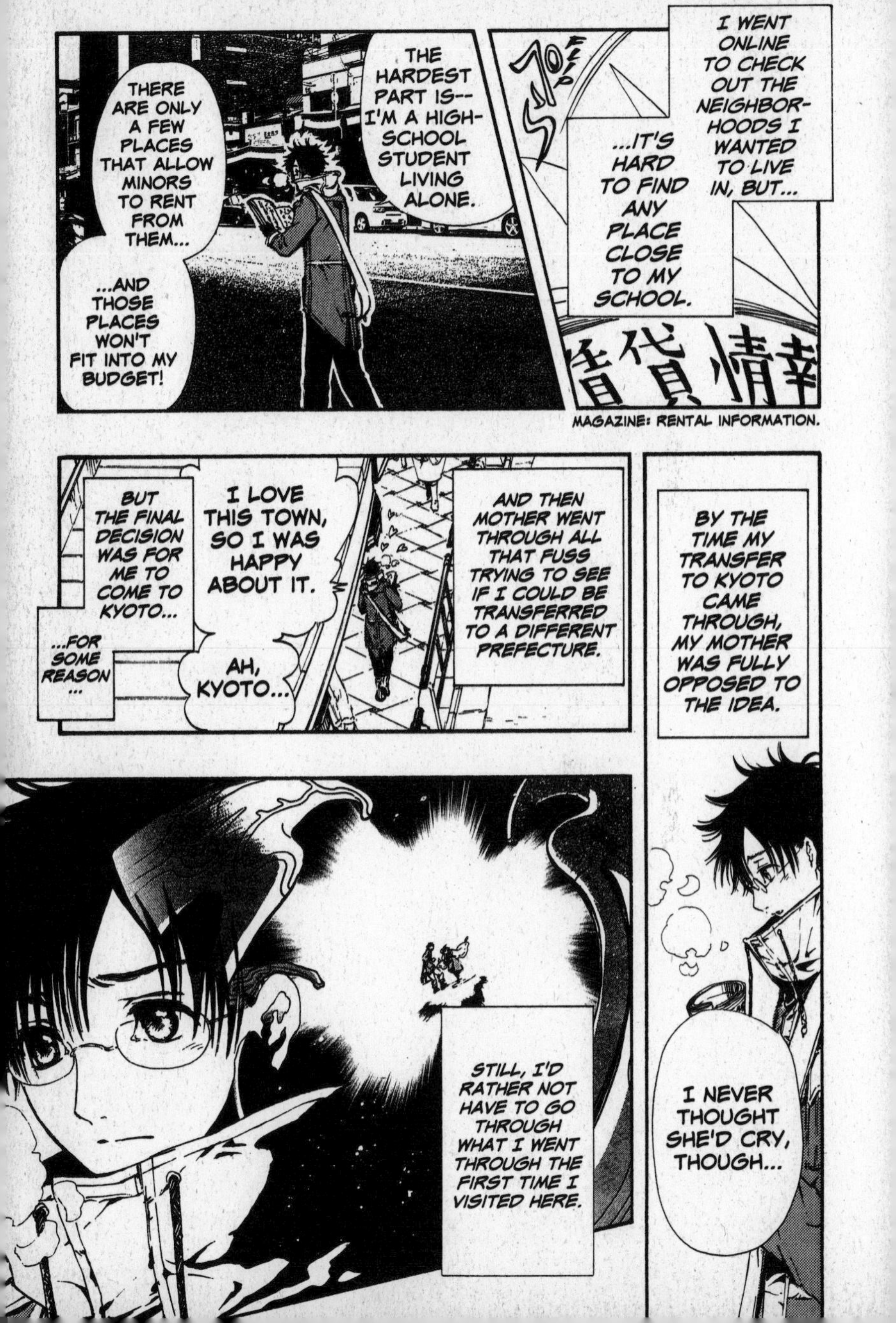
FLIP
I WENT ONLINE TO CHECK OUT THE NEIGHBOR-HOODS I WANTED TO LIVE IN, BUT...
...IT'S HARD TO FIND ANY PLACE CLOSE TO MY SCHOOL.
THE HARDEST PART IS-- I'M A HIGH-SCHOOL STUDENT LIVING ALONE.
THERE ARE ONLY A FEW PLACES THAT ALLOW MINORS TO RENT FROM THEM...
...AND THOSE PLACES WON'T FIT INTO MY BUDGET!
MAGAZINE: RENTAL INFORMATION.
BY THE TIME MY TRANSFER TO KYOTO CAME THROUGH, MY MOTHER WAS FULLY OPPOSED TO THE IDEA.
I NEVER THOUGHT SHE'D CRY, THOUGH...
AND THEN MOTHER WENT THROUGH ALL THAT FUSS TRYING TO SEE IF I COULD BE TRANSFERRED TO A DIFFERENT PREFECTURE.
BUT THE FINAL DECISION WAS FOR ME TO COME TO KYOTO...
...FOR SOME REASON...
I LOVE THIS TOWN, SO I WAS HAPPY ABOUT IT.
AH, KYOTO...
STILL, I'D RATHER NOT HAVE TO GO THROUGH WHAT I WENT THROUGH THE FIRST TIME I VISITED HERE.

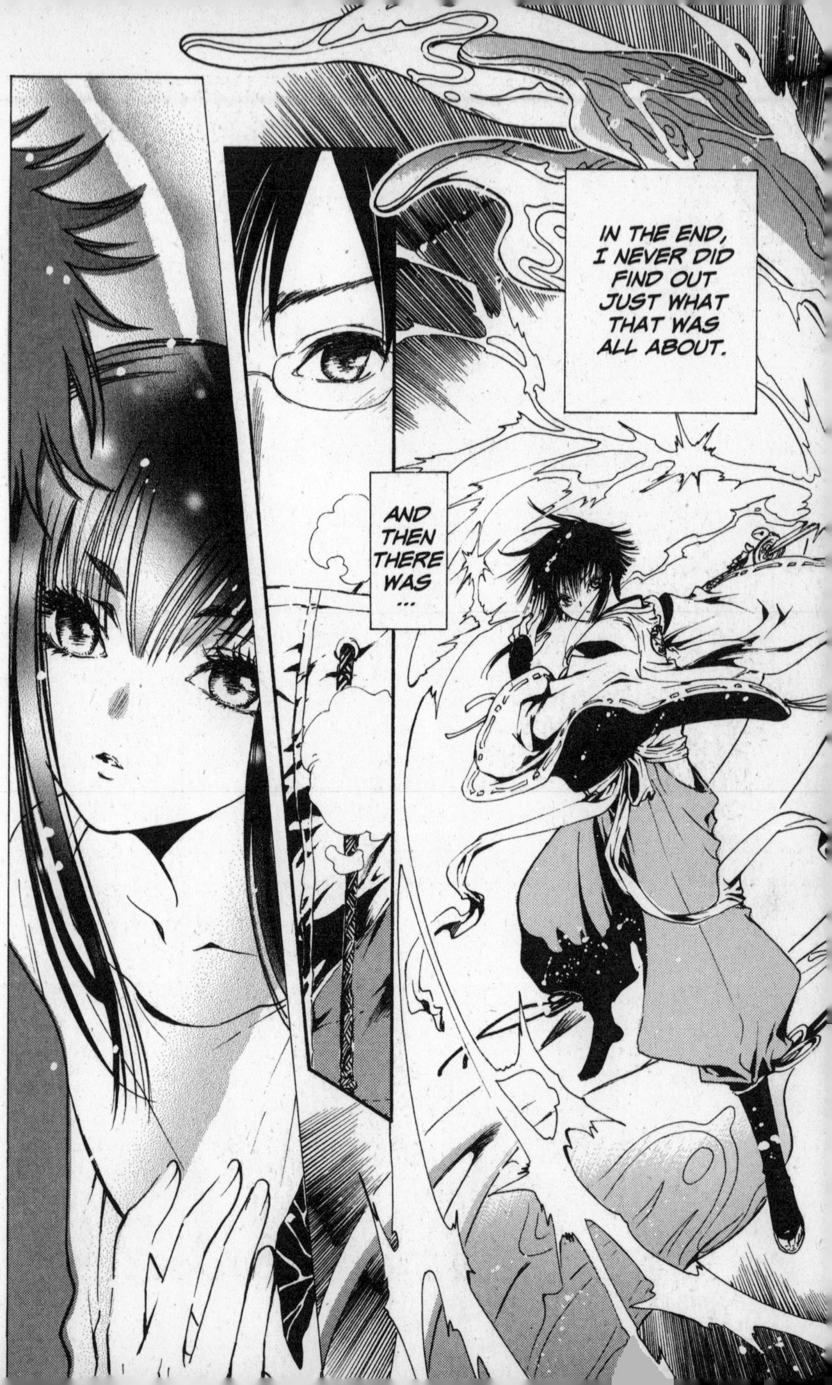
IN THE END, I NEVER DID FIND OUT JUST WHAT THAT WAS ALL ABOUT.
AND THEN THERE WAS ...

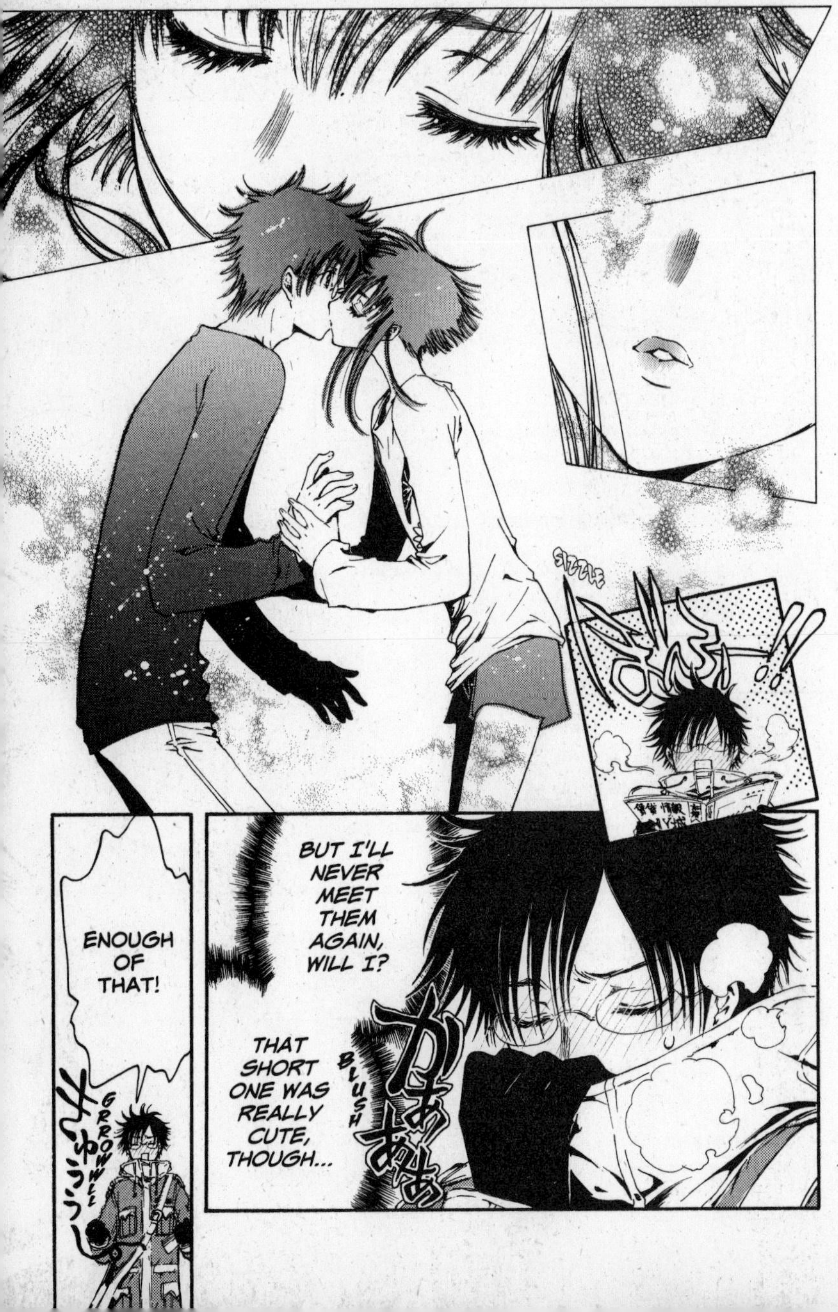
SIZZLE
BUT I'LL NEVER MEET THEM AGAIN, WILL I?
THAT SHORT ONE WAS REALLY CUTE, THOUGH...
BLUSH
ENOUGH OF THAT!
GRROWLL

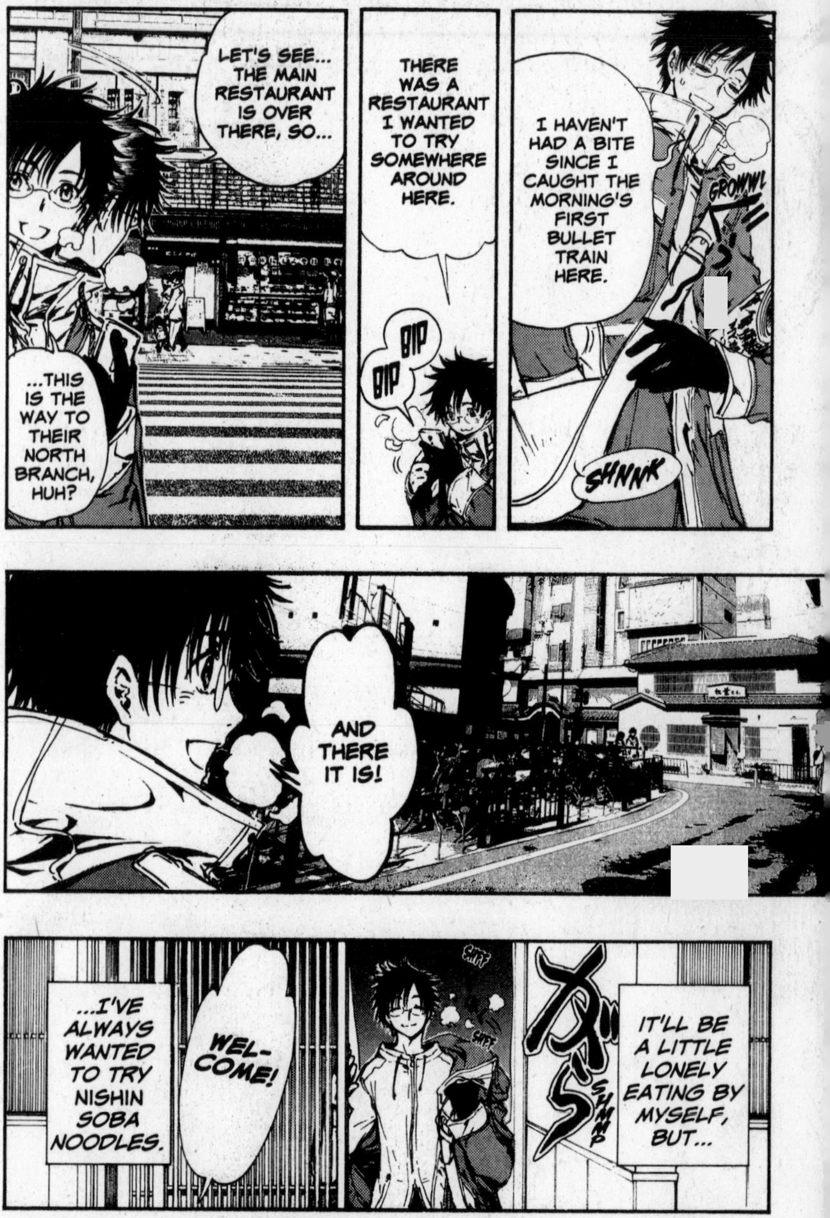
I HAVEN'T HAD A BITE SINCE I CAUGHT THE MORNING'S FIRST BULLET TRAIN HERE.
GROWWL
SHNNK
THERE WAS A RESTAURANT I WANTED TO TRY SOMEWHERE AROUND HERE.
BIP
BIP
LET'S SEE... THE MAIN RESTAURANT IS OVER THERE, SO...
...THIS IS THE WAY TO THEIR NORTH BRANCH, HUH?
AND THERE IT IS!
IT'LL BE A LITTLE LONELY EATING BY MYSELF, BUT...
SHMMP
SHFF
SHFF
WEL-COME!
...I'VE ALWAYS WANTED TO TRY NISHIN SOBA NOODLES.

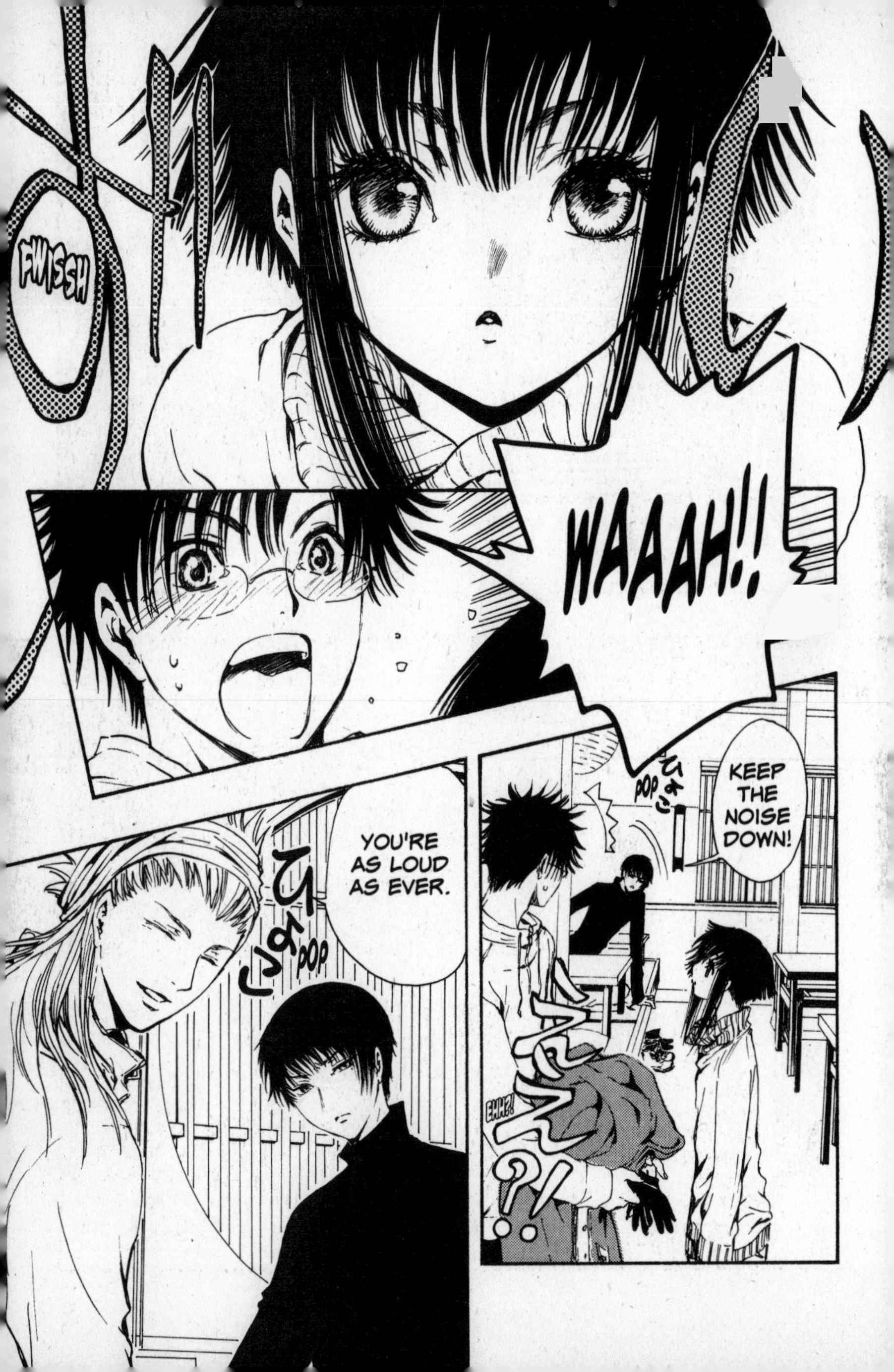
FWISSH
WAAAH!!
KEEP THE NOISE DOWN!
POP
EH!?
YOU'RE AS LOUD AS EVER.
POP

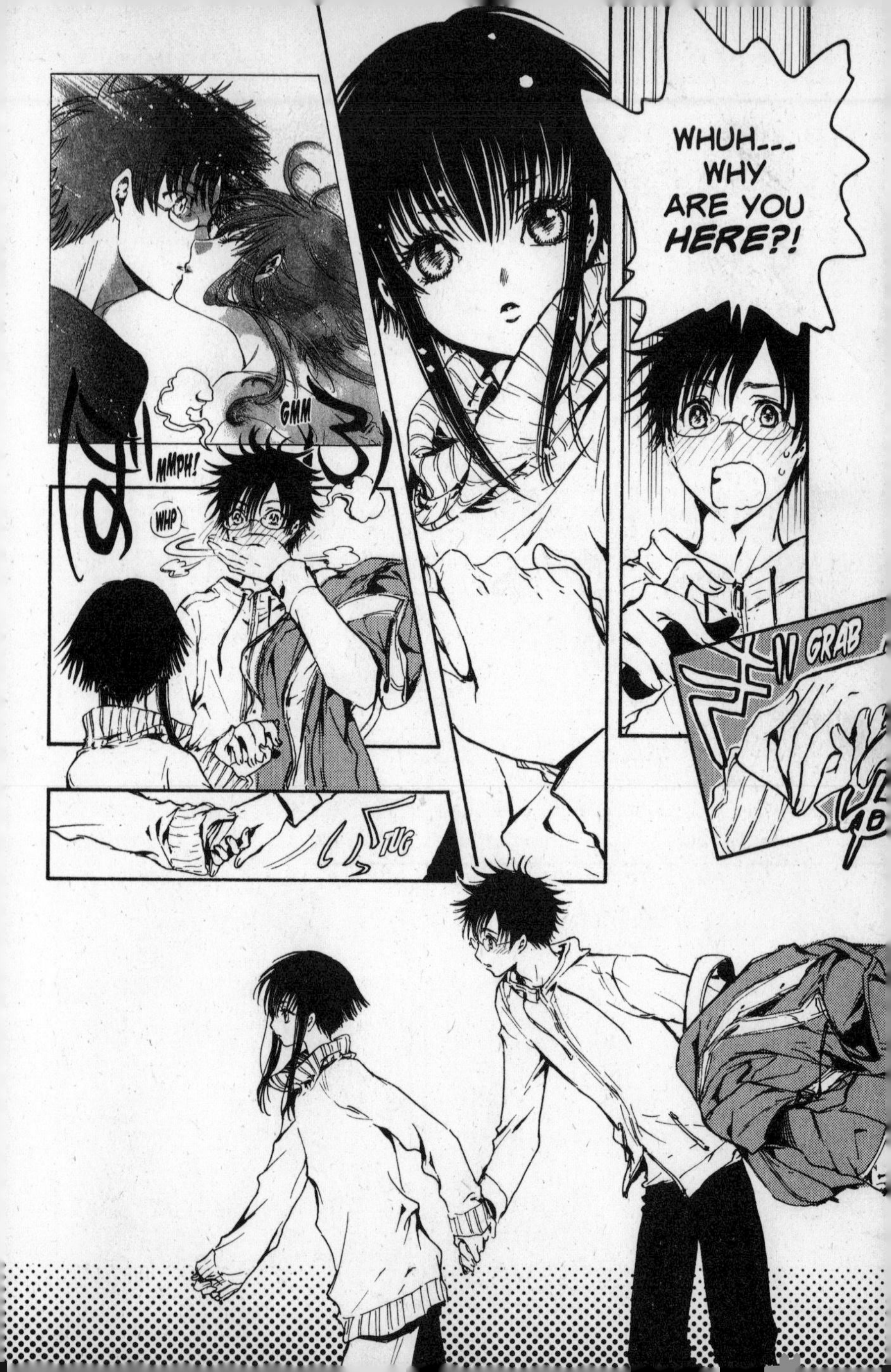
WHUH... WHY ARE YOU HERE?!
GRAB
GMM
MMPH!
WHP
TUG

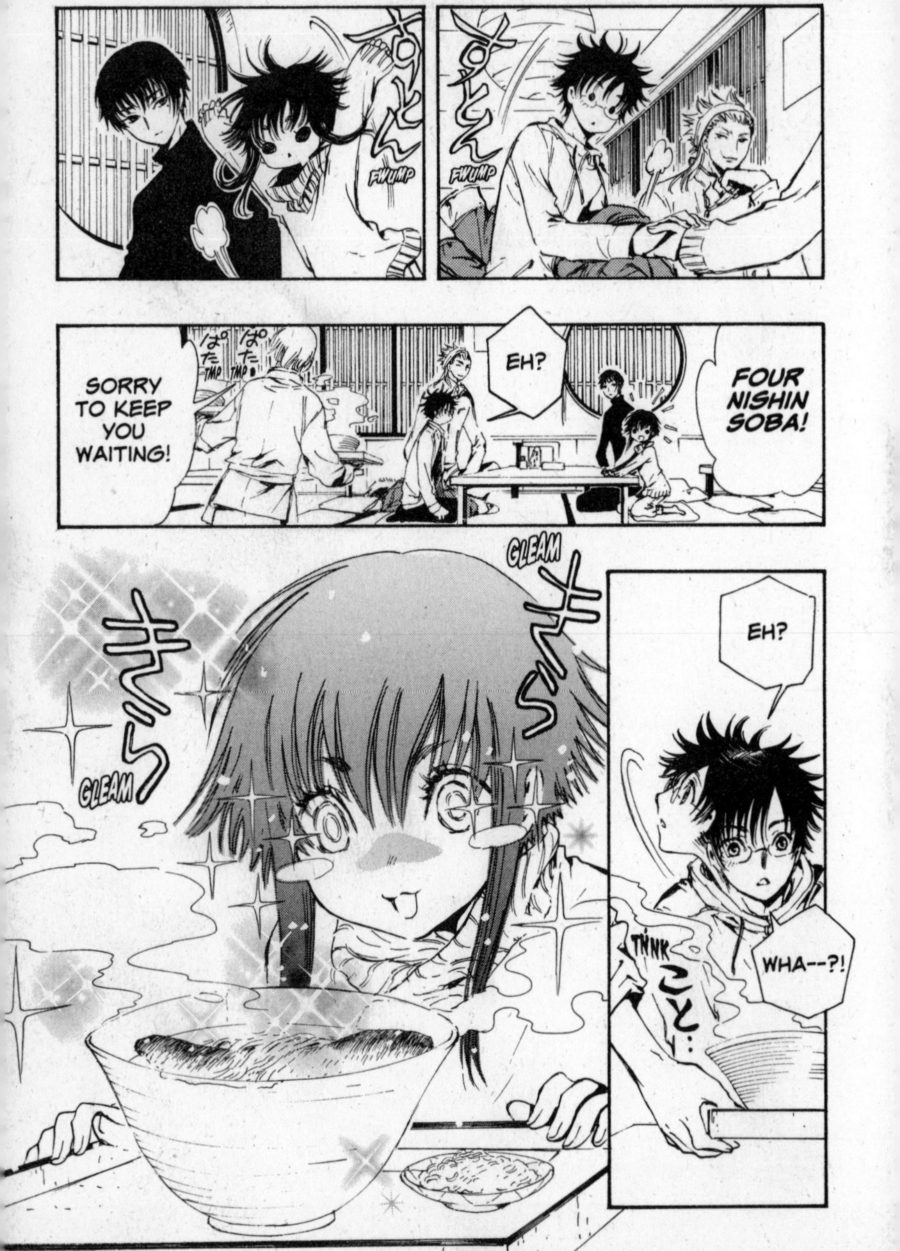
すとん
FWUMP
すとん
FWUMP
FOUR NISHIN SOBA!
EH?
ぱた
TMP
ぱた
TMP
SORRY TO KEEP YOU WAITING!
EH?
WHA--?!
こと
TINK
きら
GLEAM
きら
GLEAM

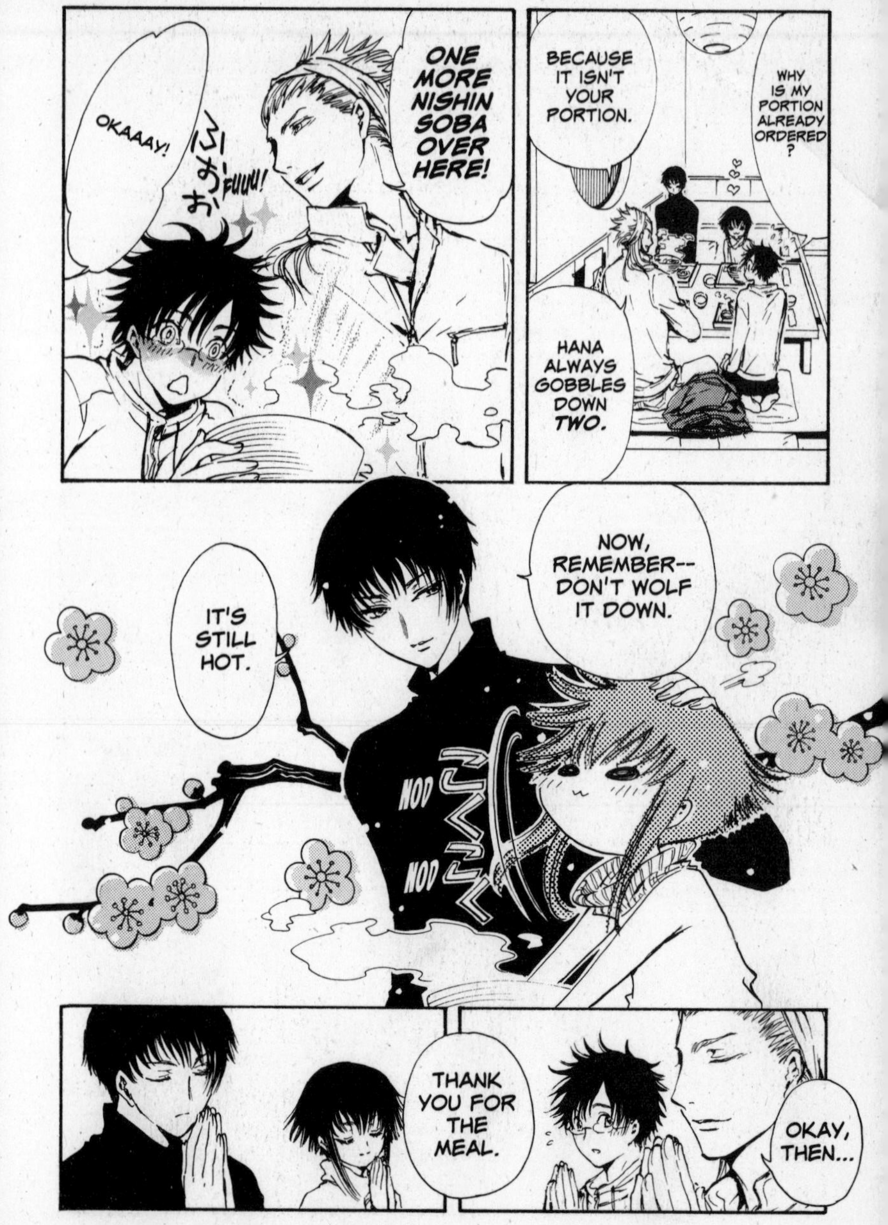
WHY IS MY PORTION ALREADY ORDERED?
BECAUSE IT ISN'T YOUR PORTION.
HANA ALWAYS GOBBLES DOWN TWO.
ONE MORE NISHIN SOBA OVER HERE!
OKAAAY!
ふおお
FUUU!
NOW, REMEMBER-- DON'T WOLF IT DOWN.
IT'S STILL HOT.
NOD
NOD
OKAY, THEN...
THANK YOU FOR THE MEAL.

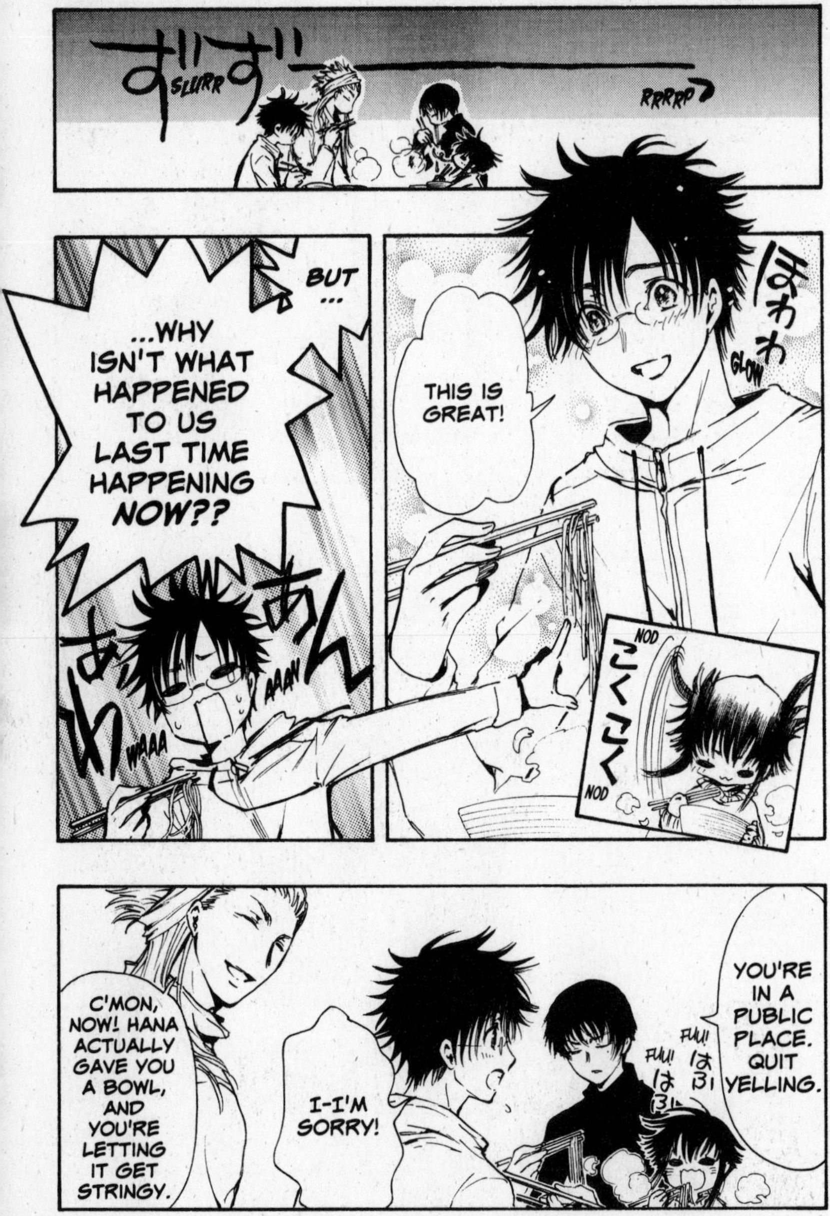
ずずー
SLURR
RRRRP
ほわわ
GLOW
THIS IS GREAT!
こくこく
NOD
NOD
BUT ...
...WHY ISN'T WHAT HAPPENED TO US LAST TIME HAPPENING NOW??
あんあわ
AAAN
WAAA
YOU'RE IN A PUBLIC PLACE. QUIT YELLING.
はふはふ
FUU!
FUU!
I-I'M SORRY!
C'MON, NOW! HANA ACTUALLY GAVE YOU A BOWL, AND YOU'RE LETTING IT GET STRINGY.

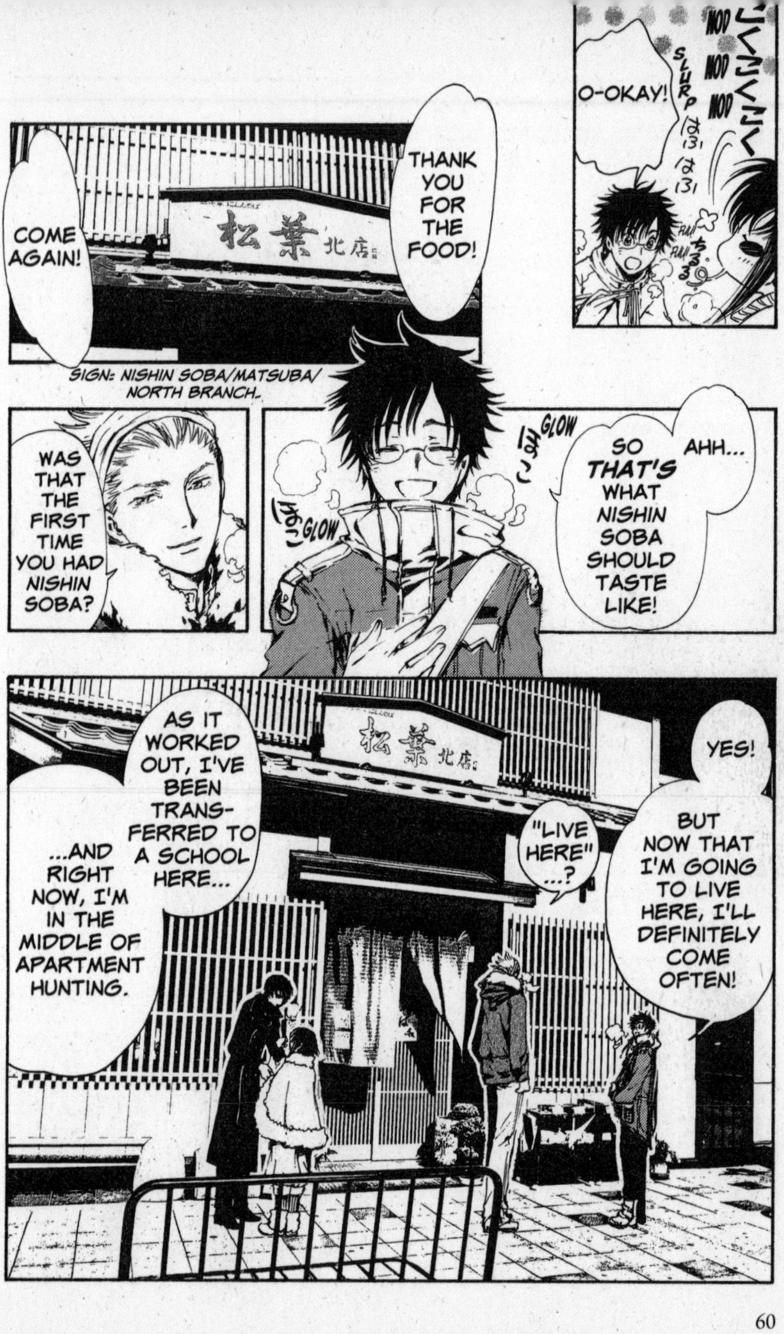
NOD NOD NOD
SLURP
O-OKAY!
THANK YOU FOR THE FOOD!
COME AGAIN!
SIGN: NISHIN SOBA/MATSUBA/ NORTH BRANCH.
GLOW
GLOW
AHH... SO THAT'S WHAT NISHIN SOBA SHOULD TASTE LIKE!
WAS THAT THE FIRST TIME YOU HAD NISHIN SOBA?
YES!
BUT NOW THAT I'M GOING TO LIVE HERE, I'LL DEFINITELY COME OFTEN!
"LIVE HERE" ...?
AS IT WORKED OUT, I'VE BEEN TRANS- FERRED TO A SCHOOL HERE...
...AND RIGHT NOW, I'M IN THE MIDDLE OF APARTMENT HUNTING.

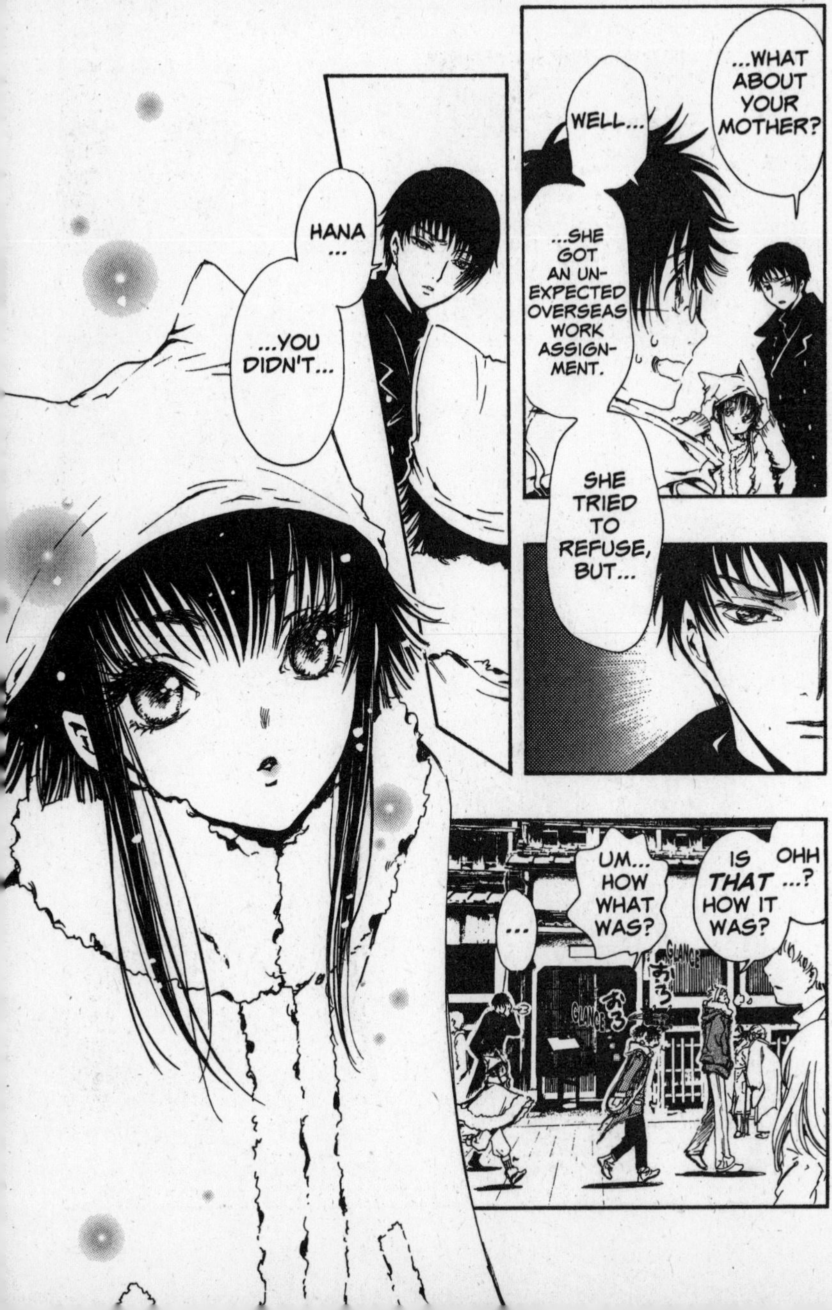
...WHAT ABOUT YOUR MOTHER?
WELL...
...SHE GOT AN UN-EXPECTED OVERSEAS WORK ASSIGN-MENT.
SHE TRIED TO REFUSE, BUT...
HANA...
...YOU DIDN'T...
OHH ...?
IS THAT HOW IT WAS?
UM... HOW WHAT WAS?
...
GLANCE
GLANCE

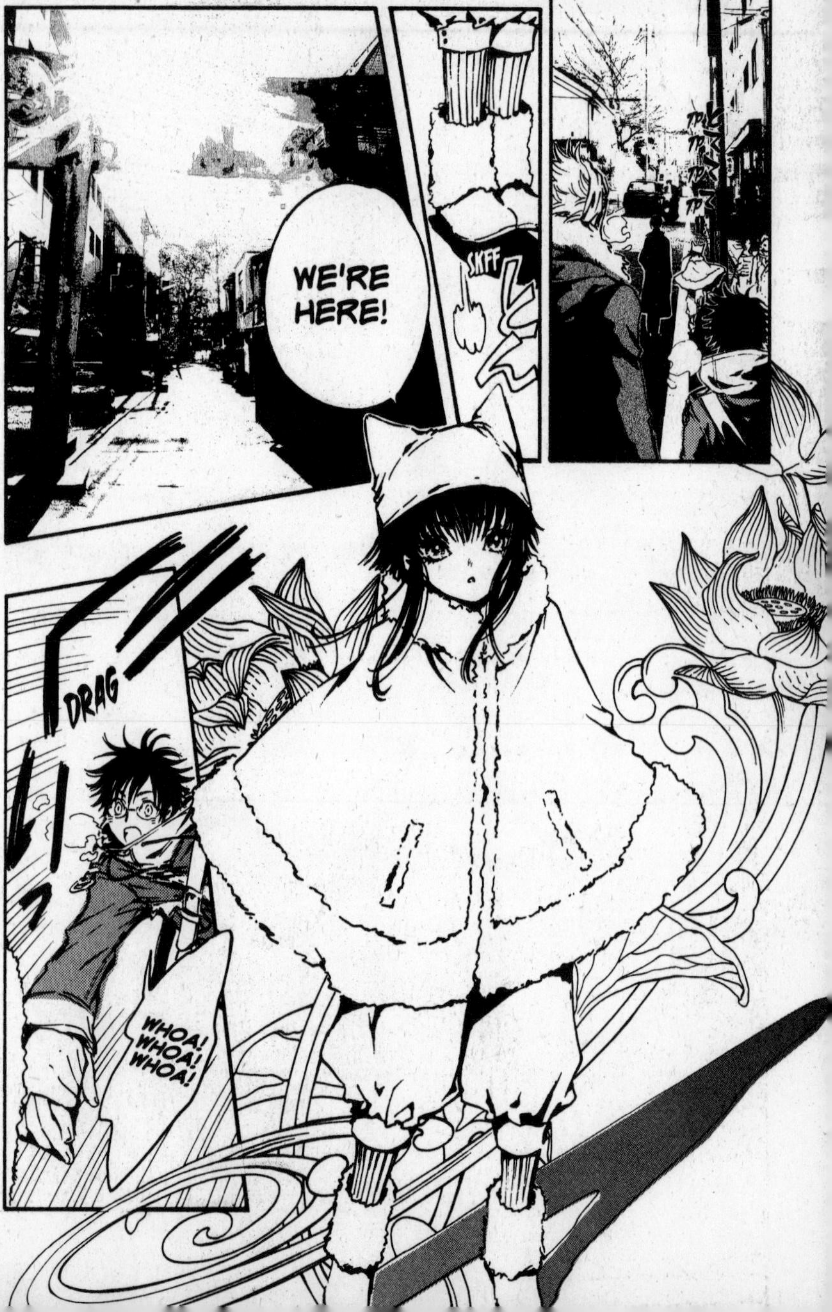

SKFF
WE'RE HERE!
DRAG
WHOA! WHOA! WHOA!

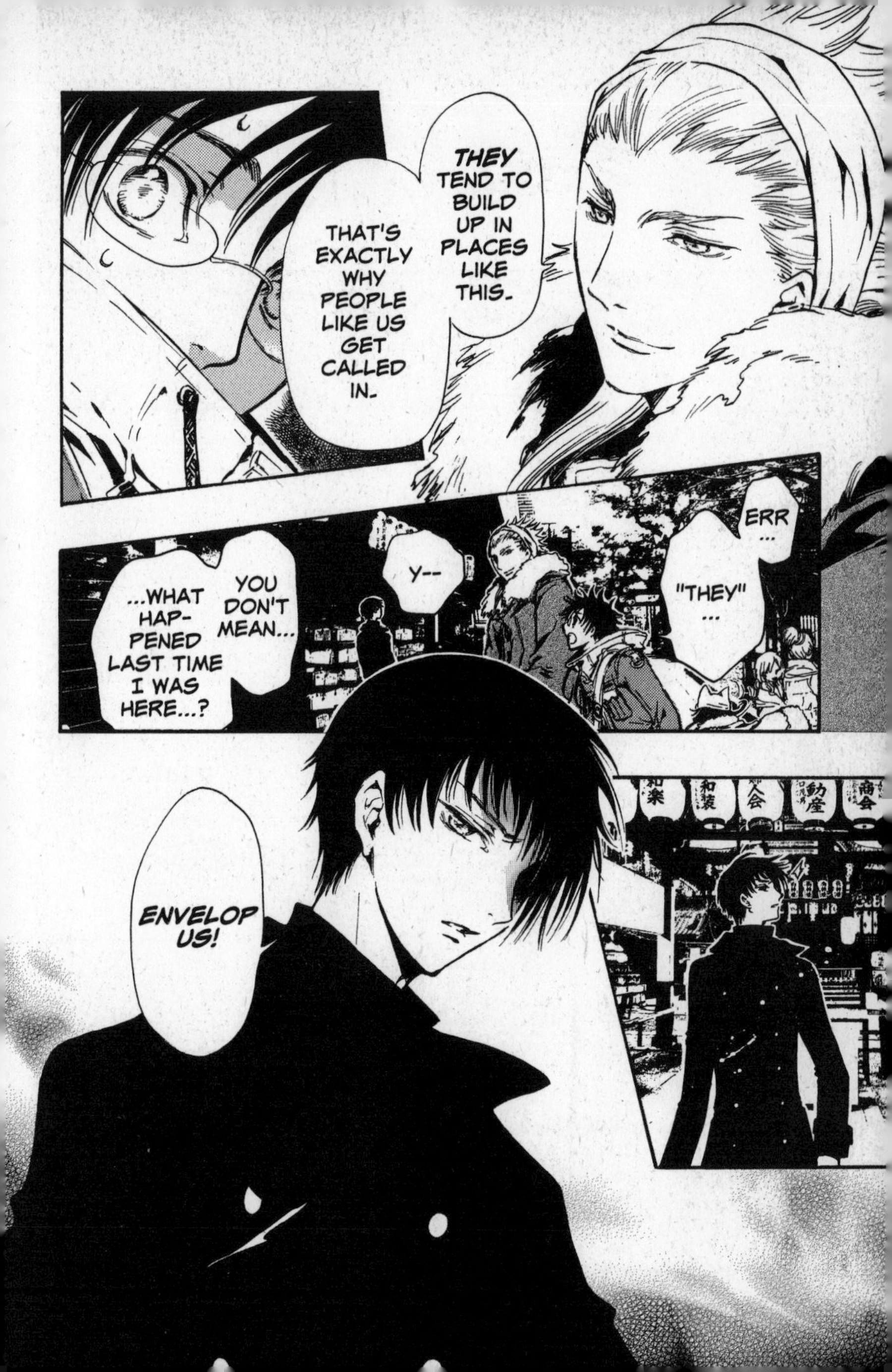
THEY TEND TO BUILD UP IN PLACES LIKE THIS.
THAT'S EXACTLY WHY PEOPLE LIKE US GET CALLED IN.
ERR... "THEY"...
Y--
YOU DON'T MEAN...
...WHAT HAPPENED LAST TIME I WAS HERE...?
ENVELOP US!

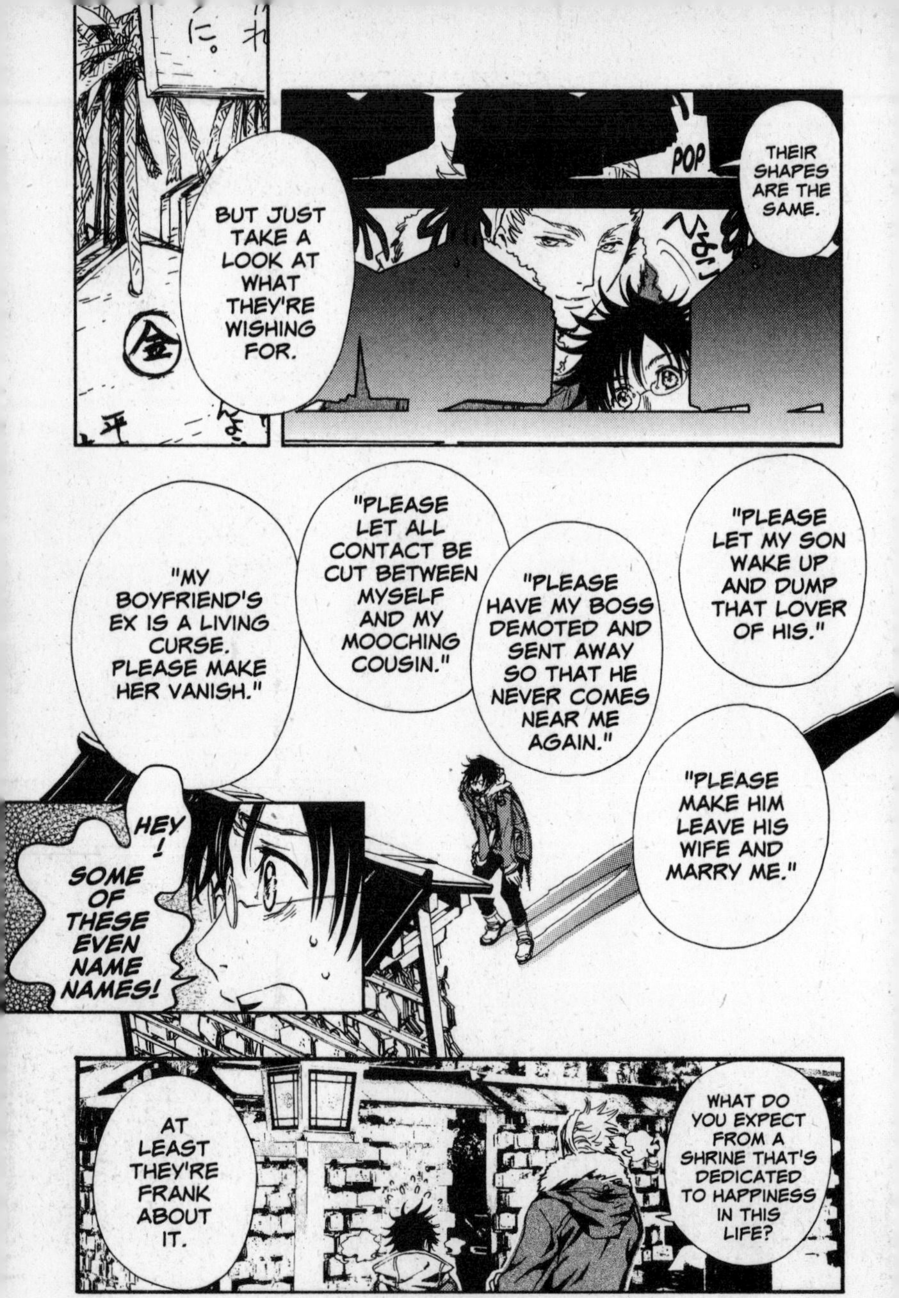

POP
THEIR SHAPES ARE THE SAME.
BUT JUST TAKE A LOOK AT WHAT THEY'RE WISHING FOR.
"PLEASE LET MY SON WAKE UP AND DUMP THAT LOVER OF HIS."
"PLEASE HAVE MY BOSS DEMOTED AND SENT AWAY SO THAT HE NEVER COMES NEAR ME AGAIN."
"PLEASE LET ALL CONTACT BE CUT BETWEEN MYSELF AND MY MOOCHING COUSIN."
"MY BOYFRIEND'S EX IS A LIVING CURSE. PLEASE MAKE HER VANISH."
"PLEASE MAKE HIM LEAVE HIS WIFE AND MARRY ME."
HEY! SOME OF THESE EVEN NAME NAMES!
WHAT DO YOU EXPECT FROM A SHRINE THAT'S DEDICATED TO HAPPINESS IN THIS LIFE?
AT LEAST THEY'RE FRANK ABOUT IT.

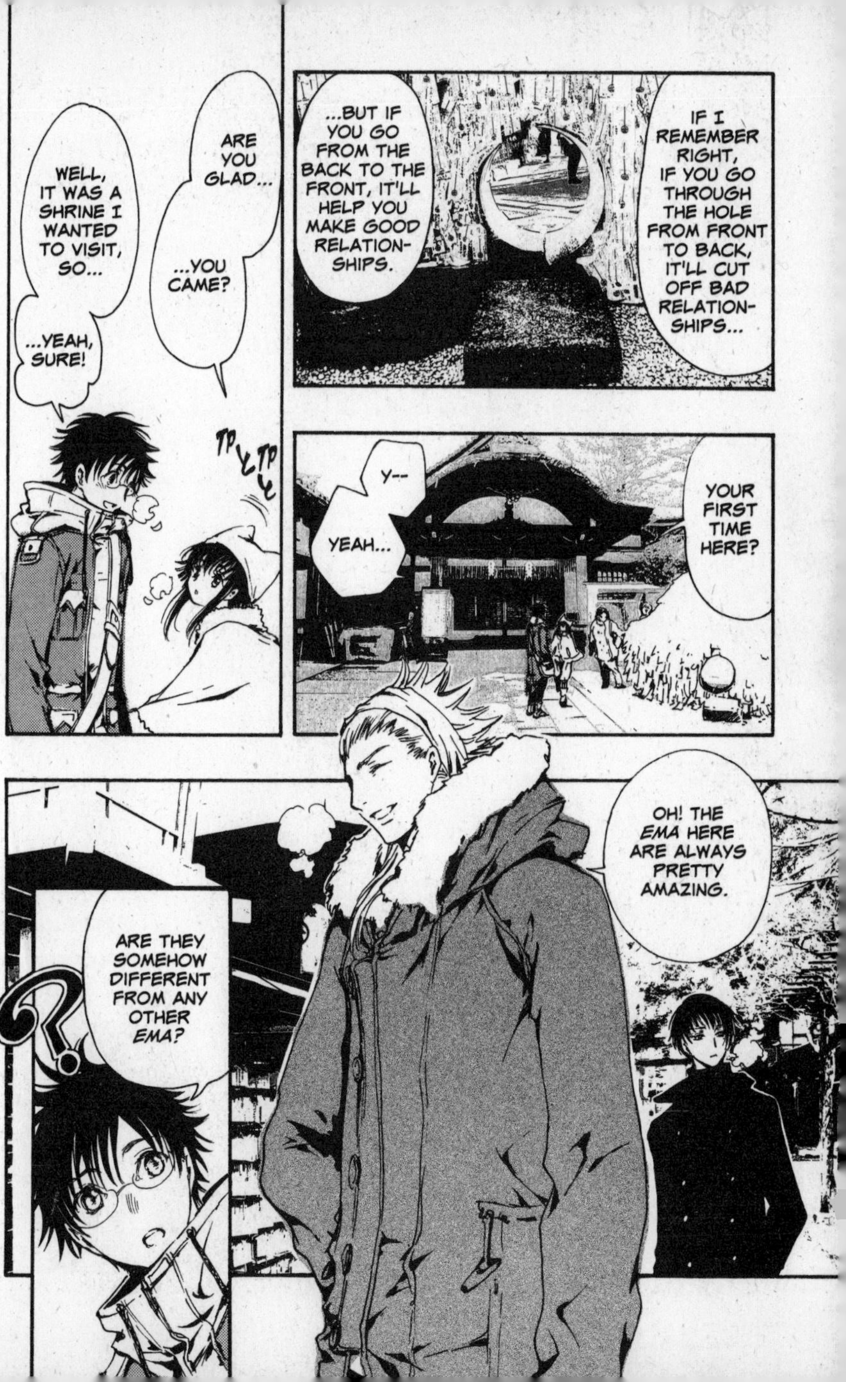
IF I REMEMBER RIGHT, IF YOU GO THROUGH THE HOLE FROM FRONT TO BACK, IT'LL CUT OFF BAD RELATIONSHIPS...
...BUT IF YOU GO FROM THE BACK TO THE FRONT, IT'LL HELP YOU MAKE GOOD RELATIONSHIPS.
YOUR FIRST TIME HERE?
Y-- YEAH...
ARE YOU GLAD... ...YOU CAME?
WELL, IT WAS A SHRINE I WANTED TO VISIT, SO...
...YEAH, SURE!
TP TP
OH! THE *EMA* HERE ARE ALWAYS PRETTY AMAZING.
ARE THEY SOMEHOW DIFFERENT FROM ANY OTHER *EMA*?

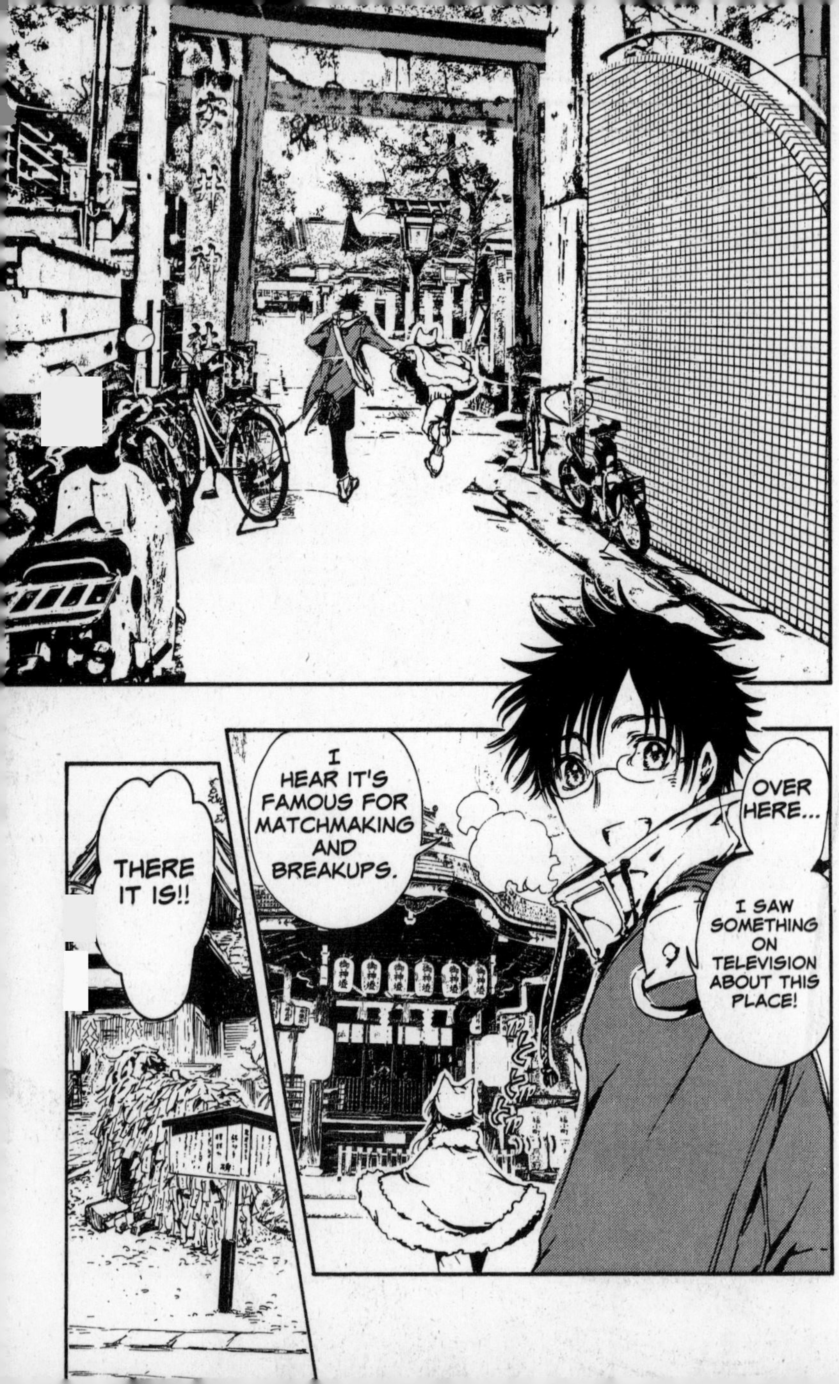
OVER HERE...
I SAW SOMETHING ON TELEVISION ABOUT THIS PLACE!
I HEAR IT'S FAMOUS FOR MATCHMAKING AND BREAKUPS.
THERE IT IS!!

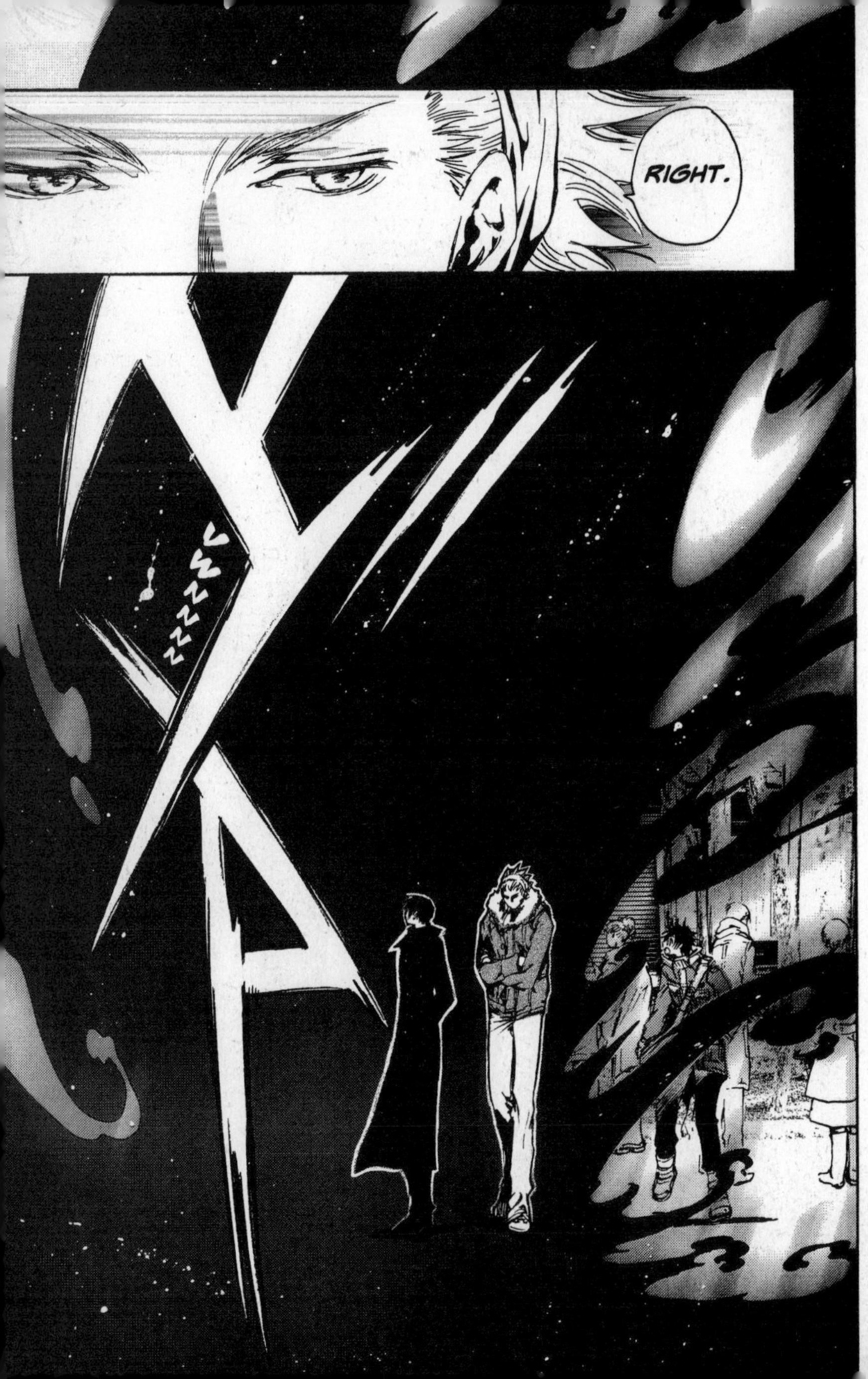
RIGHT.
VWNNNN

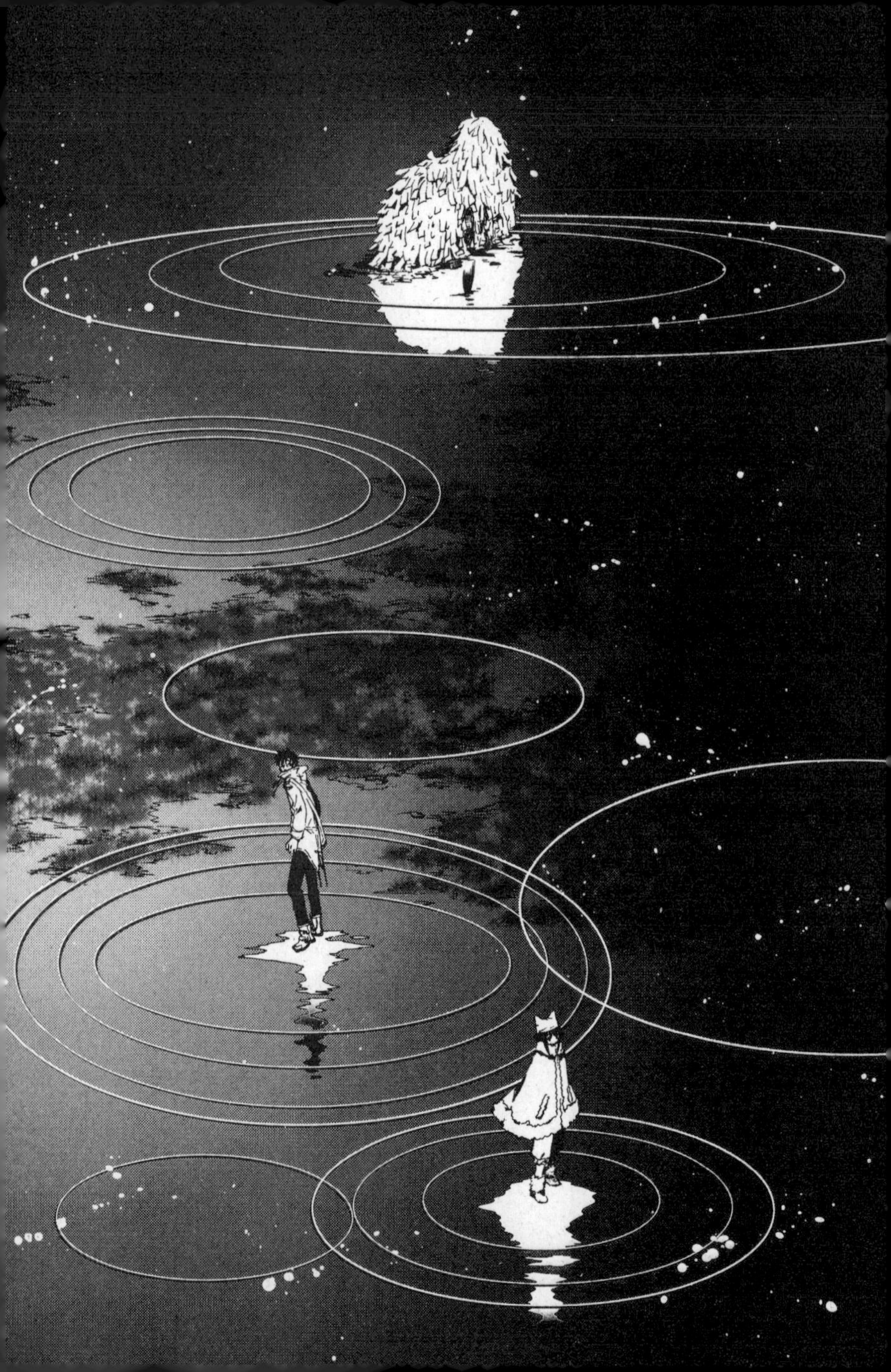

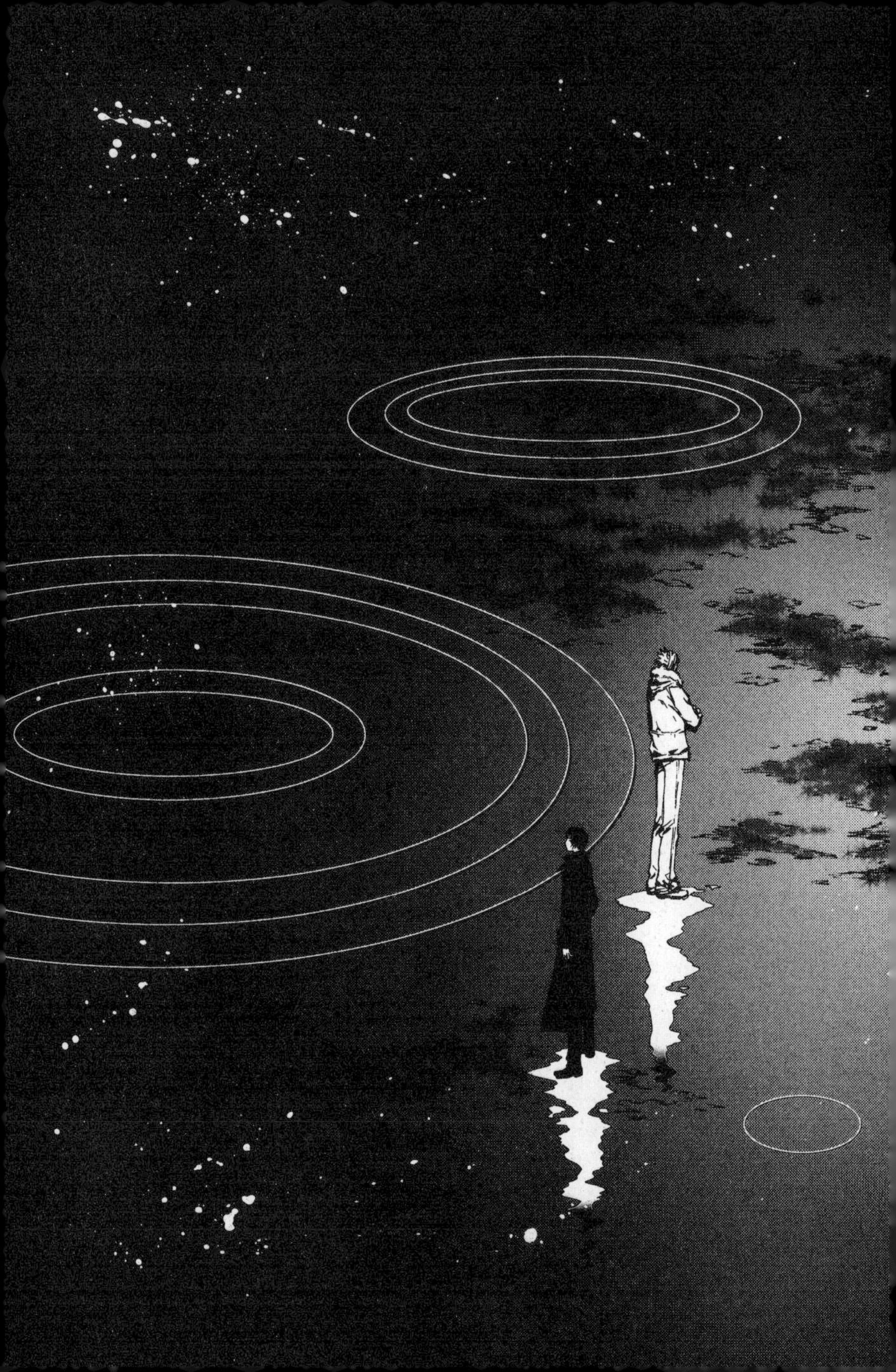

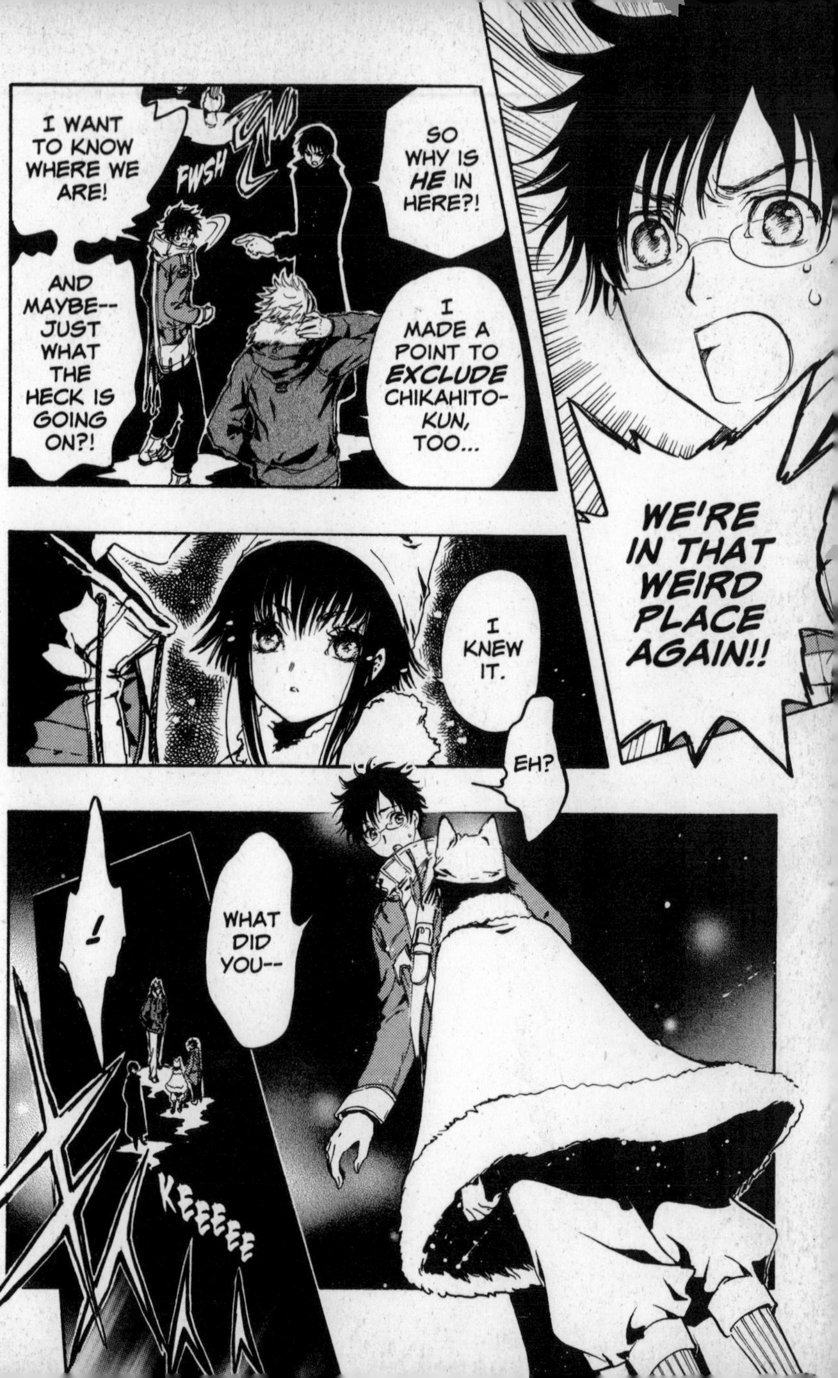
WE'RE IN THAT WEIRD PLACE AGAIN!!
SO WHY IS *HE* IN HERE?!
I WANT TO KNOW WHERE WE ARE!
FWSH
I MADE A POINT TO *EXCLUDE* CHIKAHITO-KUN, TOO...
AND MAYBE-- JUST WHAT THE HECK IS GOING ON?!
I KNEW IT.
EH?
WHAT DID YOU--
!
KEEEEEE

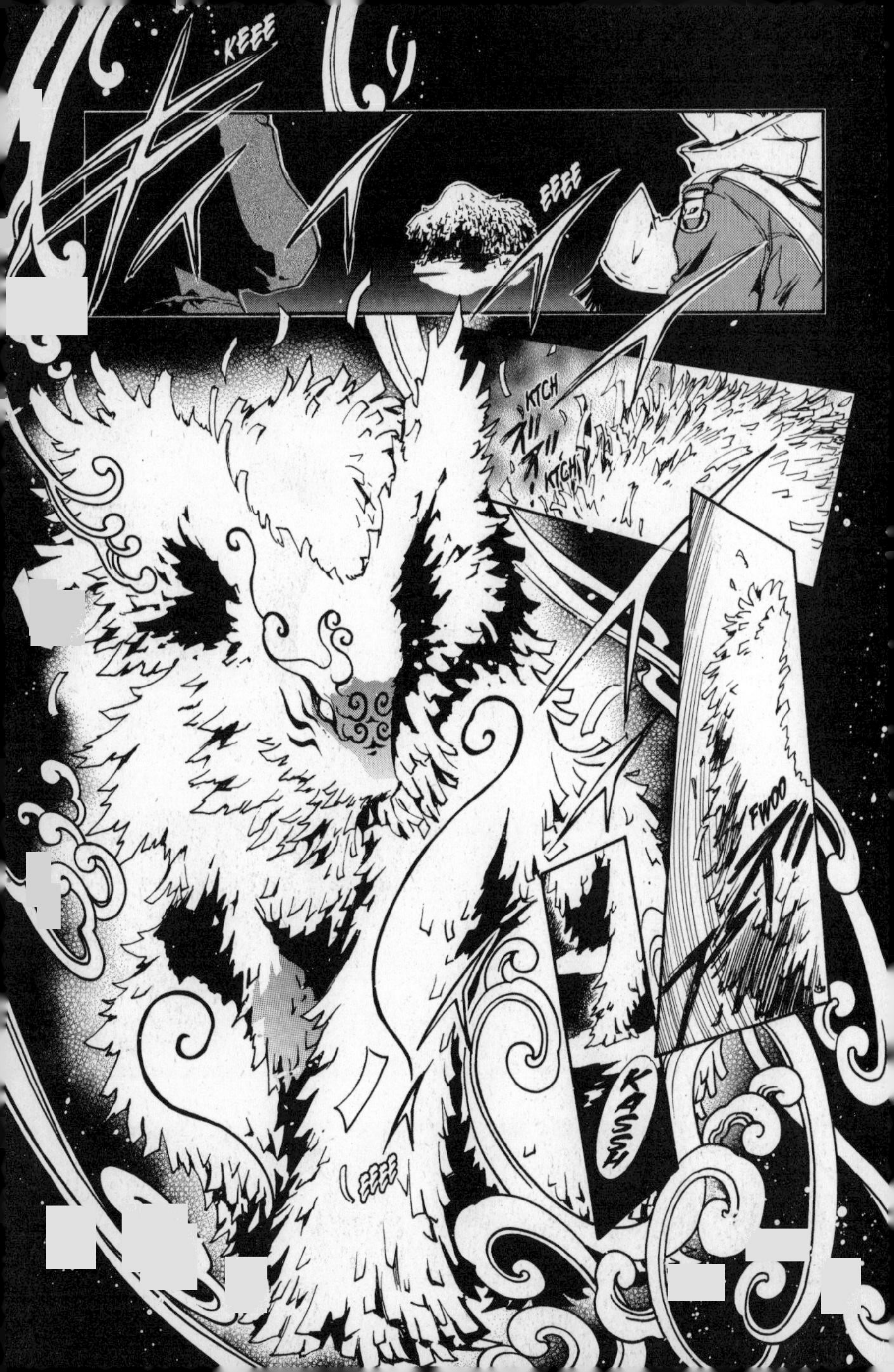
EEEE
KEEE
KTCH
KTCH
FWOO
KASSH
EEEE

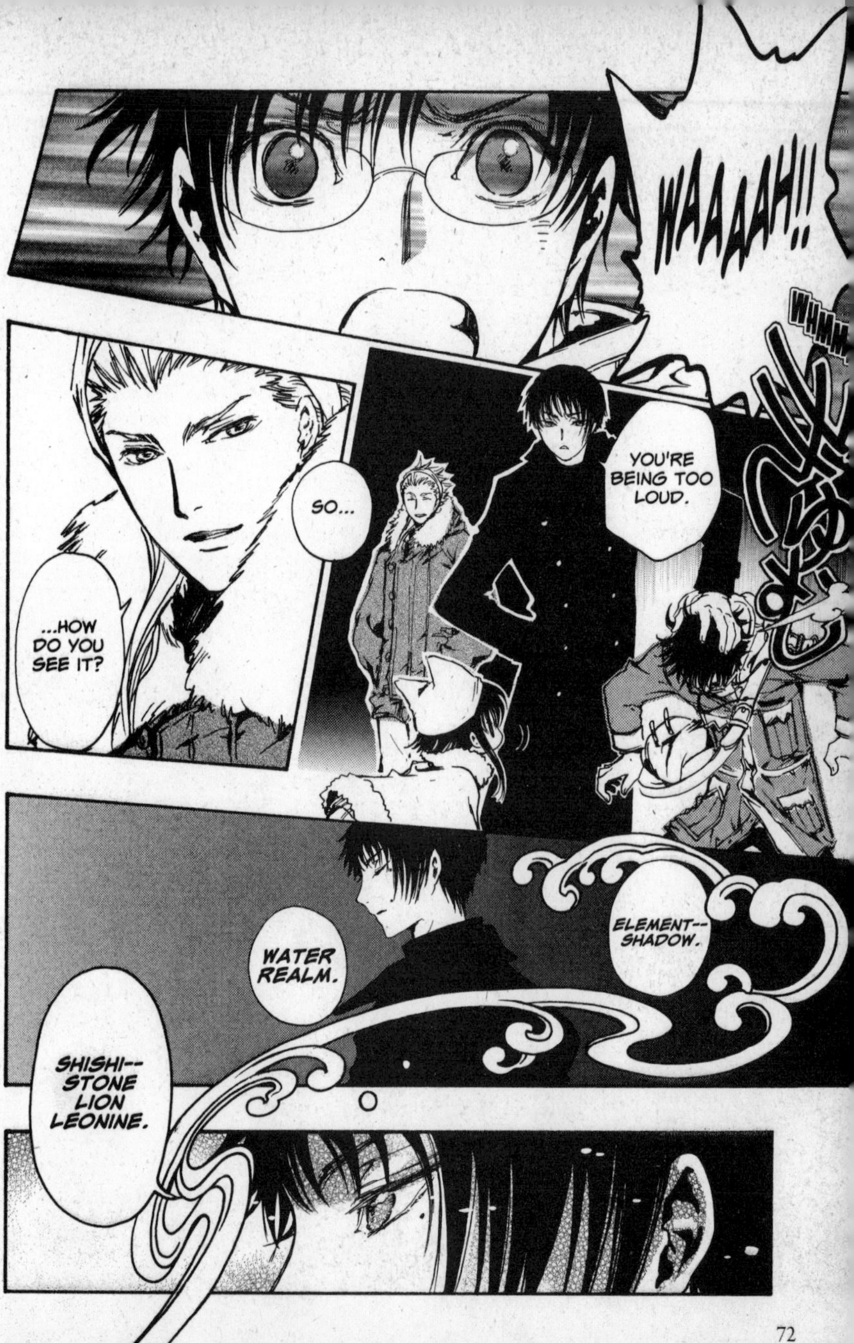
WAAAAH!!
WHMM
YOU'RE BEING TOO LOUD.
SO...
...HOW DO YOU SEE IT?
ELEMENT--SHADOW.
WATER REALM.
SHISHI--STONE LION LEONINE.

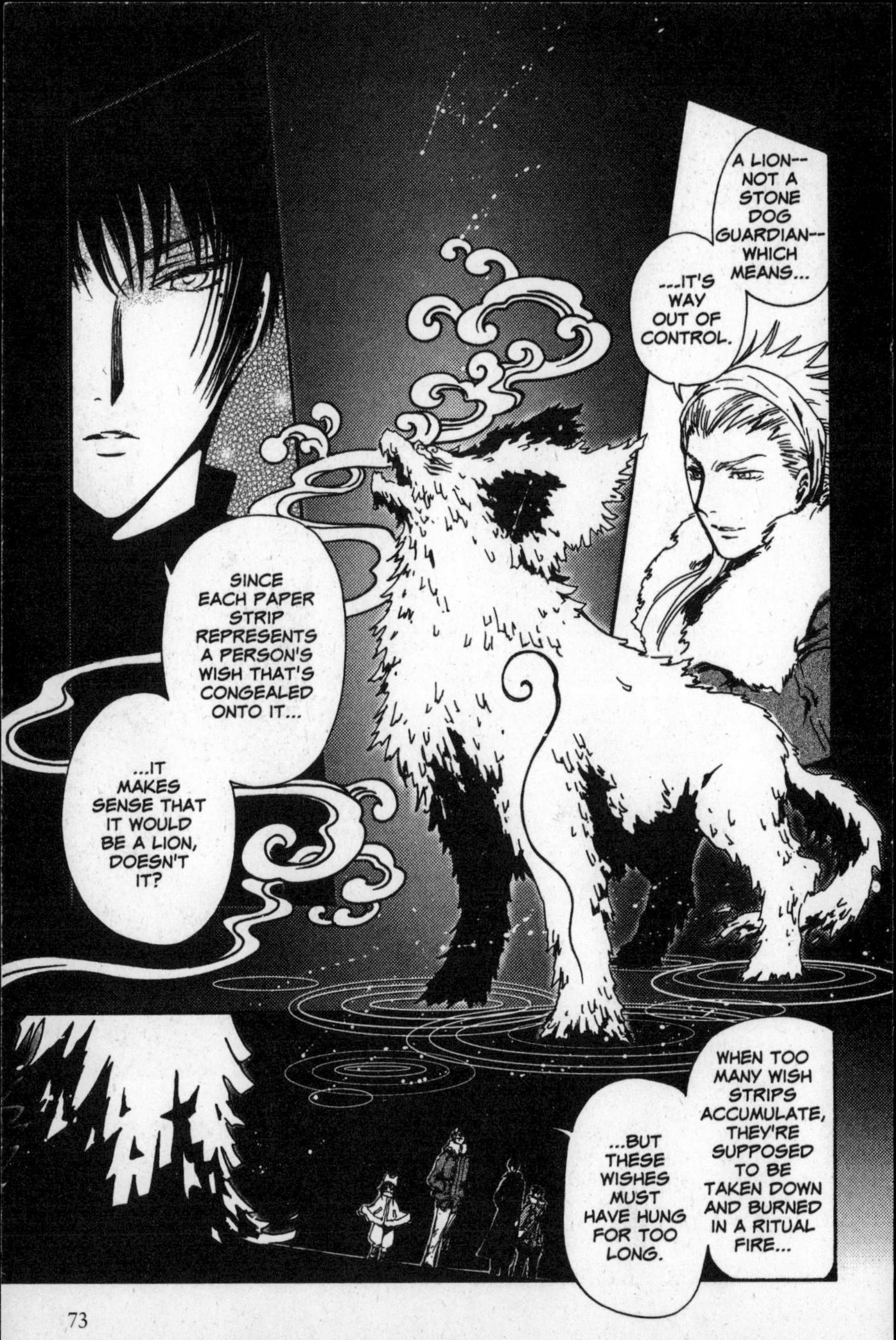
A LION-- NOT A STONE DOG GUARDIAN-- WHICH MEANS...
...IT'S WAY OUT OF CONTROL.
SINCE EACH PAPER STRIP REPRESENTS A PERSON'S WISH THAT'S CONGEALED ONTO IT...
...IT MAKES SENSE THAT IT WOULD BE A LION, DOESN'T IT?
WHEN TOO MANY WISH STRIPS ACCUMULATE, THEY'RE SUPPOSED TO BE TAKEN DOWN AND BURNED IN A RITUAL FIRE...
...BUT THESE WISHES MUST HAVE HUNG FOR TOO LONG.

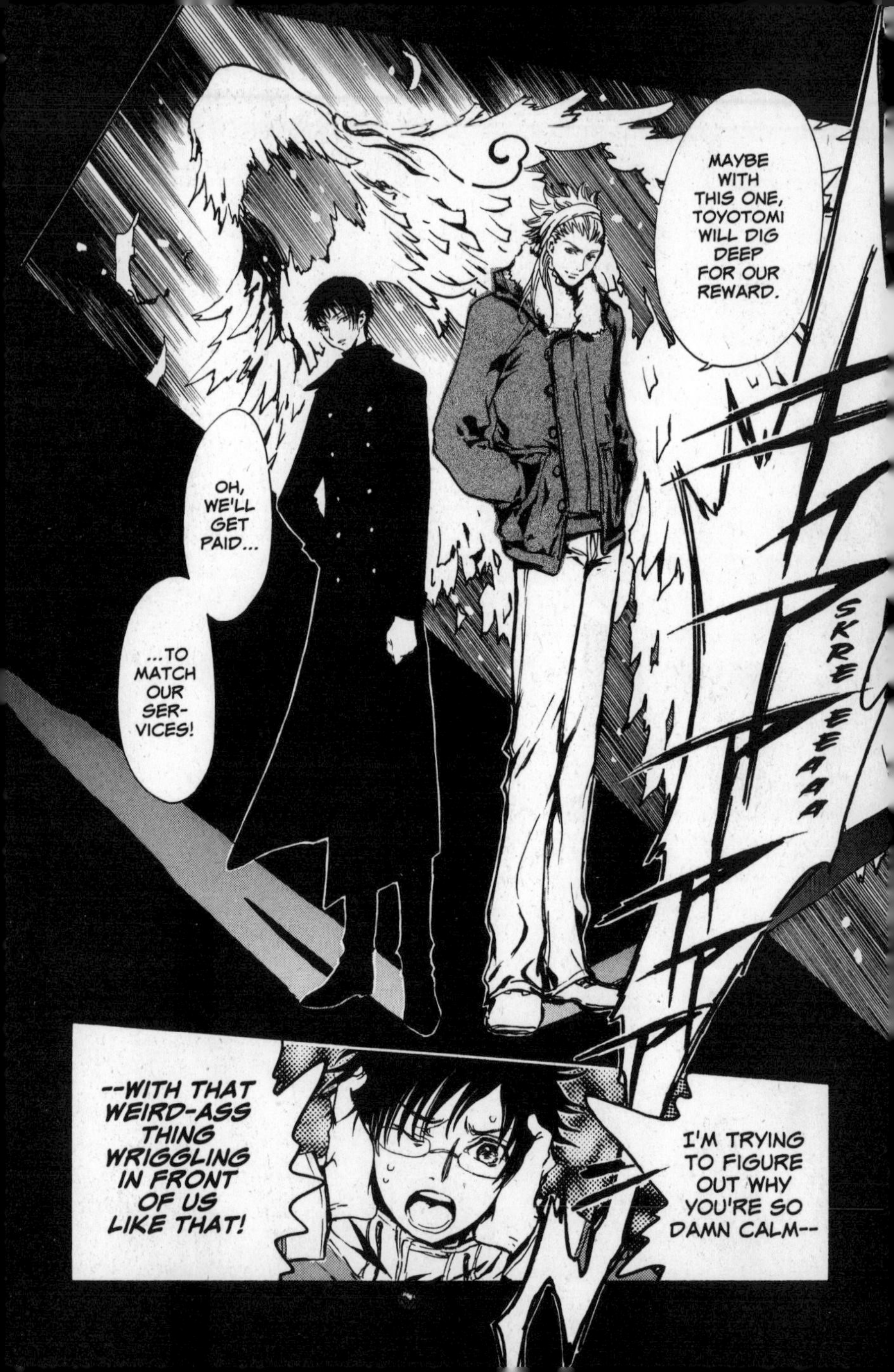
MAYBE WITH THIS ONE, TOYOTOMI WILL DIG DEEP FOR OUR REWARD.
SKREEEEAAAA
OH, WE'LL GET PAID...
...TO MATCH OUR SER-VICES!
I'M TRYING TO FIGURE OUT WHY YOU'RE SO DAMN CALM--
--WITH THAT WEIRD-ASS THING WRIGGLING IN FRONT OF US LIKE THAT!

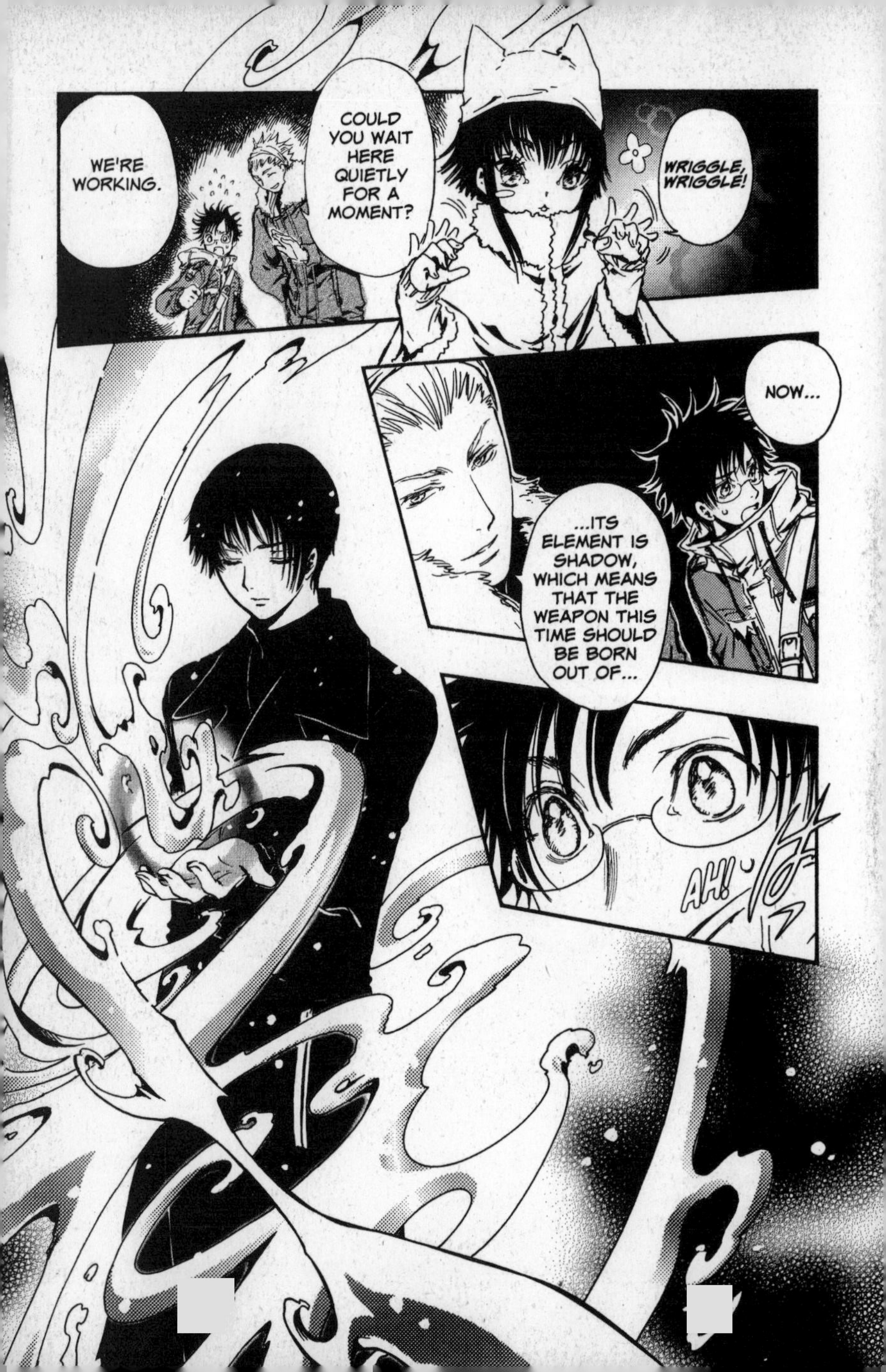
WRIGGLE, WRIGGLE!
COULD YOU WAIT HERE QUIETLY FOR A MOMENT?
WE'RE WORKING.
NOW...
...ITS ELEMENT IS SHADOW, WHICH MEANS THAT THE WEAPON THIS TIME SHOULD BE BORN OUT OF...
AH!

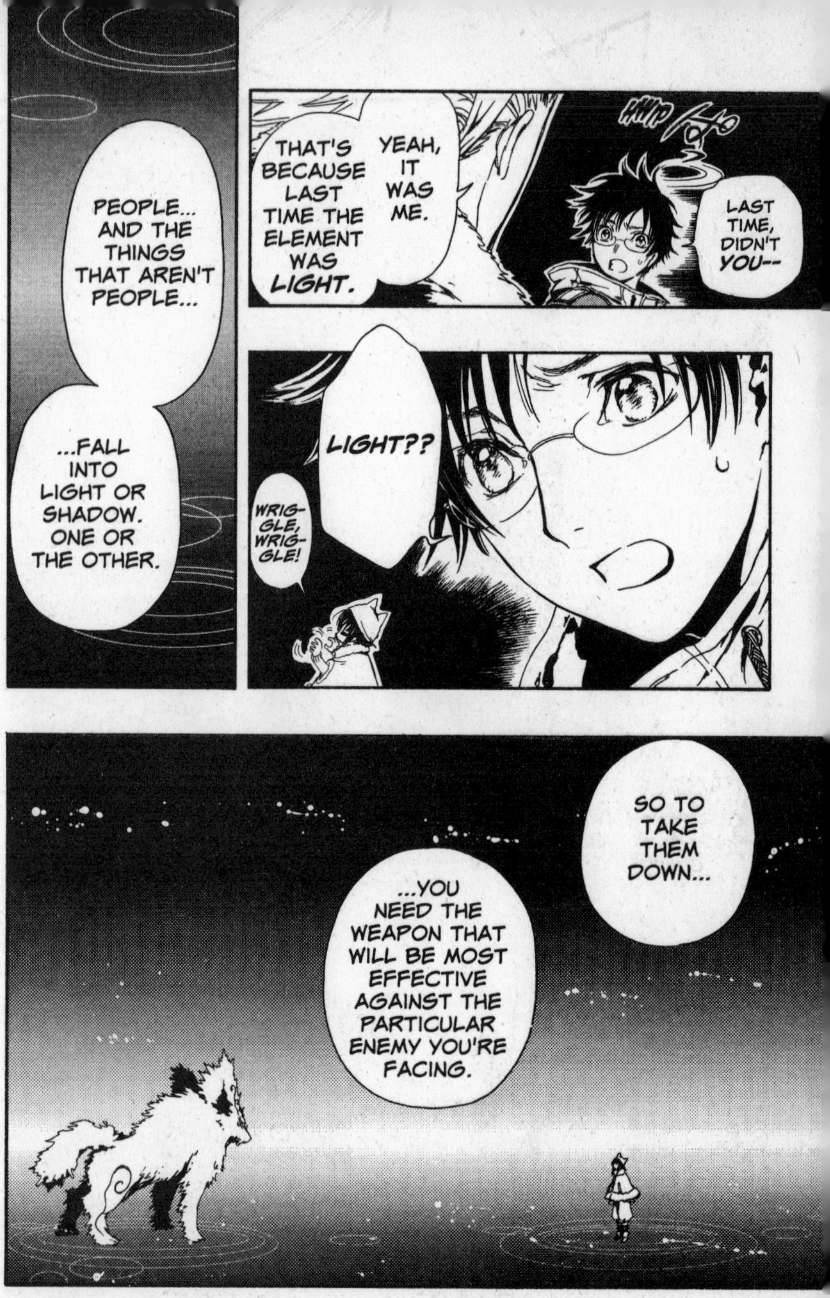
WHIP
LAST TIME, DIDN'T *YOU*--
YEAH, IT WAS ME.
THAT'S BECAUSE LAST TIME THE ELEMENT WAS *LIGHT*.
LIGHT??
WRIG-GLE, WRIG-GLE!
PEOPLE... AND THE THINGS THAT AREN'T PEOPLE...
...FALL INTO LIGHT OR SHADOW. ONE OR THE OTHER.
SO TO TAKE THEM DOWN...
...YOU NEED THE WEAPON THAT WILL BE MOST EFFECTIVE AGAINST THE PARTICULAR ENEMY YOU'RE FACING.

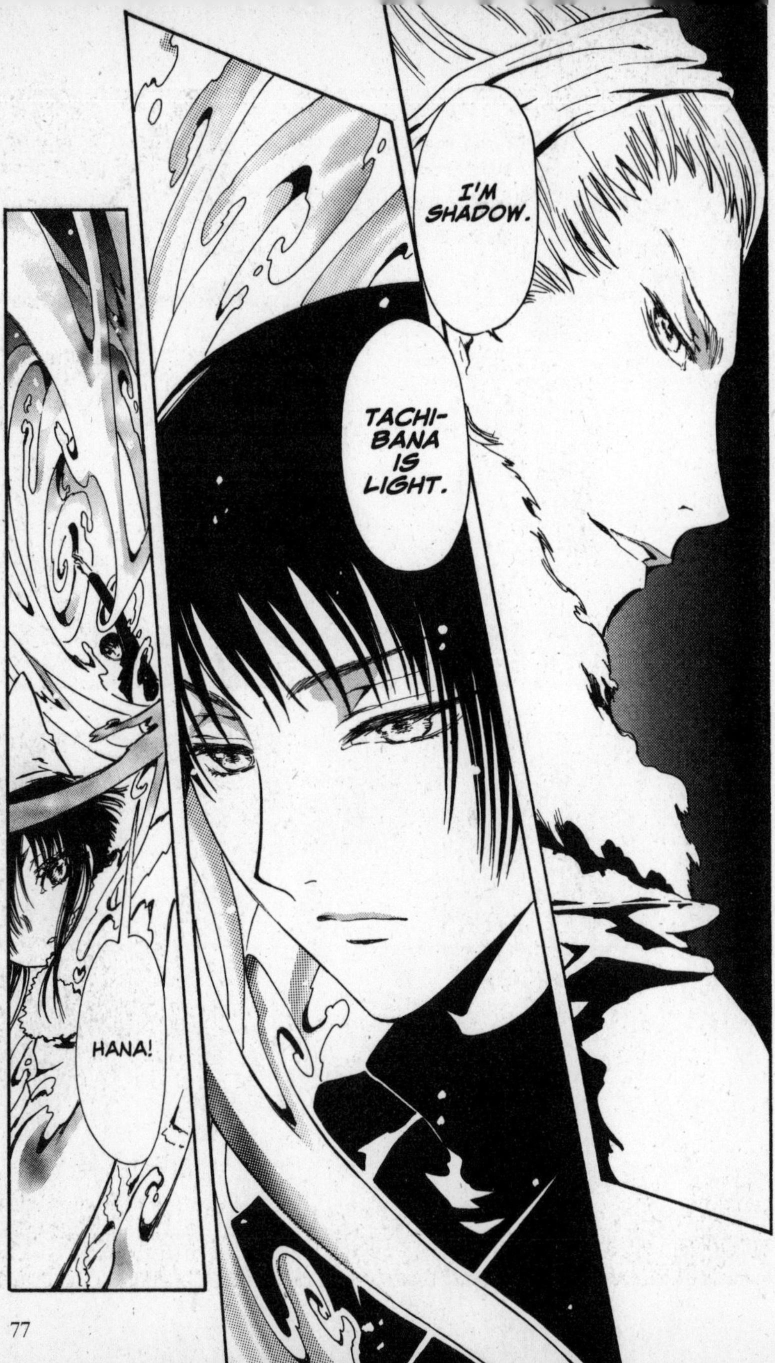
I'M SHADOW.
TACHI-BANA IS LIGHT.
HANA!

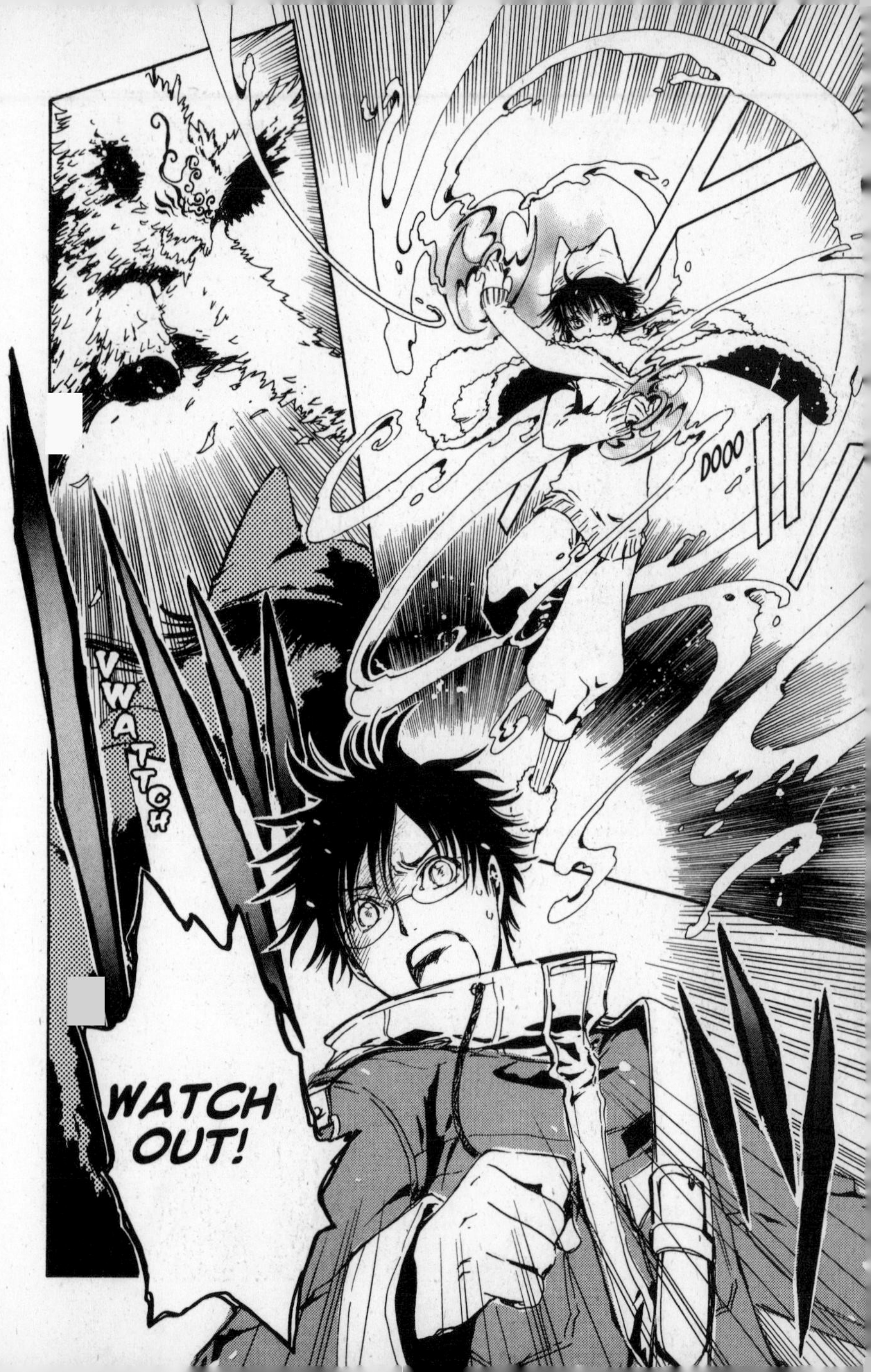
DOOO
VWATTCH
WATCH OUT!

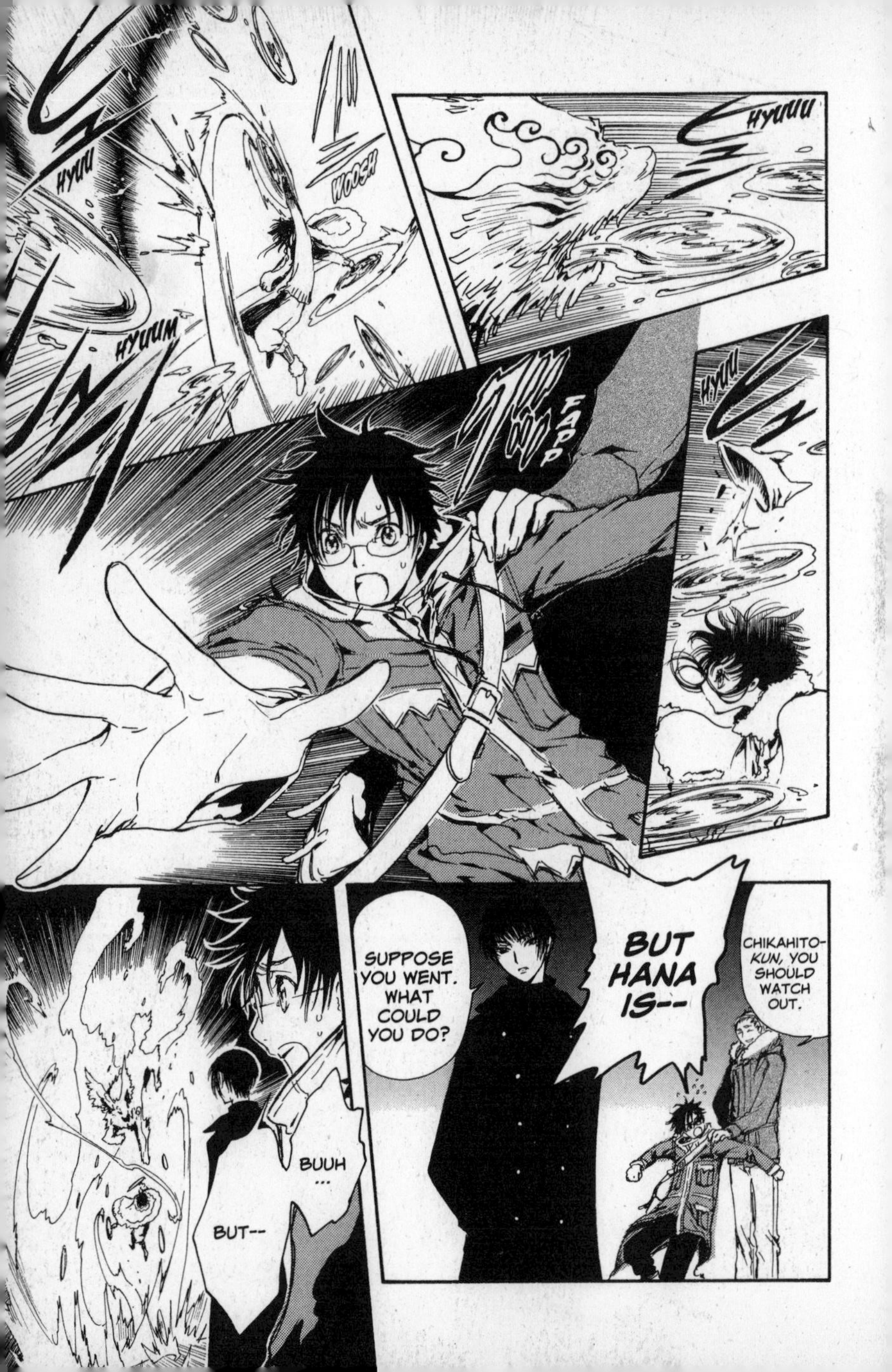
CHYUUU
HYUU
WOOSH
HYUUM
HYUU
FAPP
CHIKAHITO-KUN, YOU SHOULD WATCH OUT.
BUT HANA IS--
SUPPOSE YOU WENT. WHAT COULD YOU DO?
BUUH ...
BUT--

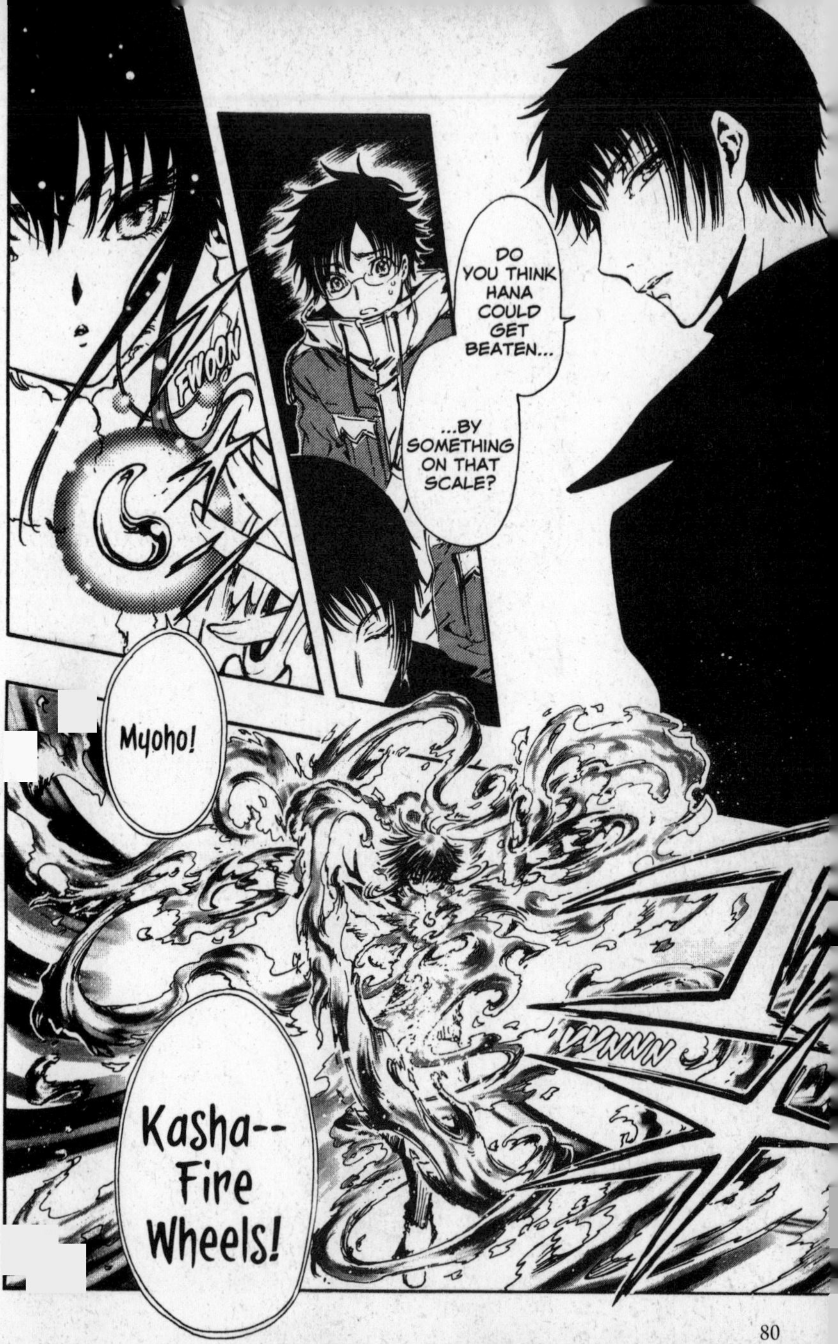
DO YOU THINK HANA COULD GET BEATEN...
...BY SOMETHING ON THAT SCALE?
FWOON
Myoho!
Kasha-- Fire Wheels!
VVNNNN

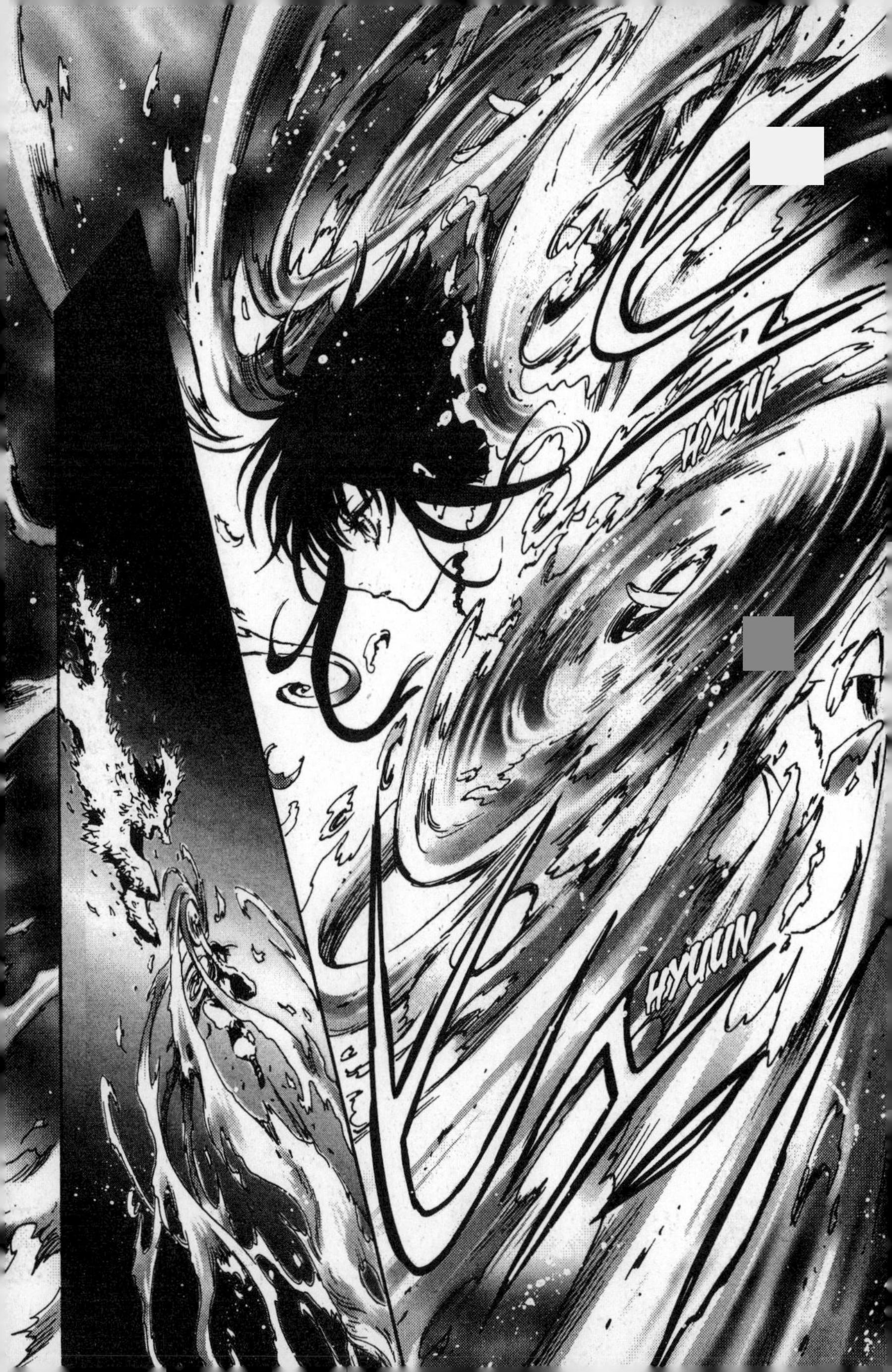
HYUU
HYUUN

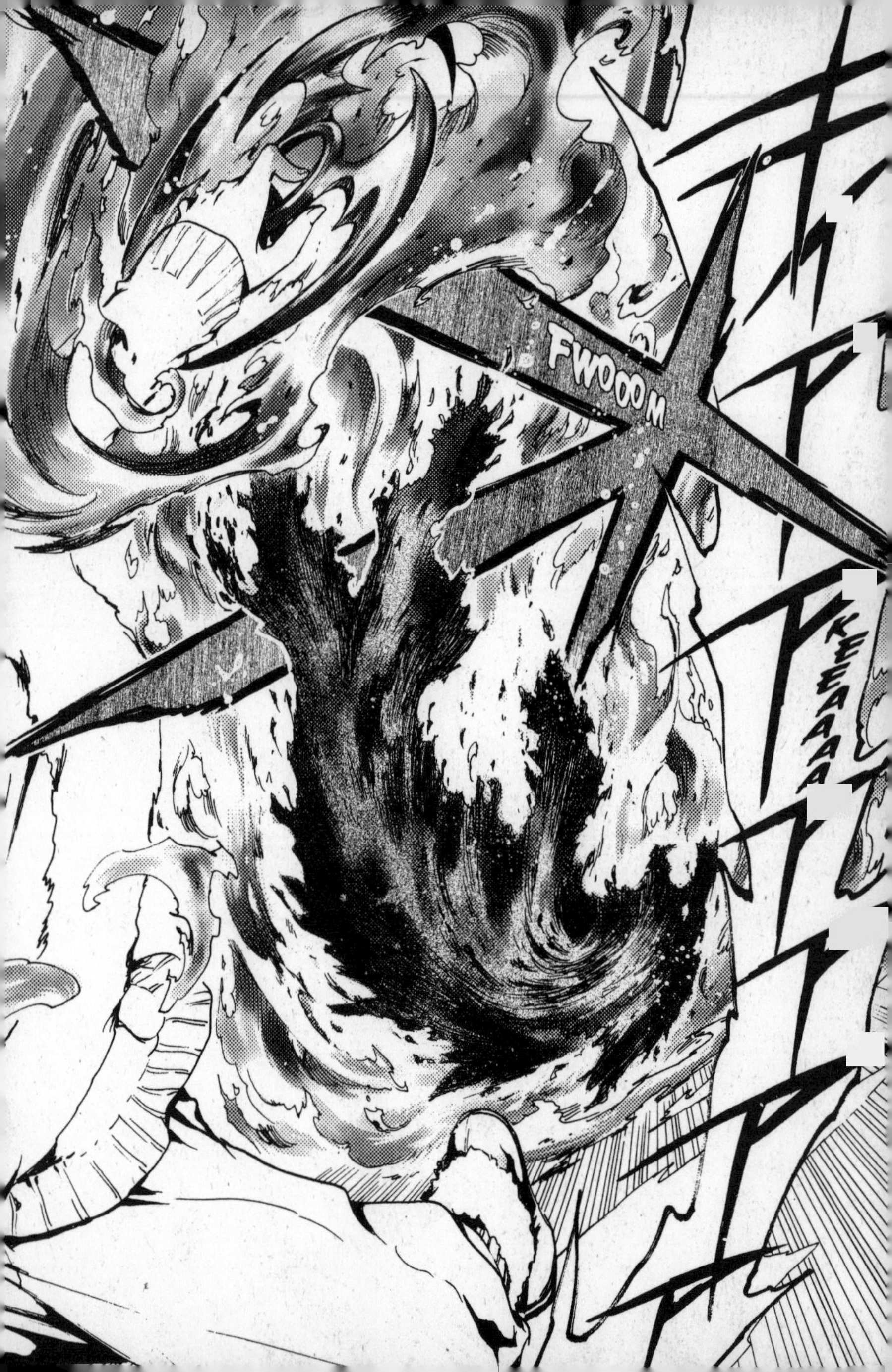
FWOOOM
KEEAAAA

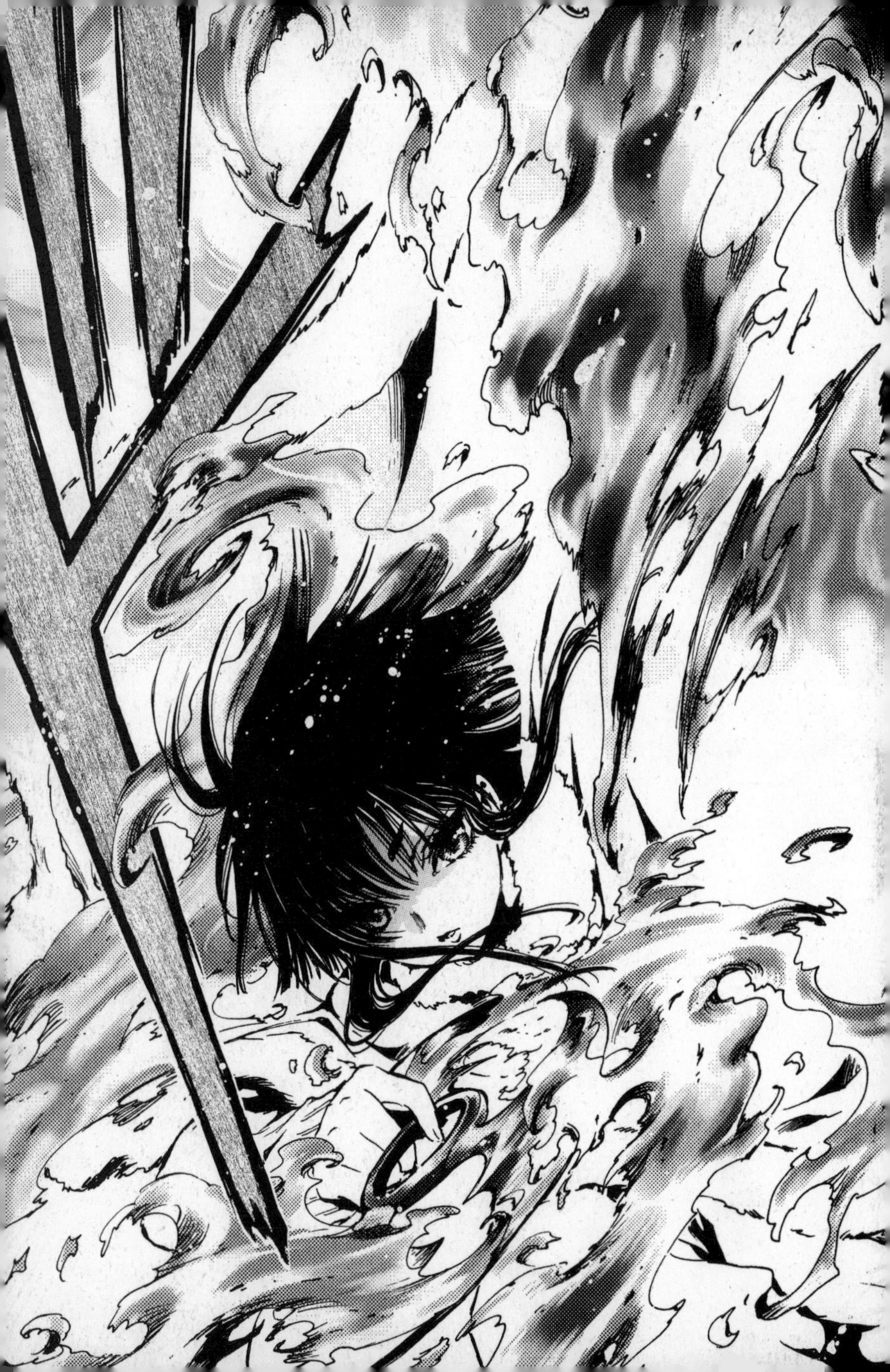

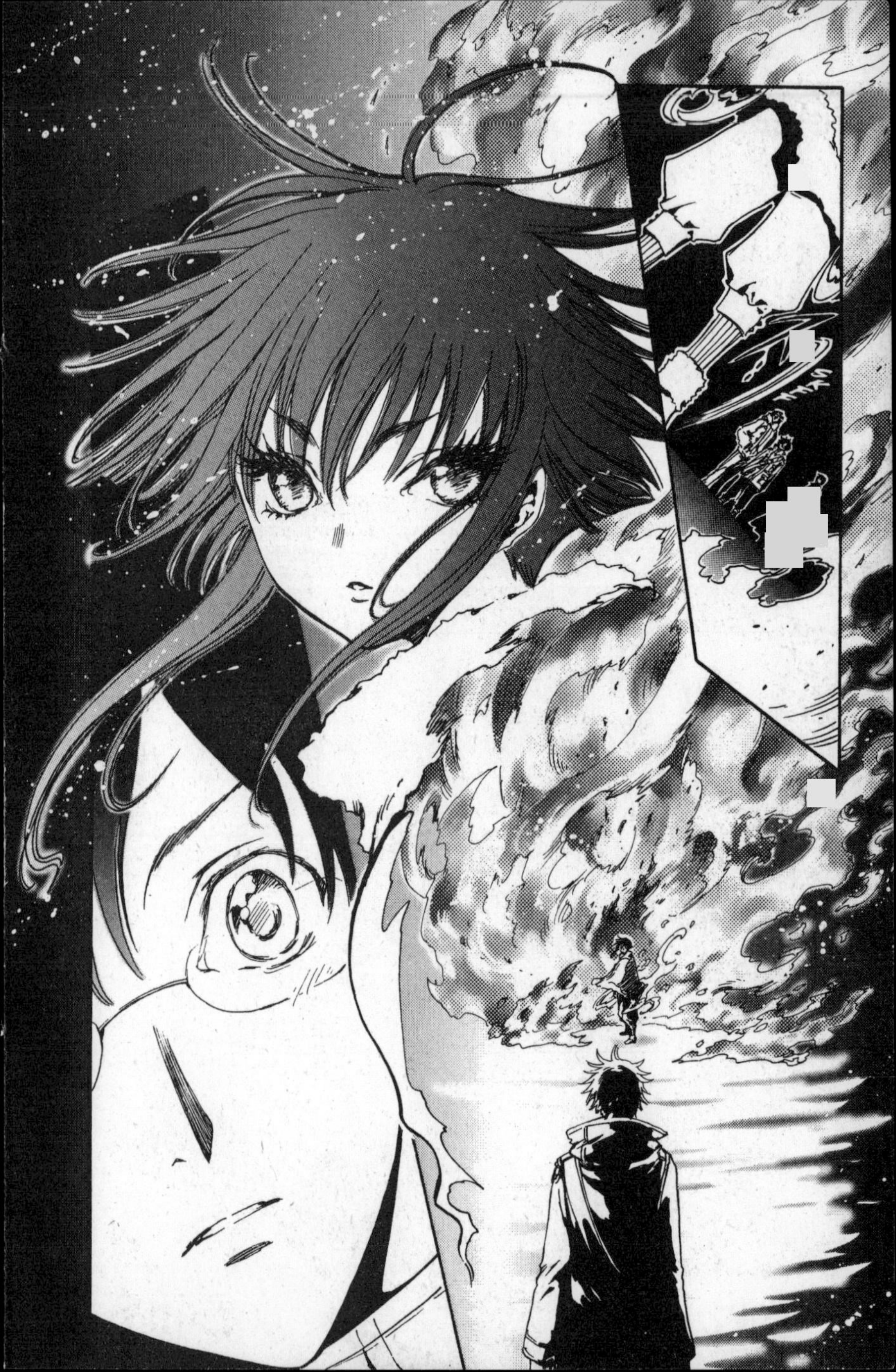

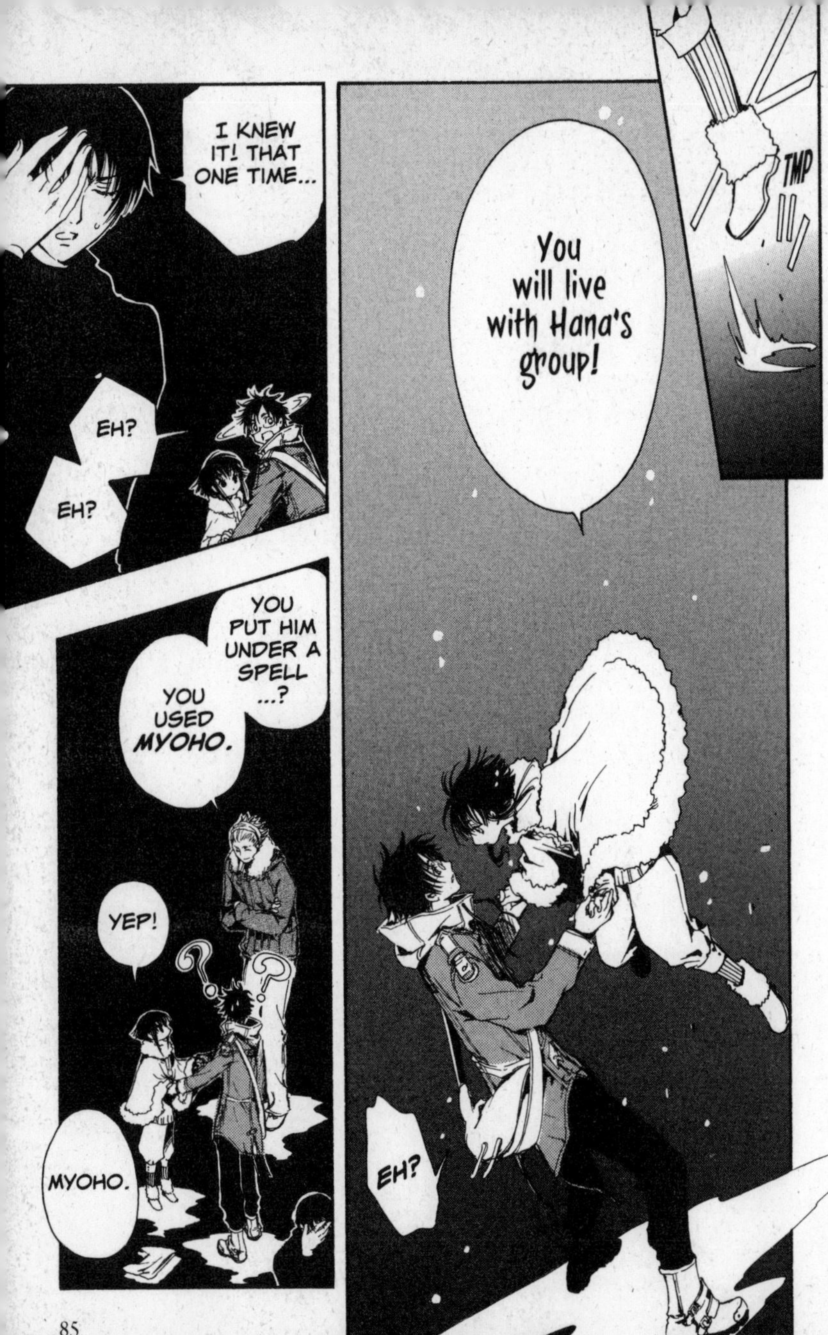
TMP
You will live with Hana's group!
EH?
I KNEW IT! THAT ONE TIME...
EH?
EH?
YOU PUT HIM UNDER A SPELL ...?
YOU USED MYOHO.
YEP!
MYOHO.

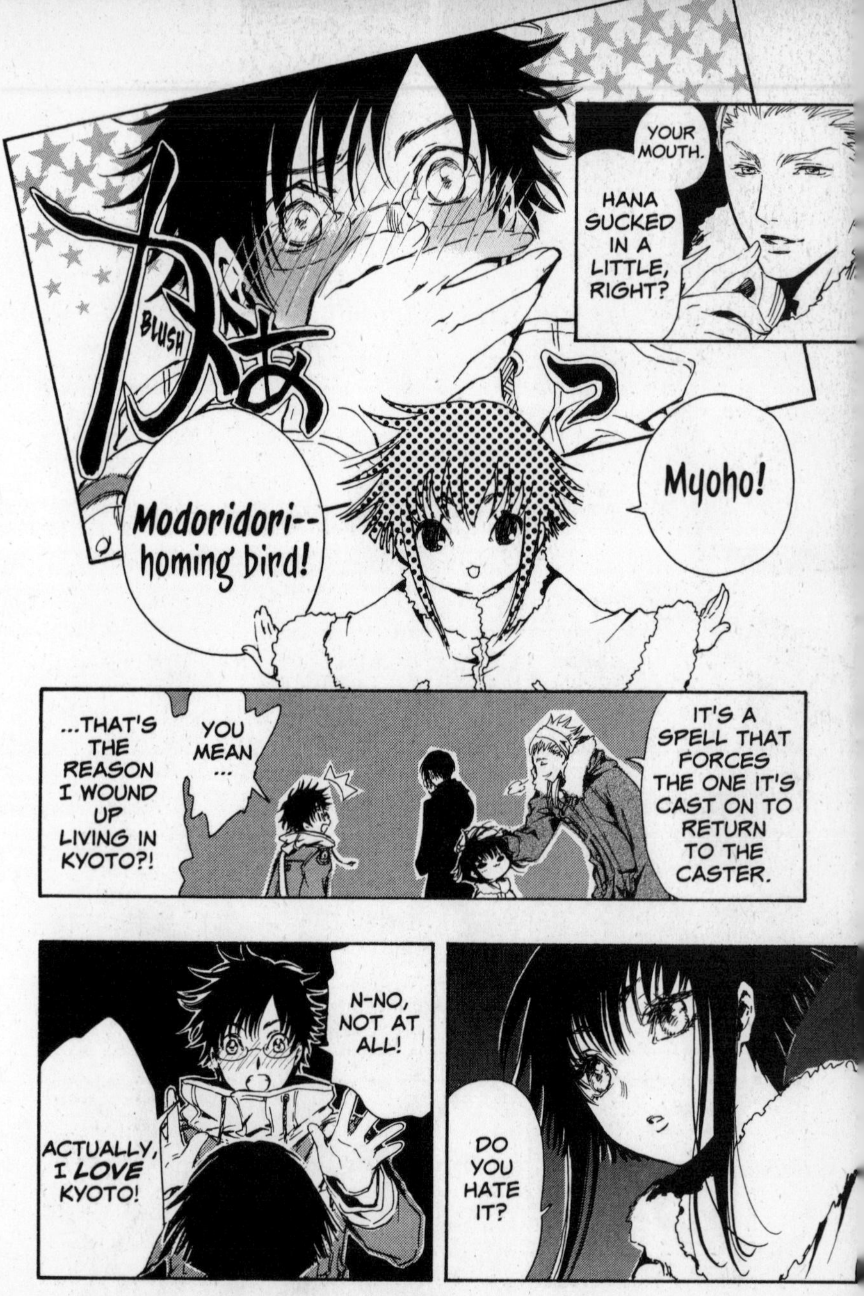
YOUR MOUTH.
HANA SUCKED IN A LITTLE, RIGHT?
BLUSH
Myoho!
Modoridori-- homing bird!
IT'S A SPELL THAT FORCES THE ONE IT'S CAST ON TO RETURN TO THE CASTER.
YOU MEAN ...
...THAT'S THE REASON I WOUND UP LIVING IN KYOTO?!
DO YOU HATE IT?
N-NO, NOT AT ALL!
ACTUALLY, I *LOVE* KYOTO!

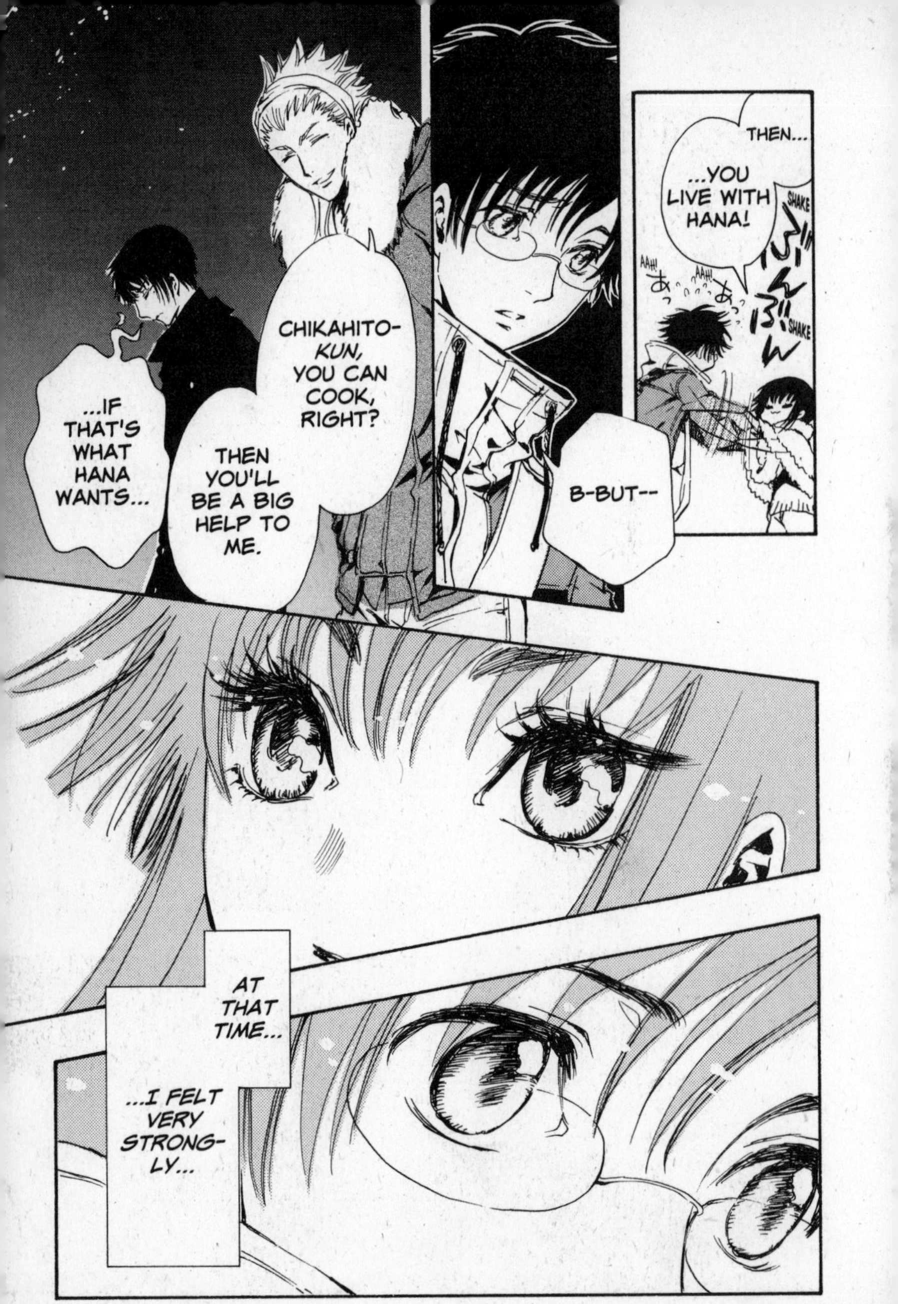
THEN...
...YOU LIVE WITH HANA!
SHAKE
SHAKE
AAH!
AAH!
B-BUT--
CHIKAHITO-KUN, YOU CAN COOK, RIGHT?
THEN YOU'LL BE A BIG HELP TO ME.
...IF THAT'S WHAT HANA WANTS...
AT THAT TIME...
...I FELT VERY STRONG-LY...

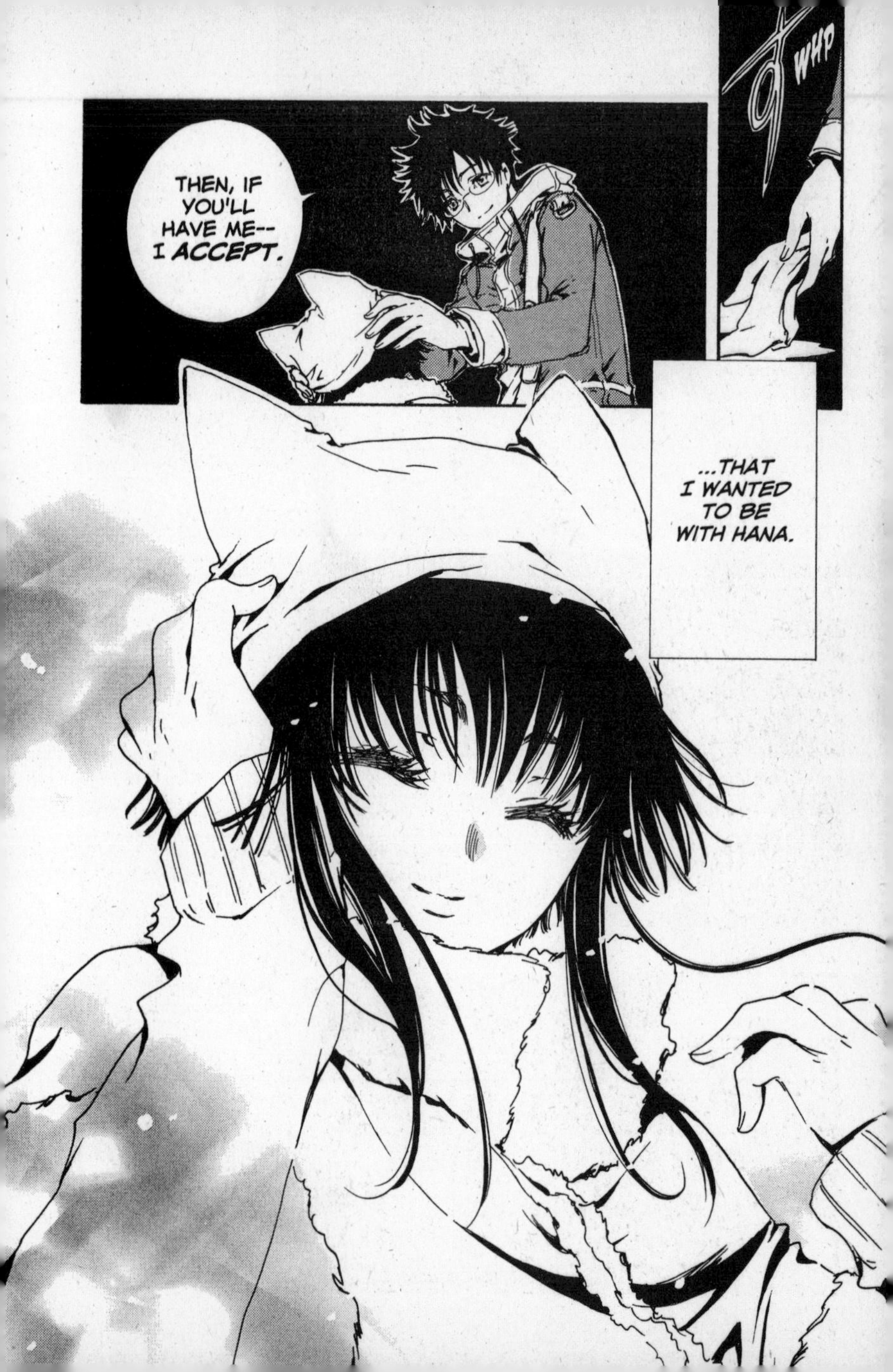
WHP
THEN, IF YOU'LL HAVE ME-- I ACCEPT.
...THAT I WANTED TO BE WITH HANA.

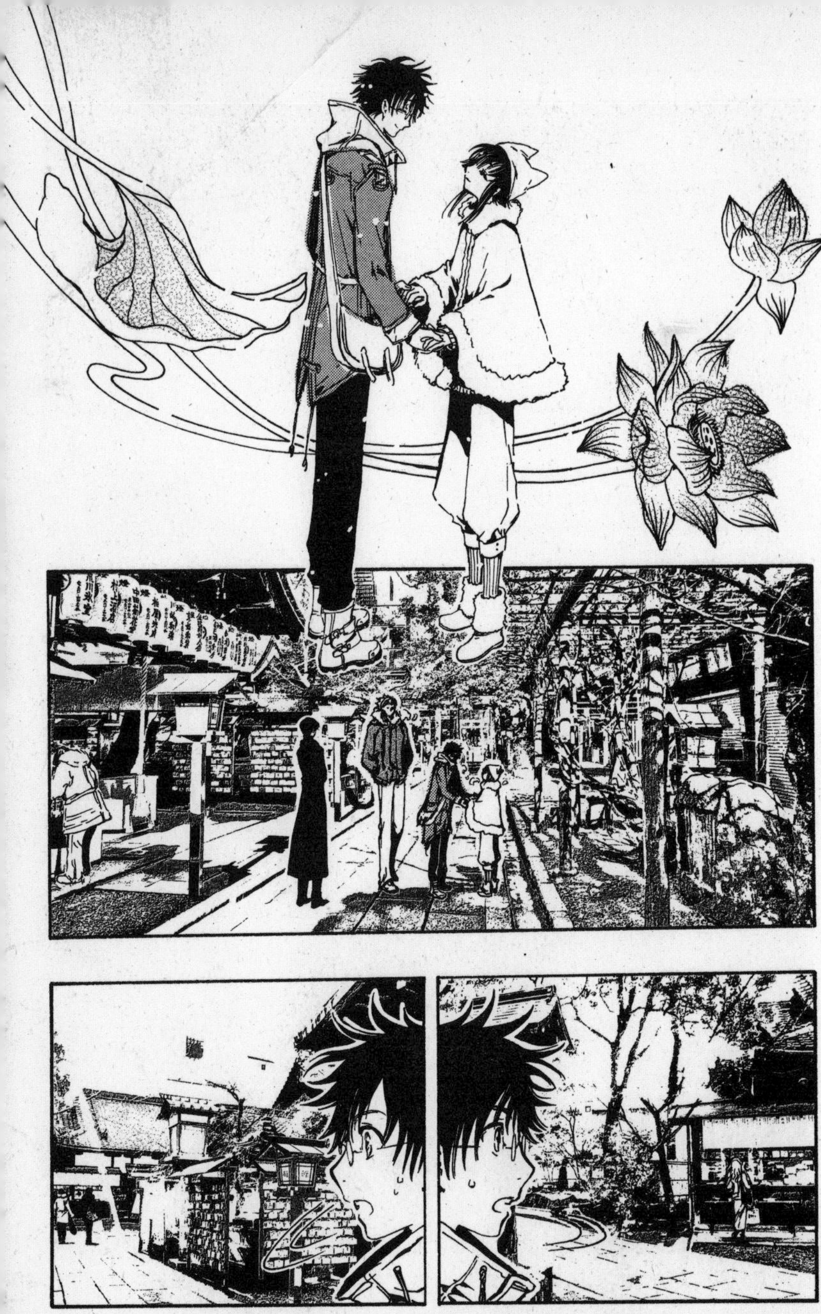

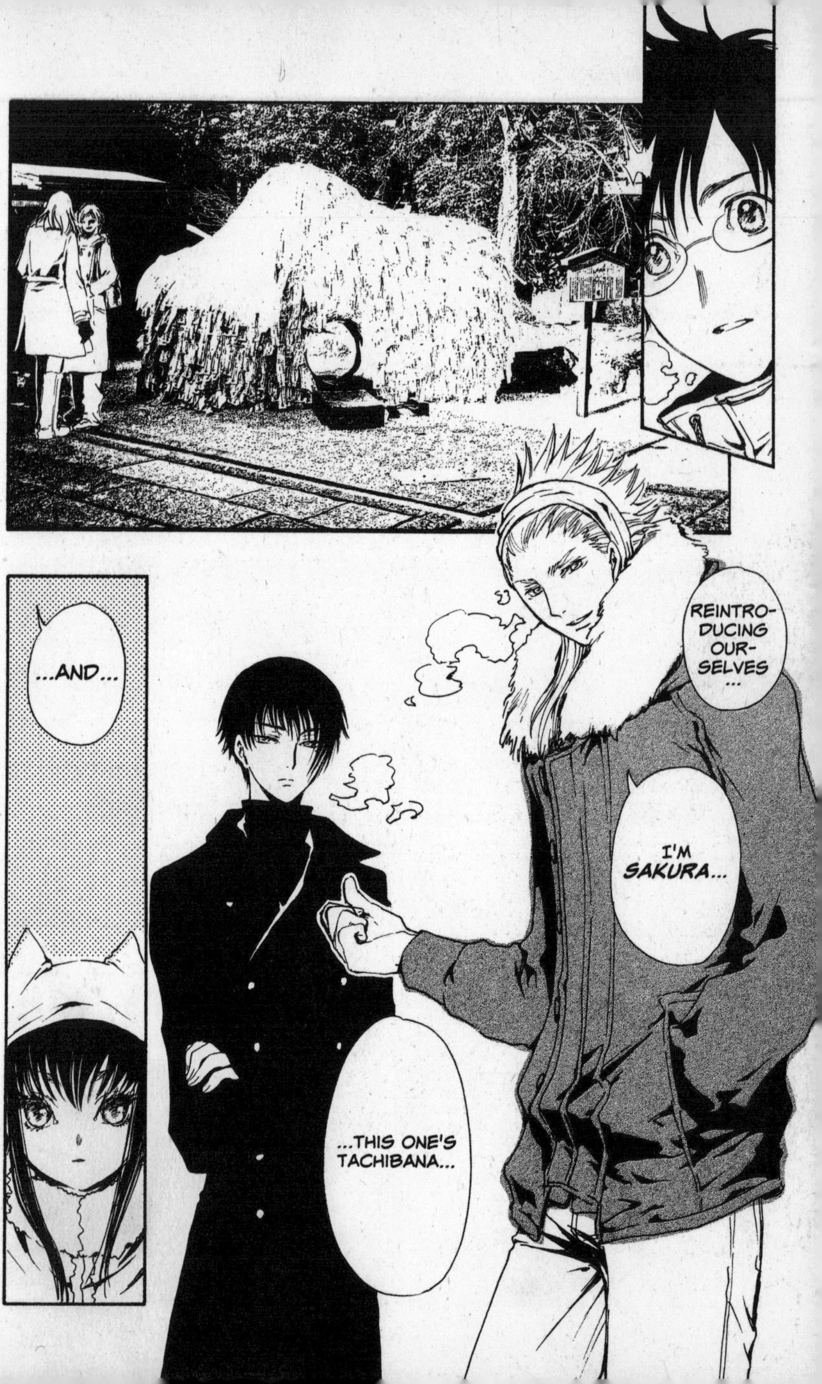
REINTRO-DUCING OUR-SELVES ...
I'M SAKURA...
...THIS ONE'S TACHIBANA...
...AND...

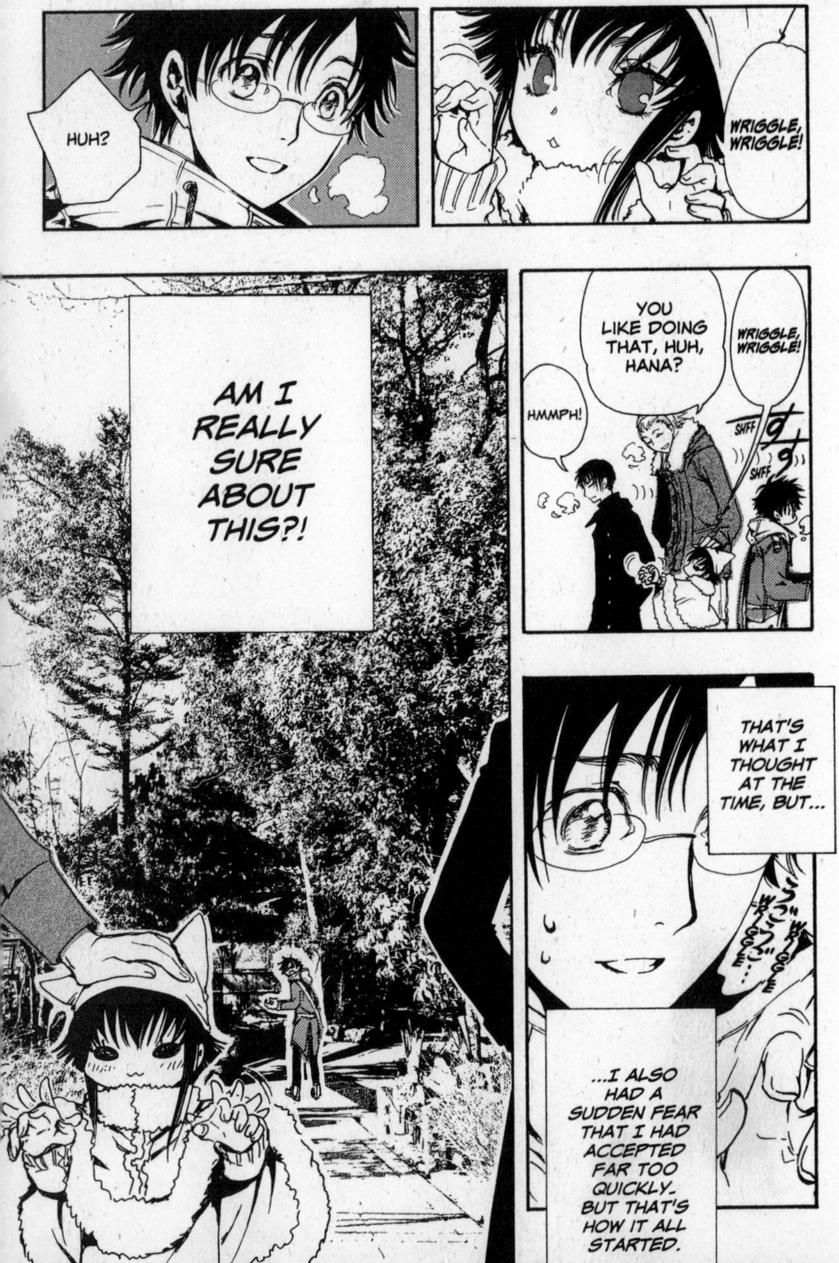
WRIGGLE, WRIGGLE!
HUH?
YOU LIKE DOING THAT, HUH, HANA?
WRIGGLE, WRIGGLE!
HMMPH!
SHFF
SHFF
THAT'S WHAT I THOUGHT AT THE TIME, BUT...
WRIGGLE WRIGGLE...
...I ALSO HAD A SUDDEN FEAR THAT I HAD ACCEPTED FAR TOO QUICKLY. BUT THAT'S HOW IT ALL STARTED.
AM I REALLY SURE ABOUT THIS?!

CHAPTER TWO: HANA AND THE URA-SHICHIKEN

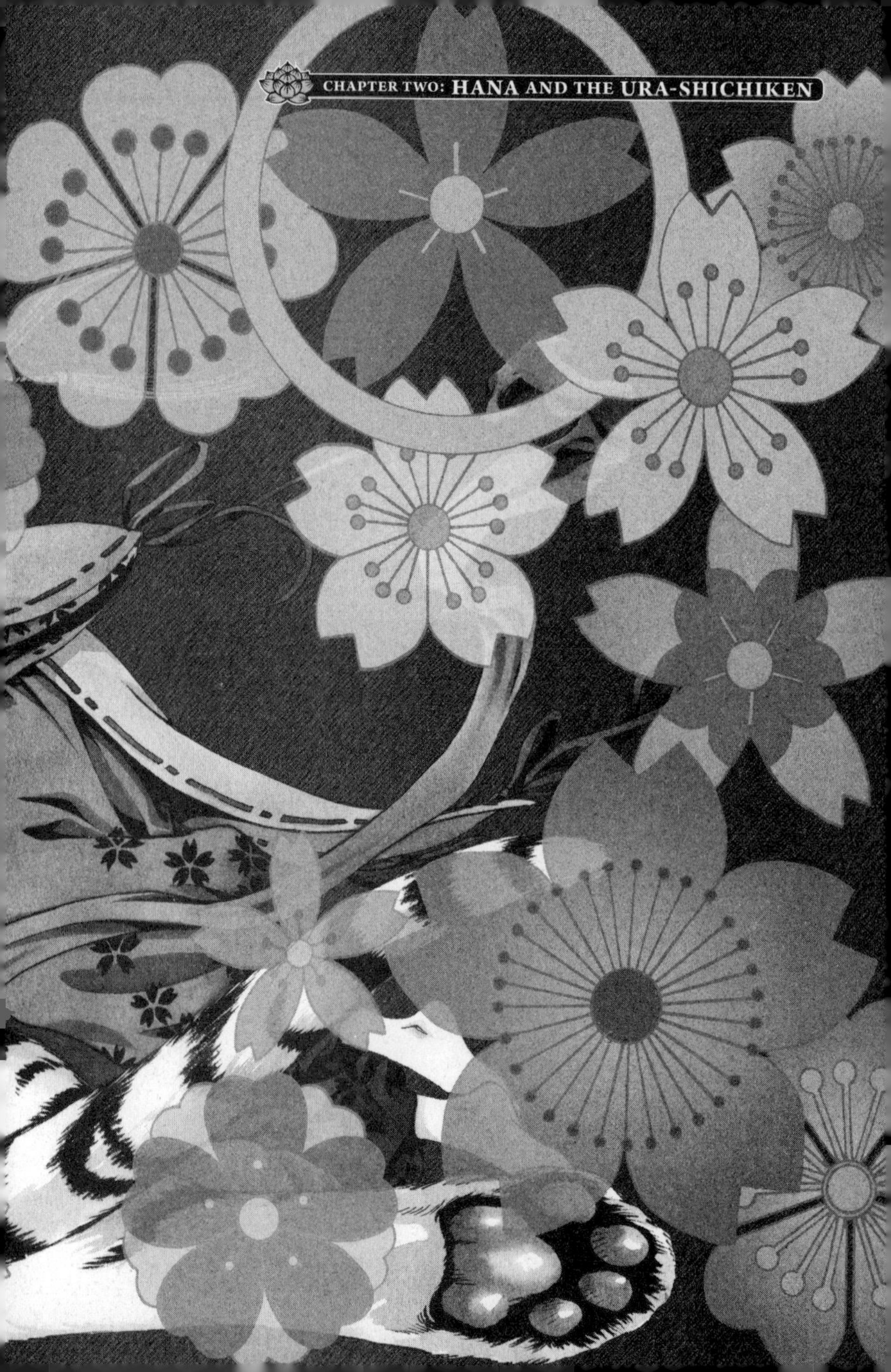

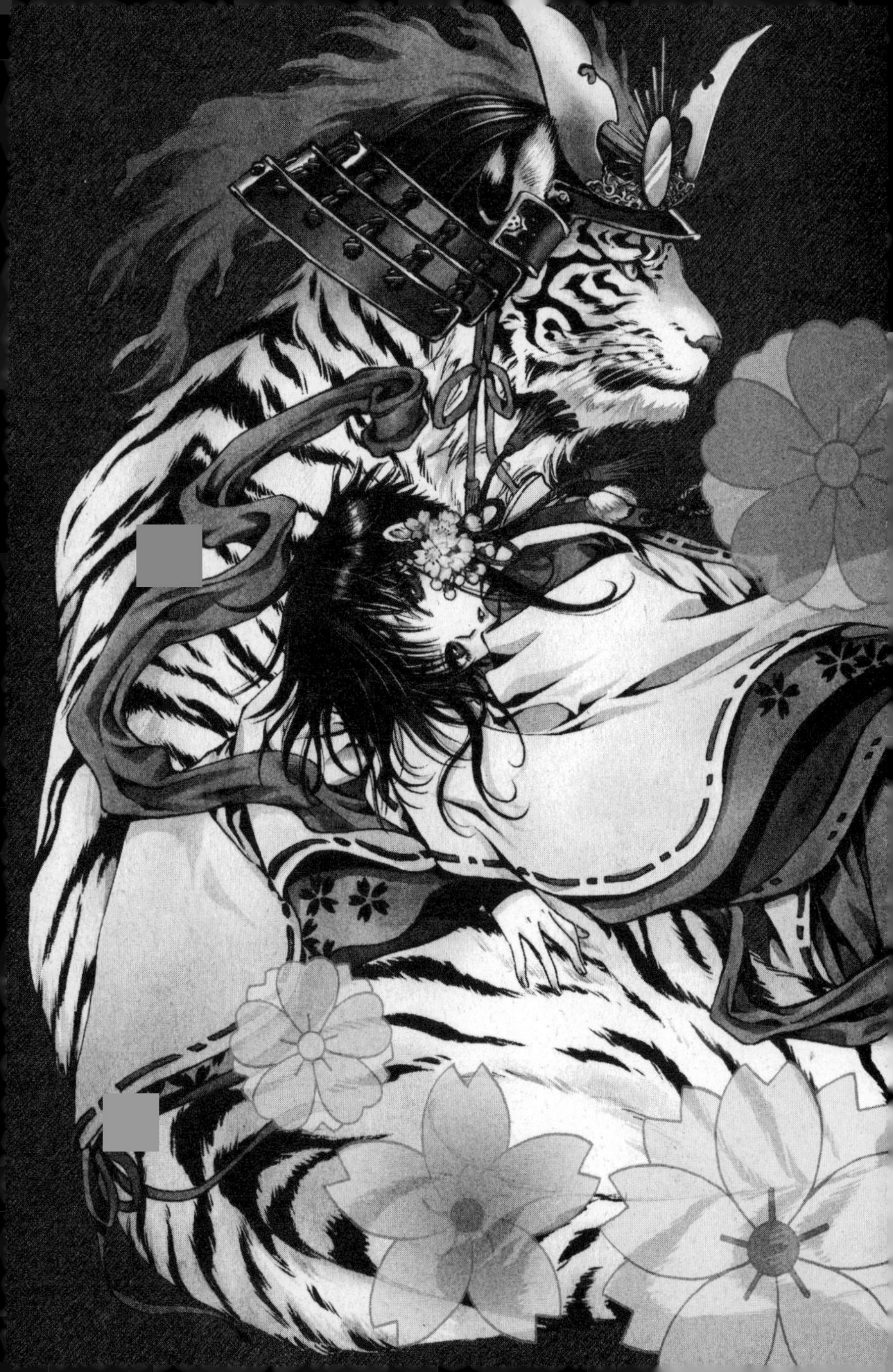

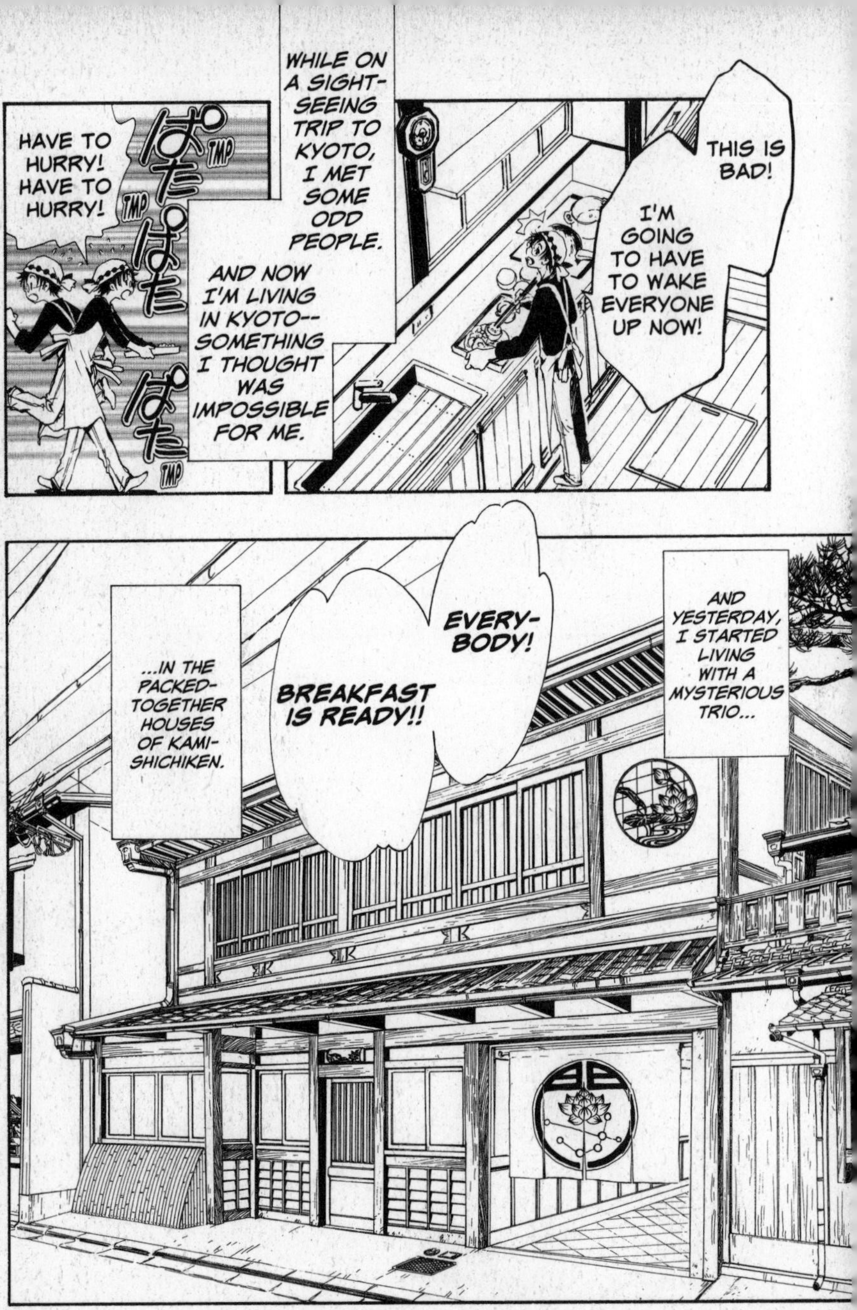
THIS IS BAD!
I'M GOING TO HAVE TO WAKE EVERYONE UP NOW!
WHILE ON A SIGHT-SEEING TRIP TO KYOTO, I MET SOME ODD PEOPLE.
AND NOW I'M LIVING IN KYOTO-- SOMETHING I THOUGHT WAS IMPOSSIBLE FOR ME.
HAVE TO HURRY! HAVE TO HURRY!
ぱた TMP
ぱた TMP
ぱた TMP
AND YESTERDAY, I STARTED LIVING WITH A MYSTERIOUS TRIO...
EVERY-BODY!
BREAKFAST IS READY!!
...IN THE PACKED-TOGETHER HOUSES OF KAMI-SHICHIKEN.

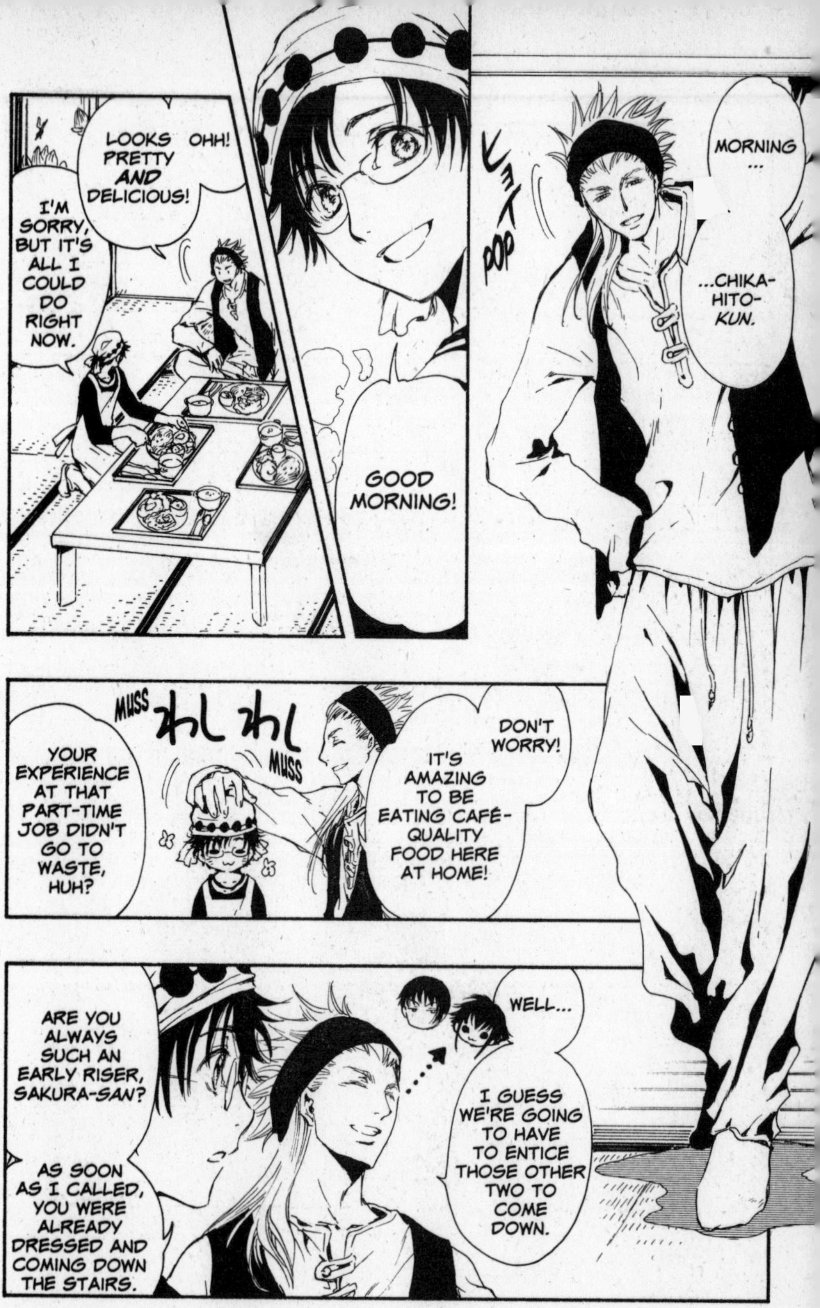
MORNING ...
...CHIKA-HITO-KUN.
POP
GOOD MORNING!
OHH! LOOKS PRETTY AND DELICIOUS!
I'M SORRY, BUT IT'S ALL I COULD DO RIGHT NOW.
DON'T WORRY! IT'S AMAZING TO BE EATING CAFÉ-QUALITY FOOD HERE AT HOME!
MUSS わしわし MUSS
YOUR EXPERIENCE AT THAT PART-TIME JOB DIDN'T GO TO WASTE, HUH?
WELL...
I GUESS WE'RE GOING TO HAVE TO ENTICE THOSE OTHER TWO TO COME DOWN.
ARE YOU ALWAYS SUCH AN EARLY RISER, SAKURA-SAN?
AS SOON AS I CALLED, YOU WERE ALREADY DRESSED AND COMING DOWN THE STAIRS.

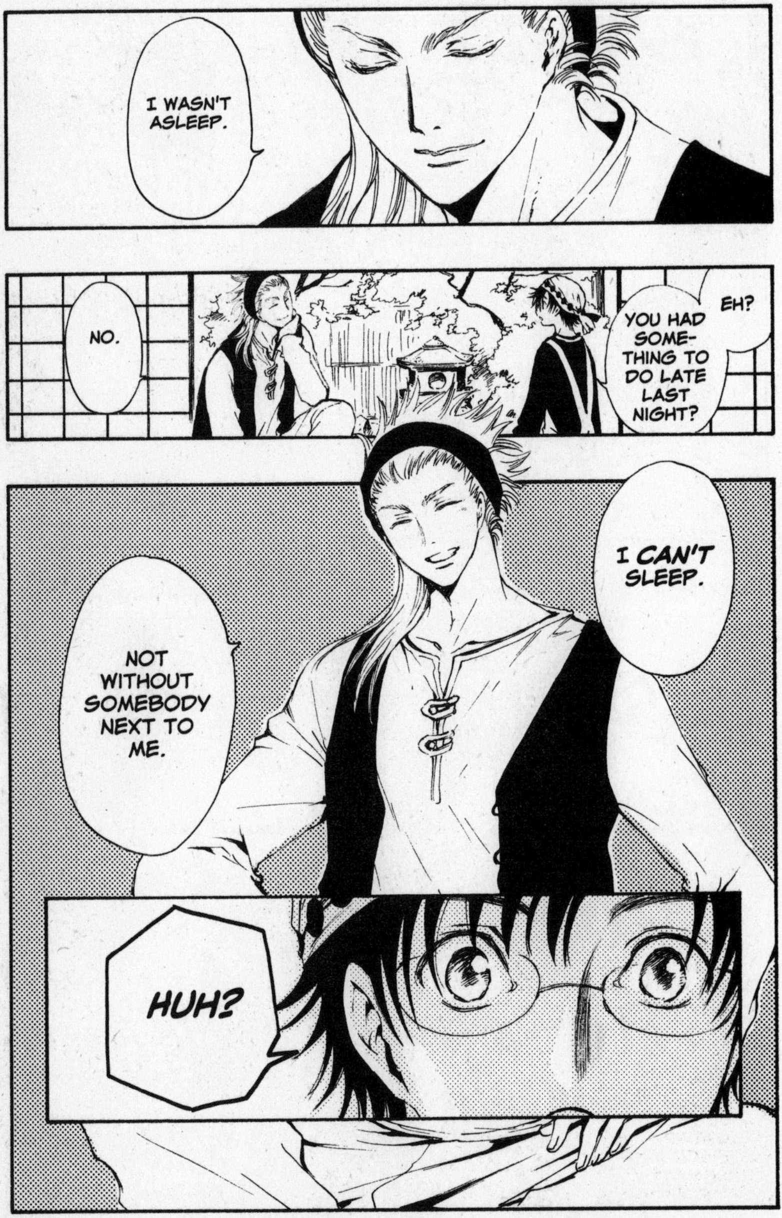
I WASN'T ASLEEP.
EH?
YOU HAD SOMETHING TO DO LATE LAST NIGHT?
NO.
I CAN'T SLEEP.
NOT WITHOUT SOMEBODY NEXT TO ME.
HUH?

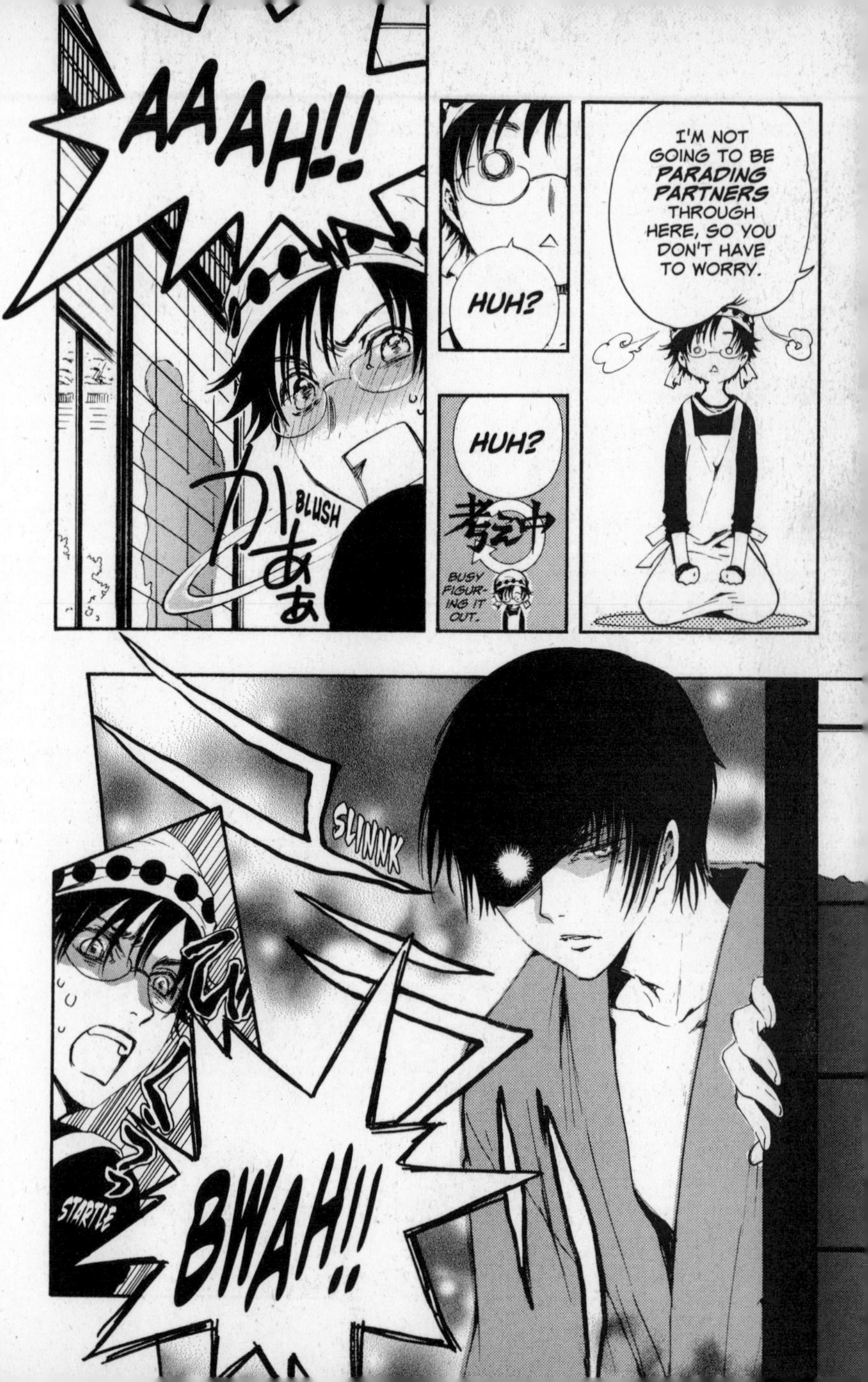
I'M NOT GOING TO BE PARADING PARTNERS THROUGH HERE, SO YOU DON'T HAVE TO WORRY.
HUH?
HUH?
考え中
BUSY FIGURING IT OUT.
AAAH!!
かぁ
BLUSH
SLINNK
BWAH!!
STARTLE

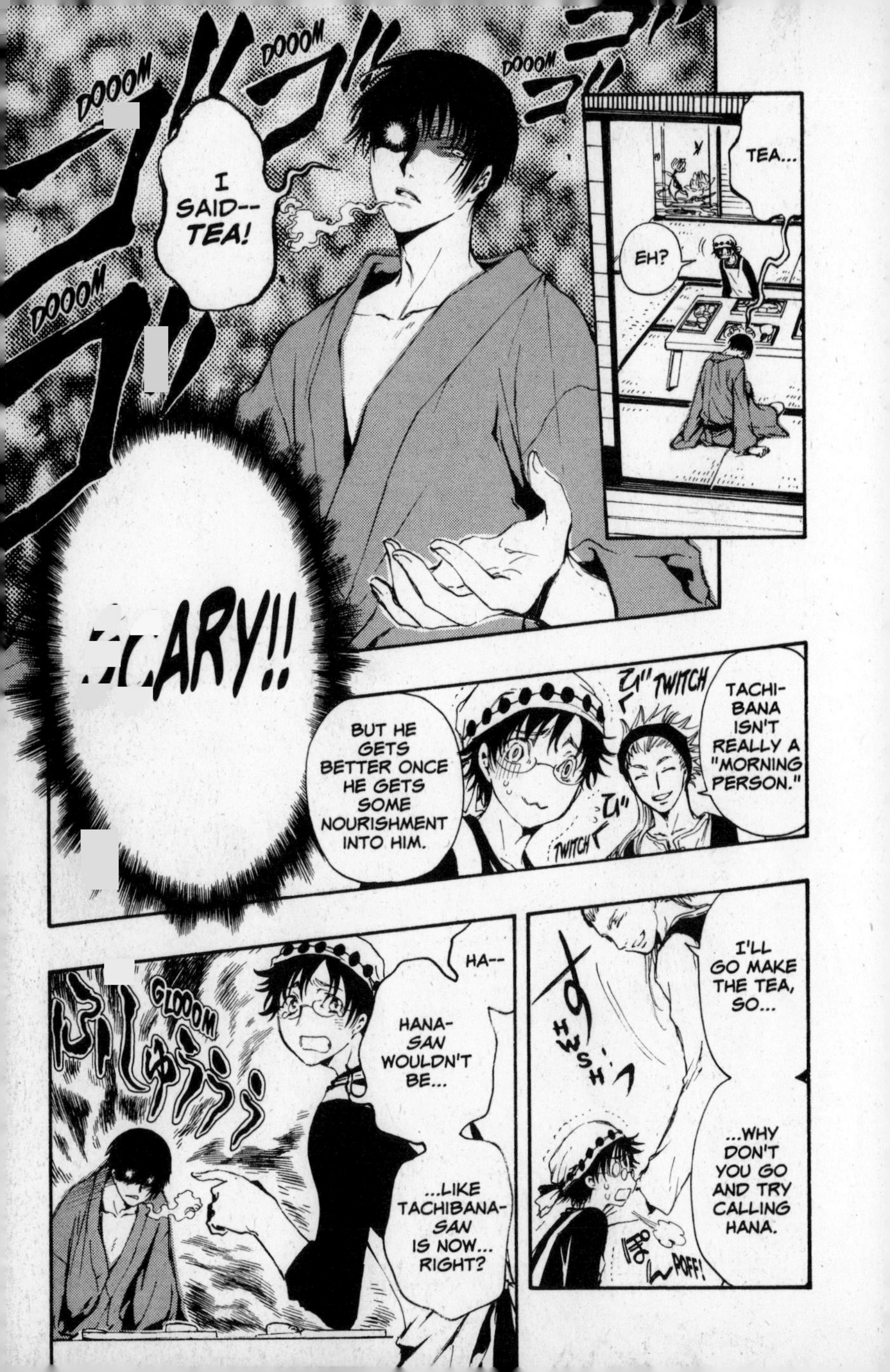
TEA...
EH?
DOOOM
DOOOM
DOOOM
I SAID--TEA!
DOOOM
SCARY!!
TACHI-BANA ISN'T REALLY A "MORNING PERSON."
TWITCH
TWITCH
BUT HE GETS BETTER ONCE HE GETS SOME NOURISHMENT INTO HIM.
I'LL GO MAKE THE TEA, SO...
HWSH
...WHY DON'T YOU GO AND TRY CALLING HANA.
POFF!
HA--
HANA-SAN WOULDN'T BE...
...LIKE TACHIBANA-SAN IS NOW... RIGHT?
GLOOOM

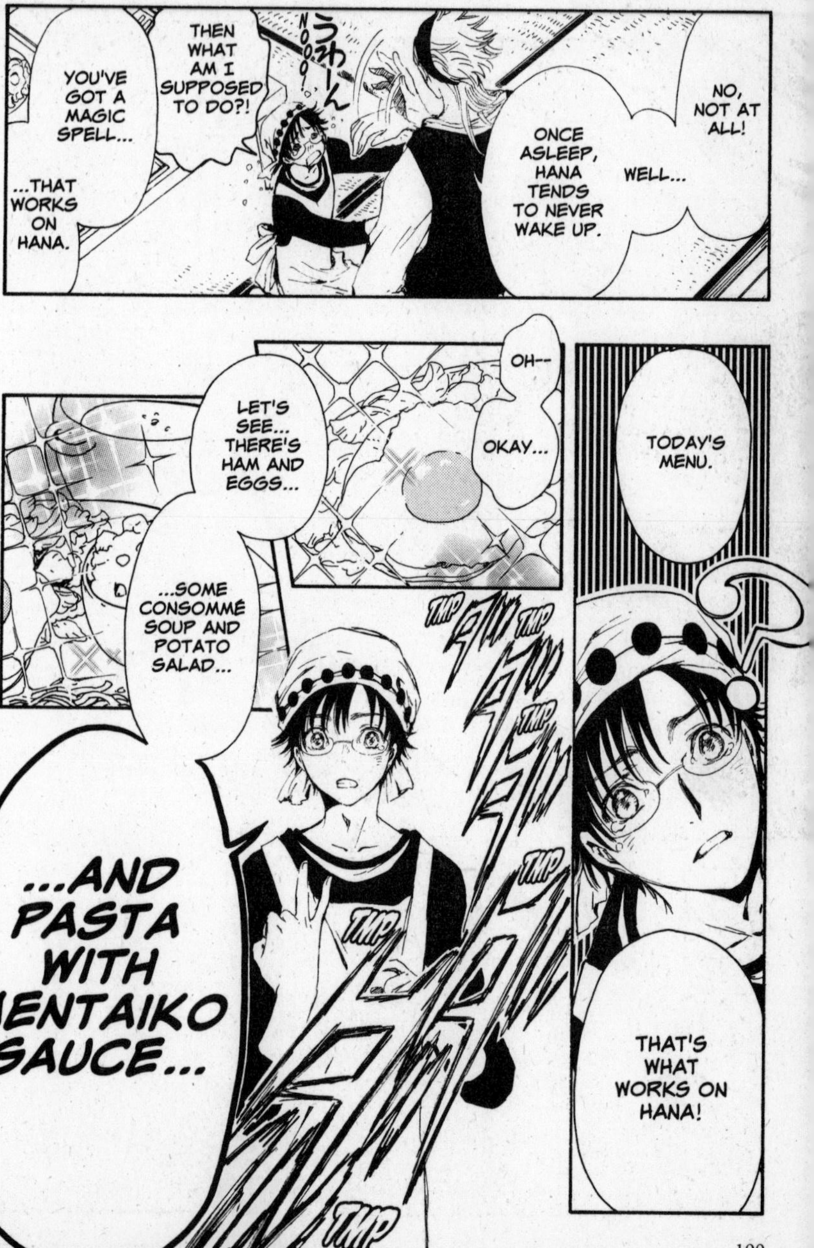
NO, NOT AT ALL!
WELL...
ONCE ASLEEP, HANA TENDS TO NEVER WAKE UP.
うわーん
NOOO!
THEN WHAT AM I SUPPOSED TO DO?!
YOU'VE GOT A MAGIC SPELL...
...THAT WORKS ON HANA.
TODAY'S MENU.
THAT'S WHAT WORKS ON HANA!
OH--
OKAY...
LET'S SEE... THERE'S HAM AND EGGS...
...SOME CONSOMMÉ SOUP AND POTATO SALAD...
TMP TMP TMP TMP TMP
...AND PASTA WITH MENTAIKO SAUCE...
TMP

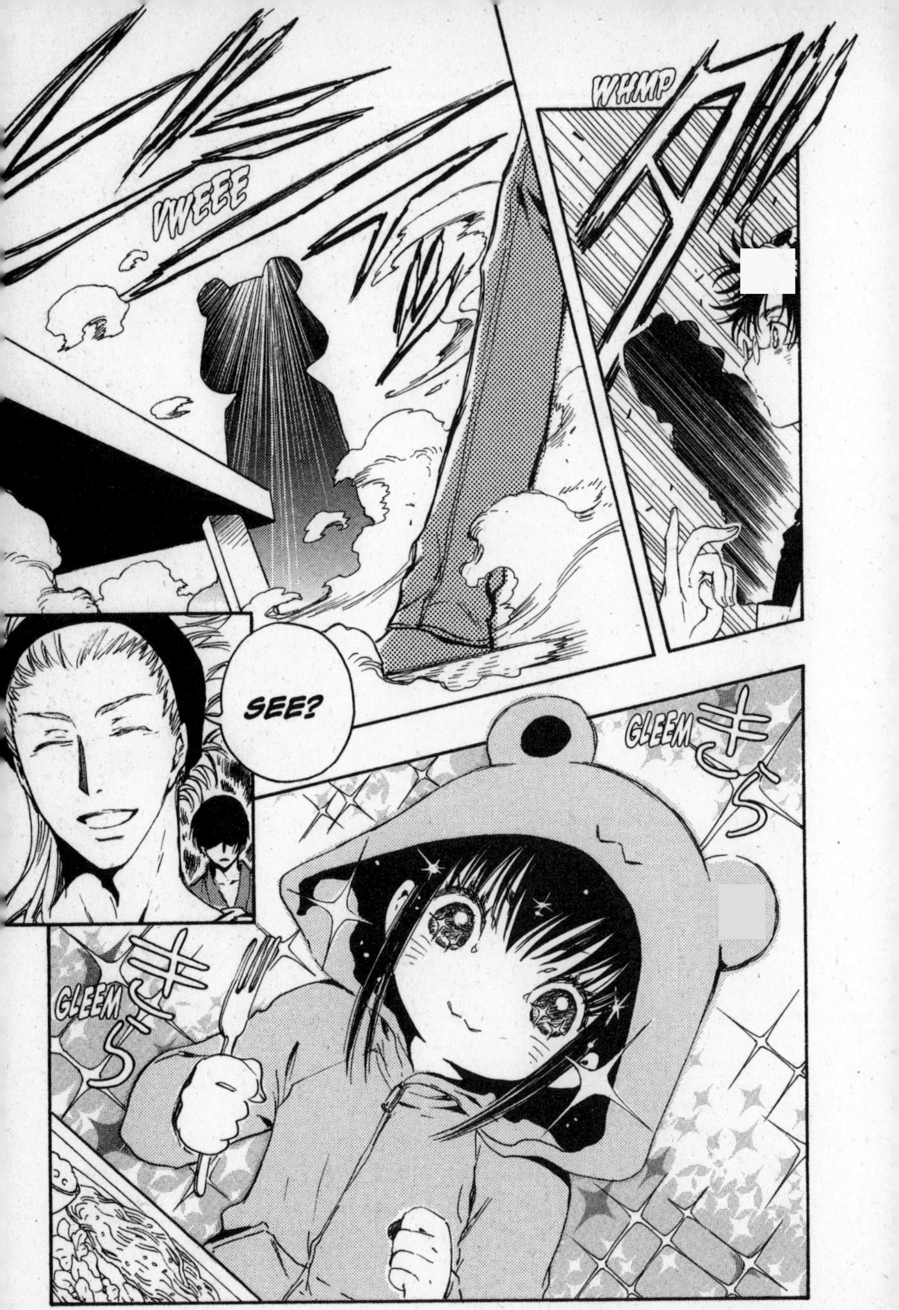
WHMP
VWEEE
GLEEM きら
GLEEM きら
SEE?

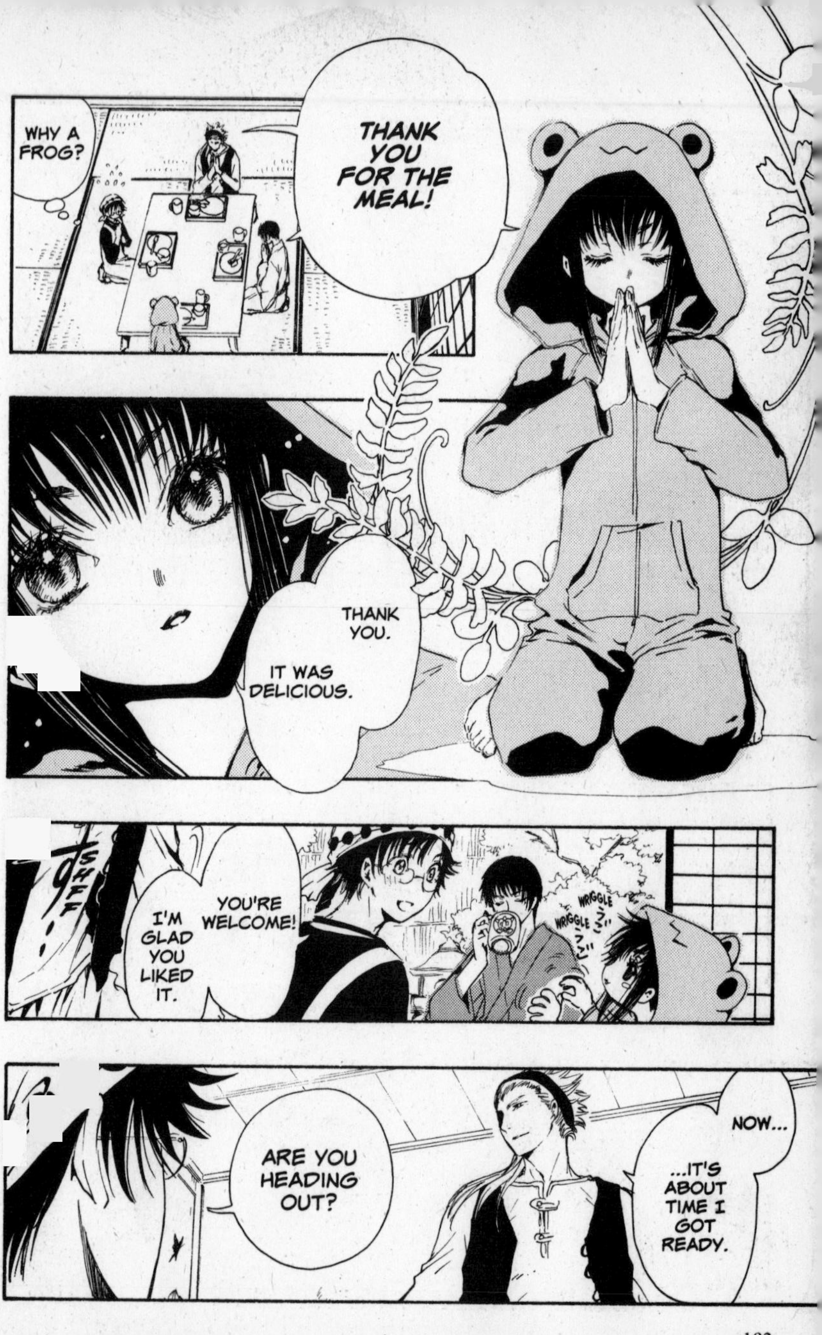
THANK YOU FOR THE MEAL!
WHY A FROG?
THANK YOU.
IT WAS DELICIOUS.
WRIGGLE WRIGGLE
YOU'RE WELCOME!
I'M GLAD YOU LIKED IT.
SHFF
NOW...
...IT'S ABOUT TIME I GOT READY.
ARE YOU HEADING OUT?

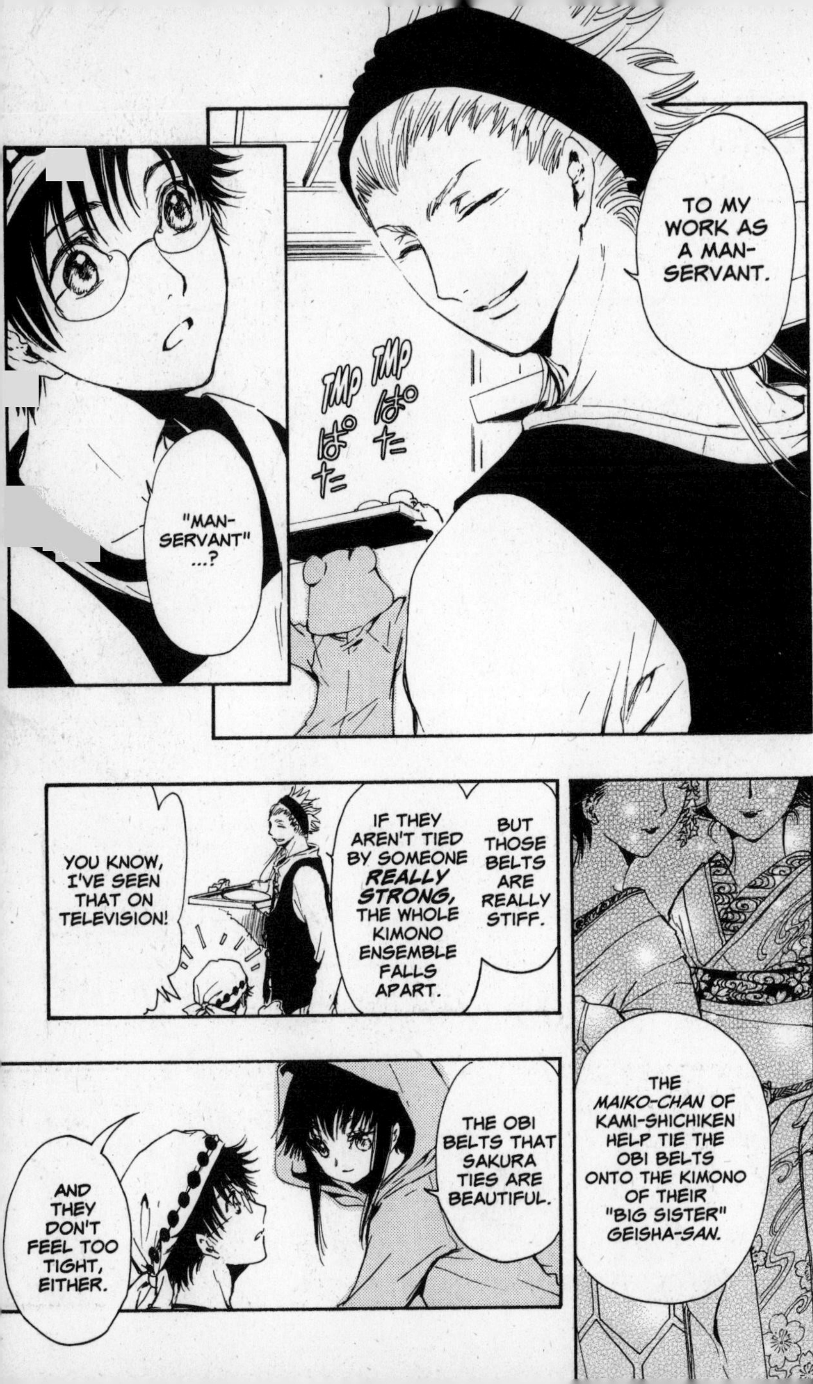
TO MY WORK AS A MAN-SERVANT.
TMP ぱた
TMP ぱた
"MAN-SERVANT" ...?
THE MAIKO-CHAN OF KAMI-SHICHIKEN HELP TIE THE OBI BELTS ONTO THE KIMONO OF THEIR "BIG SISTER" GEISHA-SAN.
BUT THOSE BELTS ARE REALLY STIFF.
IF THEY AREN'T TIED BY SOMEONE REALLY STRONG, THE WHOLE KIMONO ENSEMBLE FALLS APART.
YOU KNOW, I'VE SEEN THAT ON TELEVISION!
THE OBI BELTS THAT SAKURA TIES ARE BEAUTIFUL.
AND THEY DON'T FEEL TOO TIGHT, EITHER.

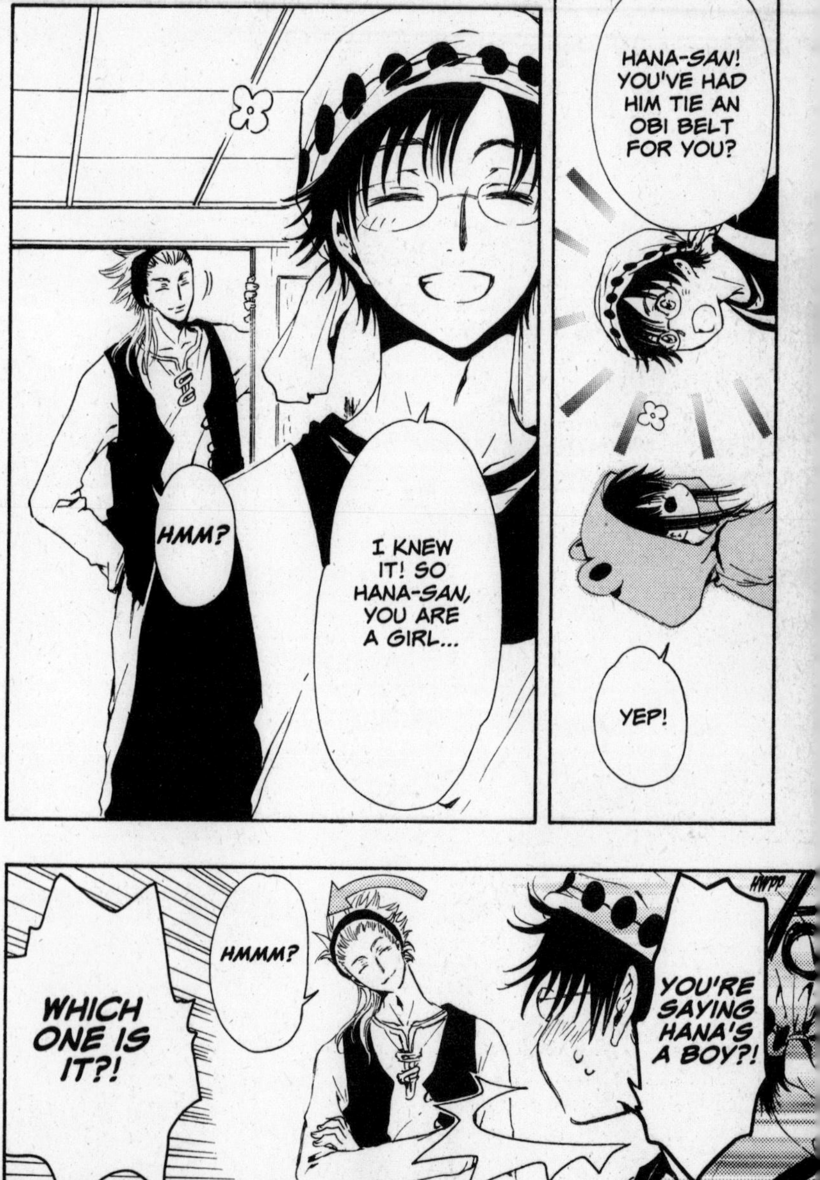
HANA-SAN! YOU'VE HAD HIM TIE AN OBI BELT FOR YOU?
YEP!
I KNEW IT! SO HANA-SAN, YOU ARE A GIRL...
HMM?
HWPP
YOU'RE SAYING HANA'S A BOY?!
HMMM?
WHICH ONE IS IT?!

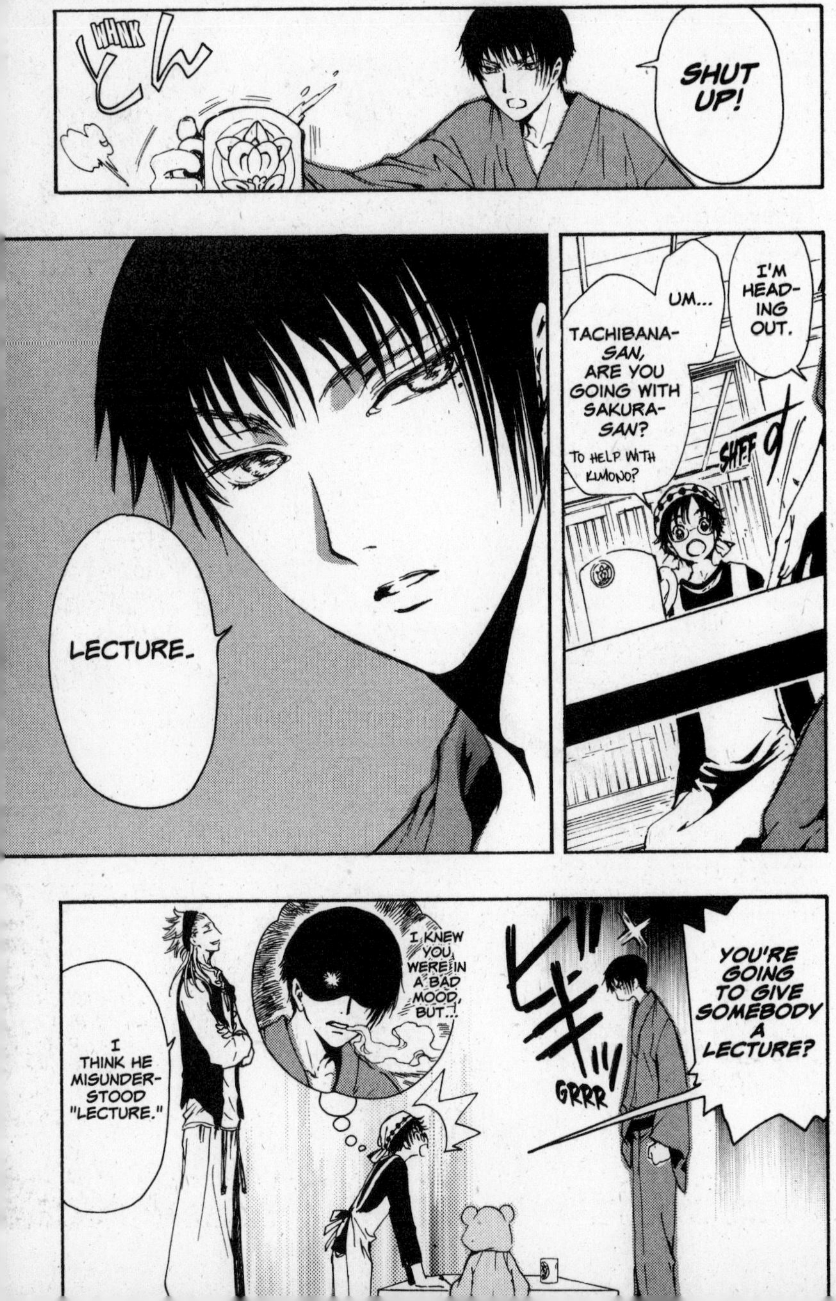
SHUT UP!
WHNK
とん
I'M HEADING OUT.
UM...
TACHIBANA-SAN, ARE YOU GOING WITH SAKURA-SAN?
TO HELP WITH KIMONO?
SHFF
LECTURE...
YOU'RE GOING TO GIVE SOMEBODY A LECTURE?
GRRR
I KNEW YOU WERE IN A BAD MOOD, BUT...!
I THINK HE MISUNDERSTOOD "LECTURE."

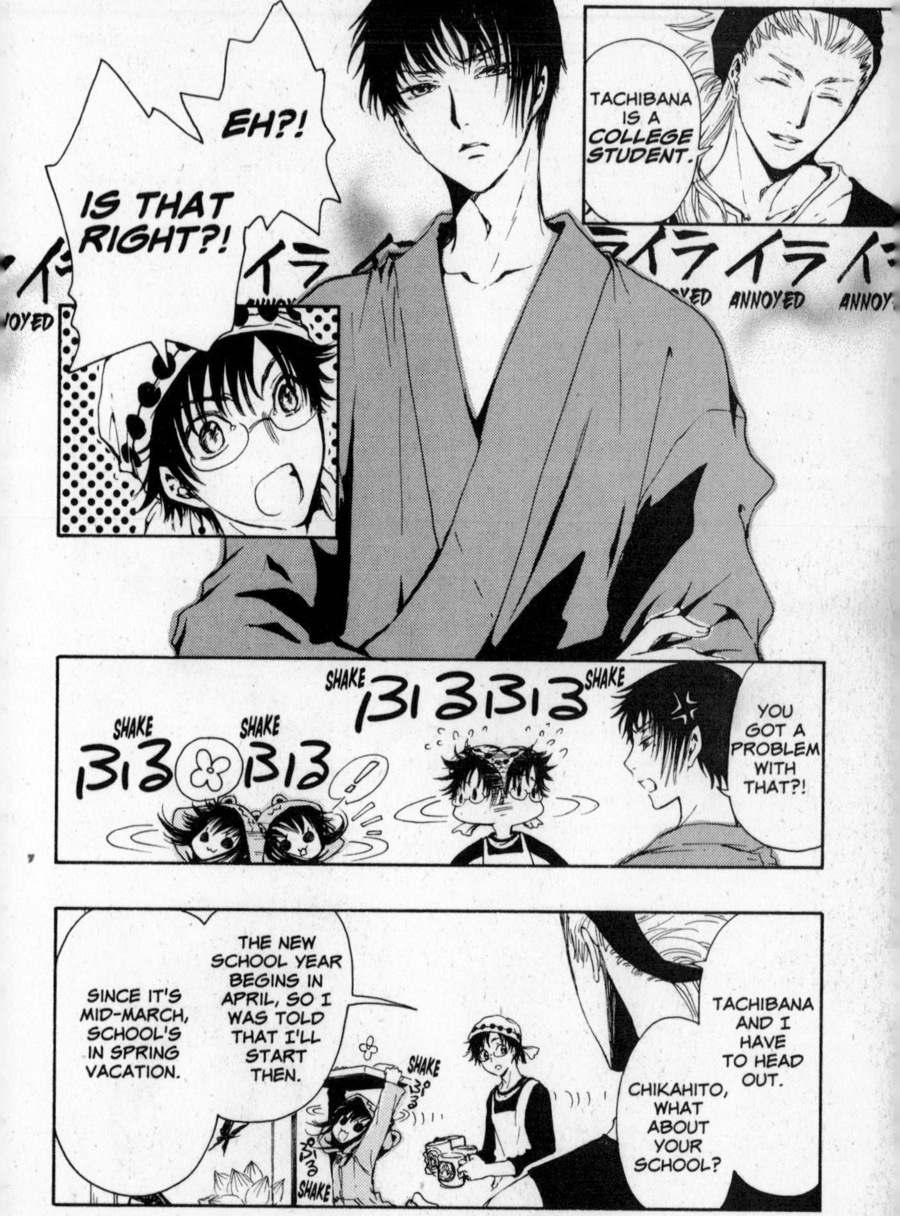
TACHIBANA IS A COLLEGE STUDENT.
EH?!
IS THAT RIGHT?!
イライラ
ANNOYED
YOU GOT A PROBLEM WITH THAT?!
ぷるぷる
SHAKE
SHAKE
ぷる
SHAKE
ぷる
SHAKE
TACHIBANA AND I HAVE TO HEAD OUT.
CHIKAHITO, WHAT ABOUT YOUR SCHOOL?
THE NEW SCHOOL YEAR BEGINS IN APRIL, SO I WAS TOLD THAT I'LL START THEN.
SINCE IT'S MID-MARCH, SCHOOL'S IN SPRING VACATION.
SHAKE
SHAKE

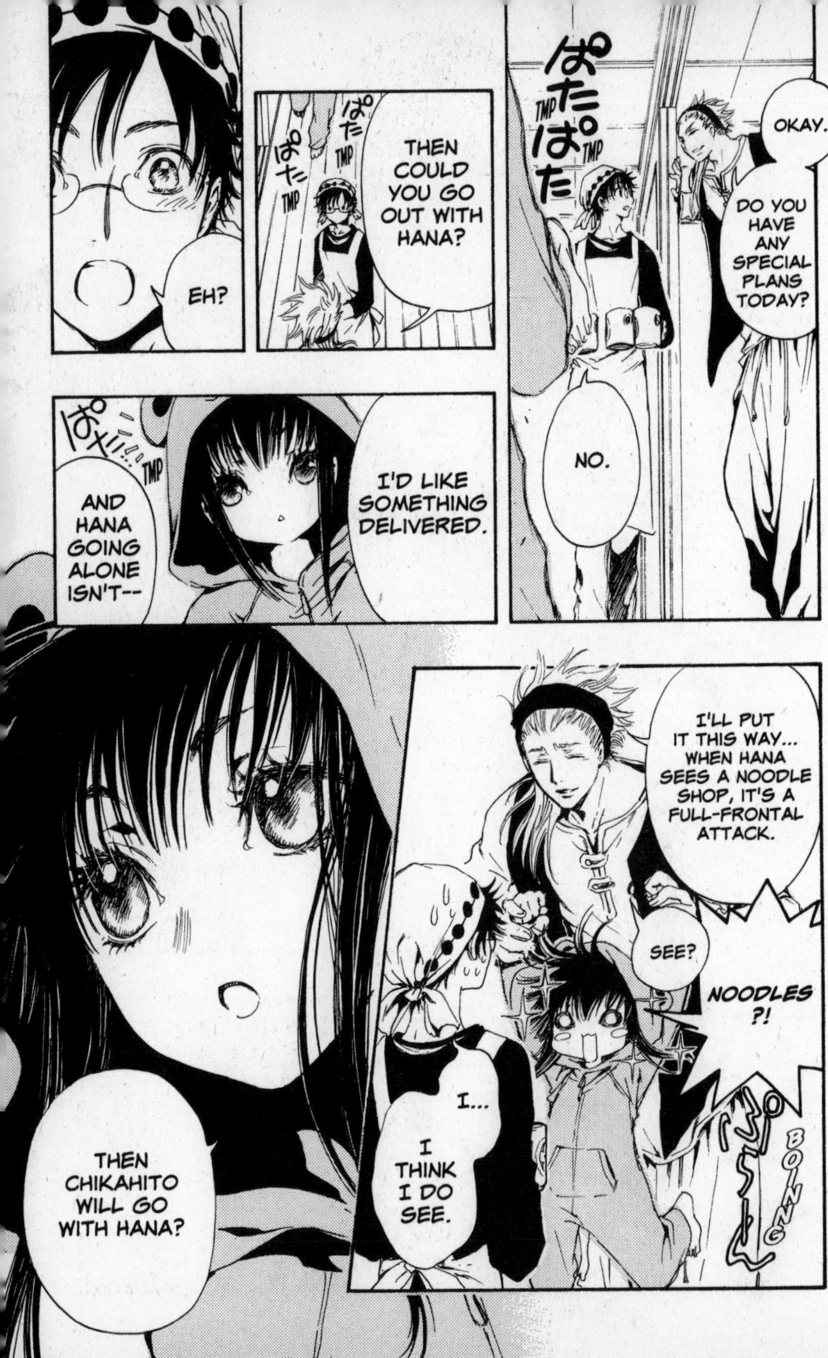
ぱたぱた
TMP
TMP
OKAY.
DO YOU HAVE ANY SPECIAL PLANS TODAY?
NO.
ぱた
TMP
ぱた
TMP
THEN COULD YOU GO OUT WITH HANA?
EH?
I'D LIKE SOMETHING DELIVERED.
TMP
AND HANA GOING ALONE ISN'T--
I'LL PUT IT THIS WAY... WHEN HANA SEES A NOODLE SHOP, IT'S A FULL-FRONTAL ATTACK.
SEE?
NOODLES?!
BOING
I...
I THINK I DO SEE.
THEN CHIKAHITO WILL GO WITH HANA?

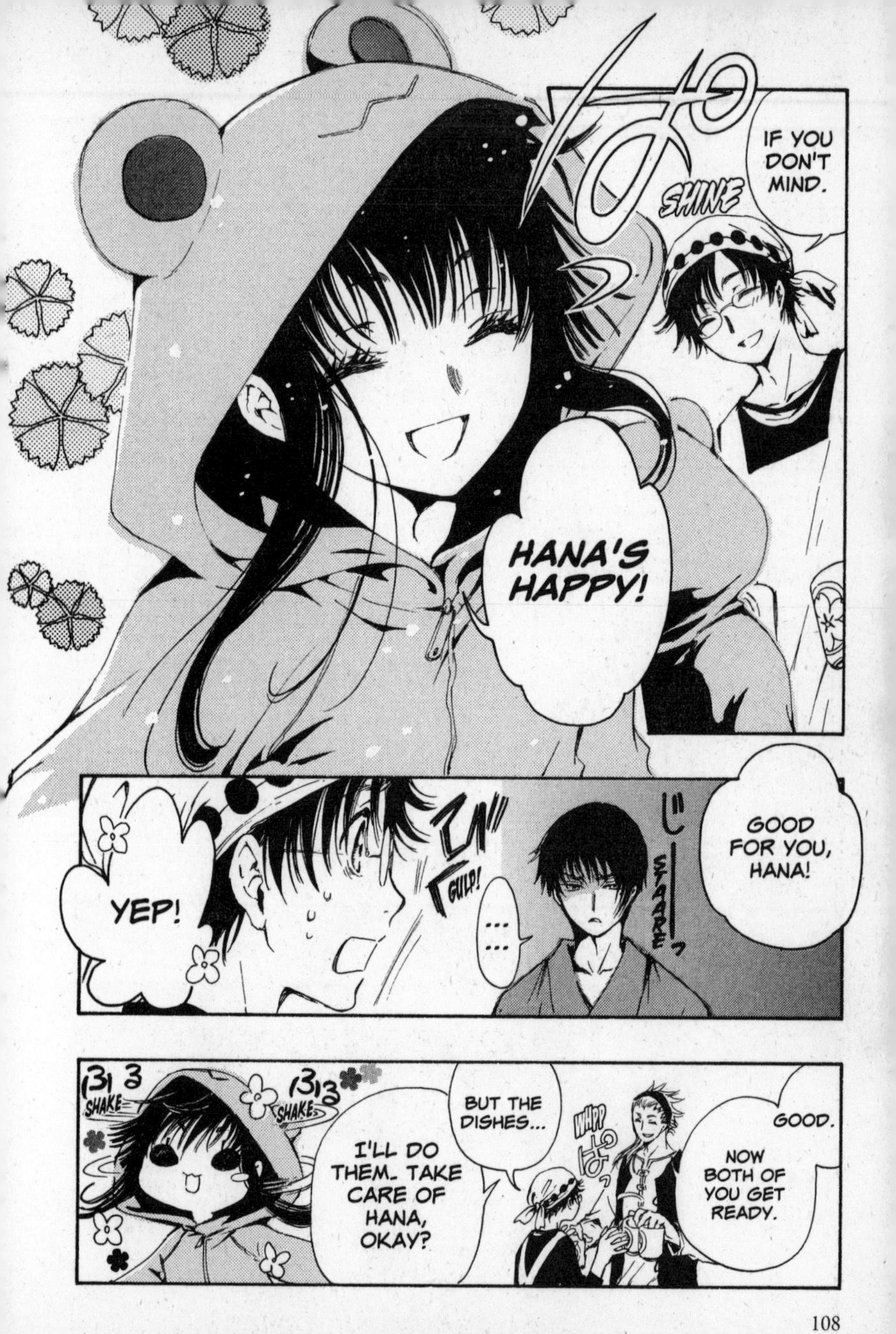
IF YOU DON'T MIND.
SHINE
HANA'S HAPPY!
GOOD FOR YOU, HANA!
STARE
......
GULP!
YEP!
GOOD.
NOW BOTH OF YOU GET READY.
WHPP
BUT THE DISHES...
I'LL DO THEM. TAKE CARE OF HANA, OKAY?
SHAKE
SHAKE

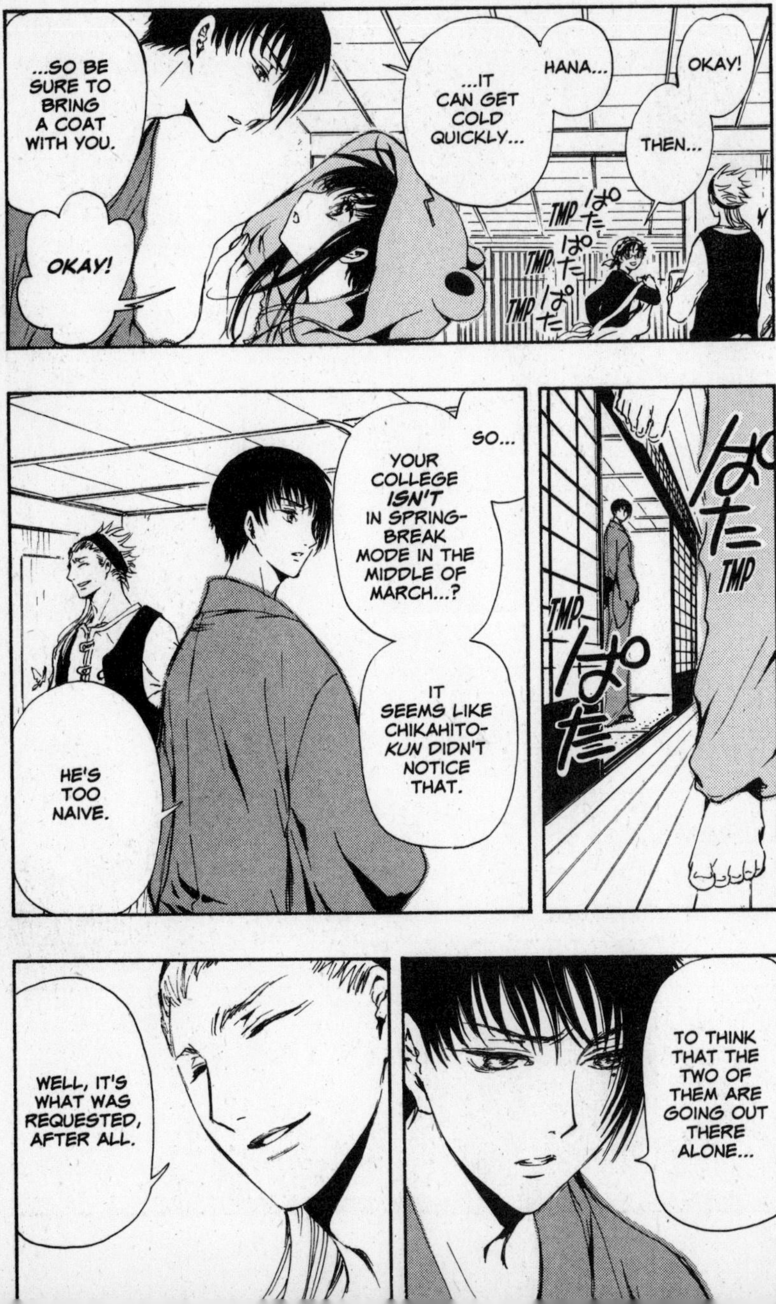
OKAY!
THEN...
HANA...
...IT CAN GET COLD QUICKLY...
...SO BE SURE TO BRING A COAT WITH YOU.
TMP ぱた
TMP ぱた
TMP ぱた
OKAY!
ぱた TMP
TMP ぱた
SO...
YOUR COLLEGE *ISN'T* IN SPRING-BREAK MODE IN THE MIDDLE OF MARCH...?
IT SEEMS LIKE CHIKAHITO-*KUN* DIDN'T NOTICE THAT.
HE'S TOO NAIVE.
TO THINK THAT THE TWO OF THEM ARE GOING OUT THERE ALONE...
WELL, IT'S WHAT WAS REQUESTED, AFTER ALL.

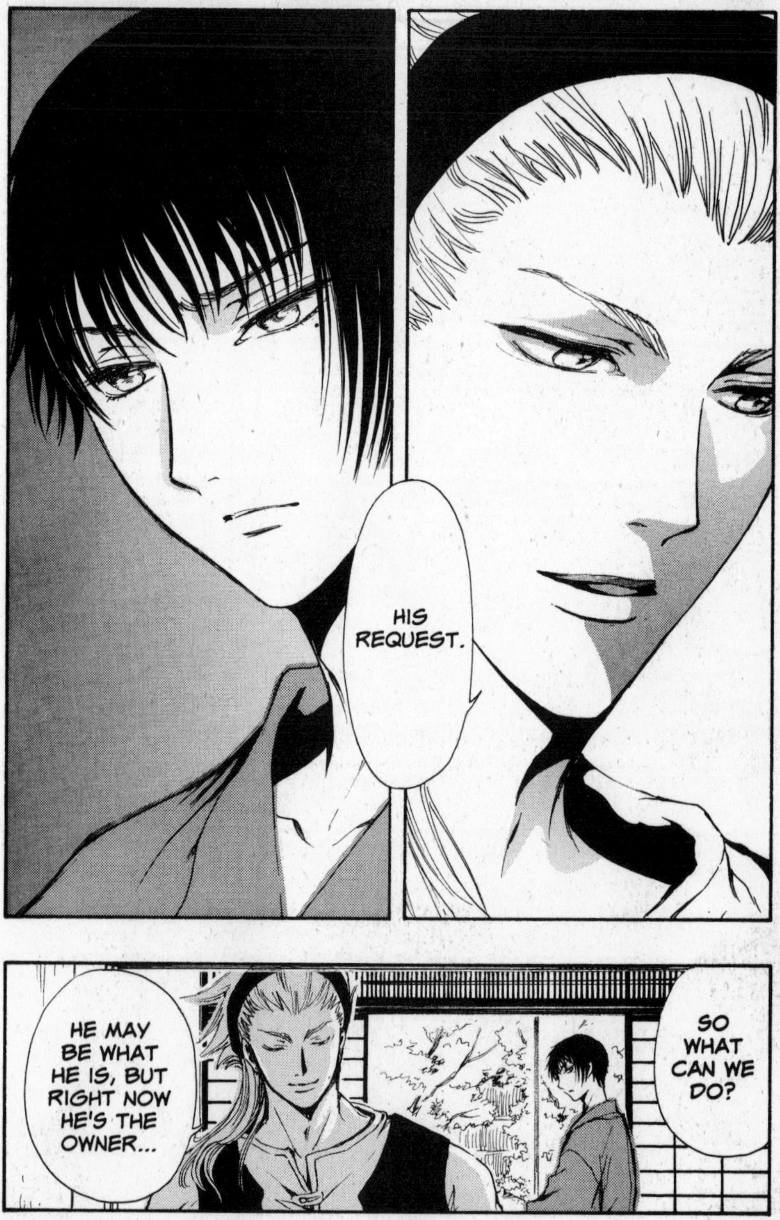
HIS REQUEST.
SO WHAT CAN WE DO?
HE MAY BE WHAT HE IS, BUT RIGHT NOW HE'S THE OWNER...

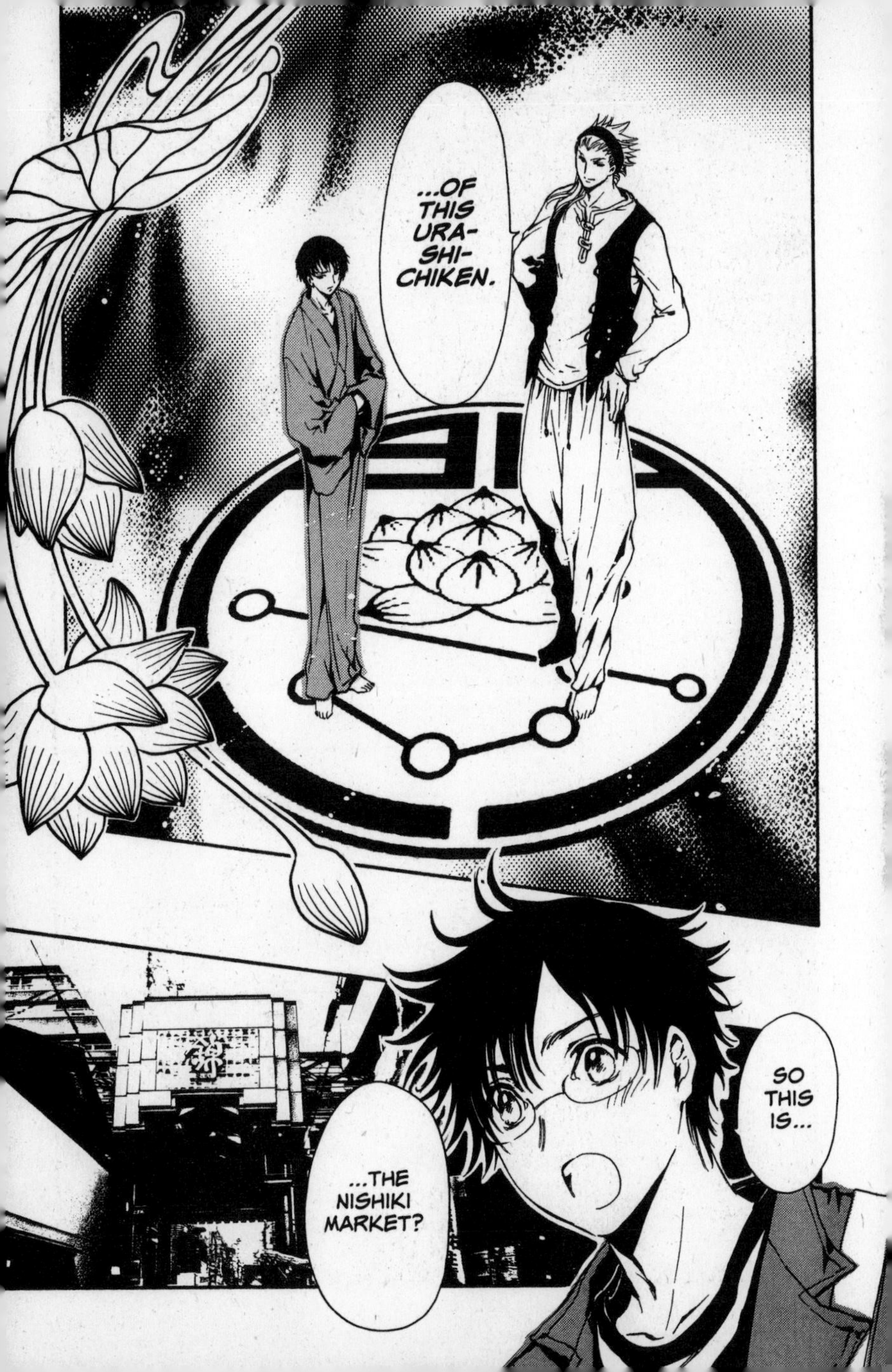
...OF THIS URA-SHI-CHIKEN.
SO THIS IS...
...THE NISHIKI MARKET?

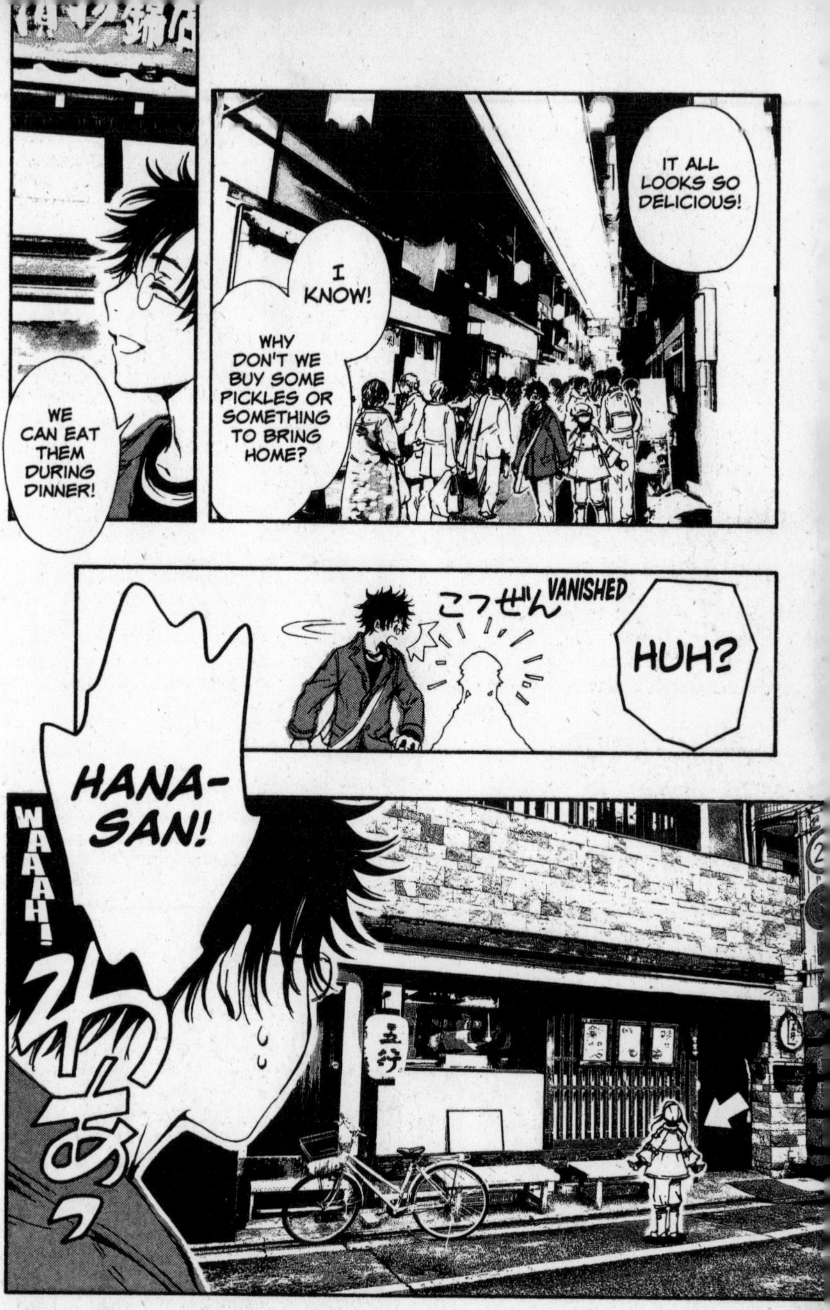
IT ALL LOOKS SO DELICIOUS!
I KNOW!
WHY DON'T WE BUY SOME PICKLES OR SOMETHING TO BRING HOME?
WE CAN EAT THEM DURING DINNER!
HUH?
こつぜん
VANISHED
HANA-SAN!
WAAAH!
わあっ

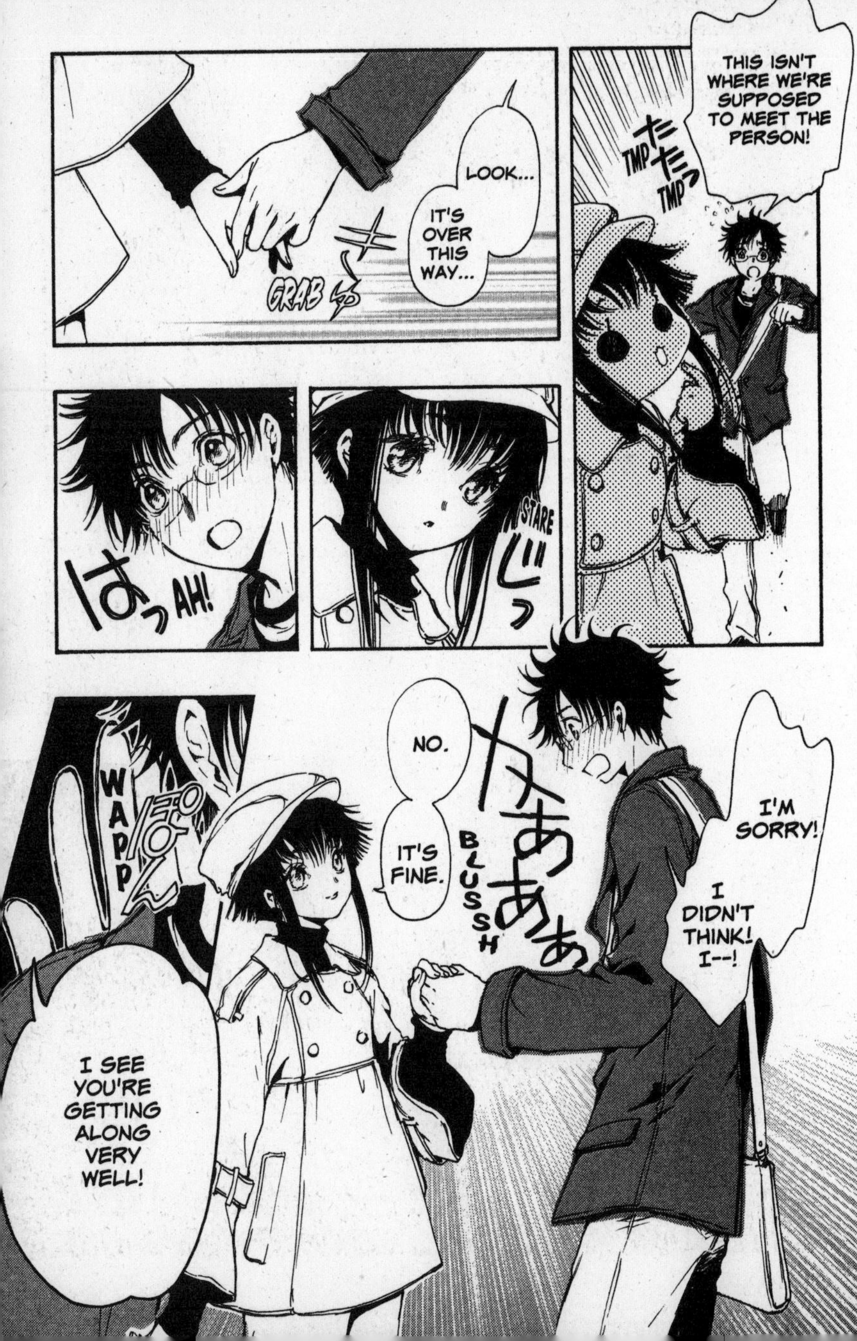
THIS ISN'T WHERE WE'RE SUPPOSED TO MEET THE PERSON!
TMP TMP
LOOK...
IT'S OVER THIS WAY...
GRAB
STARE
AH!
I'M SORRY!
I DIDN'T THINK! I--!
BLUSSH
NO.
IT'S FINE.
WAPP
I SEE YOU'RE GETTING ALONG VERY WELL!

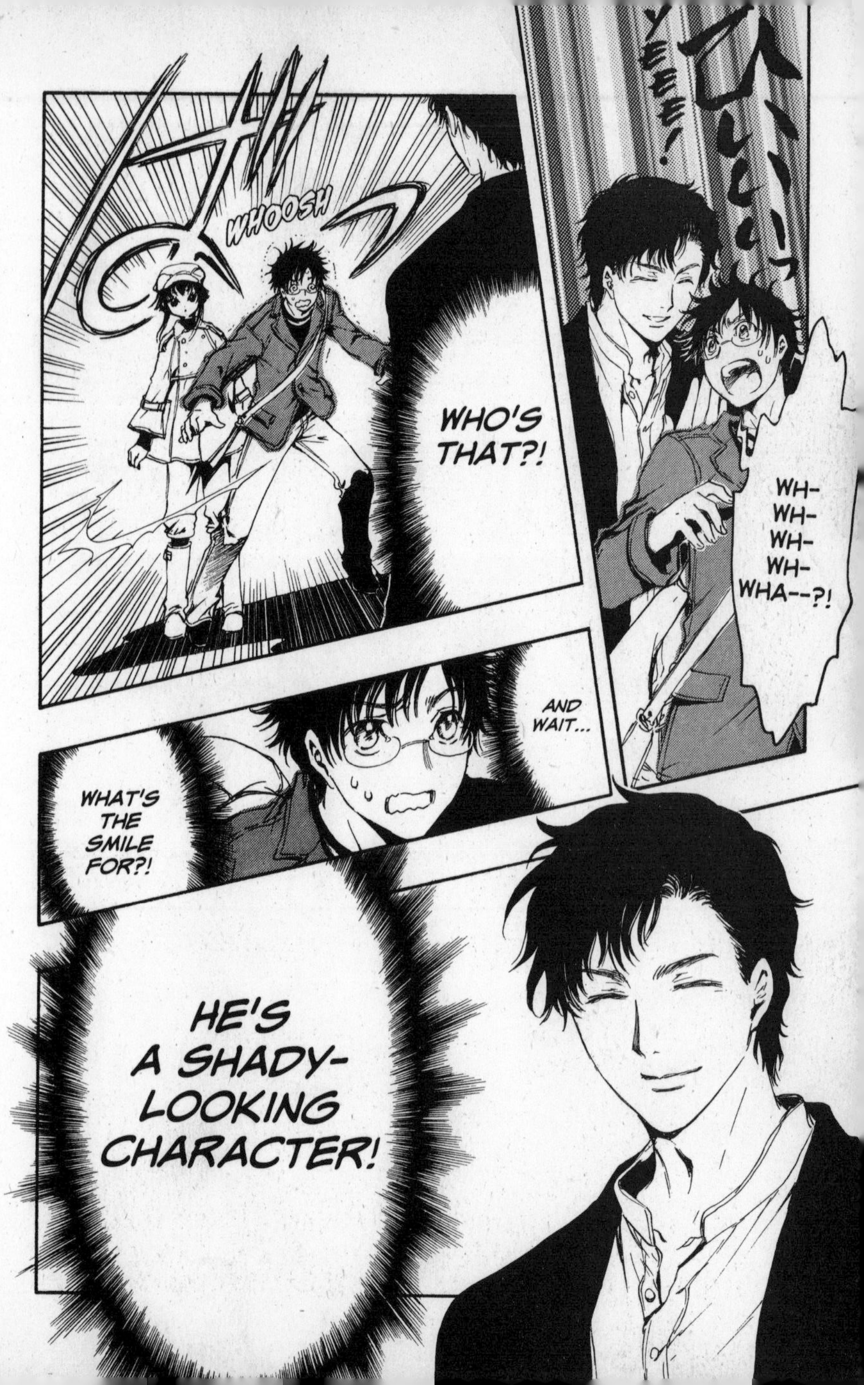
YEEEE!
WH-
WH-
WH-
WH-
WHA--?!
WHOOSH
WHO'S THAT?!
AND WAIT...
WHAT'S THE SMILE FOR?!
HE'S A SHADY-LOOKING CHARACTER!

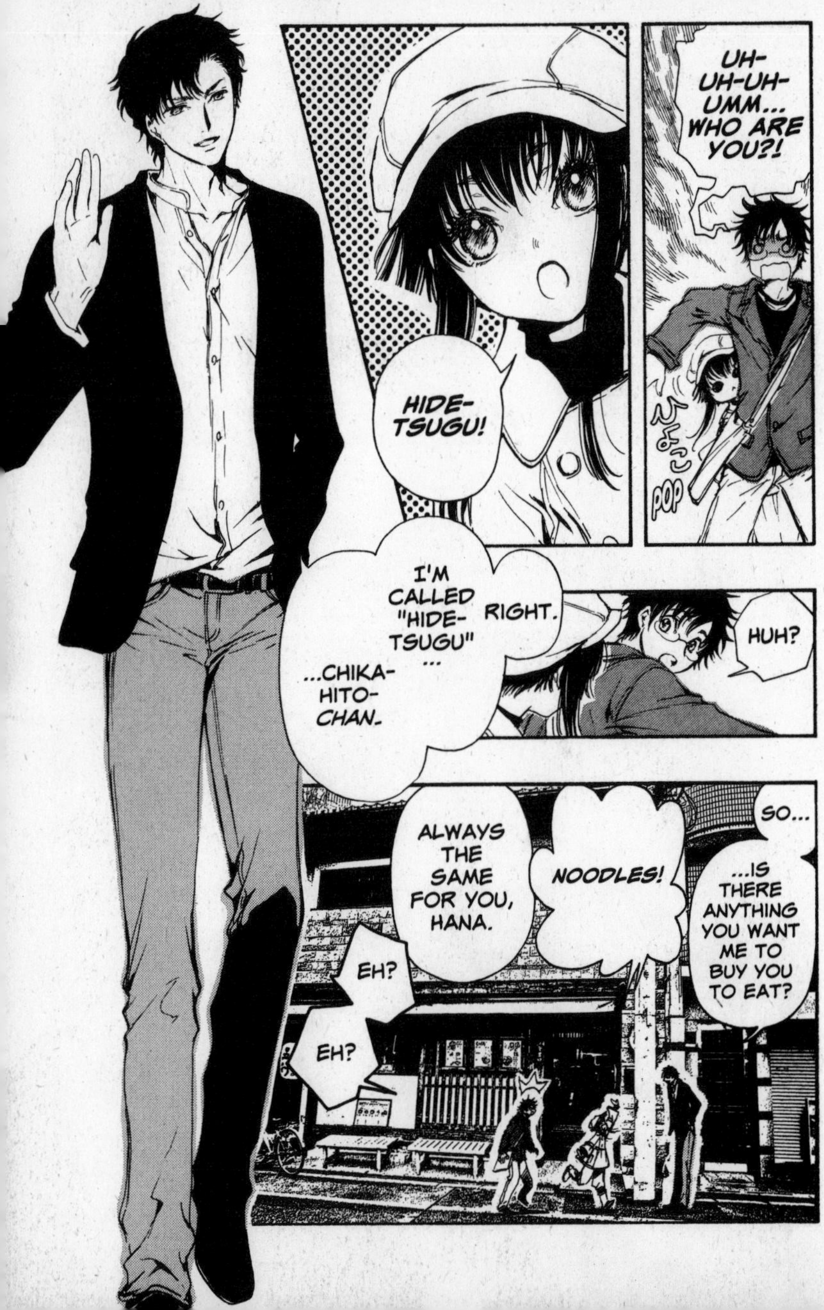
UH-UH-UH-UMM... WHO ARE YOU?!
ひょこ
POP
HIDE-TSUGU!
HUH?
RIGHT.
I'M CALLED "HIDE-TSUGU"...
...CHIKA-HITO-CHAN.
SO...
...IS THERE ANYTHING YOU WANT ME TO BUY YOU TO EAT?
NOODLES!
ALWAYS THE SAME FOR YOU, HANA.
EH?
EH?

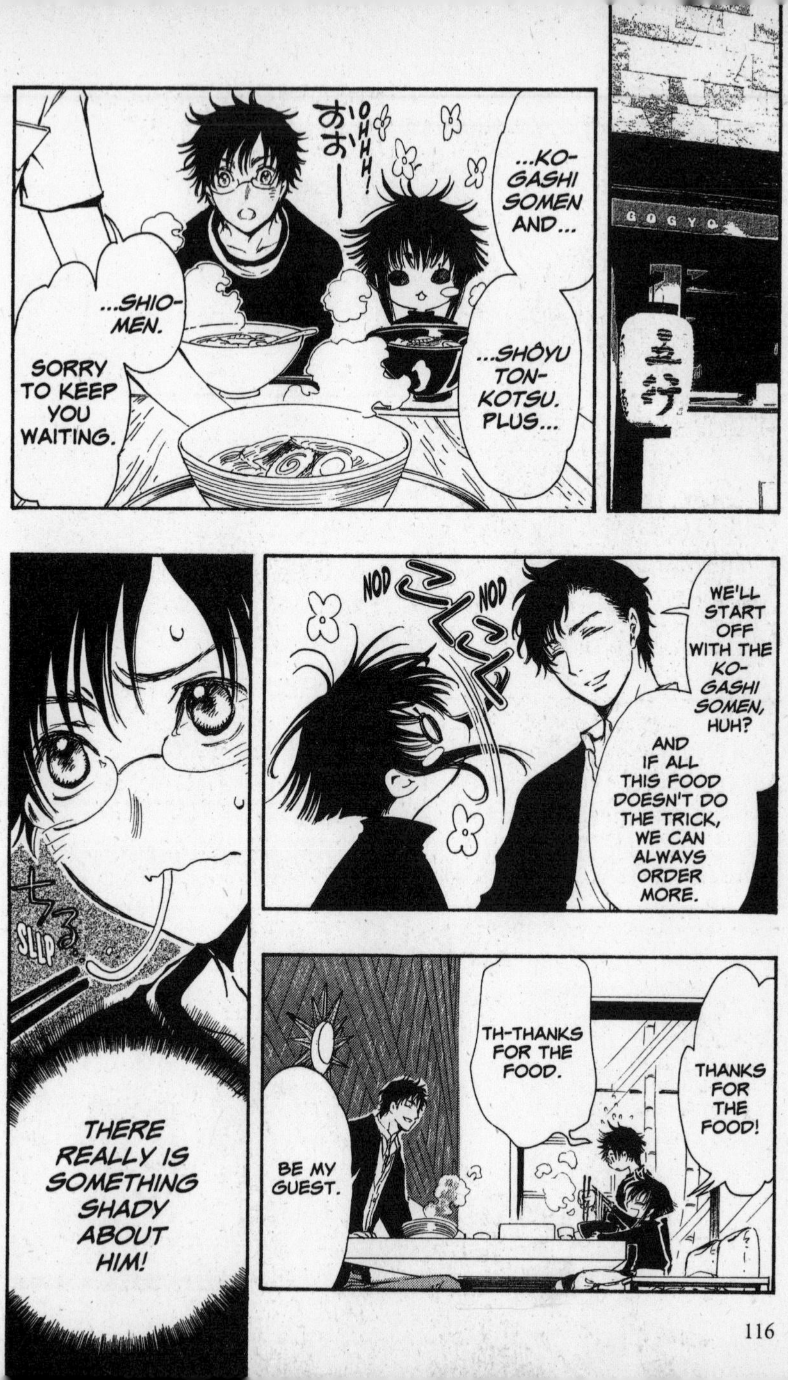
GOGYO
五行
...KO-GASHI SOMEN AND...
...SHÔYU TON-KOTSU. PLUS...
OHHH! おおー
...SHIO-MEN.
SORRY TO KEEP YOU WAITING.
WE'LL START OFF WITH THE KO-GASHI SOMEN, HUH?
AND IF ALL THIS FOOD DOESN'T DO THE TRICK, WE CAN ALWAYS ORDER MORE.
NOD NOD
THANKS FOR THE FOOD!
TH-THANKS FOR THE FOOD.
BE MY GUEST.
SLLP
THERE REALLY IS SOMETHING SHADY ABOUT HIM!

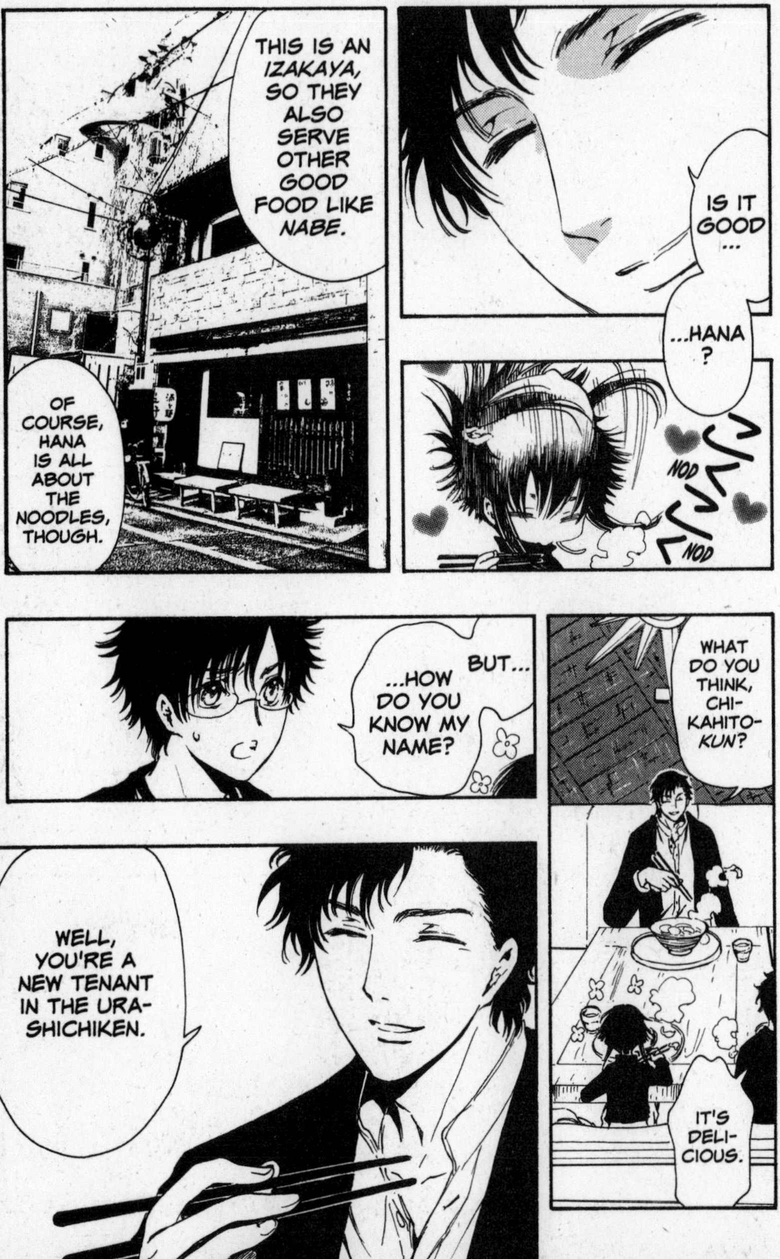
IS IT GOOD ...
...HANA ?
NOD
NOD
THIS IS AN IZAKAYA, SO THEY ALSO SERVE OTHER GOOD FOOD LIKE NABE.
OF COURSE, HANA IS ALL ABOUT THE NOODLES, THOUGH.
WHAT DO YOU THINK, CHI-KAHITO-KUN?
IT'S DELI-CIOUS.
BUT... ...HOW DO YOU KNOW MY NAME?
WELL, YOU'RE A NEW TENANT IN THE URA-SHICHIKEN.

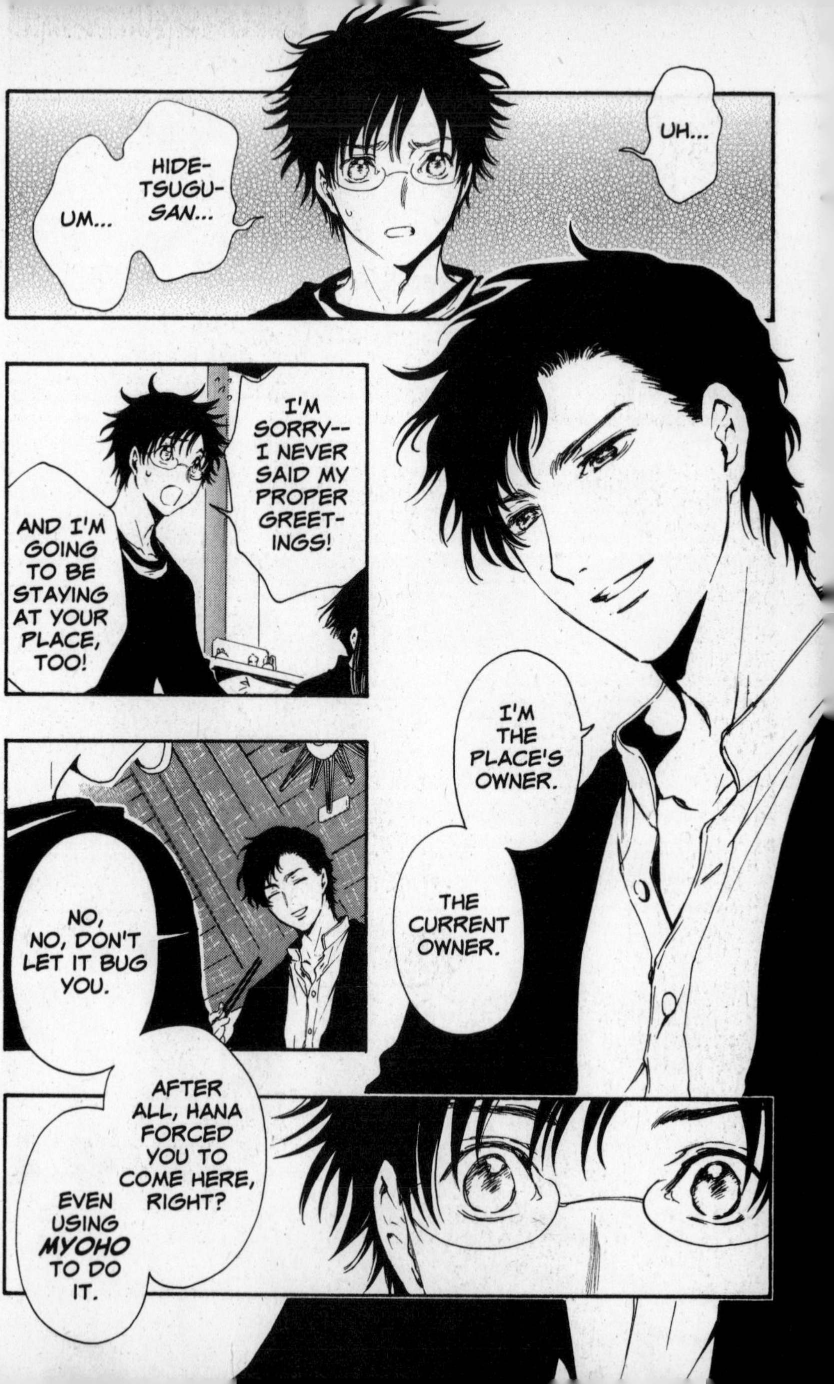
UH...
UM... HIDE-TSUGU-SAN...
I'M SORRY-- I NEVER SAID MY PROPER GREET-INGS!
AND I'M GOING TO BE STAYING AT YOUR PLACE, TOO!
I'M THE PLACE'S OWNER.
THE CURRENT OWNER.
NO, NO, DON'T LET IT BUG YOU.
AFTER ALL, HANA FORCED YOU TO COME HERE, RIGHT?
EVEN USING MYOHO TO DO IT.

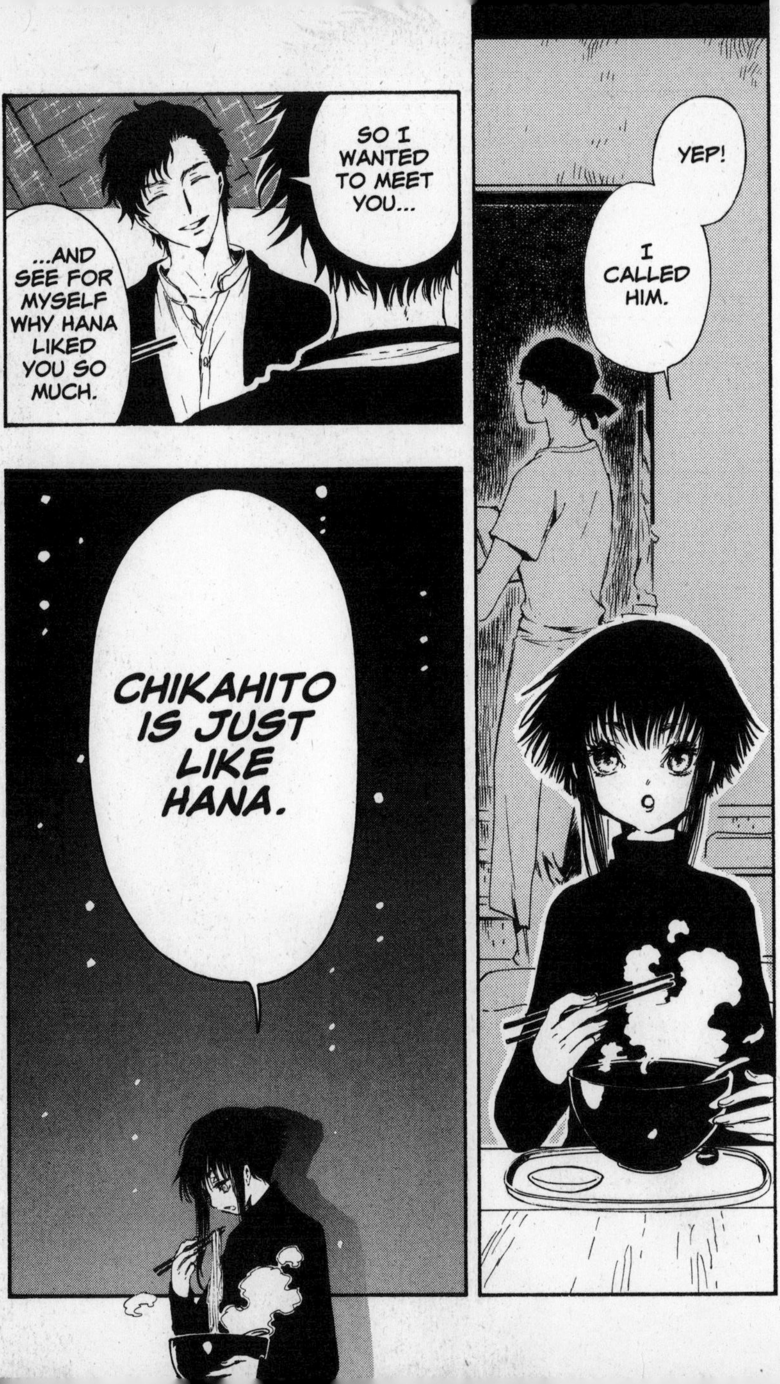
YEP!
I CALLED HIM.
SO I WANTED TO MEET YOU...
...AND SEE FOR MYSELF WHY HANA LIKED YOU SO MUCH.
CHIKAHITO IS JUST LIKE HANA.

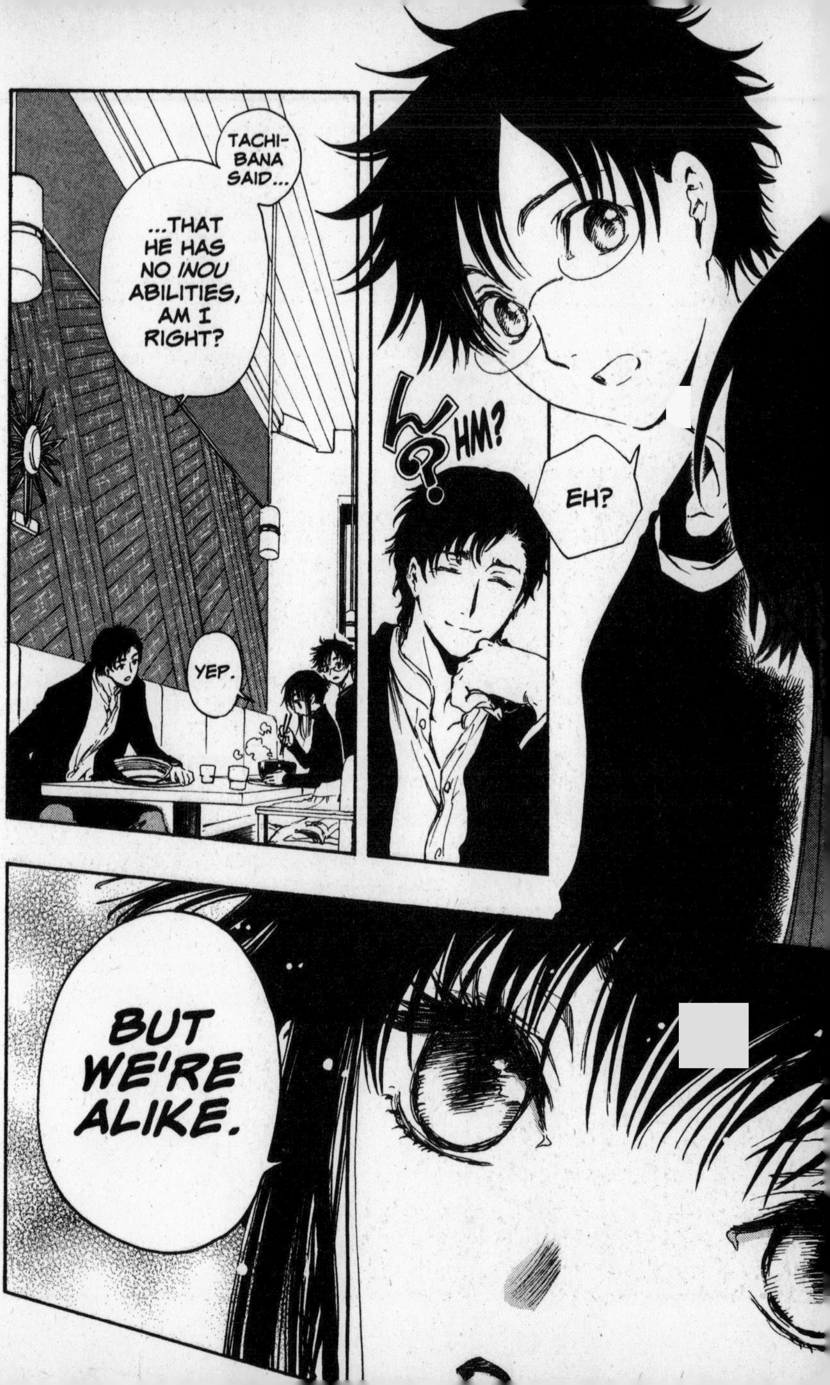
TACHIBANA SAID...
...THAT HE HAS NO *INOU* ABILITIES, AM I RIGHT?
YEP.
HM?
EH?
BUT WE'RE ALIKE.

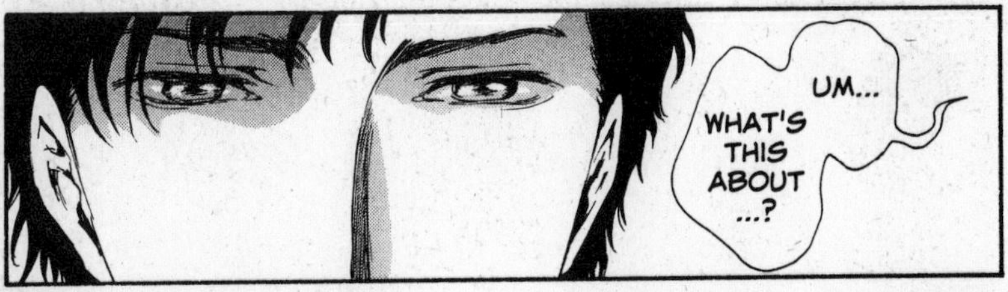
UM...
WHAT'S THIS ABOUT ...?
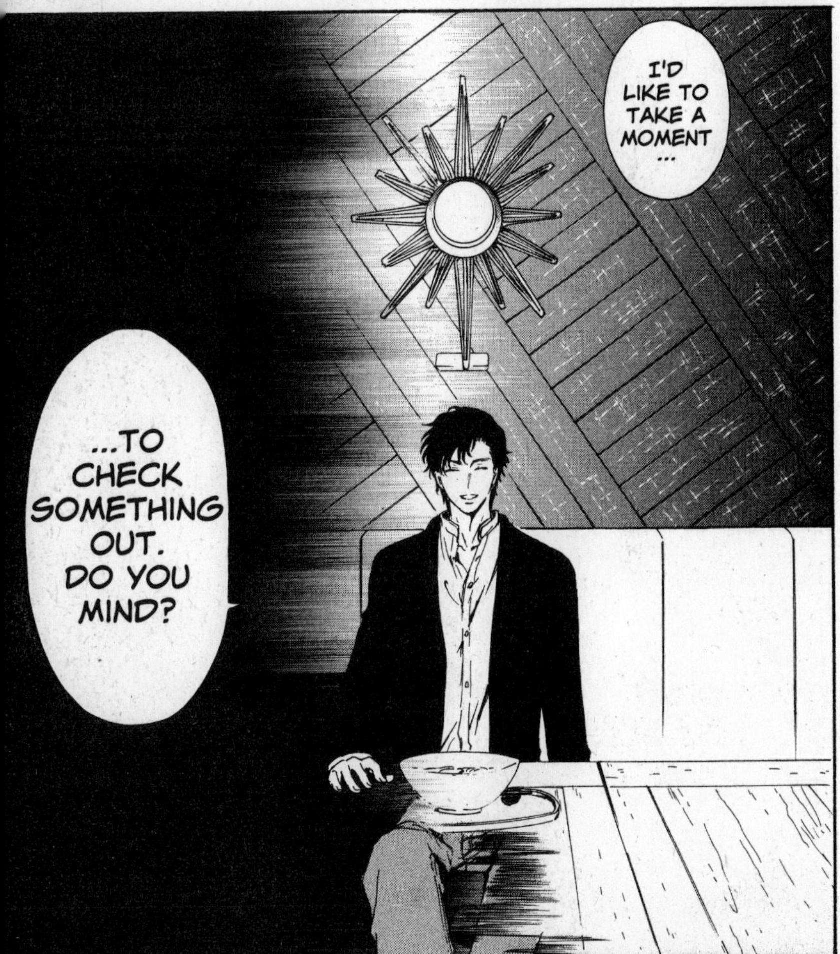
I'D LIKE TO TAKE A MOMENT ...
...TO CHECK SOMETHING OUT. DO YOU MIND?

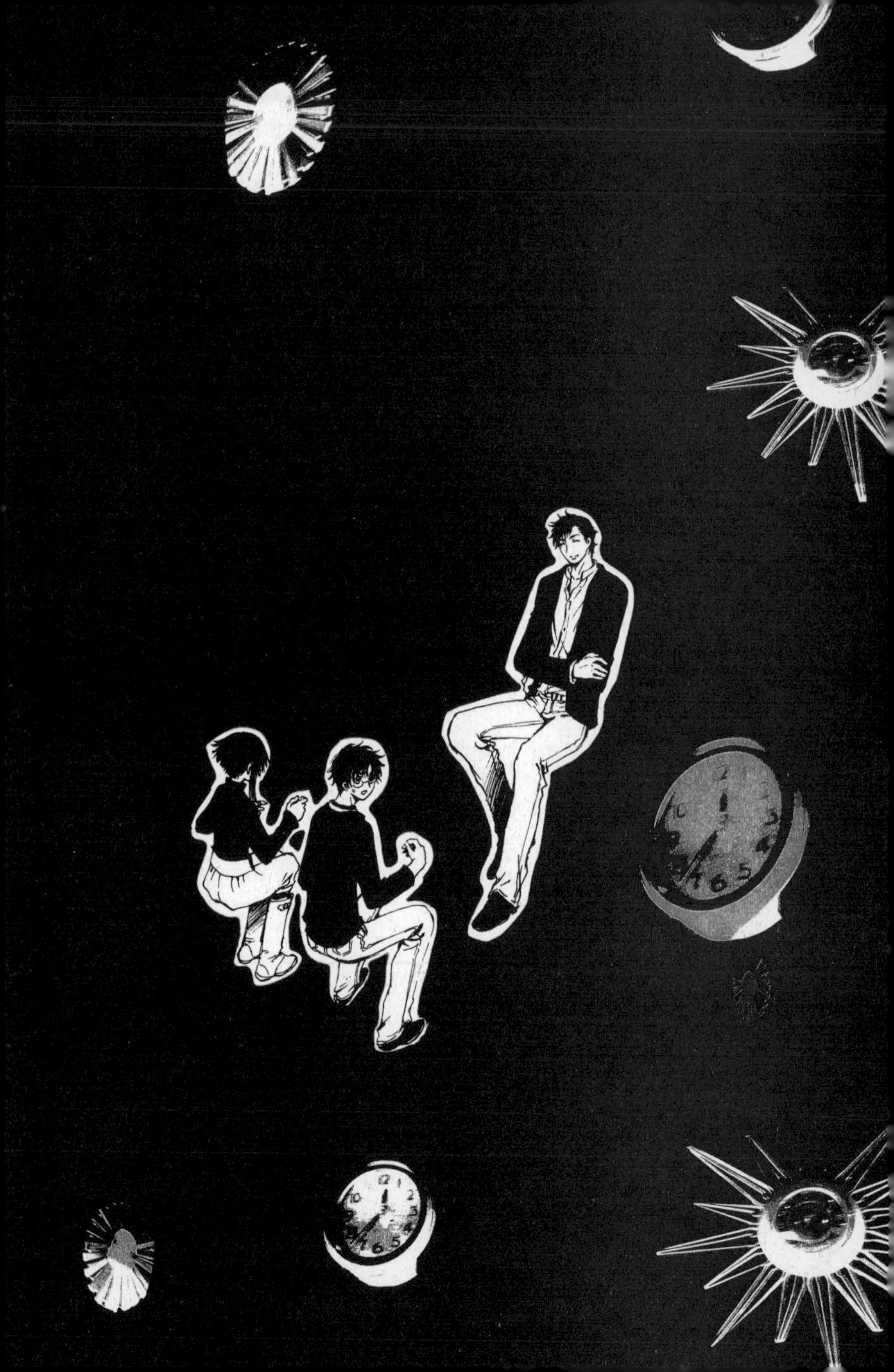

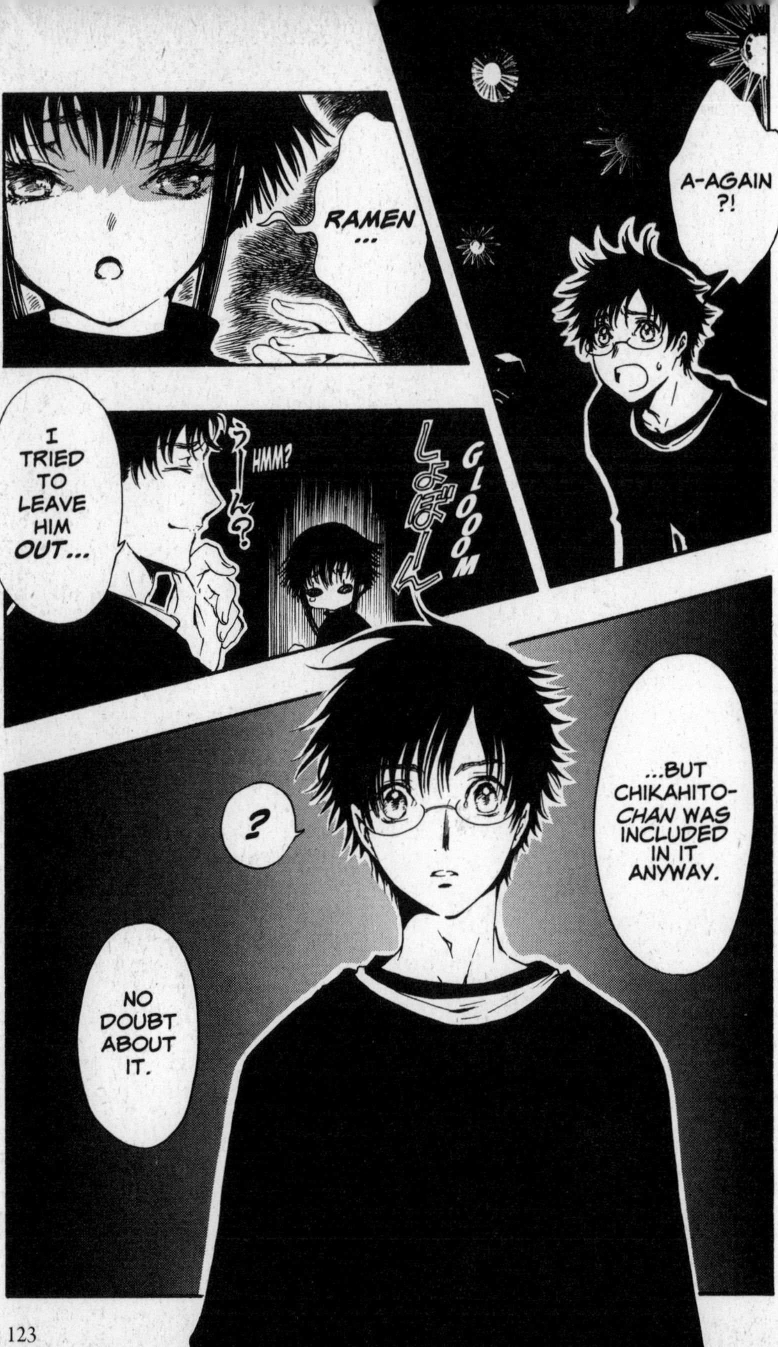
RAMEN ...
A-AGAIN ?!
しょぼーん GLOOOM
うーん? HMM?
I TRIED TO LEAVE HIM OUT...
...BUT CHIKAHITO-CHAN WAS INCLUDED IN IT ANYWAY.
?
NO DOUBT ABOUT IT.

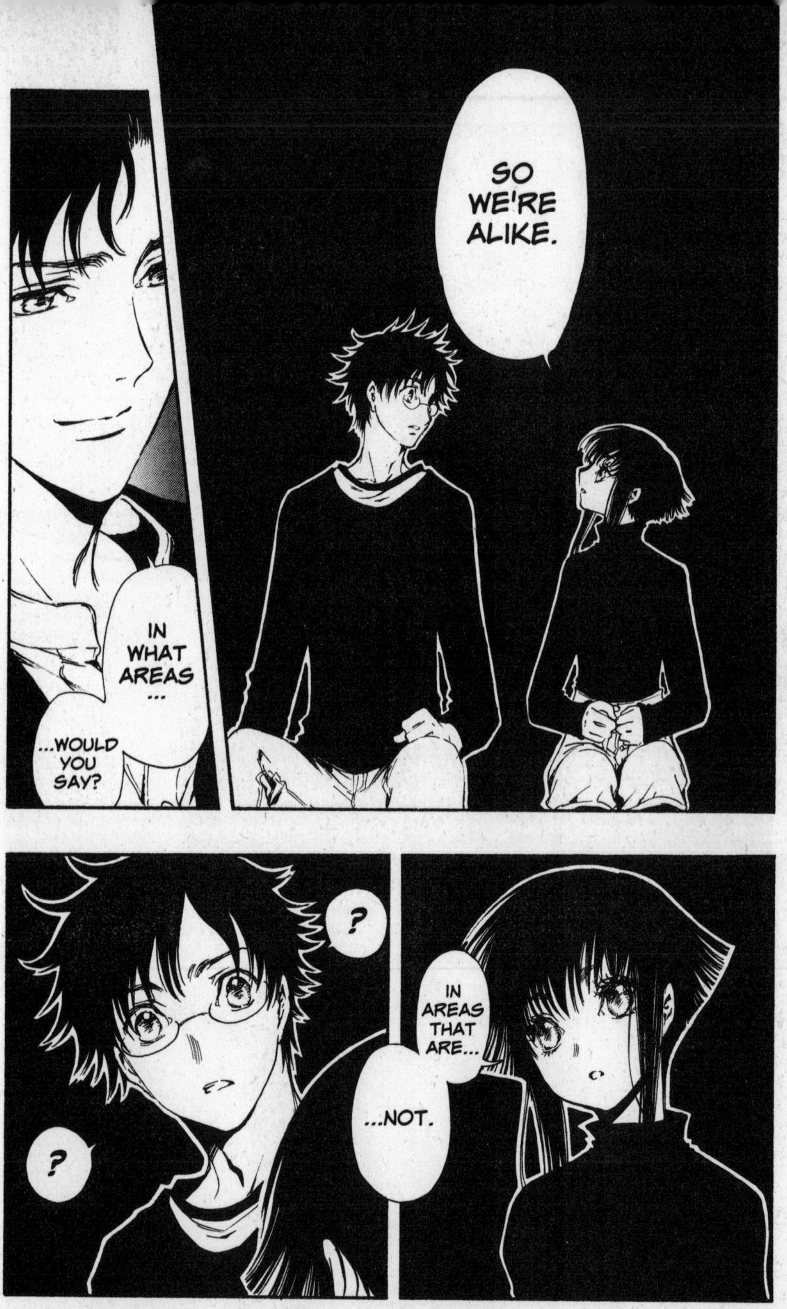
SO WE'RE ALIKE.
IN WHAT AREAS...
...WOULD YOU SAY?
IN AREAS THAT ARE...
...NOT.
?
?

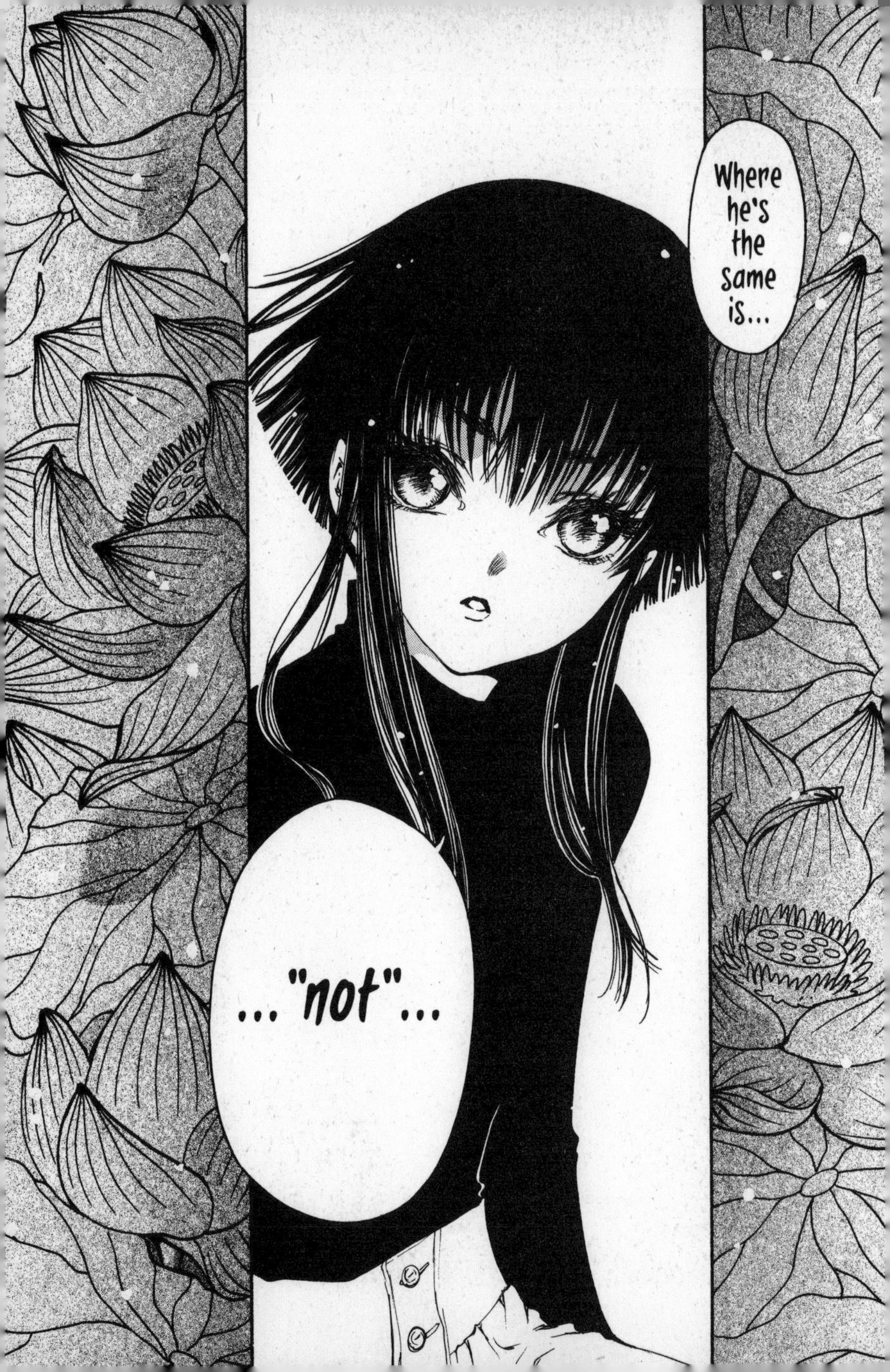
Where he's the same is...
..."not"...

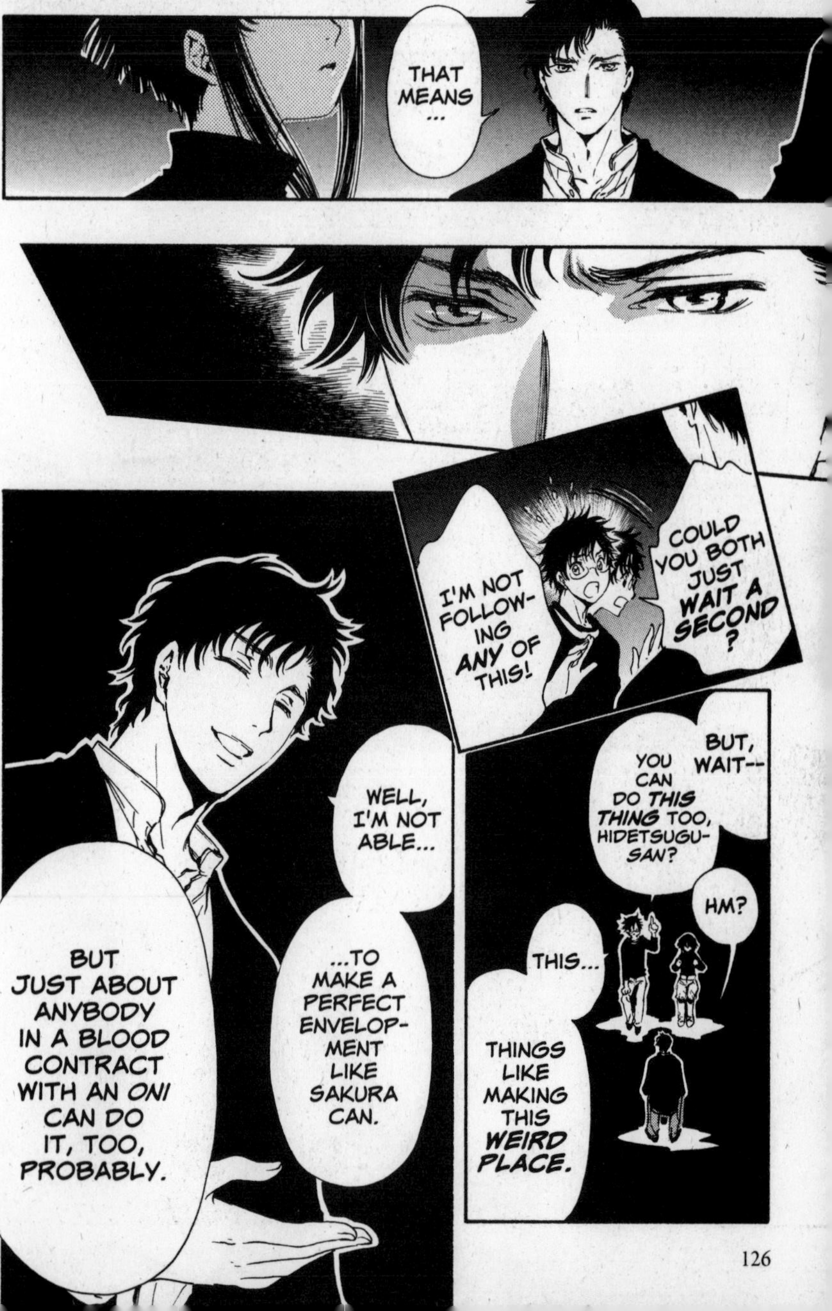
THAT MEANS ...
COULD YOU BOTH JUST WAIT A SECOND?
I'M NOT FOLLOWING ANY OF THIS!
BUT, WAIT--
YOU CAN DO THIS THING TOO, HIDETSUGU-SAN?
HM?
THIS...
THINGS LIKE MAKING THIS WEIRD PLACE.
WELL, I'M NOT ABLE...
...TO MAKE A PERFECT ENVELOPMENT LIKE SAKURA CAN.
BUT JUST ABOUT ANYBODY IN A BLOOD CONTRACT WITH AN ONI CAN DO IT, TOO, PROBABLY.

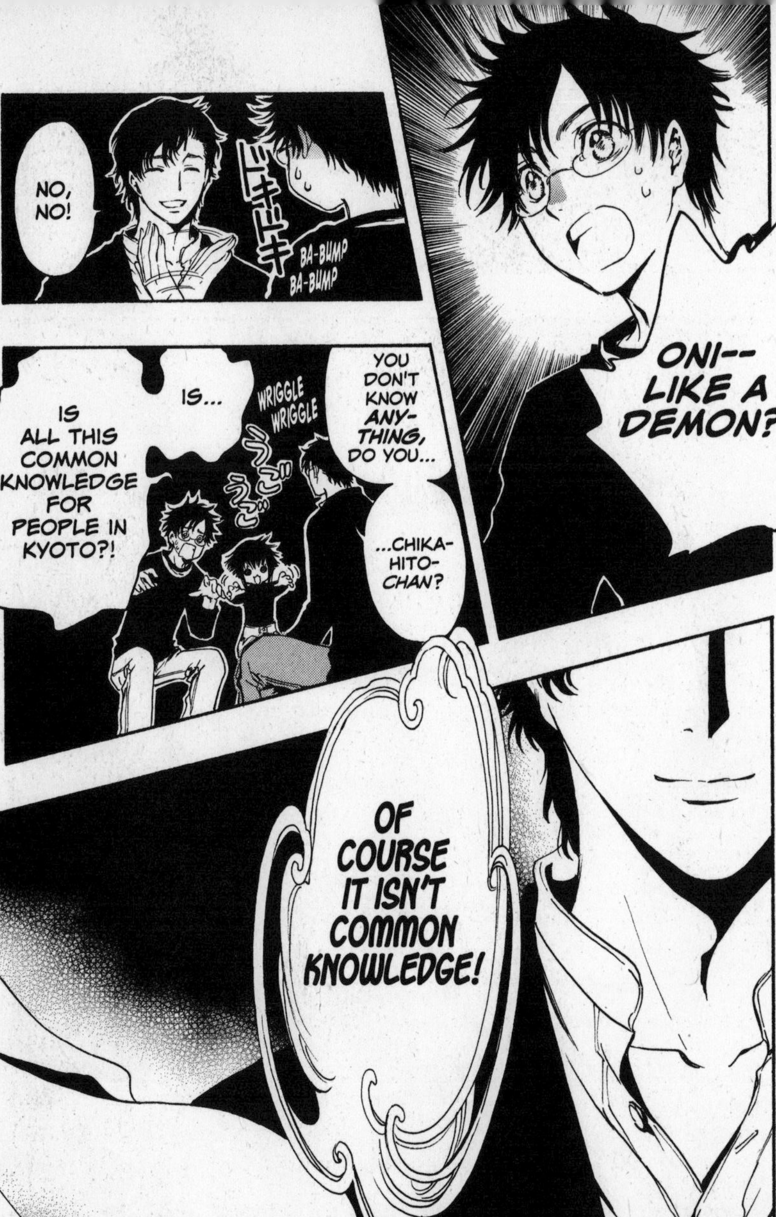

ONI-- LIKE A DEMON?!
NO, NO!
ドキドキ
BA-BUMP BA-BUMP
YOU DON'T KNOW ANYTHING, DO YOU...
...CHIKA-HITO-CHAN?
うごうご
WRIGGLE WRIGGLE
IS...
IS ALL THIS COMMON KNOWLEDGE FOR PEOPLE IN KYOTO?!
OF COURSE IT ISN'T COMMON KNOWLEDGE!

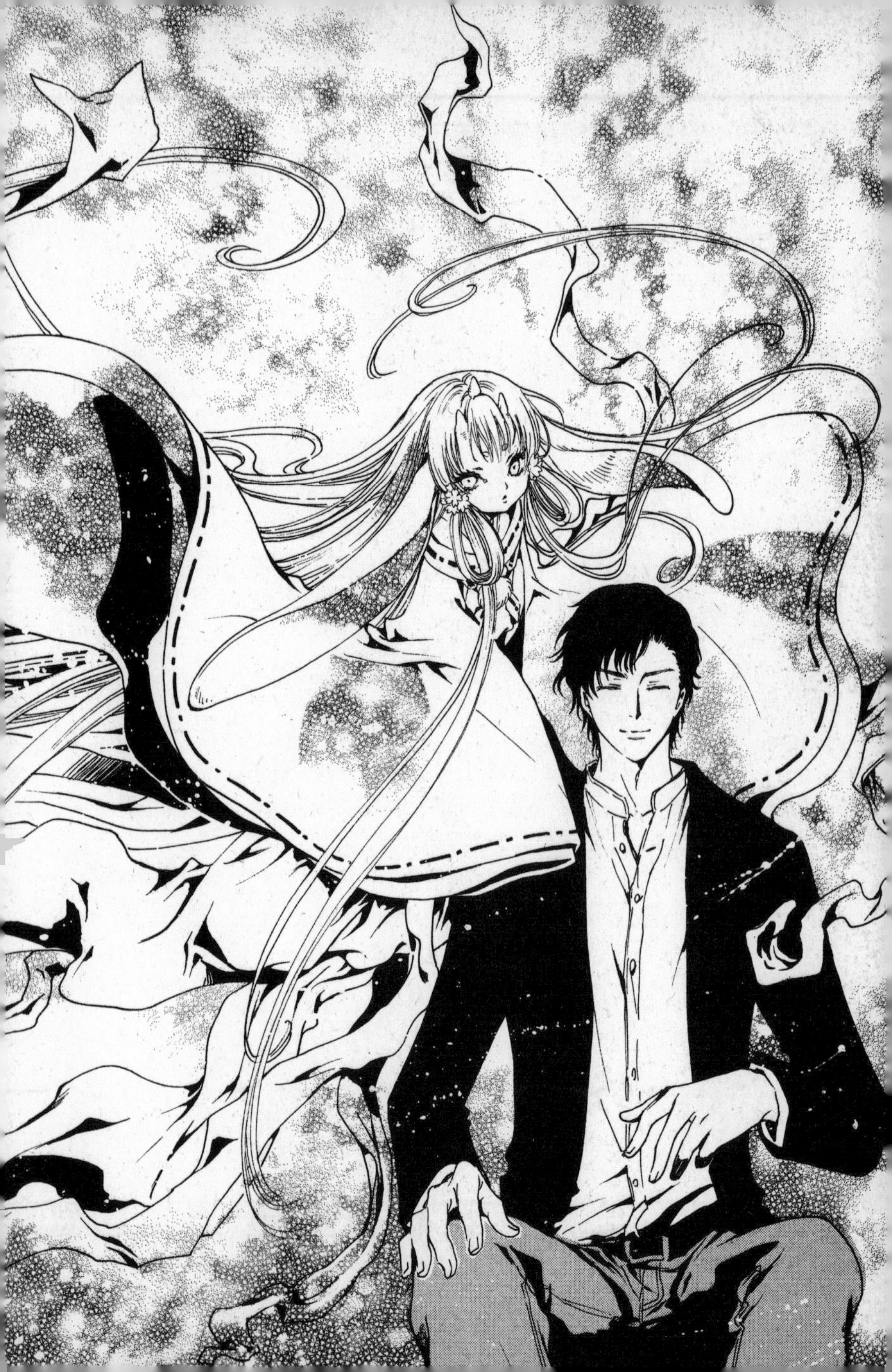

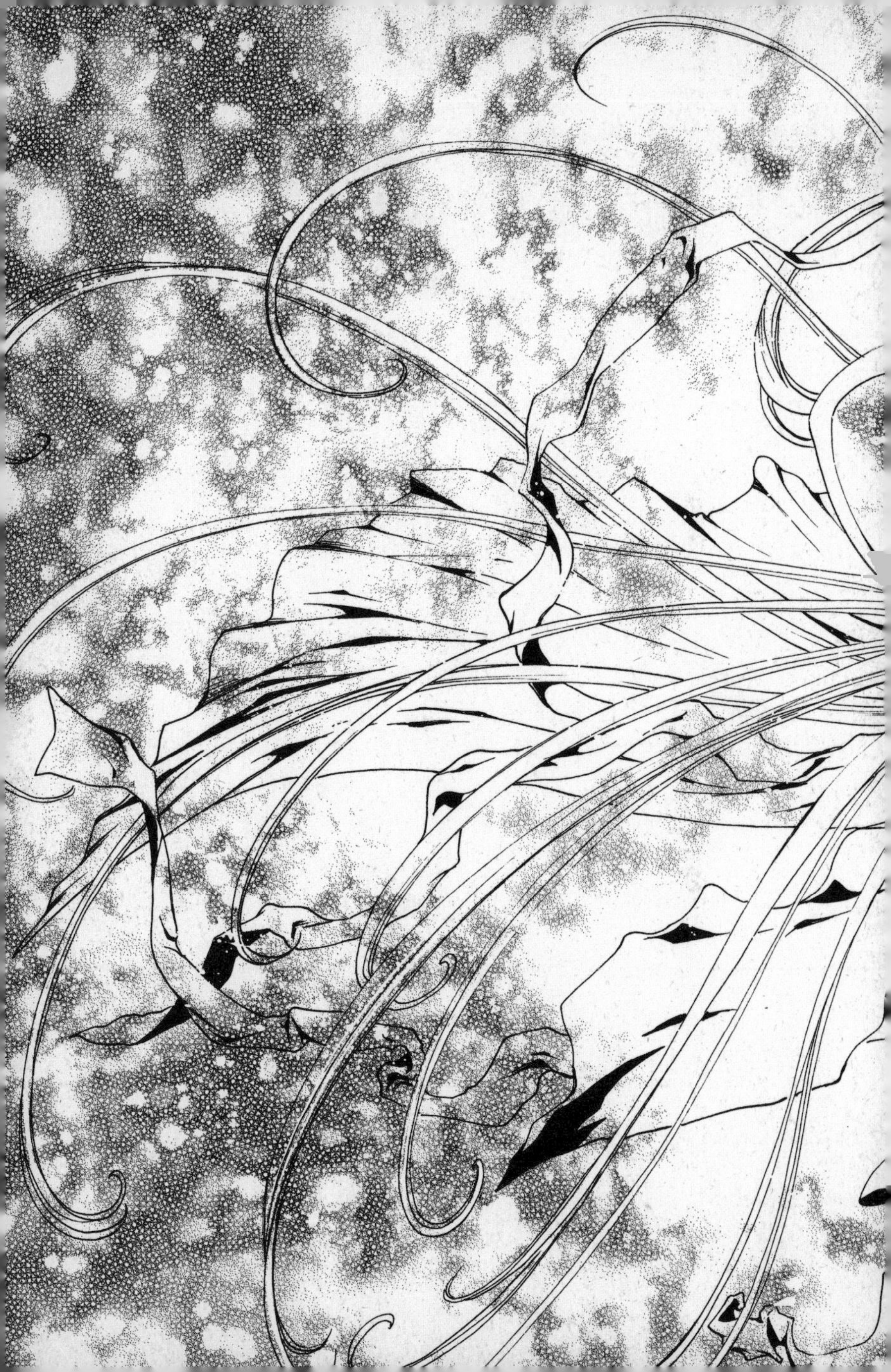

GATE 7
ゲート セブン

CHAPTER THREE: HIDETSUGU AND THE *ONI*

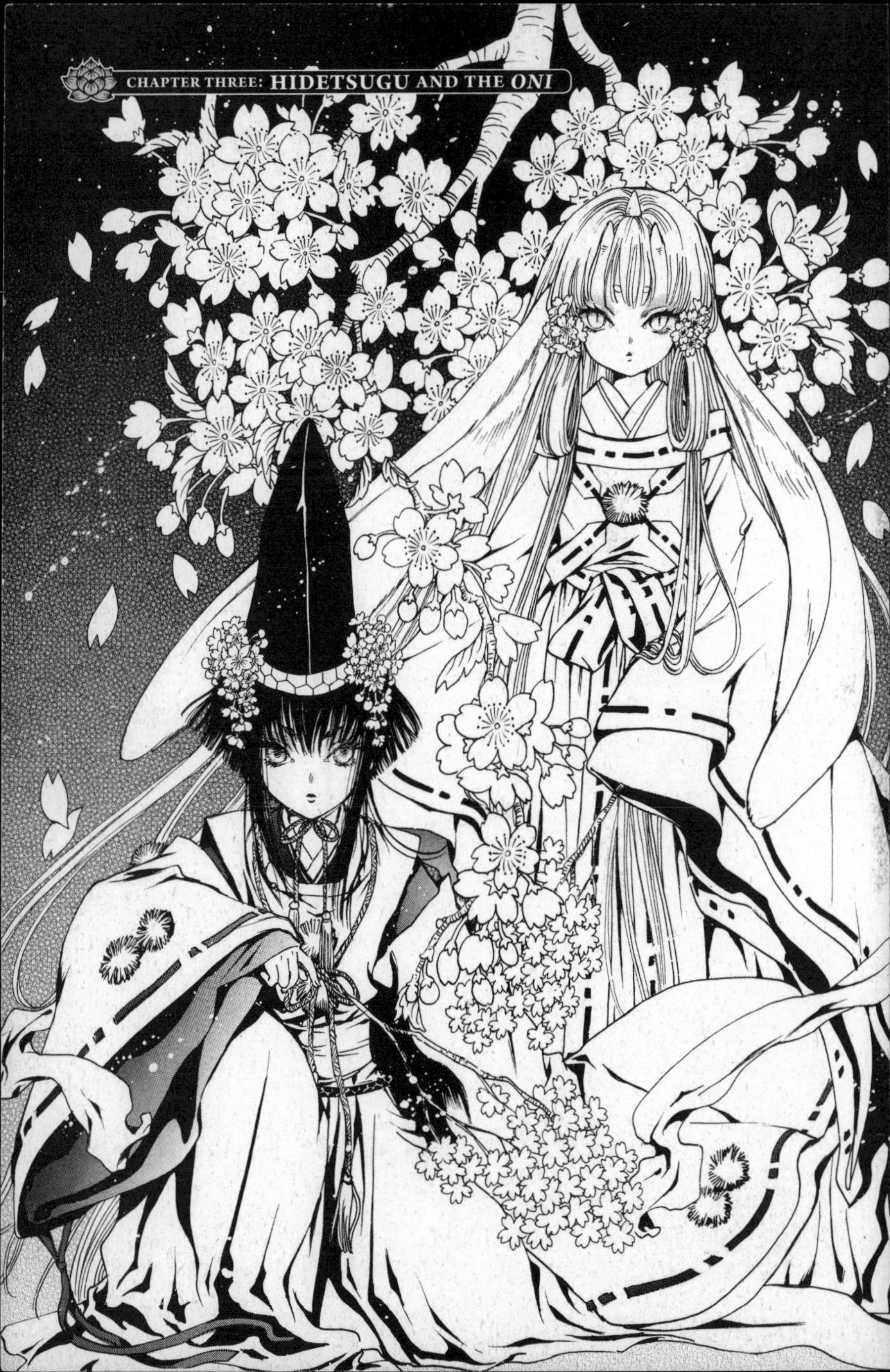

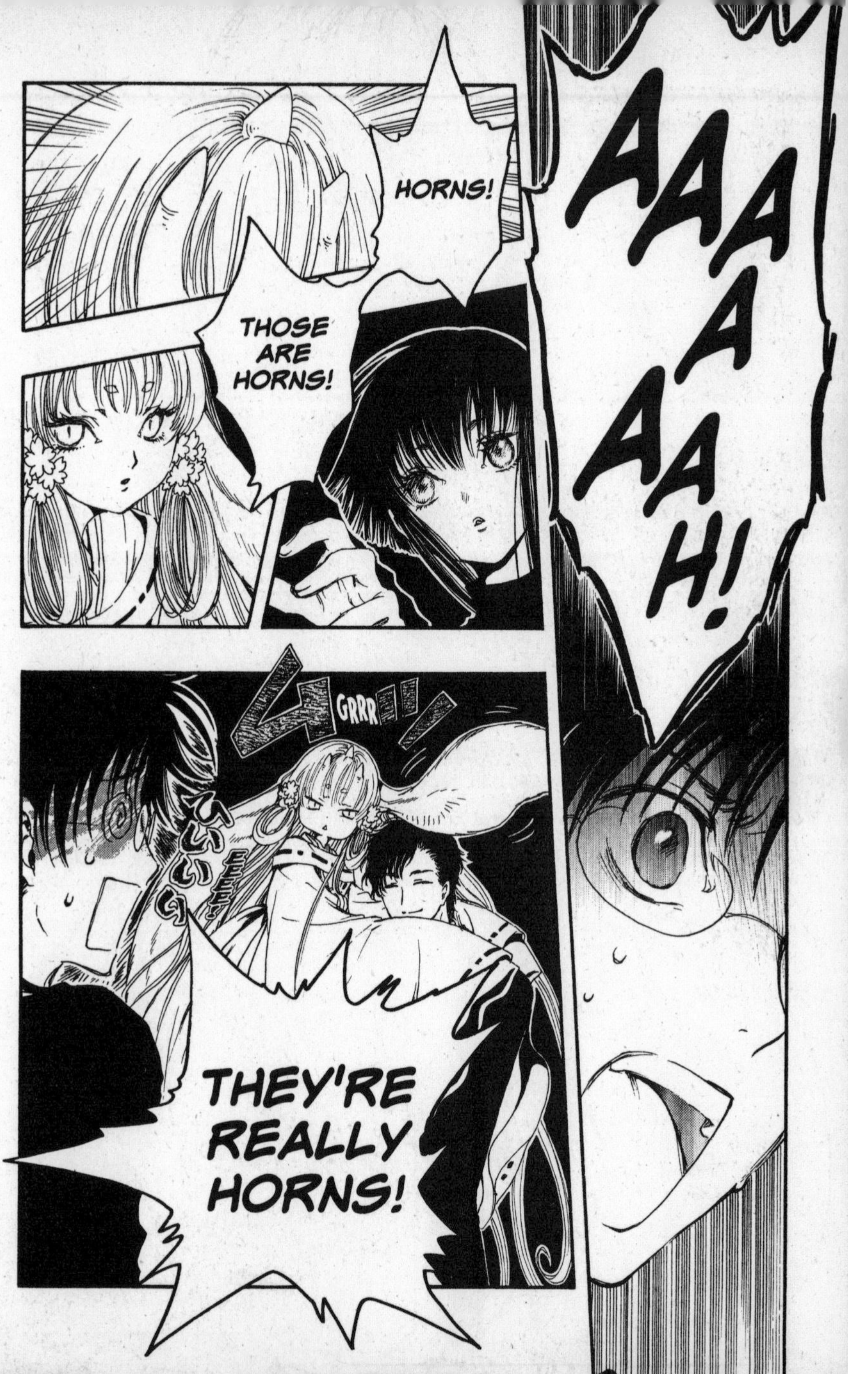

HORNS!
THOSE ARE HORNS!
GRRR
THEY'RE REALLY HORNS!
AAAAAH!

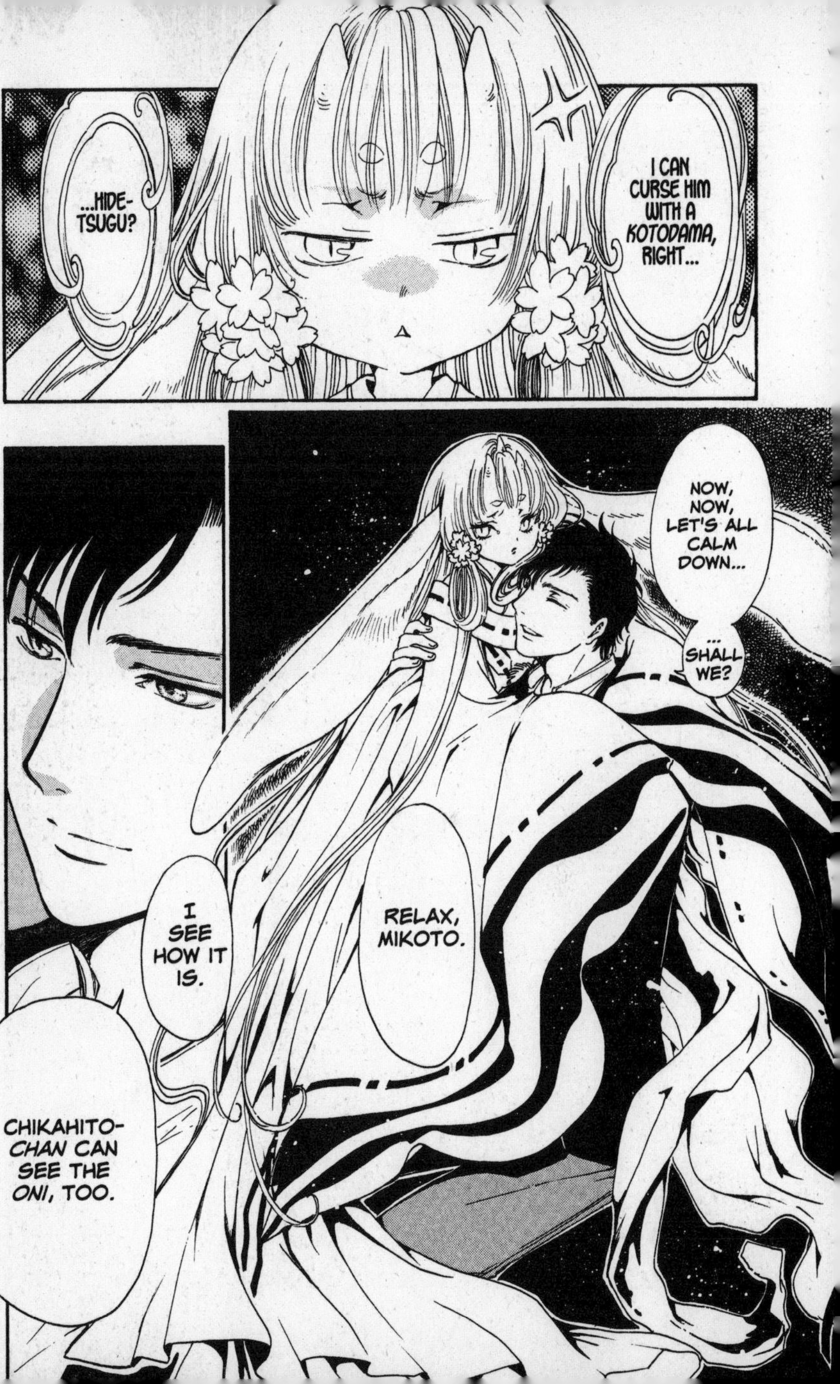
I CAN CURSE HIM WITH A KOTODAMA, RIGHT...
...HIDE-TSUGU?
NOW, NOW, LET'S ALL CALM DOWN...
...SHALL WE?
RELAX, MIKOTO.
I SEE HOW IT IS.
CHIKAHITO-CHAN CAN SEE THE *ONI*, TOO.

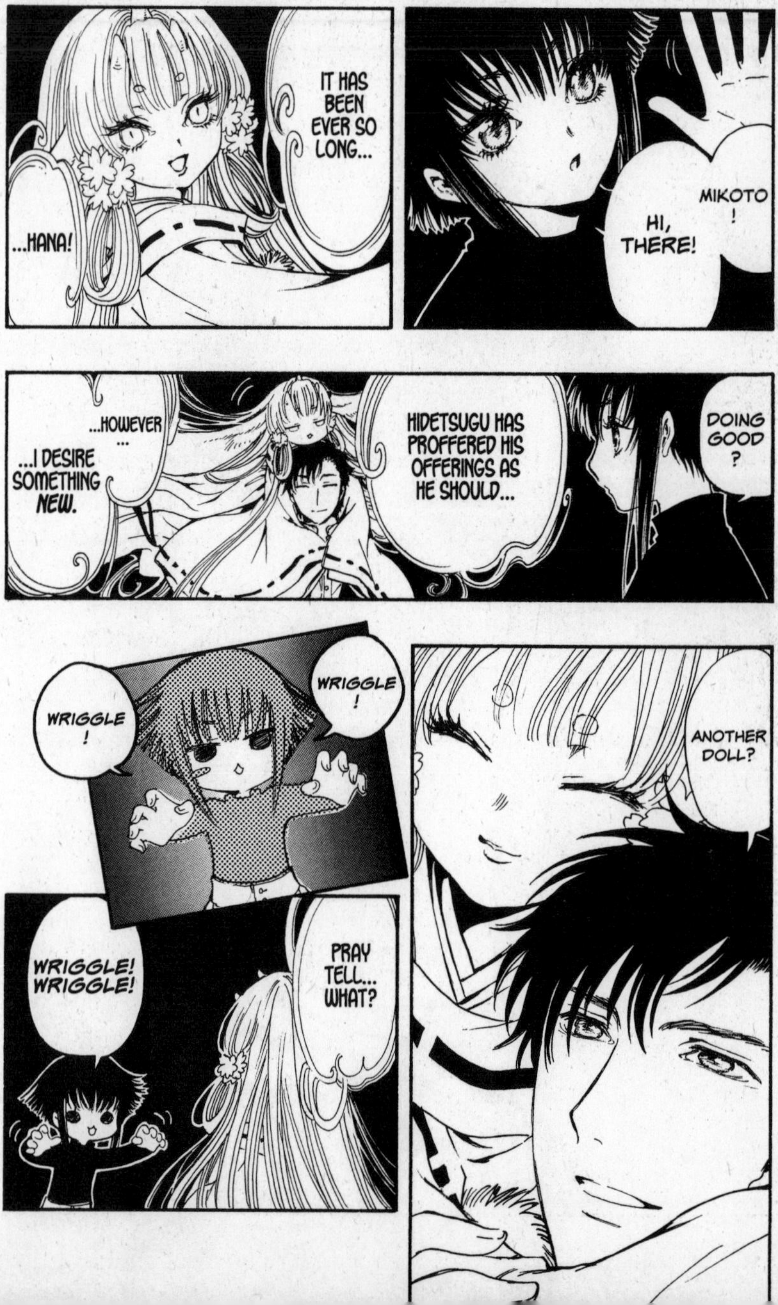

HI, THERE! MIKOTO!
IT HAS BEEN EVER SO LONG...
...HANA!
DOING GOOD?
HIDETSUGU HAS PROFFERED HIS OFFERINGS AS HE SHOULD...
...HOWEVER...
...I DESIRE SOMETHING NEW.
ANOTHER DOLL?
WRIGGLE!
WRIGGLE!
PRAY TELL... WHAT?
WRIGGLE! WRIGGLE!

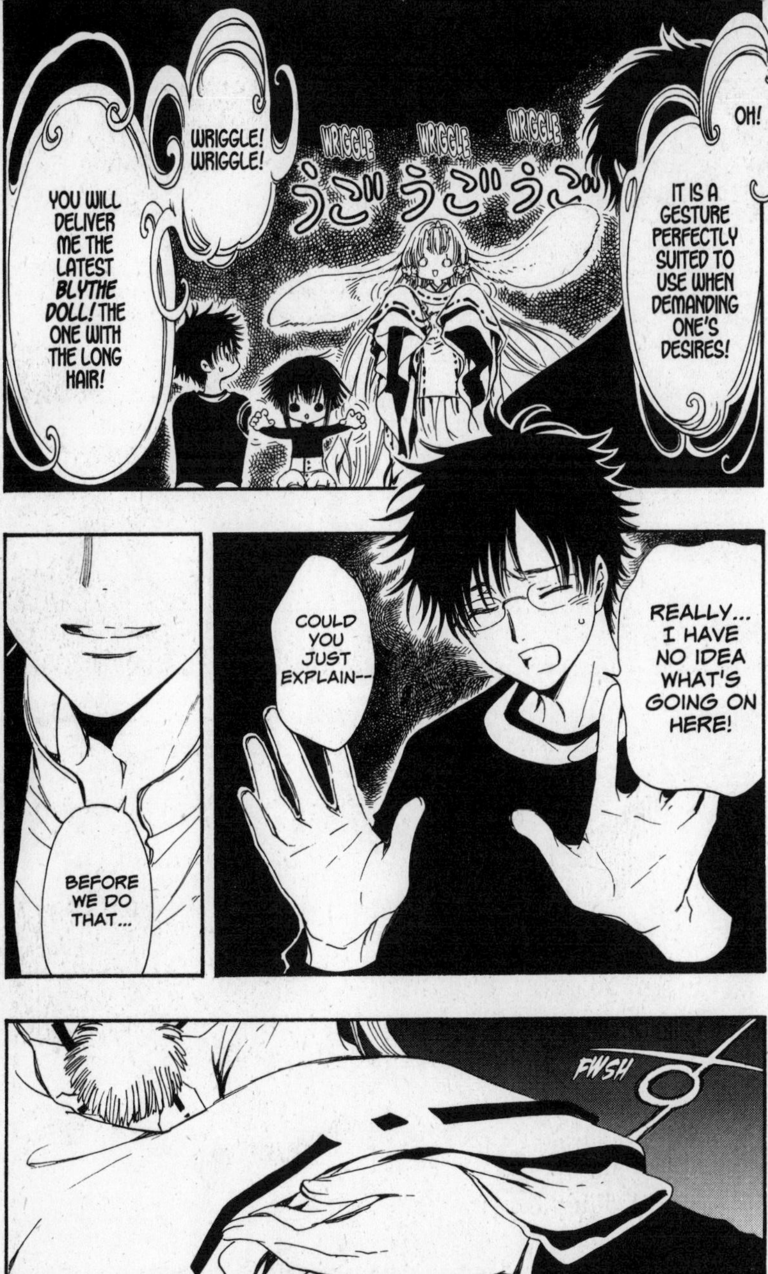
OH!
IT IS A GESTURE PERFECTLY SUITED TO USE WHEN DEMANDING ONE'S DESIRES!
WRIGGLE
WRIGGLE
WRIGGLE
うごうごうご
WRIGGLE! WRIGGLE!
YOU WILL DELIVER ME THE LATEST *BLYTHE DOLL!* THE ONE WITH THE LONG HAIR!
REALLY... I HAVE NO IDEA WHAT'S GOING ON HERE!
COULD YOU JUST EXPLAIN--
BEFORE WE DO THAT...
FWSH

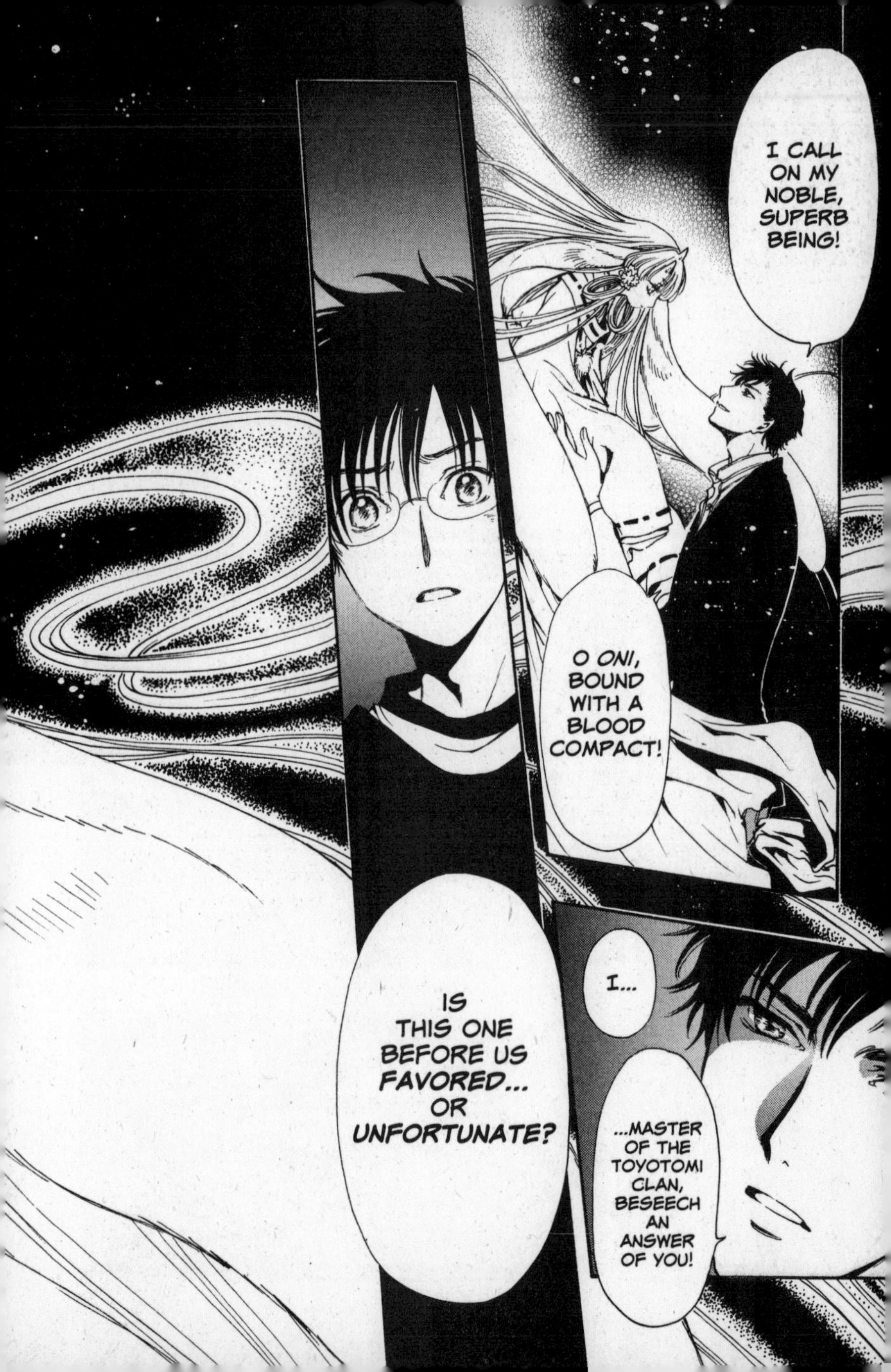
I CALL ON MY NOBLE, SUPERB BEING!
O ONI, BOUND WITH A BLOOD COMPACT!
I...
...MASTER OF THE TOYOTOMI CLAN, BESEECH AN ANSWER OF YOU!
IS THIS ONE BEFORE US FAVORED... OR UNFORTUNATE?

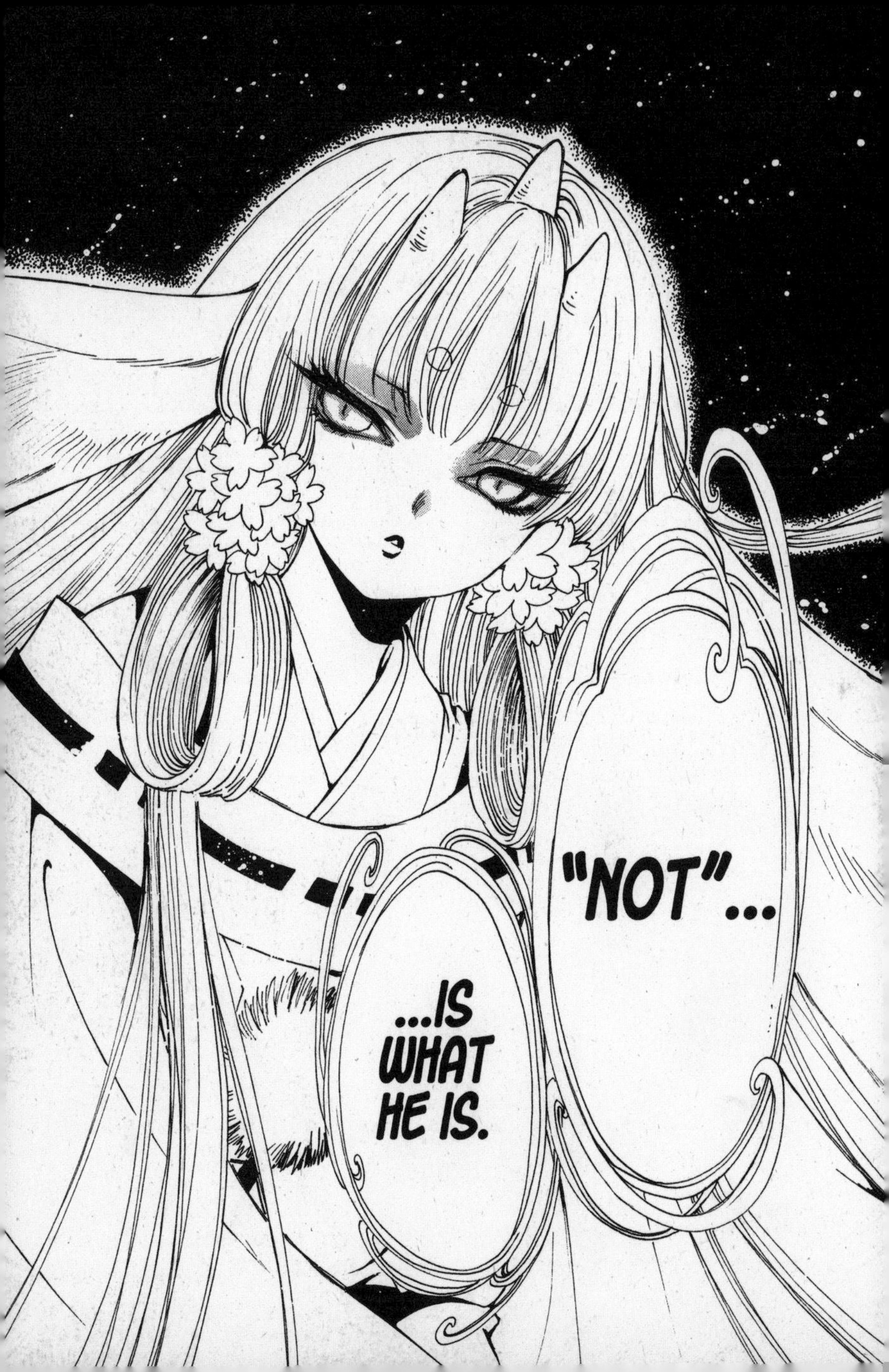
"NOT"...
...IS WHAT HE IS.

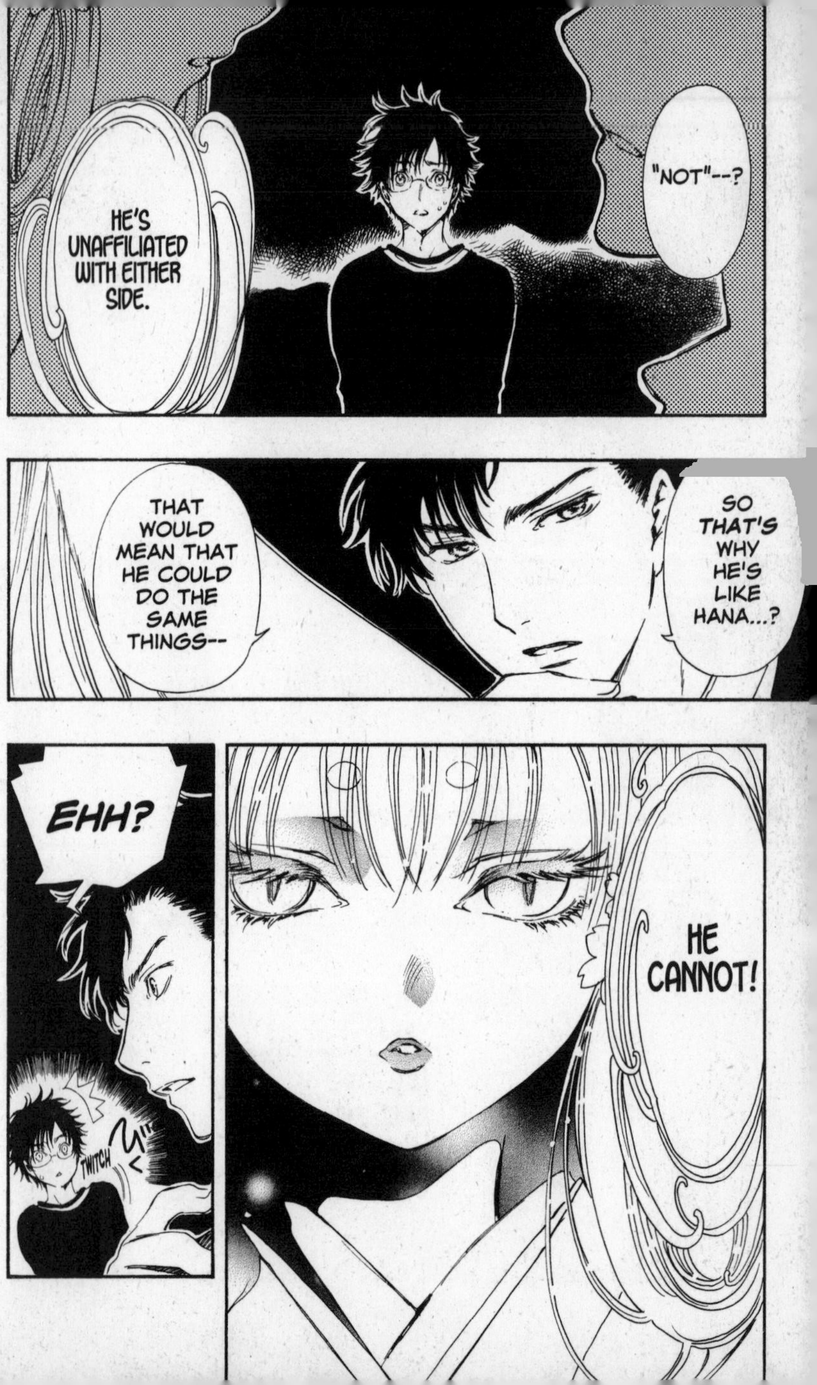
"NOT"--?
HE'S UNAFFILIATED WITH EITHER SIDE.
SO THAT'S WHY HE'S LIKE HANA...?
THAT WOULD MEAN THAT HE COULD DO THE SAME THINGS--
HE CANNOT!
EHH?
TWITCH

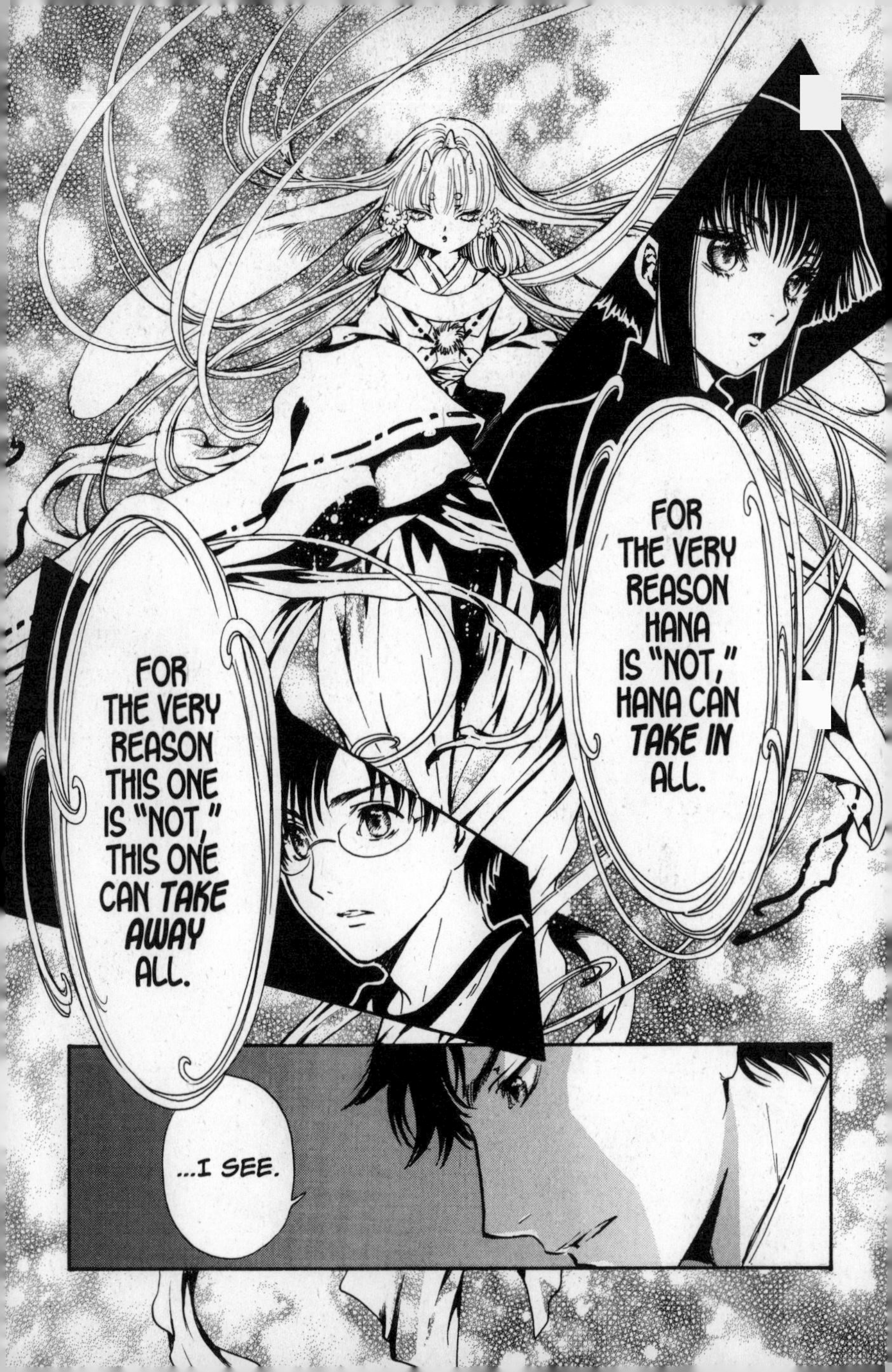
FOR THE VERY REASON HANA IS "NOT," HANA CAN TAKE IN ALL.
FOR THE VERY REASON THIS ONE IS "NOT," THIS ONE CAN TAKE AWAY ALL.
...I SEE.

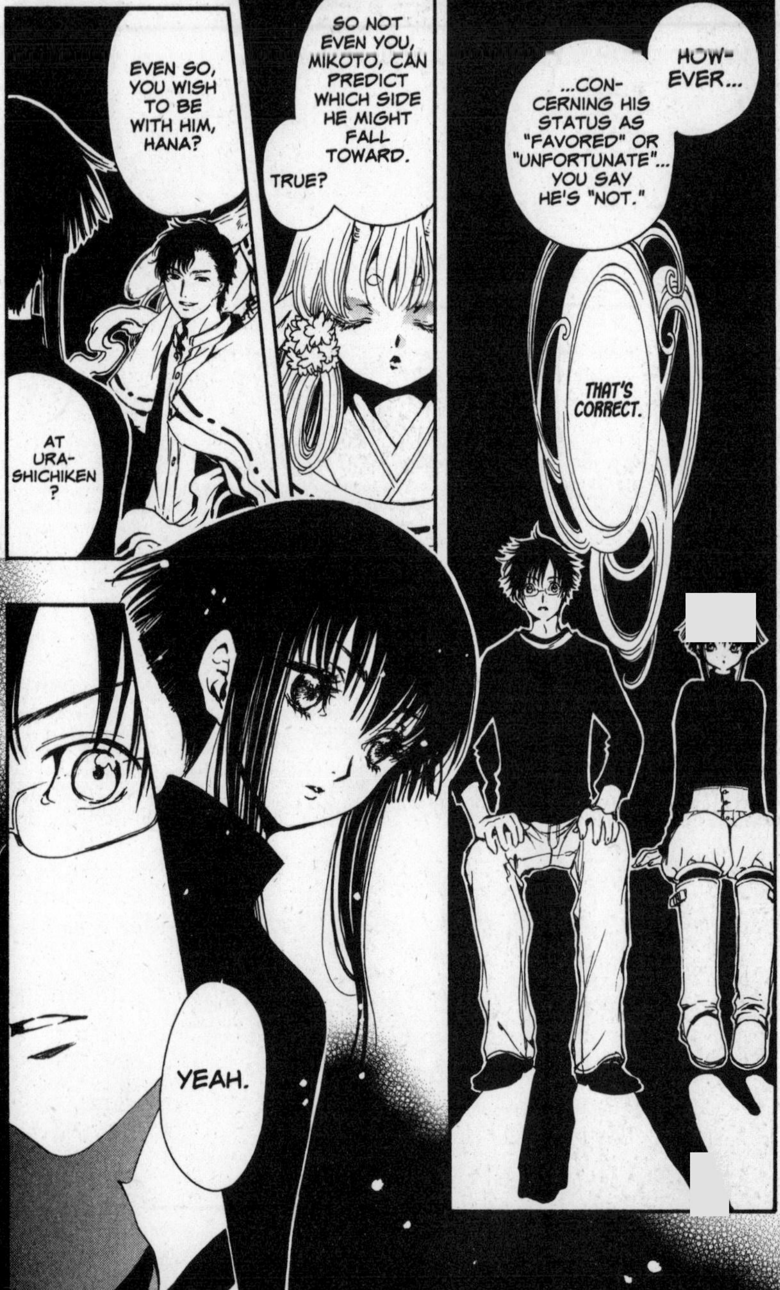
HOW-EVER...
...CON-CERNING HIS STATUS AS "FAVORED" OR "UNFORTUNATE"... YOU SAY HE'S "NOT."
THAT'S CORRECT.
SO NOT EVEN YOU, MIKOTO, CAN PREDICT WHICH SIDE HE MIGHT FALL TOWARD.
TRUE?
EVEN SO, YOU WISH TO BE WITH HIM, HANA?
AT URA-SHICHIKEN?
YEAH.

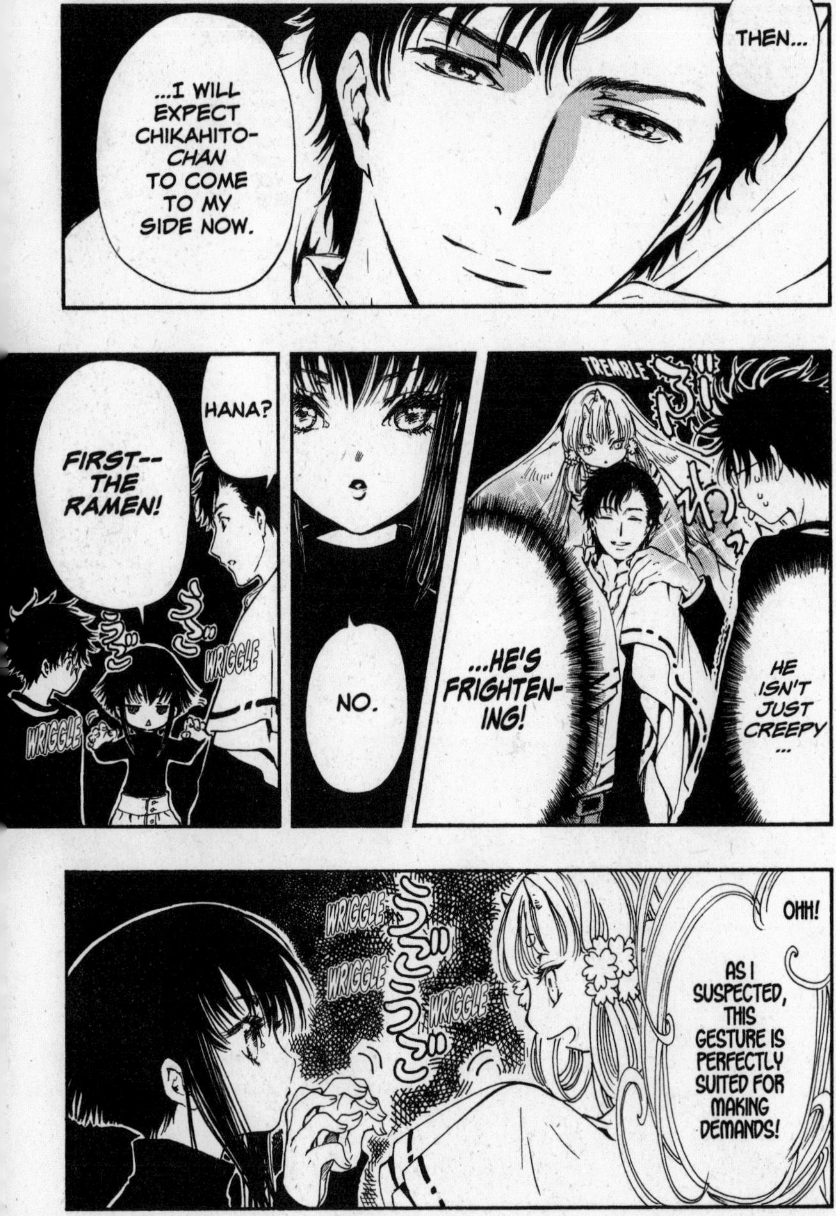
THEN...
...I WILL EXPECT CHIKAHITO-CHAN TO COME TO MY SIDE NOW.
TREMBLE
HE ISN'T JUST CREEPY ...
...HE'S FRIGHTEN-ING!
NO.
HANA?
FIRST-- THE RAMEN!
WRIGGLE
WRIGGLE
OHH!
AS I SUSPECTED, THIS GESTURE IS PERFECTLY SUITED FOR MAKING DEMANDS!
WRIGGLE
WRIGGLE
WRIGGLE

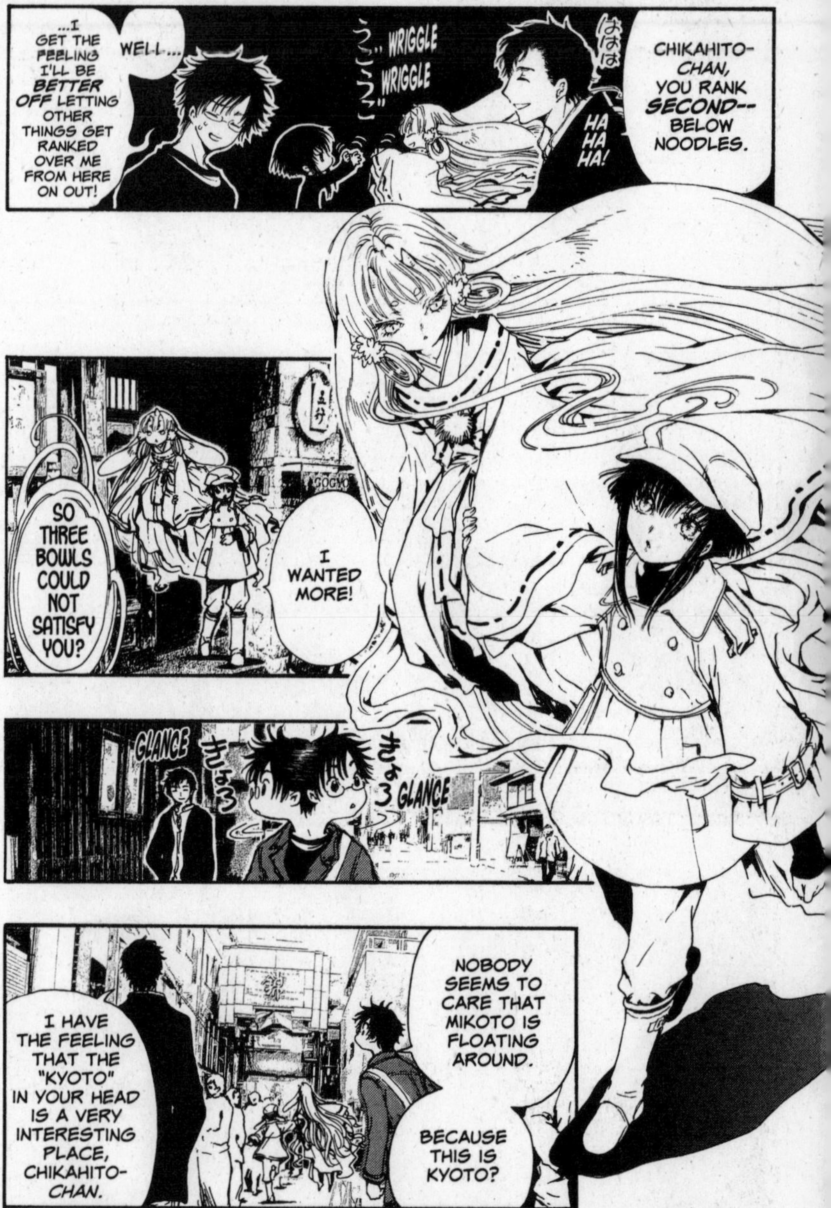
CHIKAHITO-CHAN, YOU RANK SECOND--BELOW NOODLES.
ははは
HA HA HA!
うごうご
WRIGGLE WRIGGLE
WELL...
...I GET THE FEELING I'LL BE BETTER OFF LETTING OTHER THINGS GET RANKED OVER ME FROM HERE ON OUT!
SO THREE BOWLS COULD NOT SATISFY YOU?
I WANTED MORE!
きょろ
GLANCE
きょろ
GLANCE
NOBODY SEEMS TO CARE THAT MIKOTO IS FLOATING AROUND.
BECAUSE THIS IS KYOTO?
I HAVE THE FEELING THAT THE "KYOTO" IN YOUR HEAD IS A VERY INTERESTING PLACE, CHIKAHITO-CHAN.

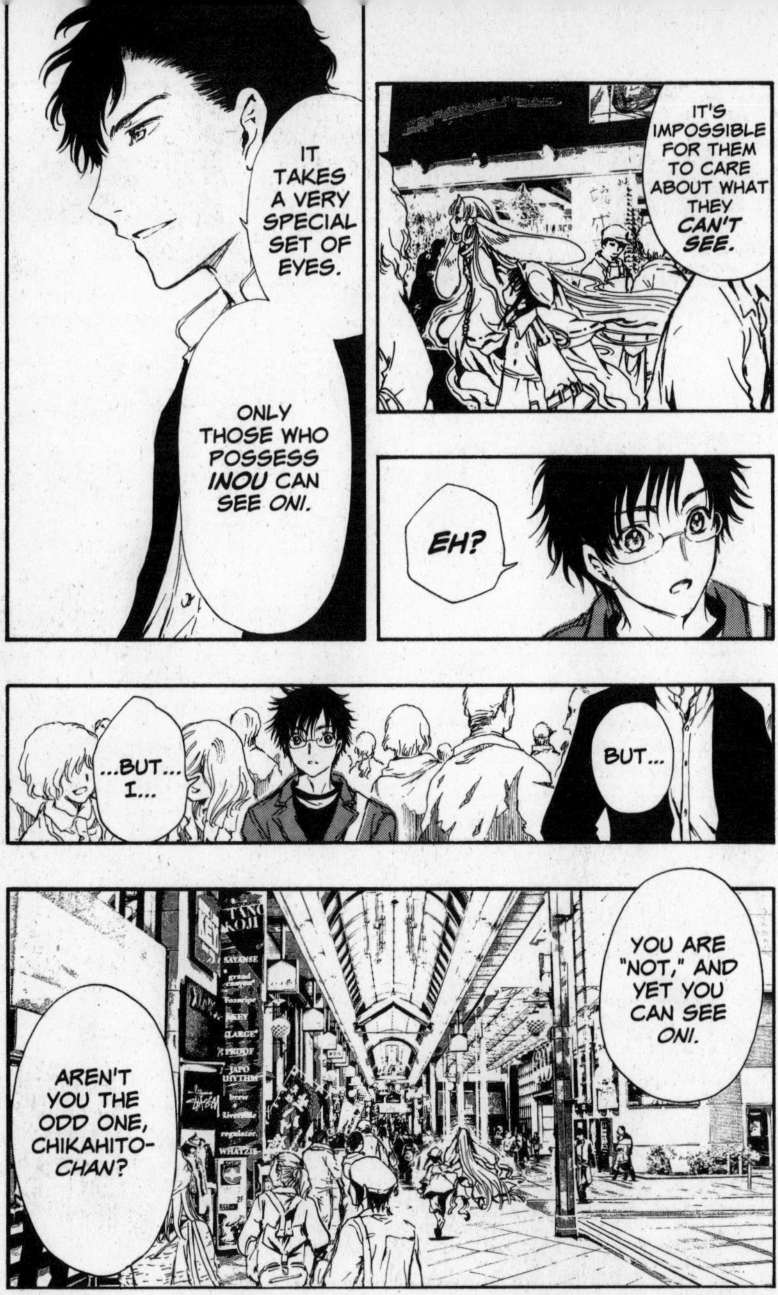
IT'S IMPOSSIBLE FOR THEM TO CARE ABOUT WHAT THEY *CAN'T SEE.*
EH?
IT TAKES A VERY SPECIAL SET OF EYES.
ONLY THOSE WHO POSSESS *INOU* CAN SEE *ONI*.
BUT...
...BUT... I...
YOU ARE "NOT," AND YET YOU CAN SEE *ONI*.
AREN'T YOU THE ODD ONE, CHIKAHITO-CHAN?

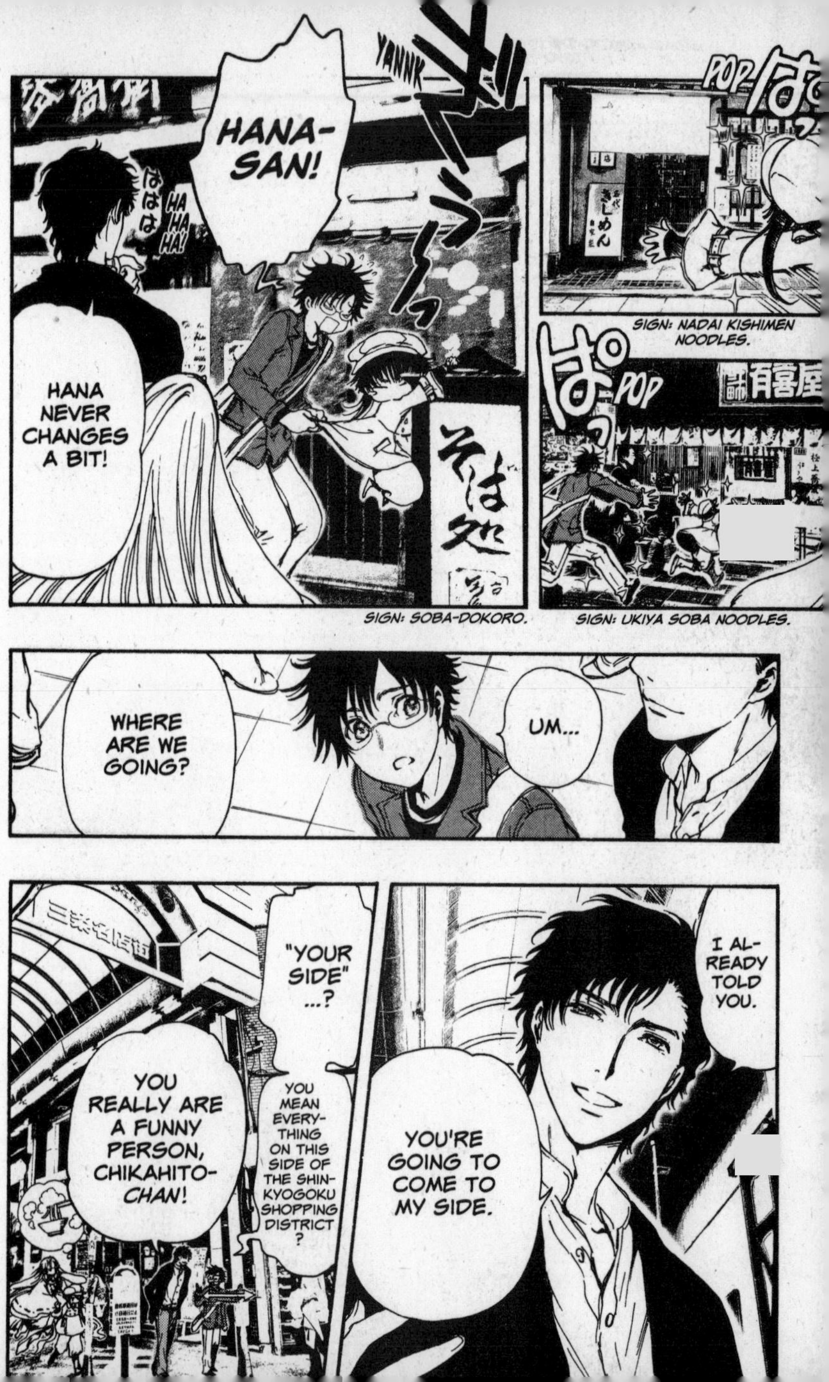
POP
SIGN: NADAI KISHIMEN NOODLES.
POP
SIGN: UKIYA SOBA NOODLES.
YANNK
HANA-SAN!
ははは
HA HA HA!
HANA NEVER CHANGES A BIT!
SIGN: SOBA-DOKORO.
UM...
WHERE ARE WE GOING?
I AL-READY TOLD YOU.
YOU'RE GOING TO COME TO MY SIDE.
"YOUR SIDE" ...?
YOU MEAN EVERY-THING ON THIS SIDE OF THE SHIN-KYOGOKU SHOPPING DISTRICT?
YOU REALLY ARE A FUNNY PERSON, CHIKAHITO-CHAN!

GRAVE MARKER: THE TOMB OF HIDETSUGU TOYOTOMI.

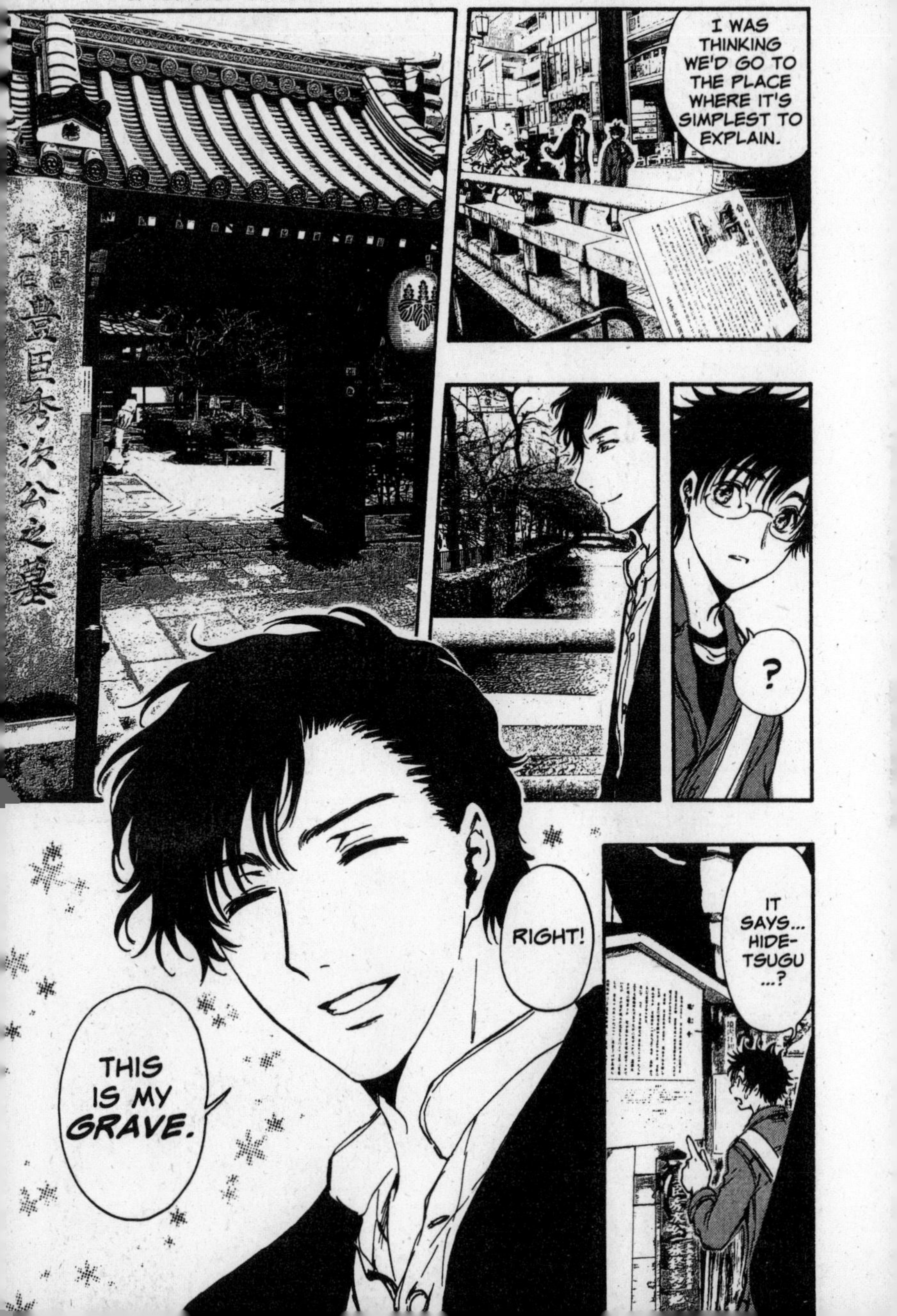
I WAS THINKING WE'D GO TO THE PLACE WHERE IT'S SIMPLEST TO EXPLAIN.
?
IT SAYS... HIDE-TSUGU ...?
RIGHT!
THIS IS MY GRAVE.

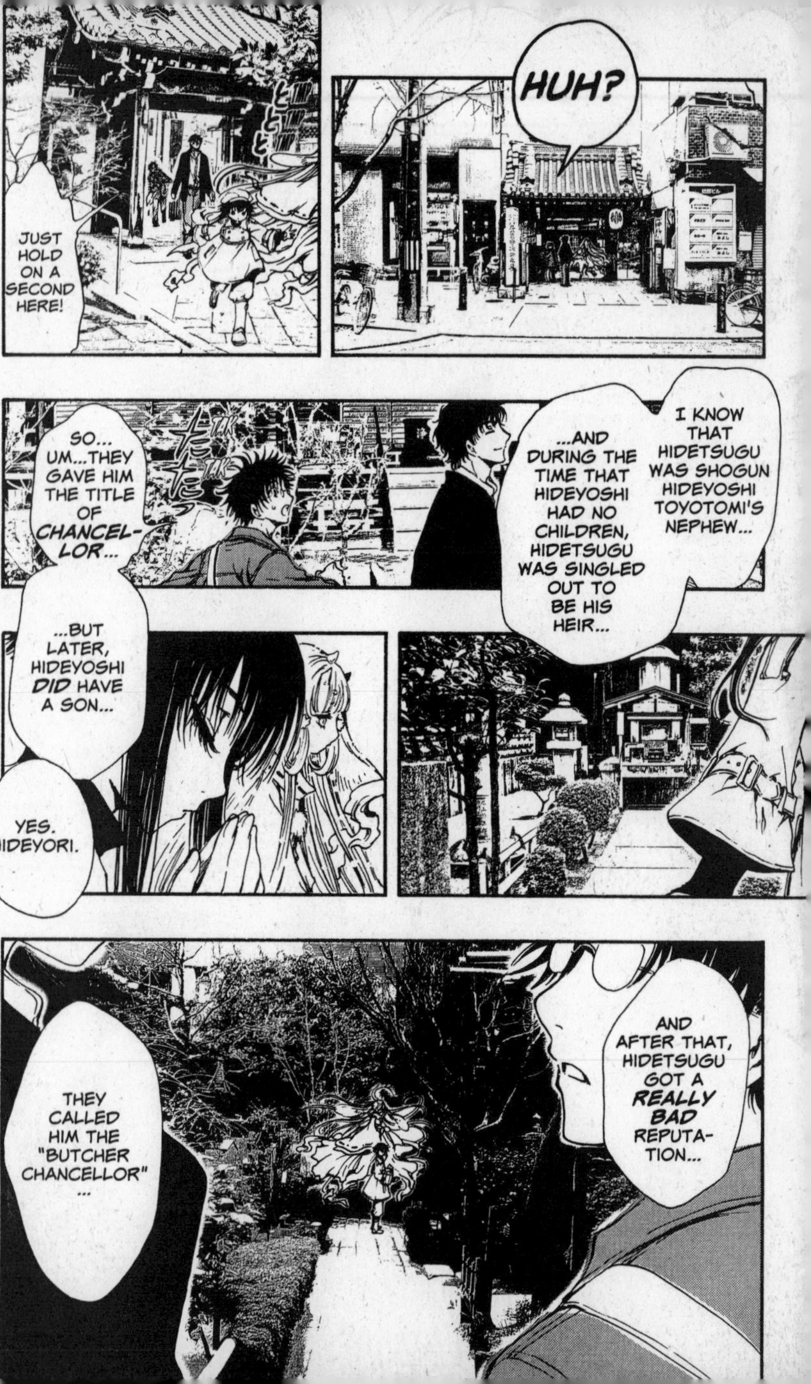
HUH?
JUST HOLD ON A SECOND HERE!
I KNOW THAT HIDETSUGU WAS SHOGUN HIDEYOSHI TOYOTOMI'S NEPHEW...
...AND DURING THE TIME THAT HIDEYOSHI HAD NO CHILDREN, HIDETSUGU WAS SINGLED OUT TO BE HIS HEIR...
SO... UM...THEY GAVE HIM THE TITLE OF CHANCELLOR...
...BUT LATER, HIDEYOSHI DID HAVE A SON...
YES. HIDEYORI.
AND AFTER THAT, HIDETSUGU GOT A REALLY BAD REPUTATION...
THEY CALLED HIM THE "BUTCHER CHANCELLOR" ...

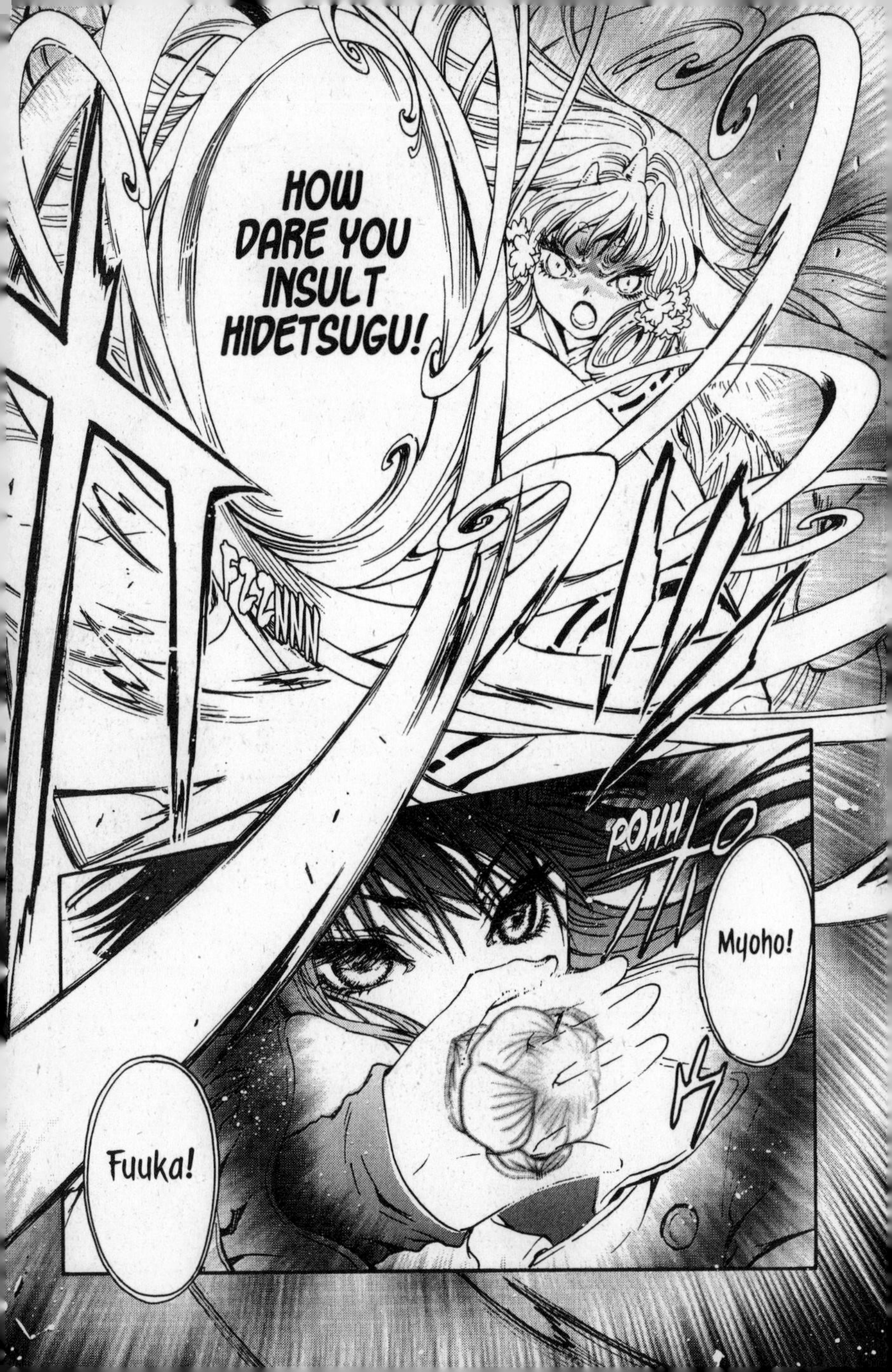
HOW DARE YOU INSULT HIDETSUGU!
FZZNNN
POHH
Myoho!
Fuuka!

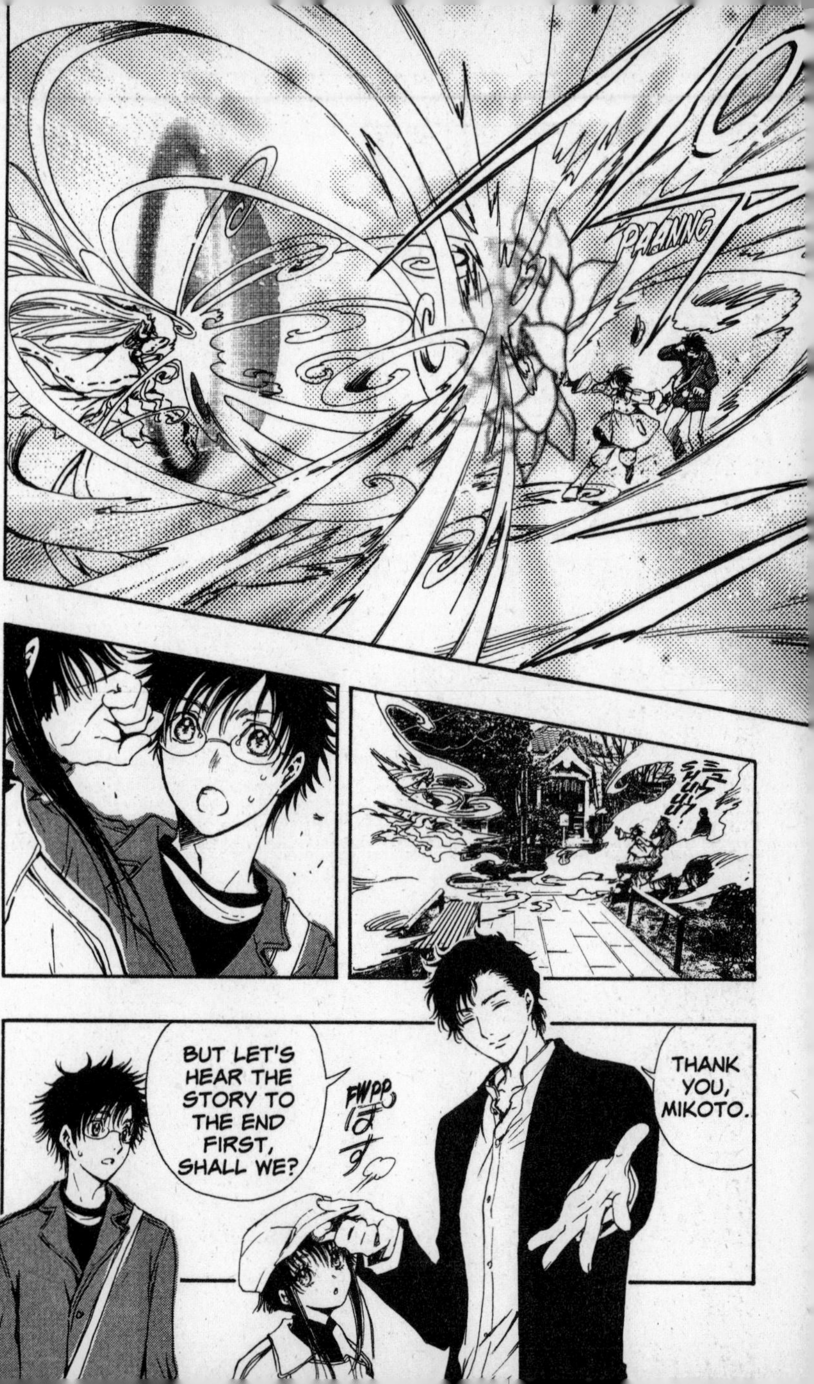
PAANNG
SHUUUU!
THANK YOU, MIKOTO.
FWPP
BUT LET'S HEAR THE STORY TO THE END FIRST, SHALL WE?

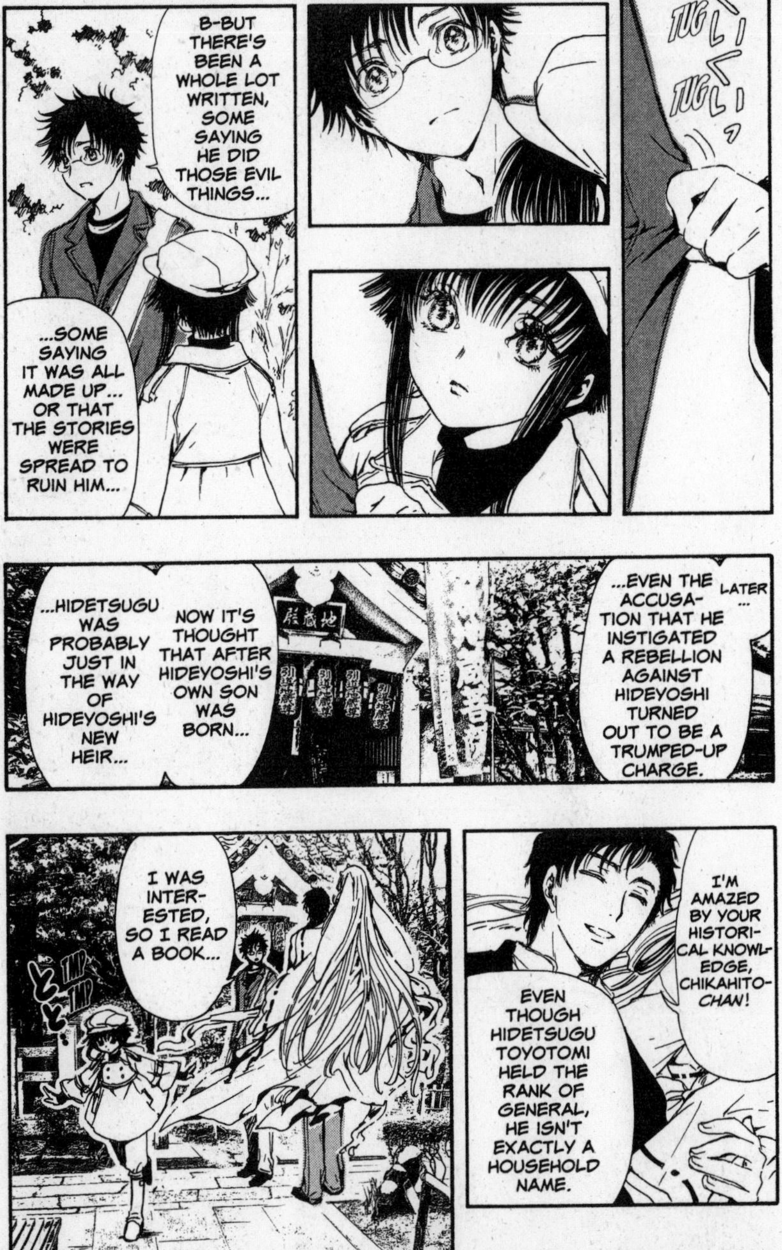
TUG
TUG
B-BUT THERE'S BEEN A WHOLE LOT WRITTEN, SOME SAYING HE DID THOSE EVIL THINGS...
...SOME SAYING IT WAS ALL MADE UP... OR THAT THE STORIES WERE SPREAD TO RUIN HIM...
LATER...
...EVEN THE ACCUSATION THAT HE INSTIGATED A REBELLION AGAINST HIDEYOSHI TURNED OUT TO BE A TRUMPED-UP CHARGE.
NOW IT'S THOUGHT THAT AFTER HIDEYOSHI'S OWN SON WAS BORN...
...HIDETSUGU WAS PROBABLY JUST IN THE WAY OF HIDEYOSHI'S NEW HEIR...
I'M AMAZED BY YOUR HISTORICAL KNOWLEDGE, CHIKAHITO-CHAN!
EVEN THOUGH HIDETSUGU TOYOTOMI HELD THE RANK OF GENERAL, HE ISN'T EXACTLY A HOUSEHOLD NAME.
I WAS INTERESTED, SO I READ A BOOK...
TMP TMP

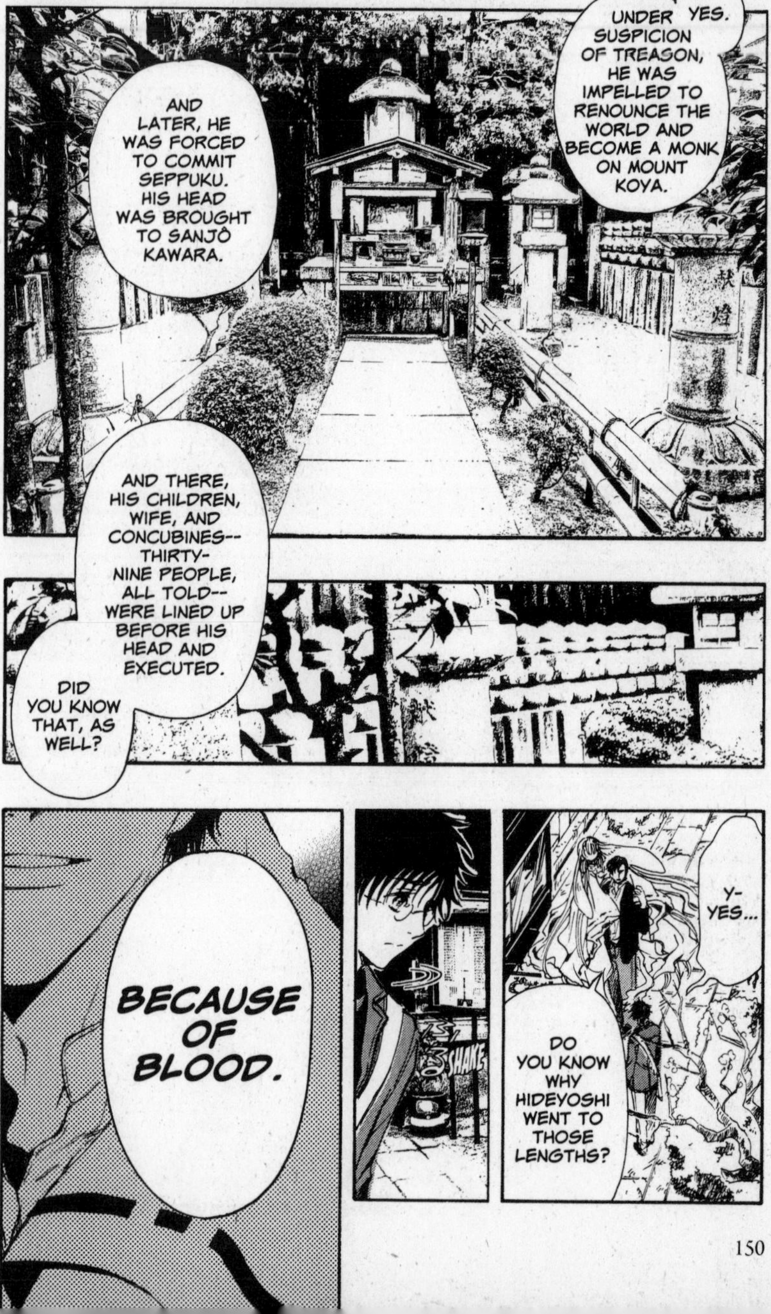
YES.
UNDER SUSPICION OF TREASON, HE WAS IMPELLED TO RENOUNCE THE WORLD AND BECOME A MONK ON MOUNT KOYA.
AND LATER, HE WAS FORCED TO COMMIT SEPPUKU. HIS HEAD WAS BROUGHT TO SANJÔ KAWARA.
AND THERE, HIS CHILDREN, WIFE, AND CONCUBINES--THIRTY-NINE PEOPLE, ALL TOLD--WERE LINED UP BEFORE HIS HEAD AND EXECUTED.
DID YOU KNOW THAT, AS WELL?
Y-YES...
DO YOU KNOW WHY HIDEYOSHI WENT TO THOSE LENGTHS?
SHAKE
BECAUSE OF BLOOD.

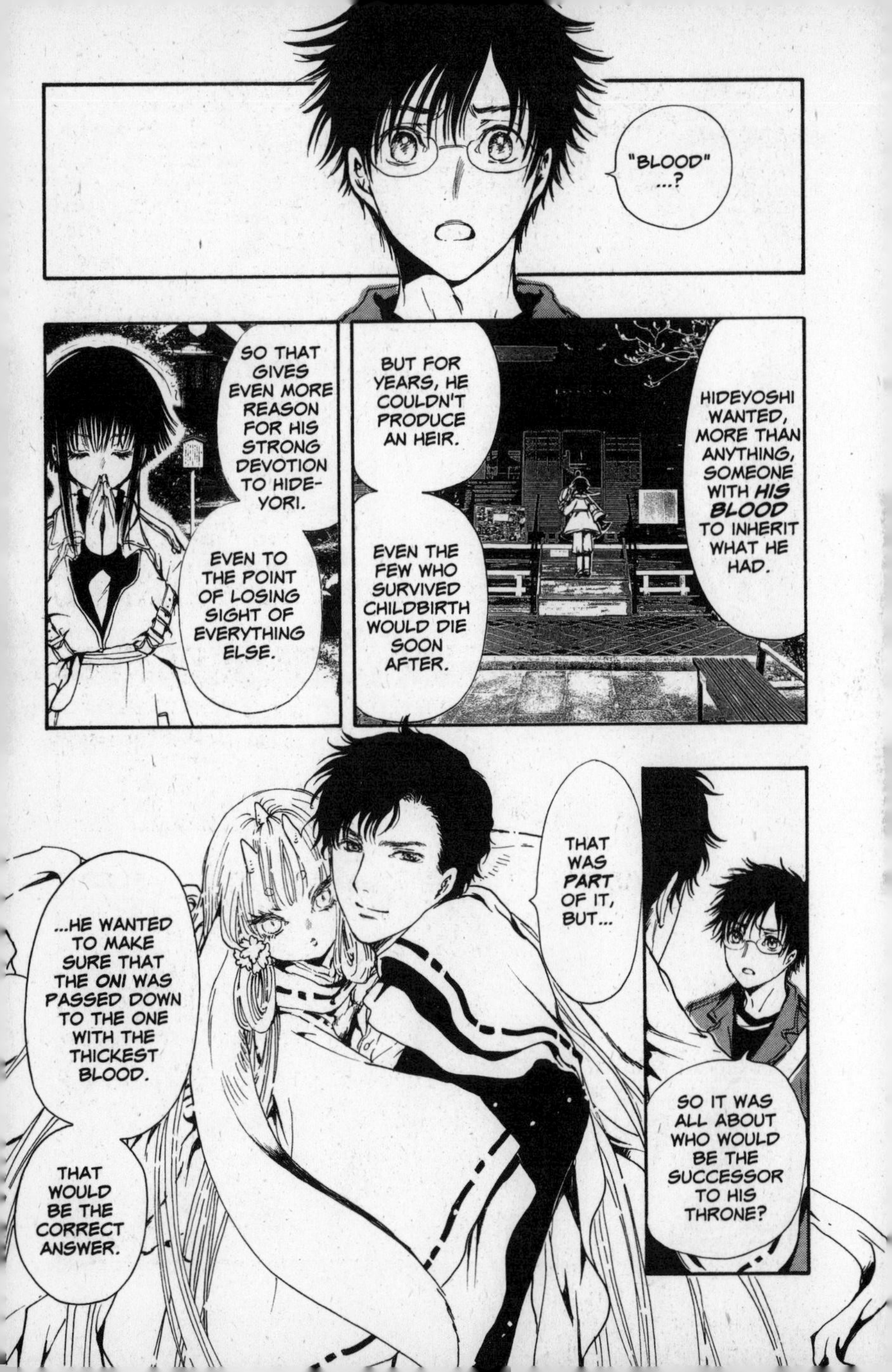
"BLOOD" ...?
HIDEYOSHI WANTED, MORE THAN ANYTHING, SOMEONE WITH ***HIS BLOOD*** TO INHERIT WHAT HE HAD.
BUT FOR YEARS, HE COULDN'T PRODUCE AN HEIR.
EVEN THE FEW WHO SURVIVED CHILDBIRTH WOULD DIE SOON AFTER.
SO THAT GIVES EVEN MORE REASON FOR HIS STRONG DEVOTION TO HIDE-YORI.
EVEN TO THE POINT OF LOSING SIGHT OF EVERYTHING ELSE.
SO IT WAS ALL ABOUT WHO WOULD BE THE SUCCESSOR TO HIS THRONE?
THAT WAS ***PART*** OF IT, BUT...
...HE WANTED TO MAKE SURE THAT THE ***ONI*** WAS PASSED DOWN TO THE ONE WITH THE THICKEST BLOOD.
THAT WOULD BE THE CORRECT ANSWER.

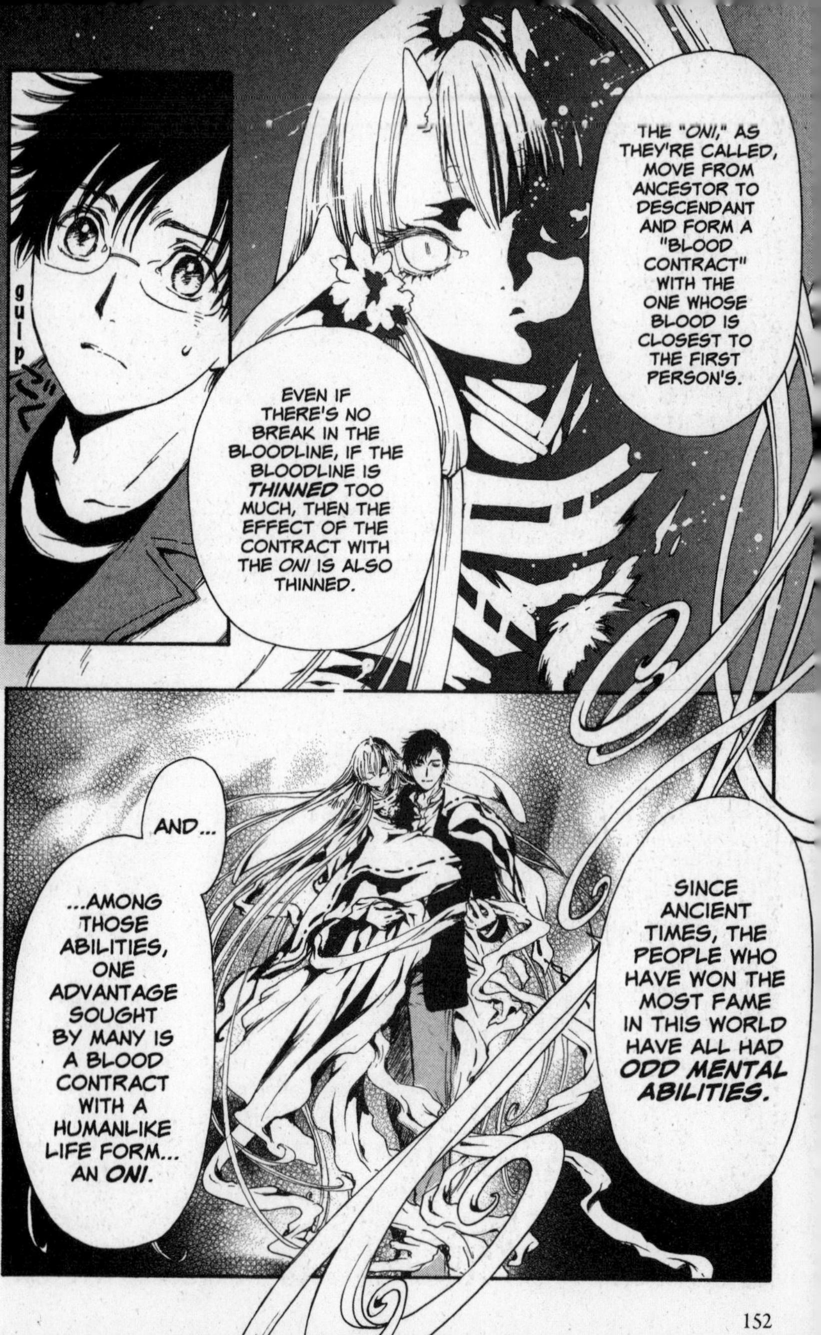
THE "ONI," AS THEY'RE CALLED, MOVE FROM ANCESTOR TO DESCENDANT AND FORM A "BLOOD CONTRACT" WITH THE ONE WHOSE BLOOD IS CLOSEST TO THE FIRST PERSON'S.
EVEN IF THERE'S NO BREAK IN THE BLOODLINE, IF THE BLOODLINE IS THINNED TOO MUCH, THEN THE EFFECT OF THE CONTRACT WITH THE ONI IS ALSO THINNED.
gulp
SINCE ANCIENT TIMES, THE PEOPLE WHO HAVE WON THE MOST FAME IN THIS WORLD HAVE ALL HAD ODD MENTAL ABILITIES.
AND...
...AMONG THOSE ABILITIES, ONE ADVANTAGE SOUGHT BY MANY IS A BLOOD CONTRACT WITH A HUMANLIKE LIFE FORM... AN ONI.

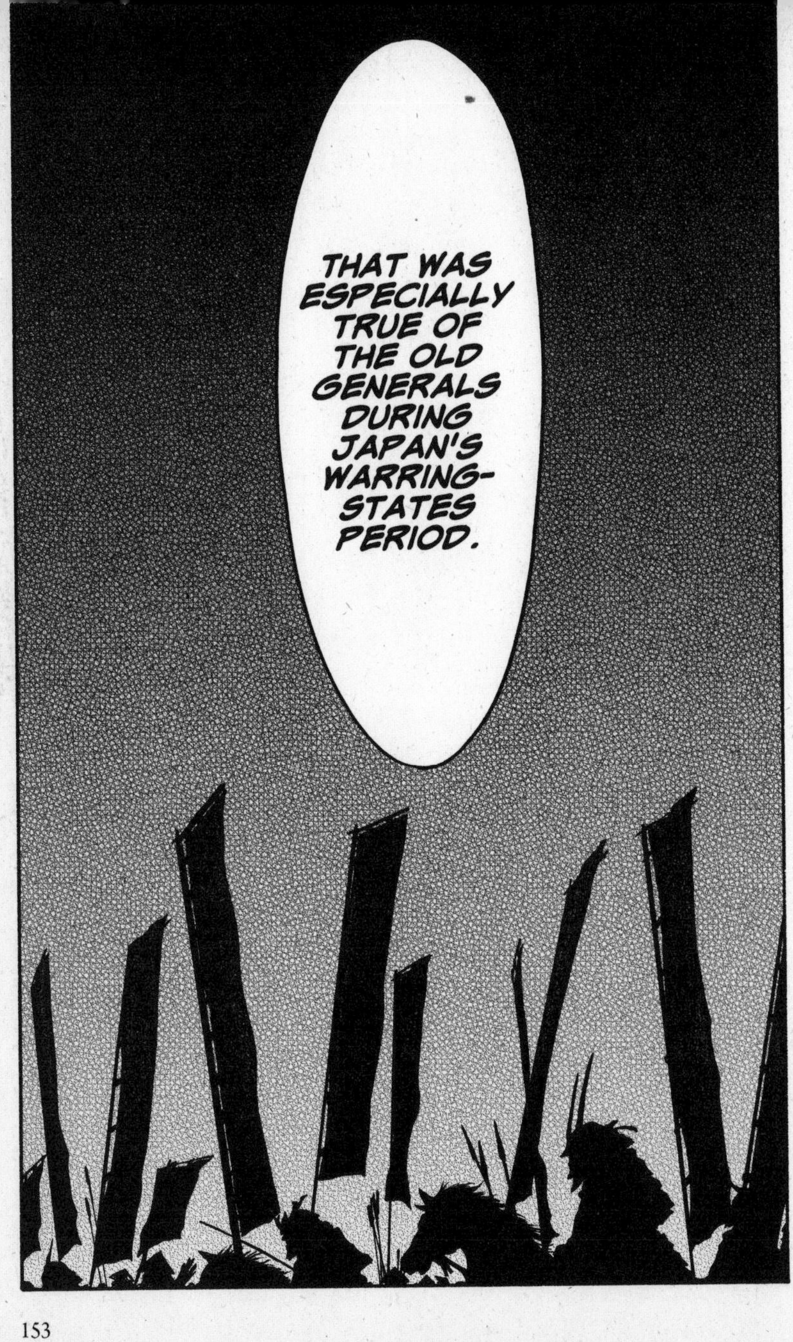
THAT WAS ESPECIALLY TRUE OF THE OLD GENERALS DURING JAPAN'S WARRING-STATES PERIOD.

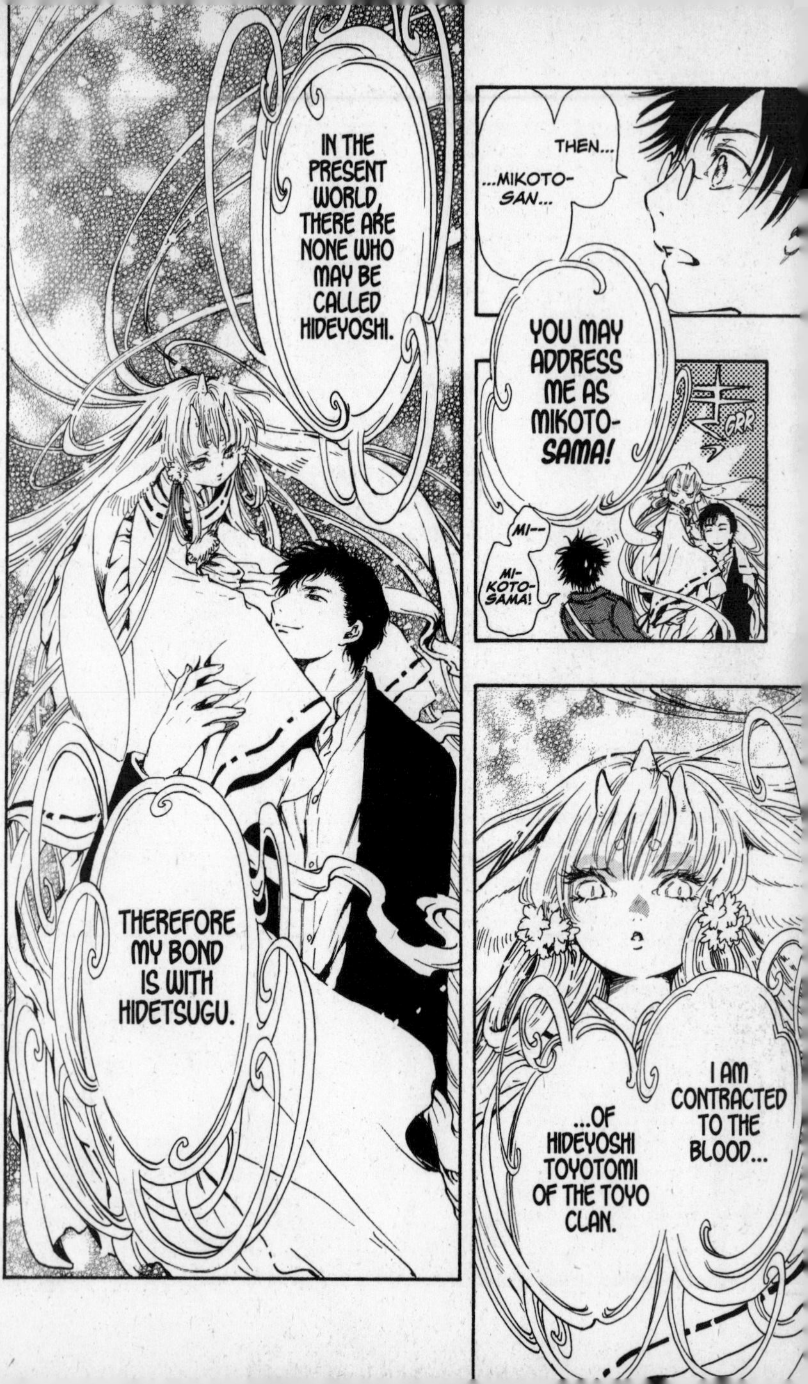
THEN...
...MIKOTO-SAN...
YOU MAY ADDRESS ME AS MIKOTO-SAMA!
GRR
MI--
MI-KOTO-SAMA!
I AM CONTRACTED TO THE BLOOD...
...OF HIDEYOSHI TOYOTOMI OF THE TOYO CLAN.
IN THE PRESENT WORLD, THERE ARE NONE WHO MAY BE CALLED HIDEYOSHI.
THEREFORE MY BOND IS WITH HIDETSUGU.

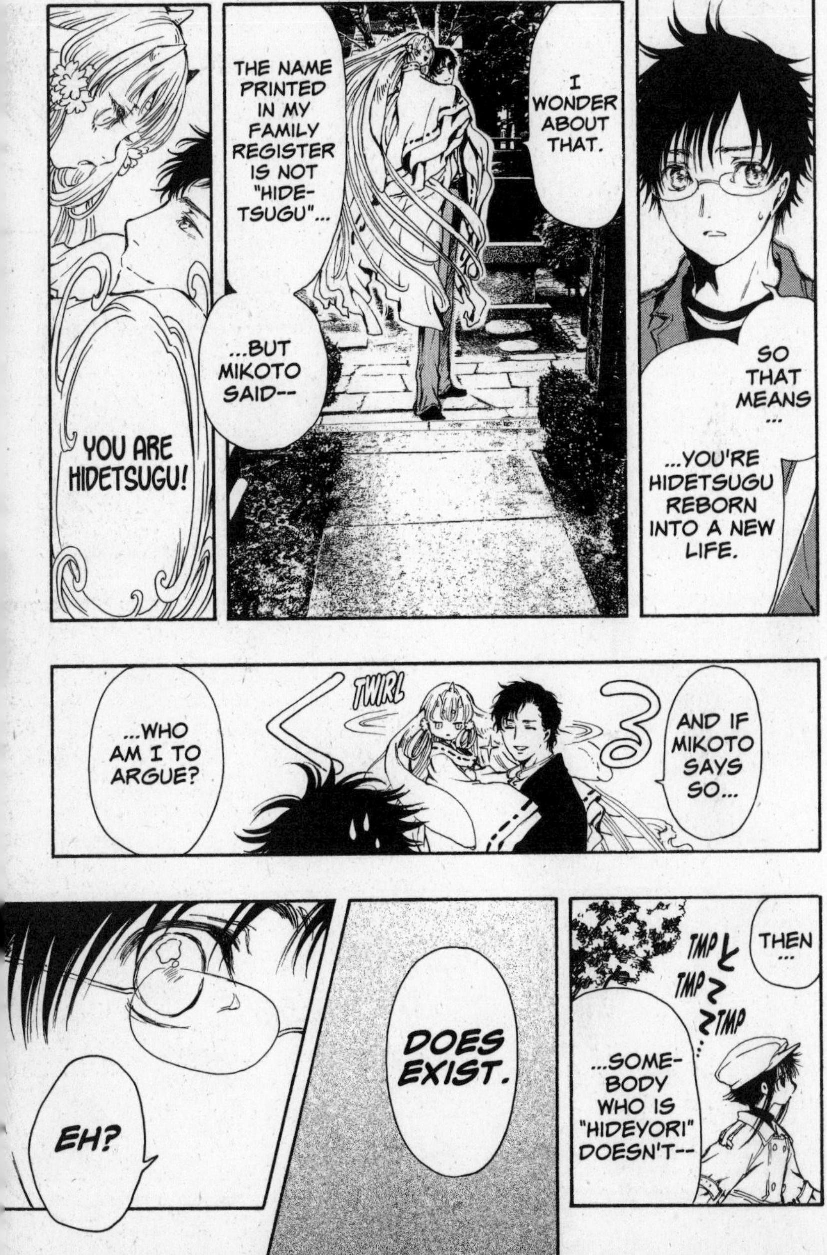
SO THAT MEANS...
...YOU'RE HIDETSUGU REBORN INTO A NEW LIFE.
I WONDER ABOUT THAT.
THE NAME PRINTED IN MY FAMILY REGISTER IS NOT "HIDE-TSUGU"...
...BUT MIKOTO SAID--
YOU ARE HIDETSUGU!
AND IF MIKOTO SAYS SO...
TWIRL
...WHO AM I TO ARGUE?
THEN...
TMP TMP TMP
...SOME-BODY WHO IS "HIDEYORI" DOESN'T--
DOES EXIST.
EH?

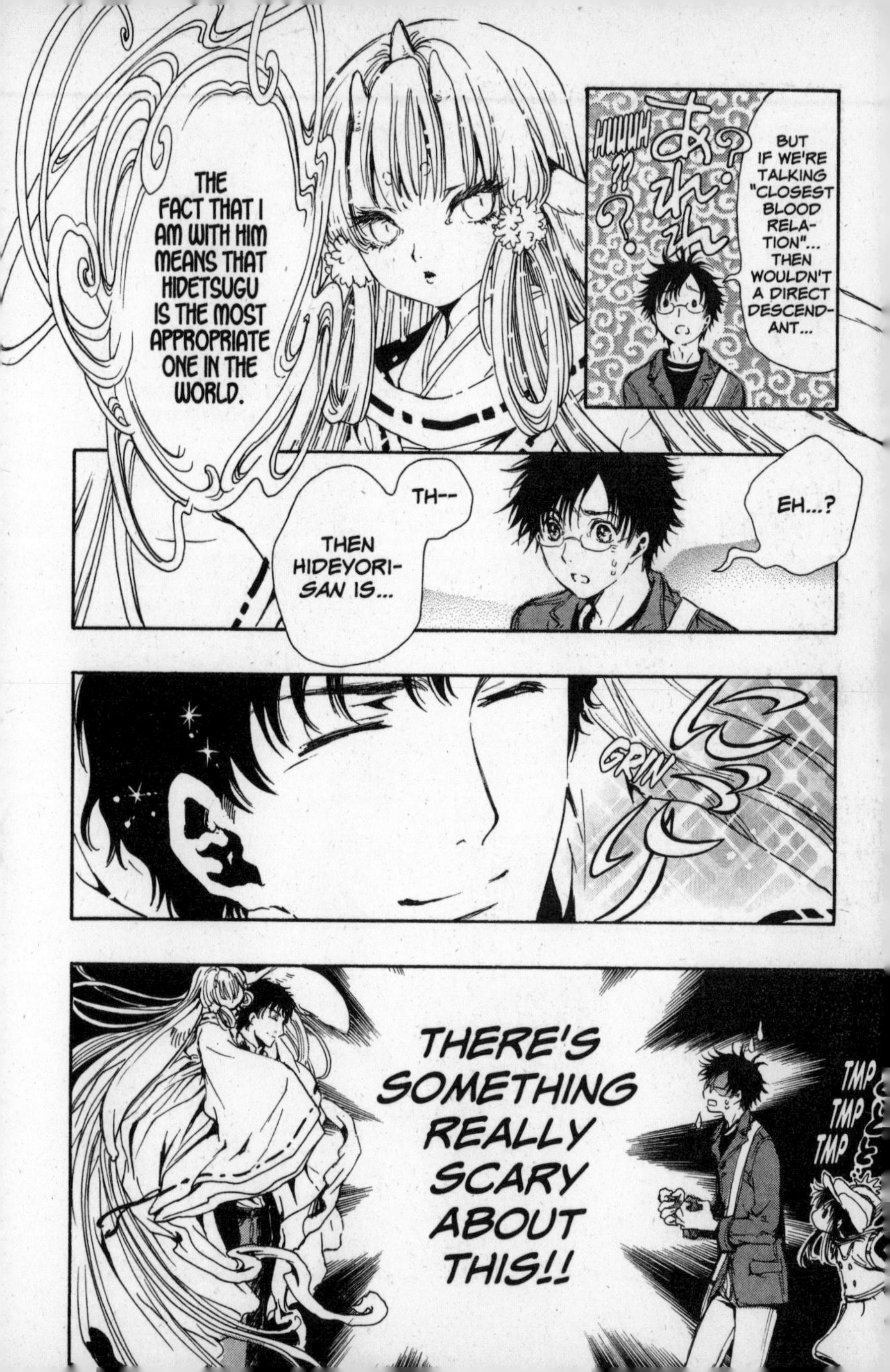
HUUUH
BUT IF WE'RE TALKING "CLOSEST BLOOD RELATION"... THEN WOULDN'T A DIRECT DESCENDANT...
THE FACT THAT I AM WITH HIM MEANS THAT HIDETSUGU IS THE MOST APPROPRIATE ONE IN THE WORLD.
EH...?
TH--
THEN HIDEYORI-SAN IS...
GRIN
TMP TMP TMP
THERE'S SOMETHING REALLY SCARY ABOUT THIS!!

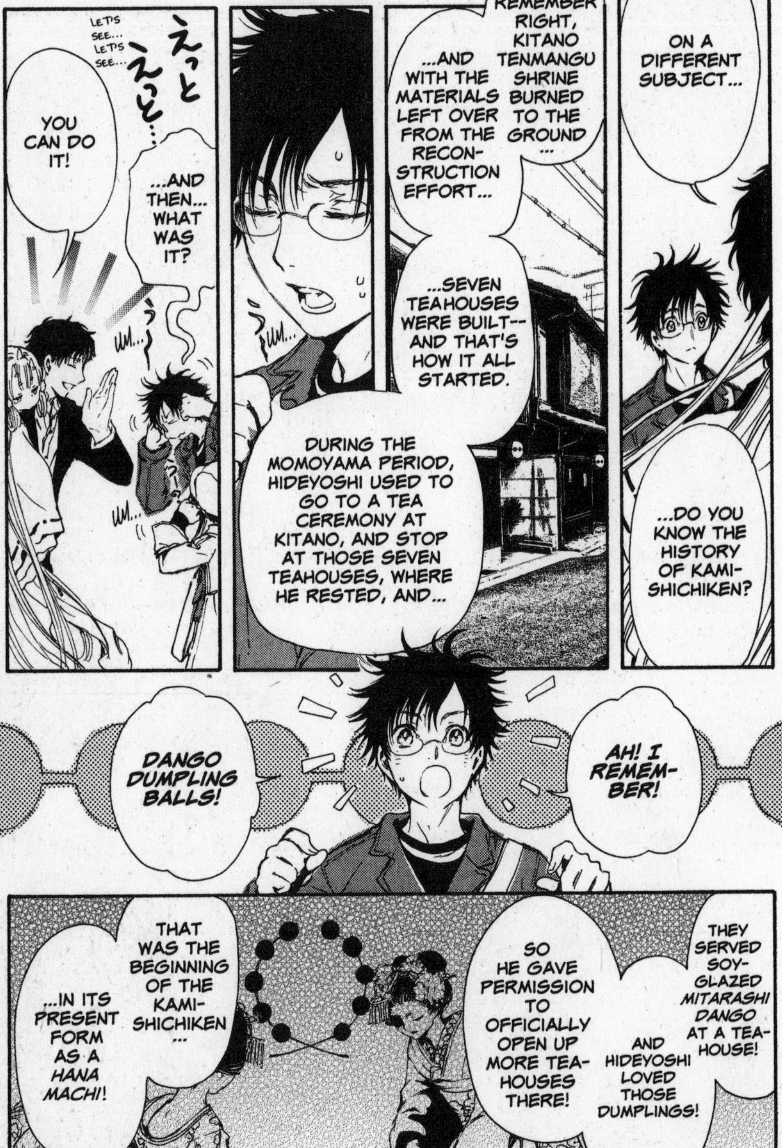
ON A DIFFERENT SUBJECT...
...DO YOU KNOW THE HISTORY OF KAMI-SHICHIKEN?
IF I REMEMBER RIGHT, KITANO TENMANGU SHRINE BURNED TO THE GROUND...
...AND WITH THE MATERIALS LEFT OVER FROM THE RECON-STRUCTION EFFORT...
...SEVEN TEAHOUSES WERE BUILT--AND THAT'S HOW IT ALL STARTED.
DURING THE MOMOYAMA PERIOD, HIDEYOSHI USED TO GO TO A TEA CEREMONY AT KITANO, AND STOP AT THOSE SEVEN TEAHOUSES, WHERE HE RESTED, AND...
UM...
えっとえっと...
LET'S SEE... LET'S SEE...
...AND THEN... WHAT WAS IT?
YOU CAN DO IT!
UM...
UM...
AH! I REMEM-BER!
DANGO DUMPLING BALLS!
THEY SERVED SOY-GLAZED *MITARASHI DANGO* AT A TEA-HOUSE!
AND HIDEYOSHI LOVED THOSE DUMPLINGS!
SO HE GAVE PERMISSION TO OFFICIALLY OPEN UP MORE TEA-HOUSES THERE!
THAT WAS THE BEGINNING OF THE KAMI-SHICHIKEN...
...IN ITS PRESENT FORM AS A *HANA MACHI*!

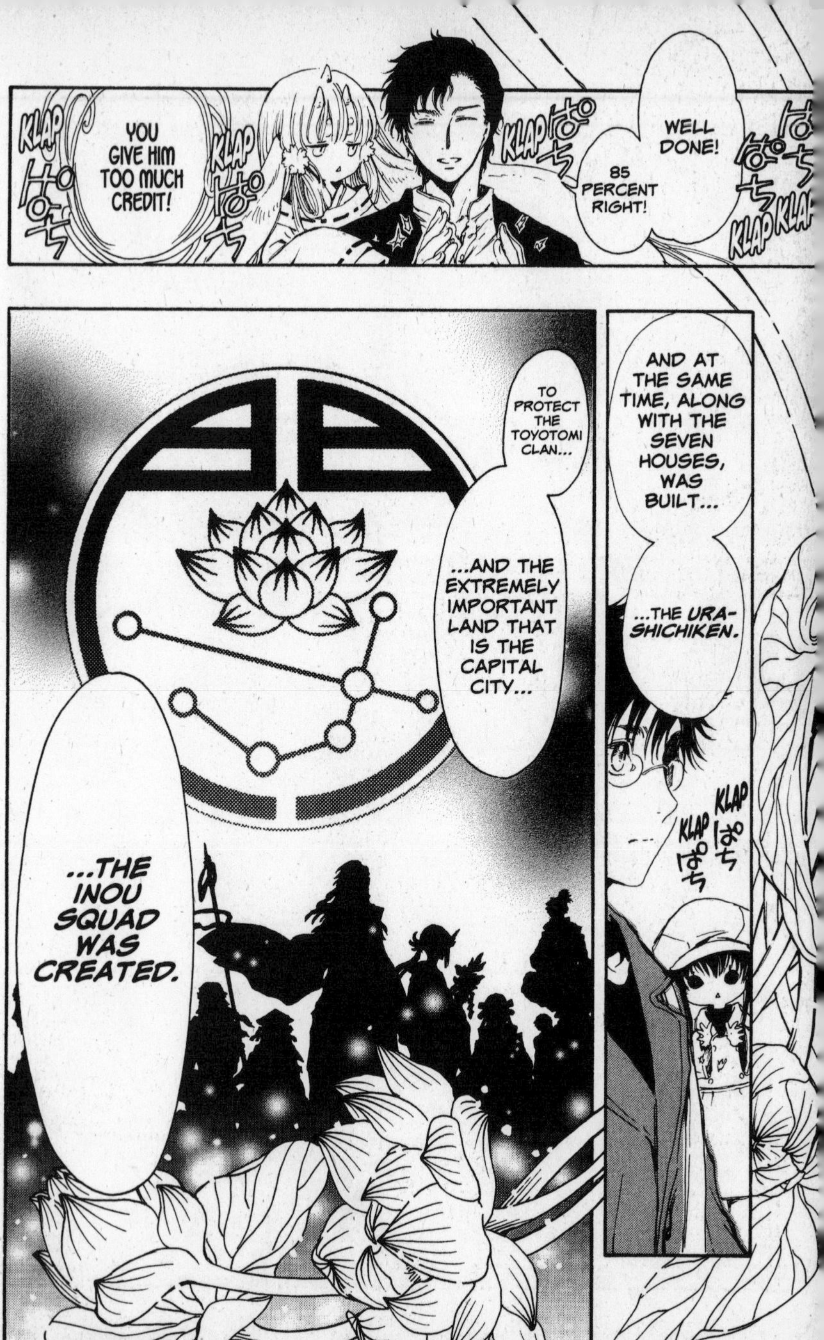
はぱち KLAP KLAP
WELL DONE!
85 PERCENT RIGHT!
KLAP ぱち
KLAP ぱち
YOU GIVE HIM TOO MUCH CREDIT!
KLAP ぱち
AND AT THE SAME TIME, ALONG WITH THE SEVEN HOUSES, WAS BUILT...
...THE URA-SHICHIKEN.

KLAP ぱち
KLAP ぱち
TO PROTECT THE TOYOTOMI CLAN...
...AND THE EXTREMELY IMPORTANT LAND THAT IS THE CAPITAL CITY...
...THE INOU SQUAD WAS CREATED.

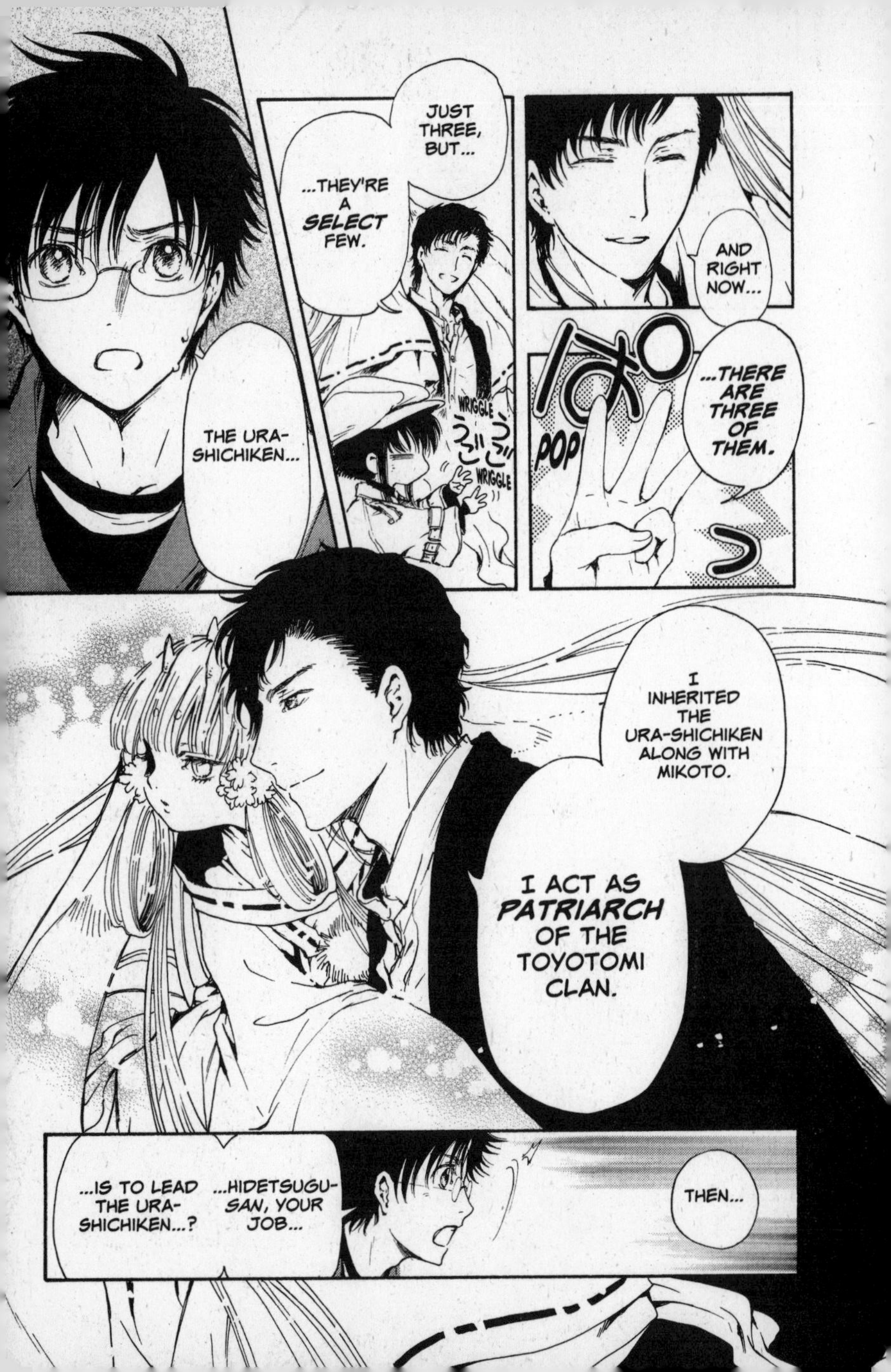
AND RIGHT NOW...
ぱっ
POP
...THERE ARE THREE OF THEM.
JUST THREE, BUT...
...THEY'RE A *SELECT* FEW.
WRIGGLE
うごうご
WRIGGLE
THE URA-SHICHIKEN...
I INHERITED THE URA-SHICHIKEN ALONG WITH MIKOTO.
I ACT AS *PATRIARCH* OF THE TOYOTOMI CLAN.
THEN...
...HIDETSUGU-SAN, YOUR JOB...
...IS TO LEAD THE URA-SHICHIKEN...?

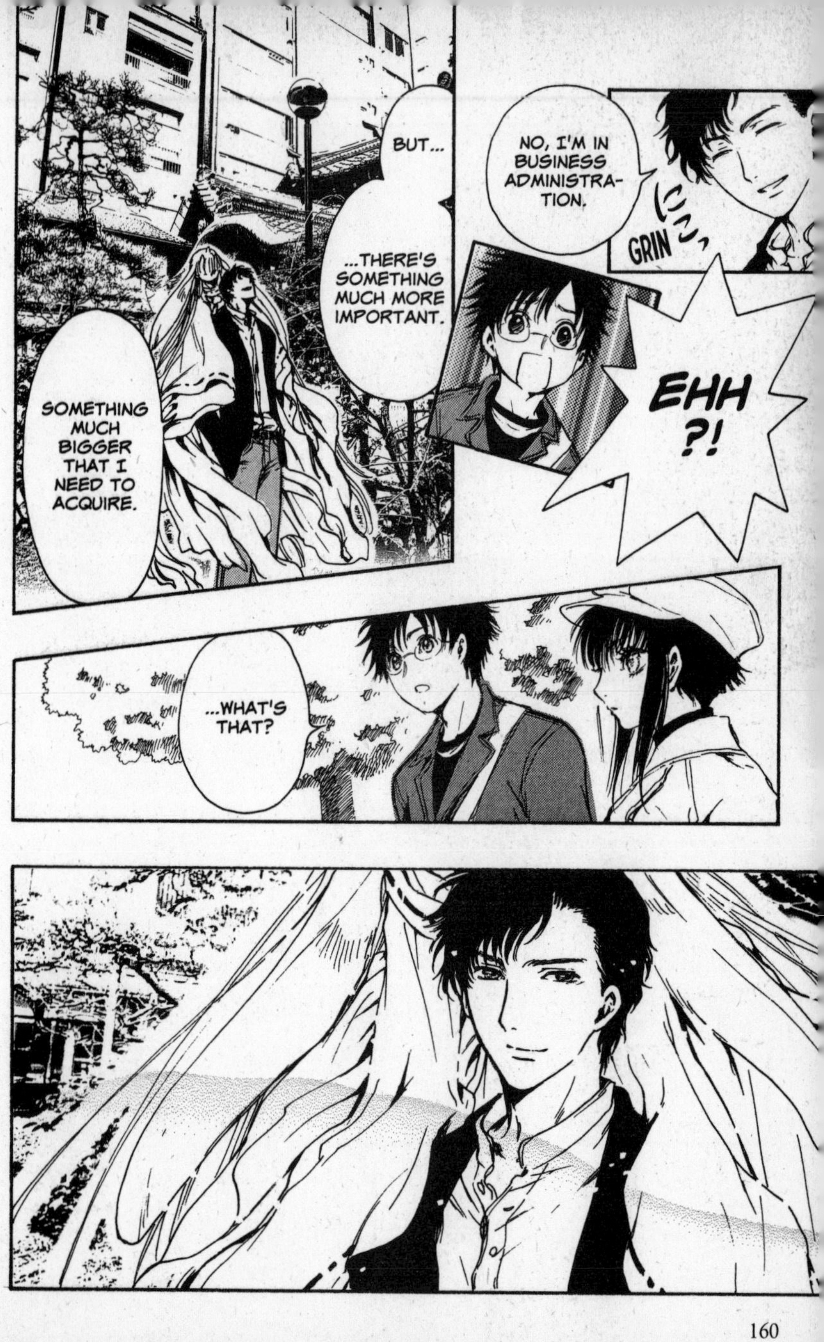
NO, I'M IN BUSINESS ADMINISTRA- TION.
GRIN
EHH ?!
BUT...
...THERE'S SOMETHING MUCH MORE IMPORTANT.
SOMETHING MUCH BIGGER THAT I NEED TO ACQUIRE.
...WHAT'S THAT?

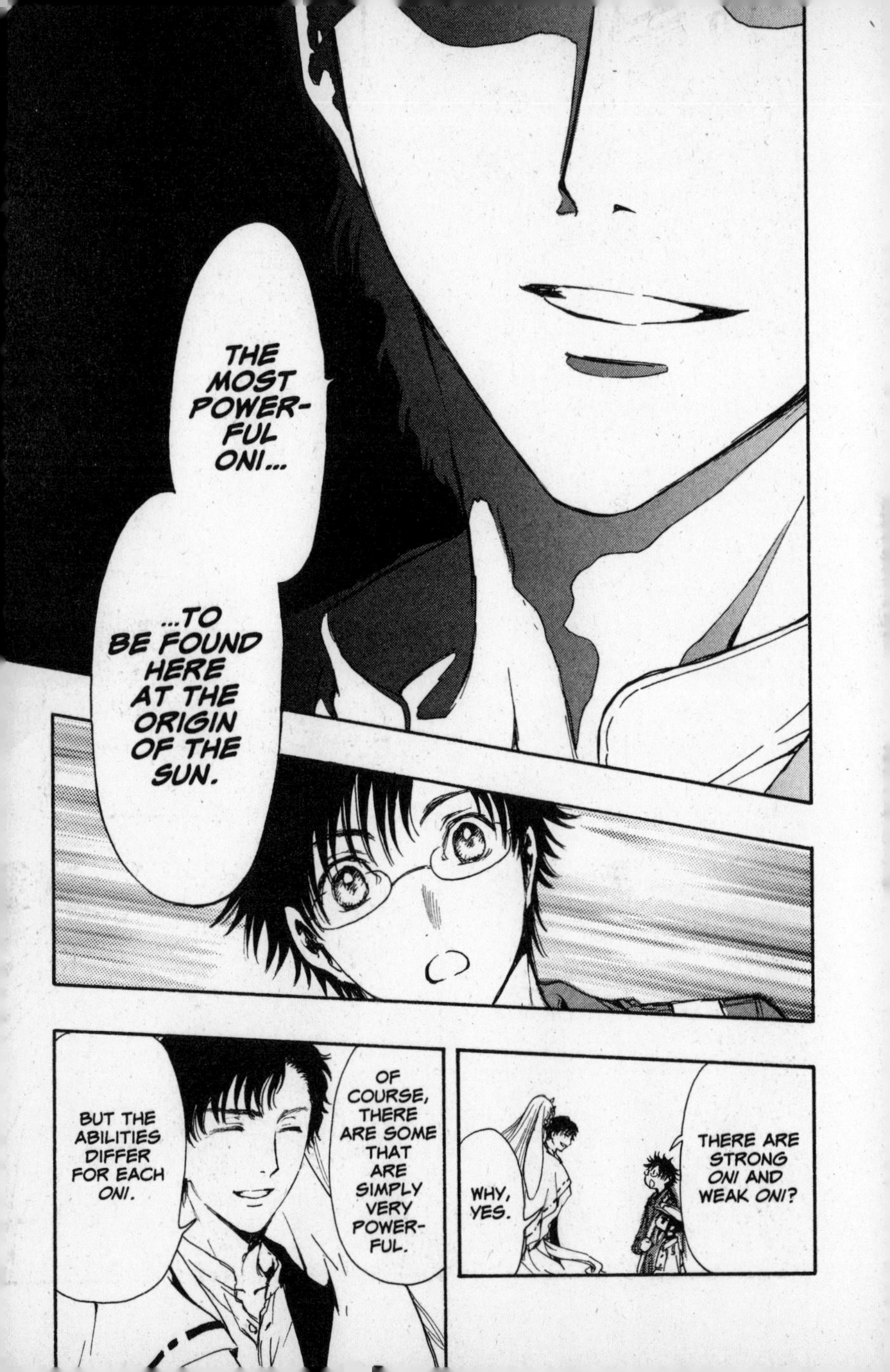
THE MOST POWERFUL ONI...
...TO BE FOUND HERE AT THE ORIGIN OF THE SUN.
THERE ARE STRONG *ONI* AND WEAK *ONI*?
WHY, YES.
OF COURSE, THERE ARE SOME THAT ARE SIMPLY VERY POWERFUL.
BUT THE ABILITIES DIFFER FOR EACH *ONI*.

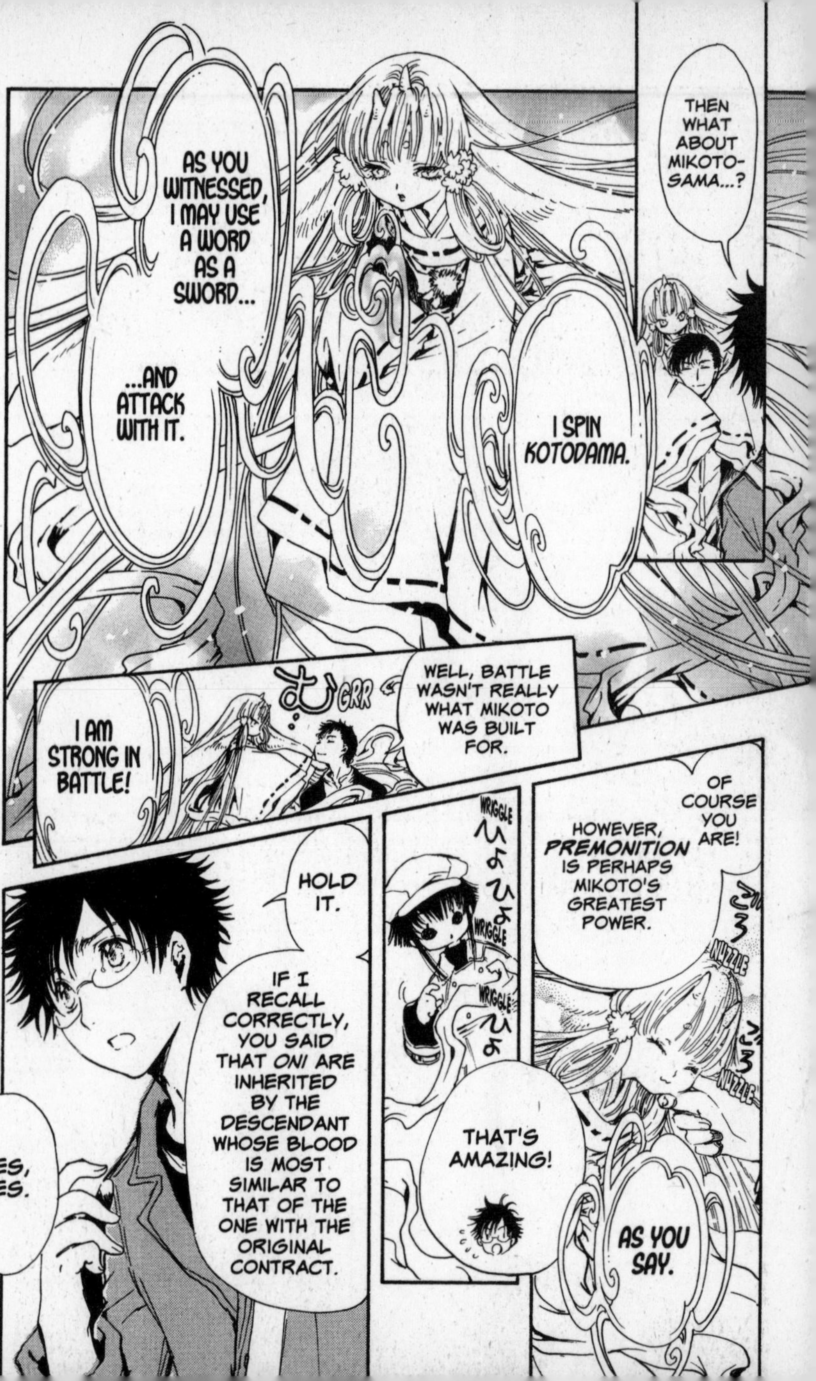
THEN WHAT ABOUT MIKOTO-SAMA...?
I SPIN KOTODAMA.
AS YOU WITNESSED, I MAY USE A WORD AS A SWORD...
...AND ATTACK WITH IT.
WELL, BATTLE WASN'T REALLY WHAT MIKOTO WAS BUILT FOR.
GRR
I AM STRONG IN BATTLE!
OF COURSE YOU ARE!
HOWEVER, *PREMONITION* IS PERHAPS MIKOTO'S GREATEST POWER.
NUZZLE
NUZZLE
AS YOU SAY.
WRIGGLE
WRIGGLE
WRIGGLE
THAT'S AMAZING!
HOLD IT.
IF I RECALL CORRECTLY, YOU SAID THAT *ONI* ARE INHERITED BY THE DESCENDANT WHOSE BLOOD IS MOST SIMILAR TO THAT OF THE ONE WITH THE ORIGINAL CONTRACT.
YES, YES.

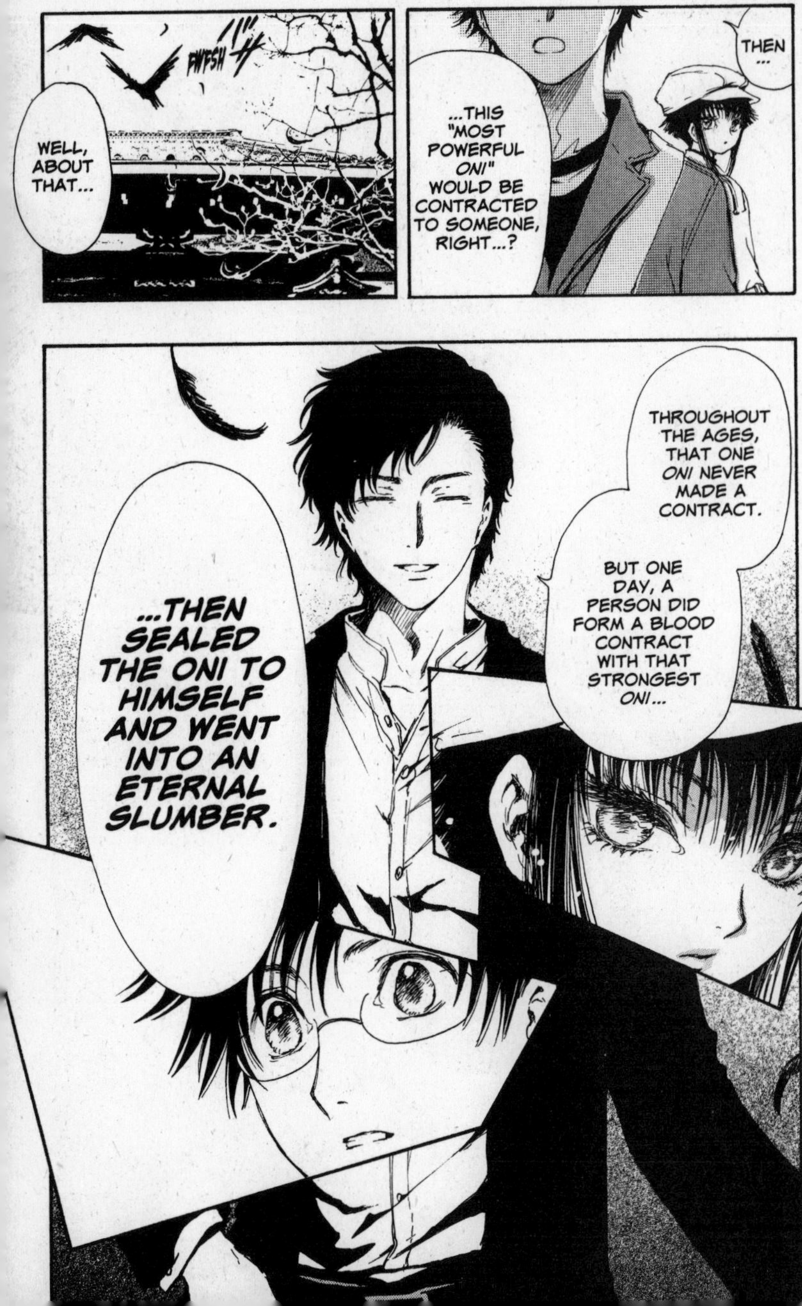
THEN ...
...THIS "MOST POWERFUL ONI" WOULD BE CONTRACTED TO SOMEONE, RIGHT...?
PWFSH
WELL, ABOUT THAT...
THROUGHOUT THE AGES, THAT ONE ONI NEVER MADE A CONTRACT.
BUT ONE DAY, A PERSON DID FORM A BLOOD CONTRACT WITH THAT STRONGEST ONI...
...THEN SEALED THE ONI TO HIMSELF AND WENT INTO AN ETERNAL SLUMBER.

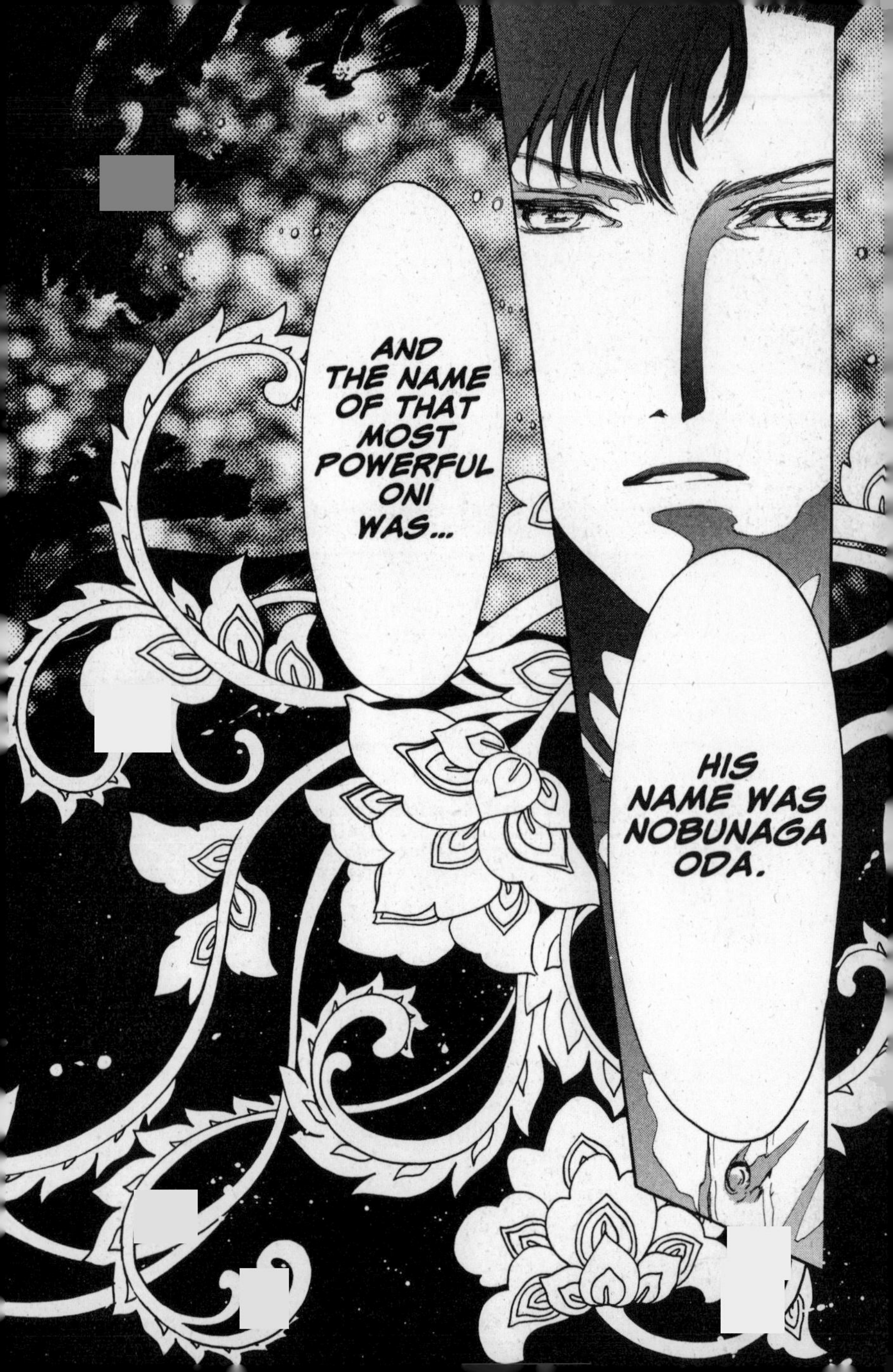
AND THE NAME OF THAT MOST POWERFUL ONI WAS...
HIS NAME WAS NOBUNAGA ODA.

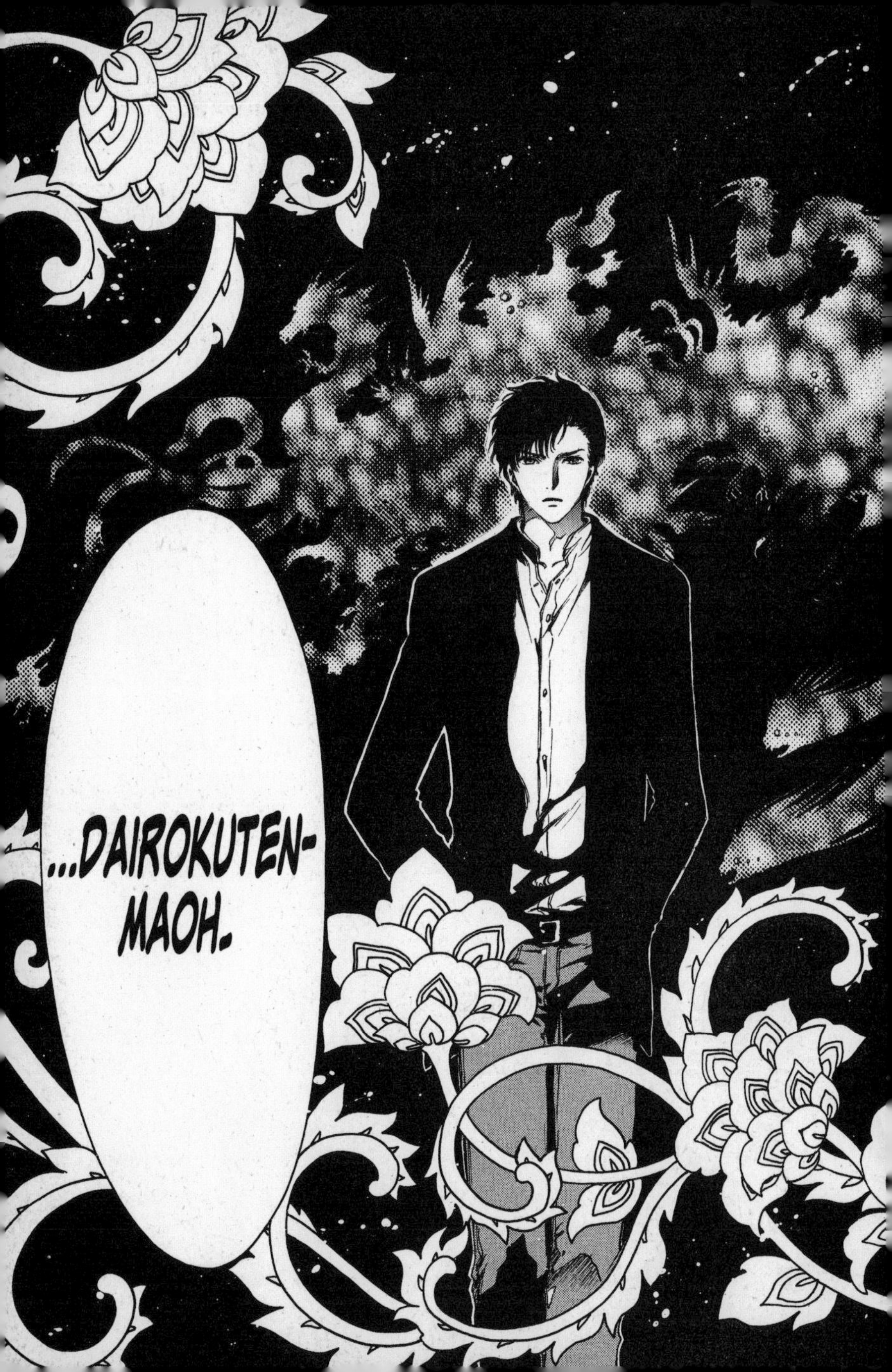
...DAIROKUTEN-
MAOH.

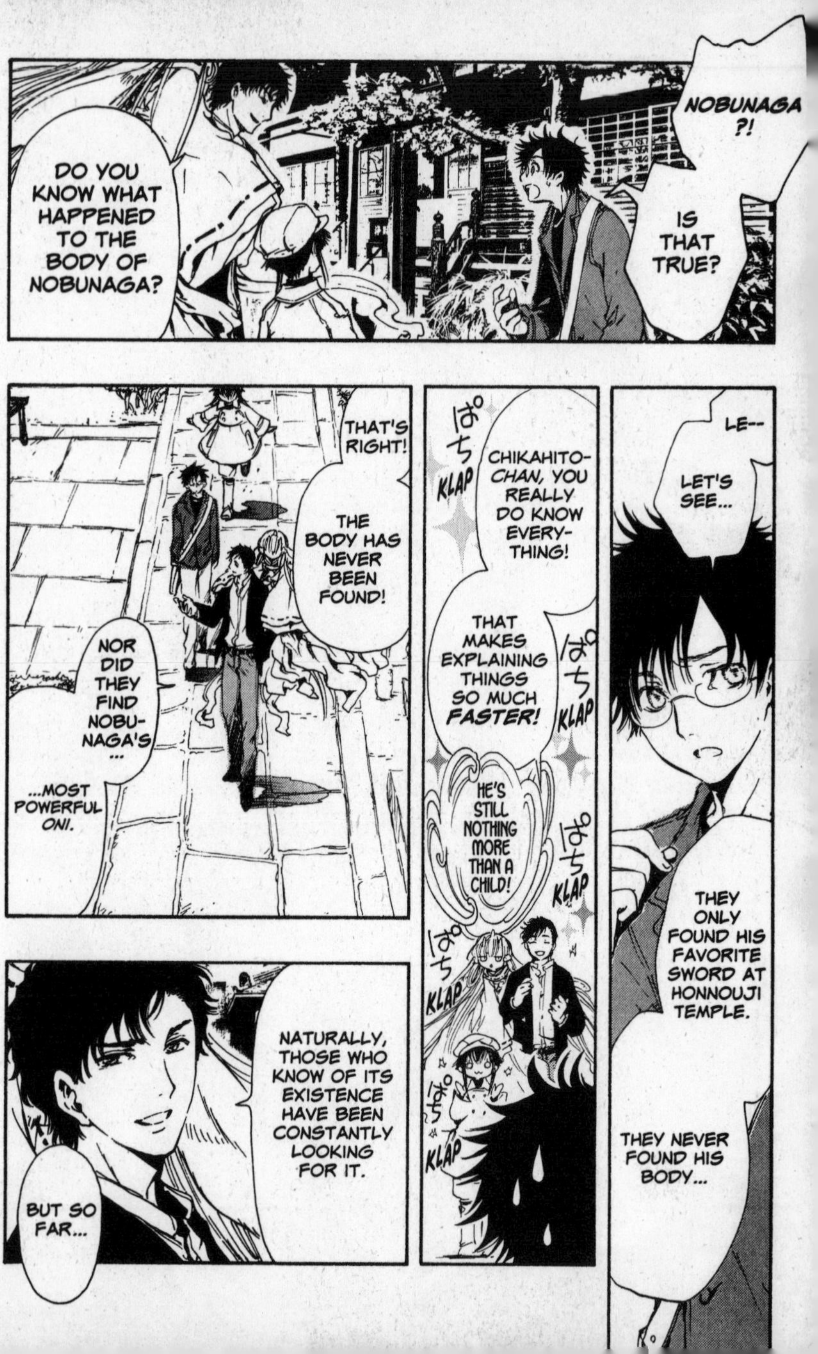

NOBUNAGA ?!
IS THAT TRUE?
DO YOU KNOW WHAT HAPPENED TO THE BODY OF NOBUNAGA?
LE--
LET'S SEE...
THEY ONLY FOUND HIS FAVORITE SWORD AT HONNOUJI TEMPLE.
THEY NEVER FOUND HIS BODY...
ぱち KLAP
CHIKAHITO-CHAN, YOU REALLY DO KNOW EVERY-THING!
ぱち KLAP
THAT MAKES EXPLAINING THINGS SO MUCH FASTER!
ぱち KLAP
HE'S STILL NOTHING MORE THAN A CHILD!
ぱち KLAP
ぱち KLAP
THAT'S RIGHT!
THE BODY HAS NEVER BEEN FOUND!
NOR DID THEY FIND NOBU-NAGA'S ...
...MOST POWERFUL ONI.
NATURALLY, THOSE WHO KNOW OF ITS EXISTENCE HAVE BEEN CONSTANTLY LOOKING FOR IT.
BUT SO FAR...

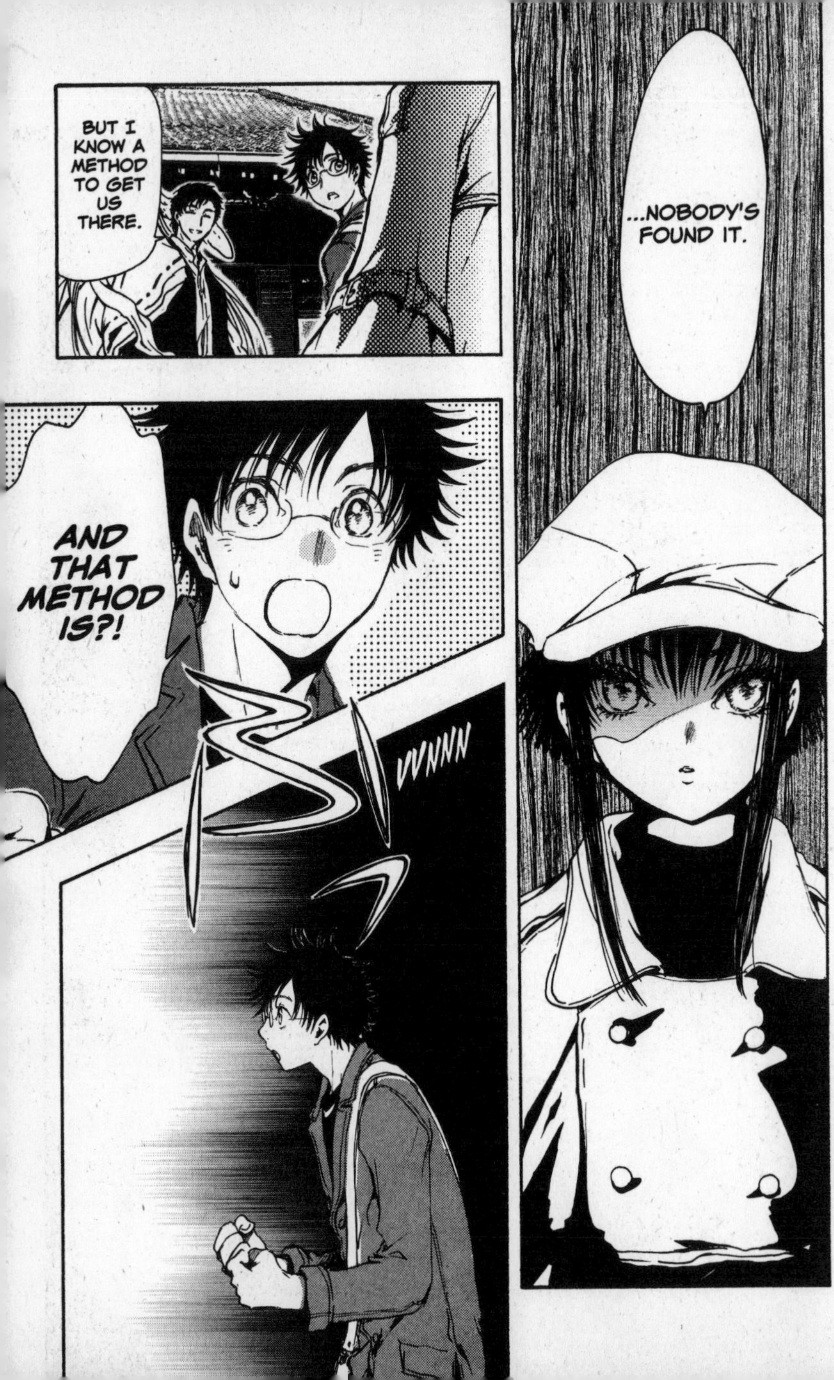
...NOBODY'S FOUND IT.
BUT I KNOW A METHOD TO GET US THERE.
AND THAT METHOD IS?!
VVNNN

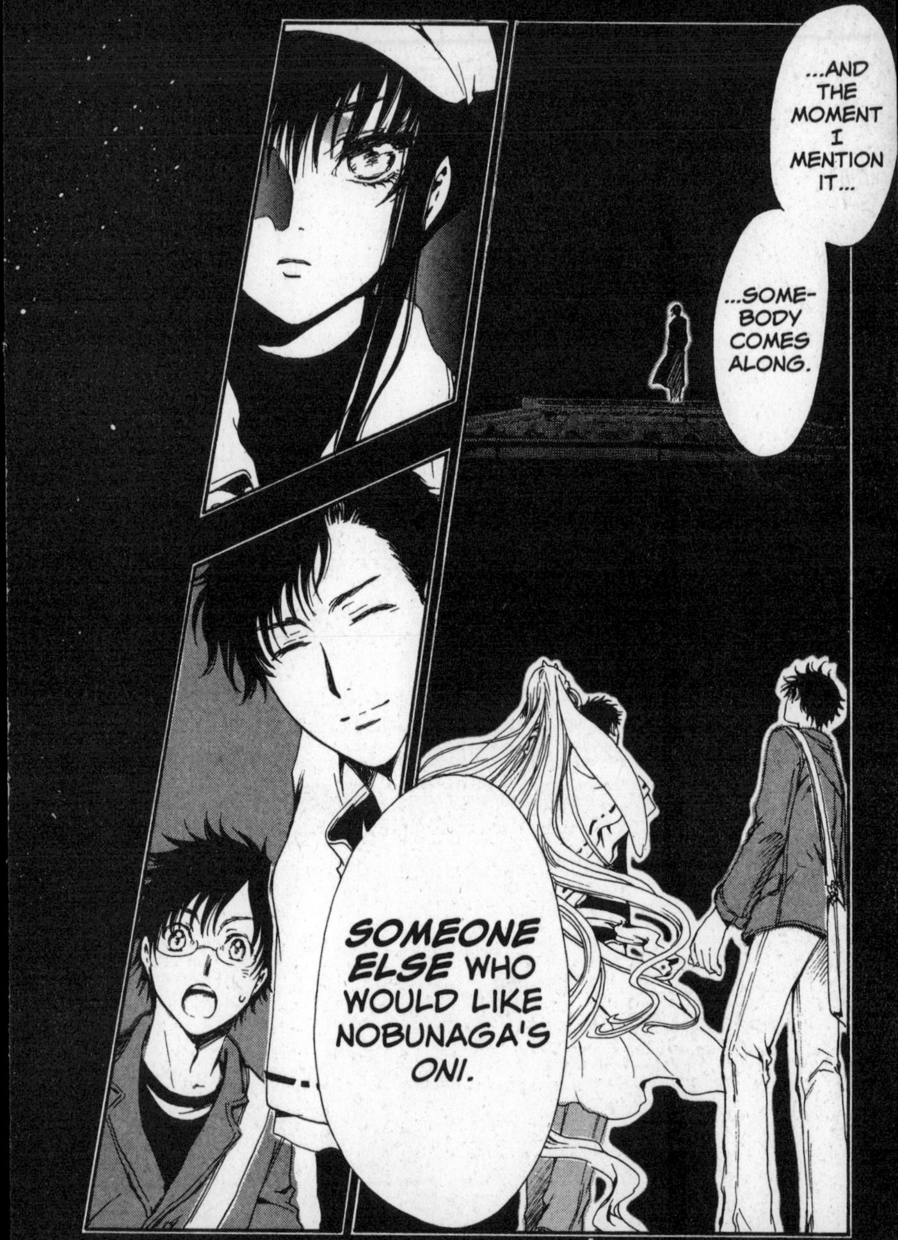
...AND THE MOMENT I MENTION IT...
...SOME-BODY COMES ALONG.
SOMEONE ELSE WHO WOULD LIKE NOBUNAGA'S ONI.

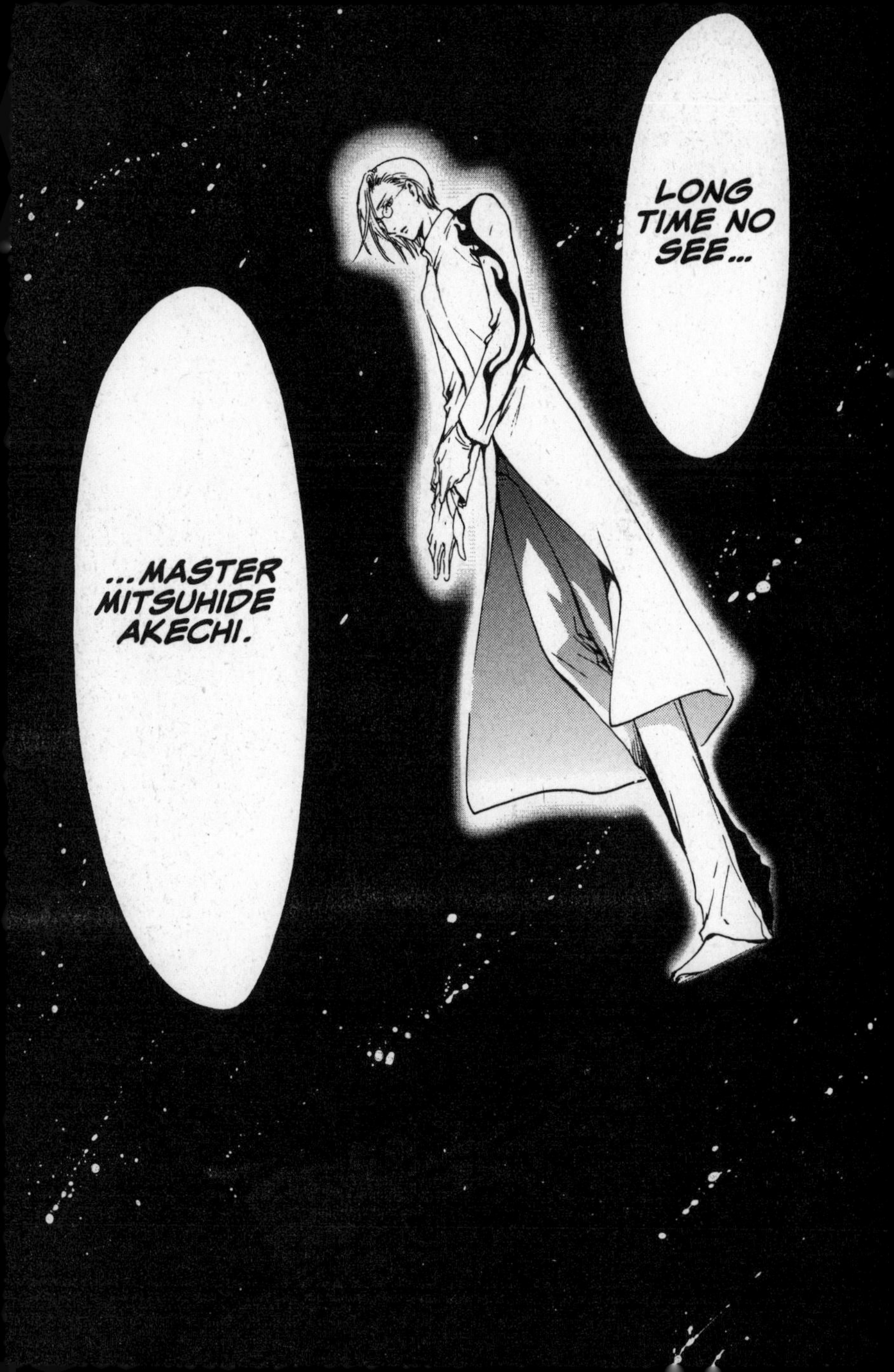
LONG TIME NO SEE...
...MASTER MITSUHIDE AKECHI.

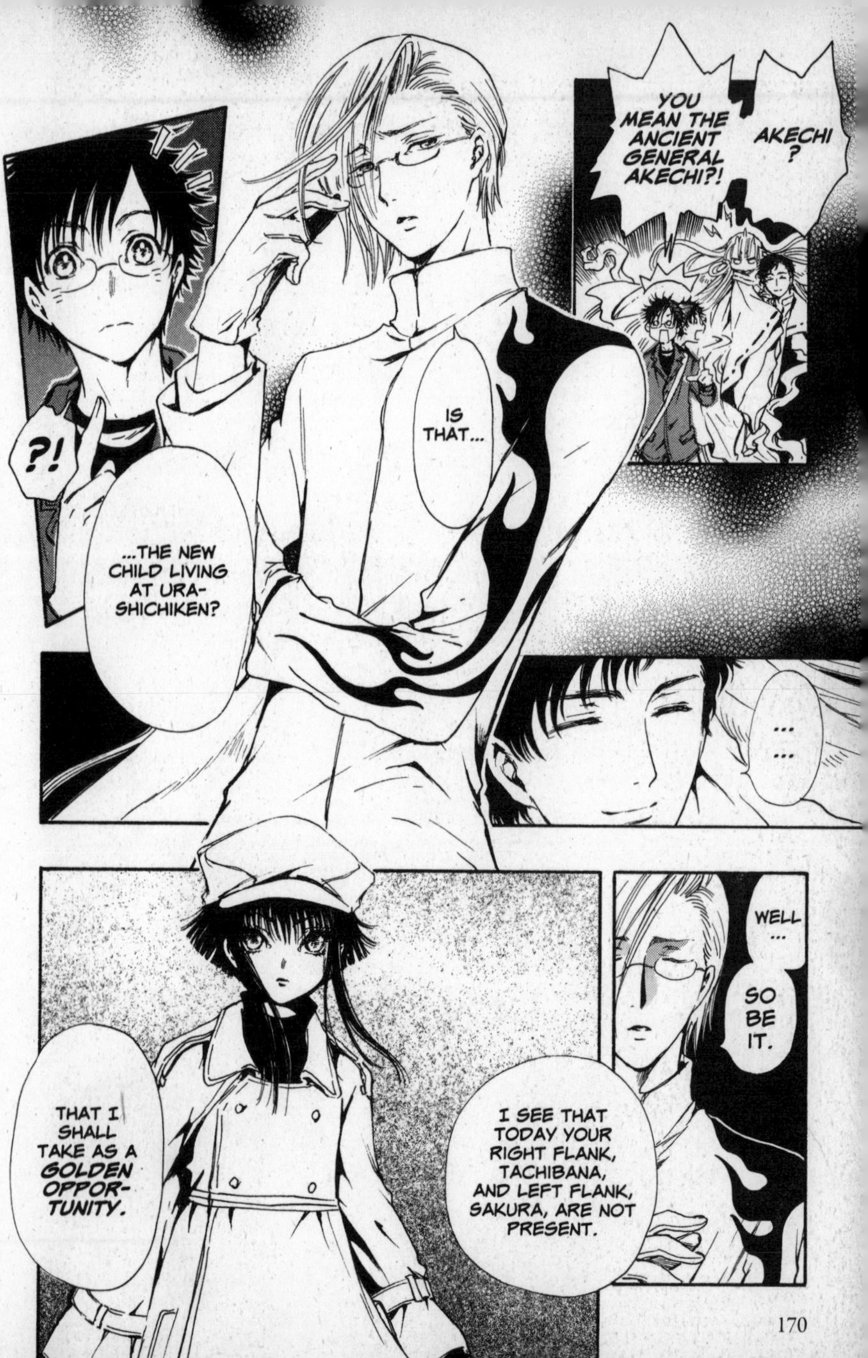
AKECHI ?
YOU MEAN THE ANCIENT GENERAL AKECHI?!
IS THAT...
?!
...THE NEW CHILD LIVING AT URA-SHICHIKEN?
... ...
WELL ...
SO BE IT.
I SEE THAT TODAY YOUR RIGHT FLANK, TACHIBANA, AND LEFT FLANK, SAKURA, ARE NOT PRESENT.
THAT I SHALL TAKE AS A *GOLDEN OPPORTUNITY.*

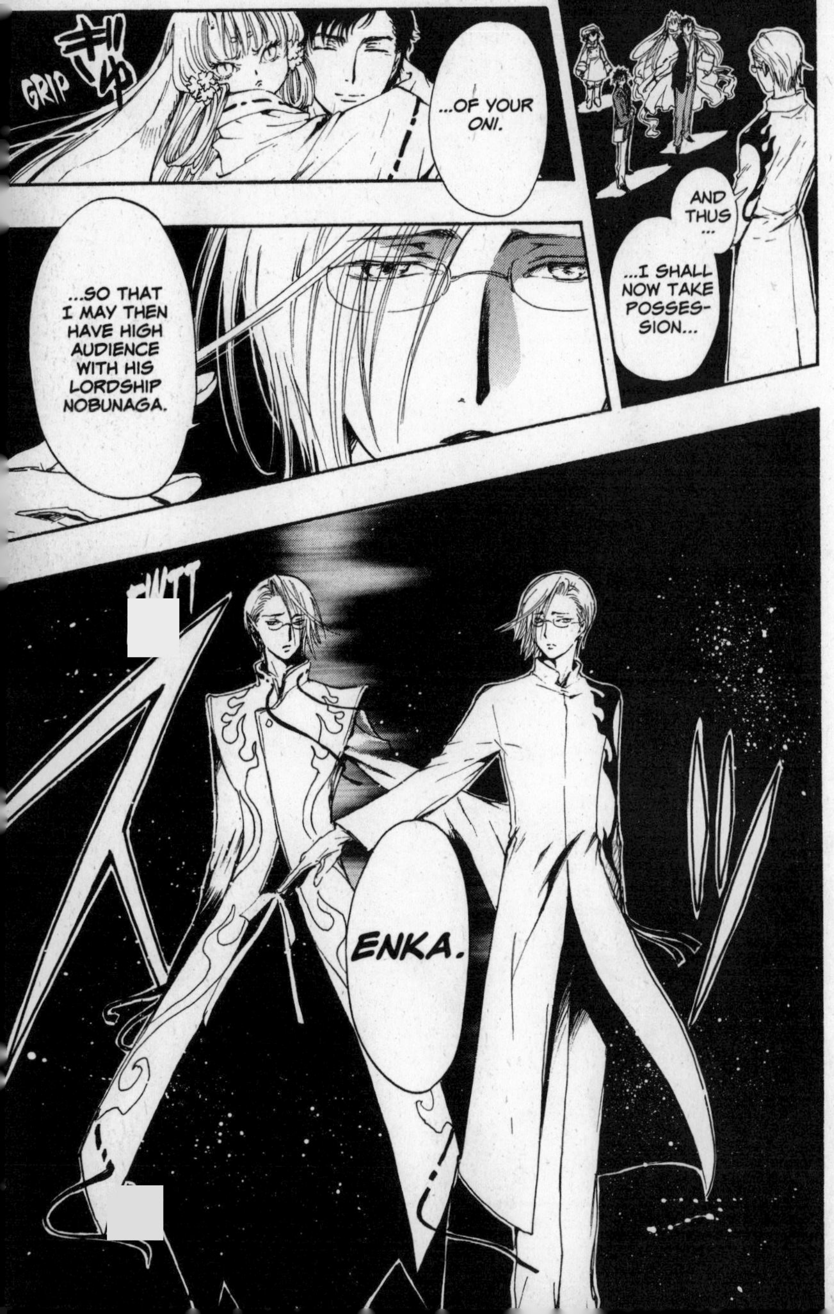
AND THUS ...
...I SHALL NOW TAKE POSSESSION...
...OF YOUR ONI.
GRIP
...SO THAT I MAY THEN HAVE HIGH AUDIENCE WITH HIS LORDSHIP NOBUNAGA.
ENKA.

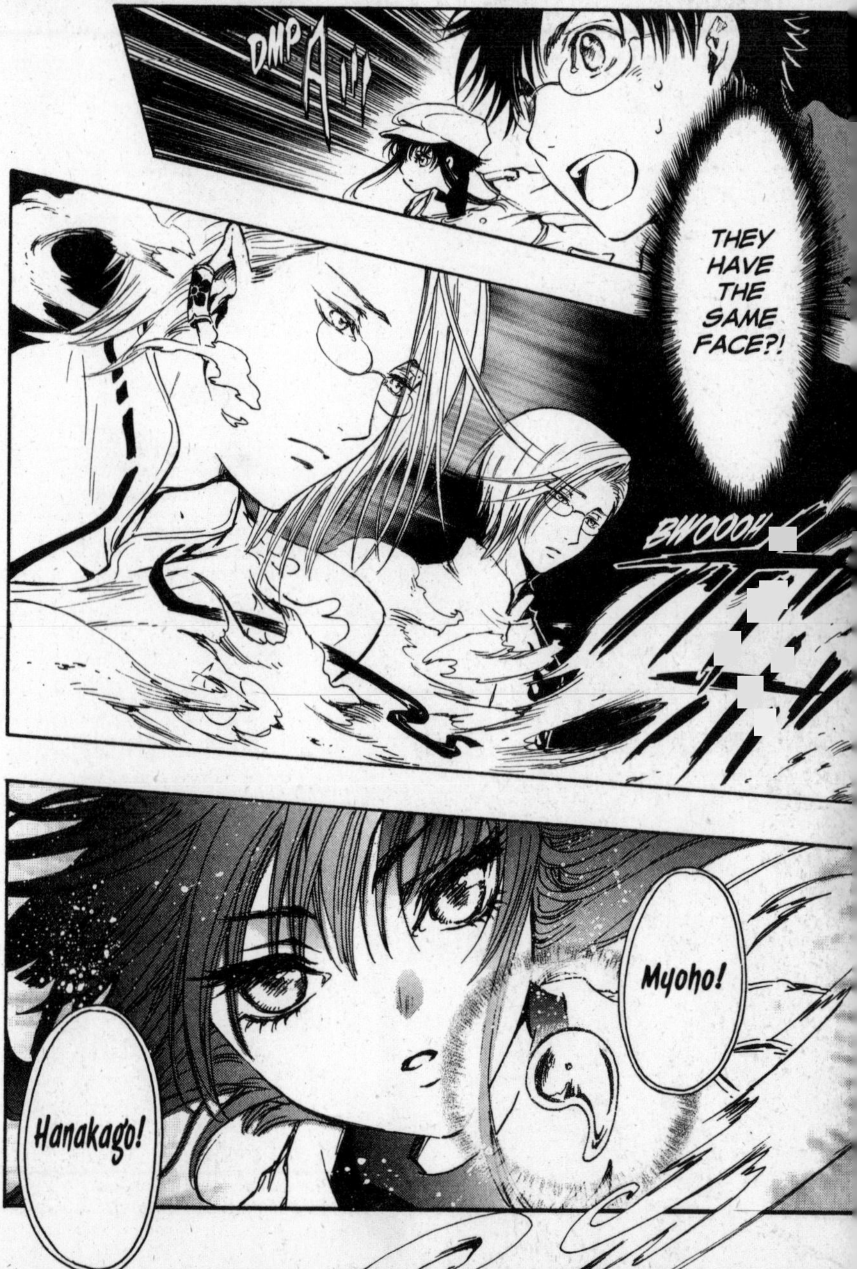
DMP
THEY HAVE THE SAME FACE?!
BWOOOH
Myoho!
Hanakago!

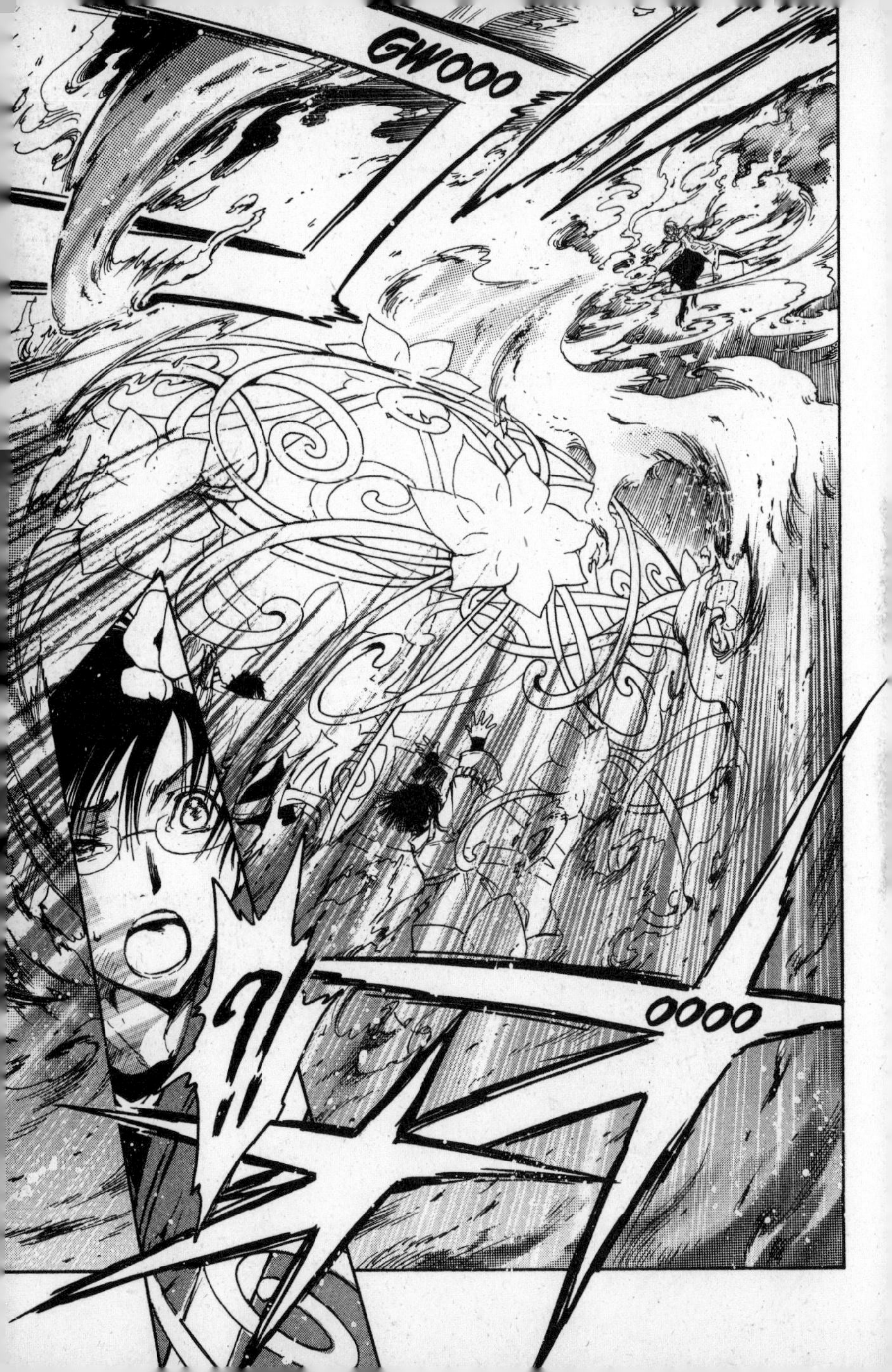

GWOOO
?!
OOOO

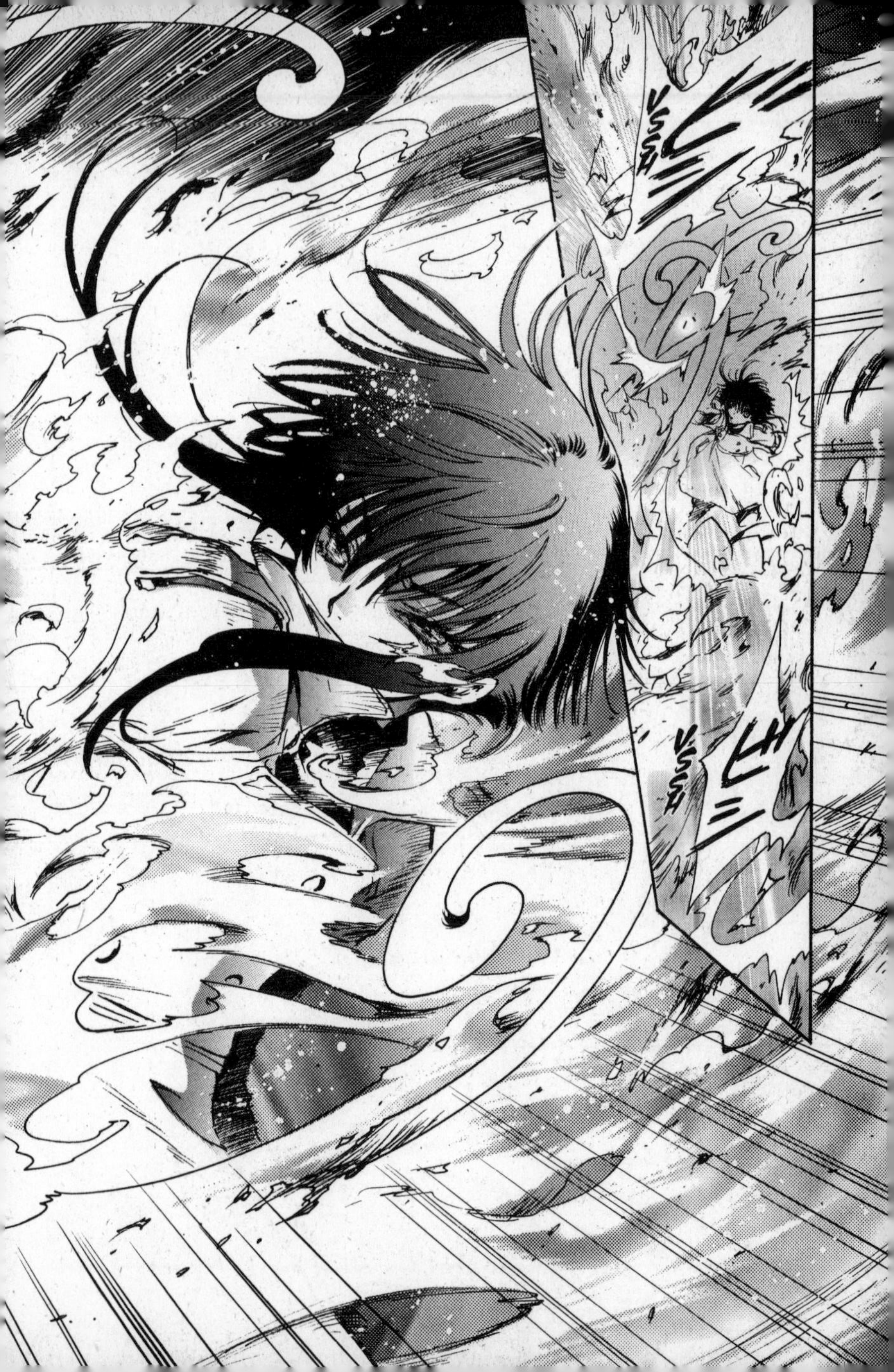
VSSH
VSSH

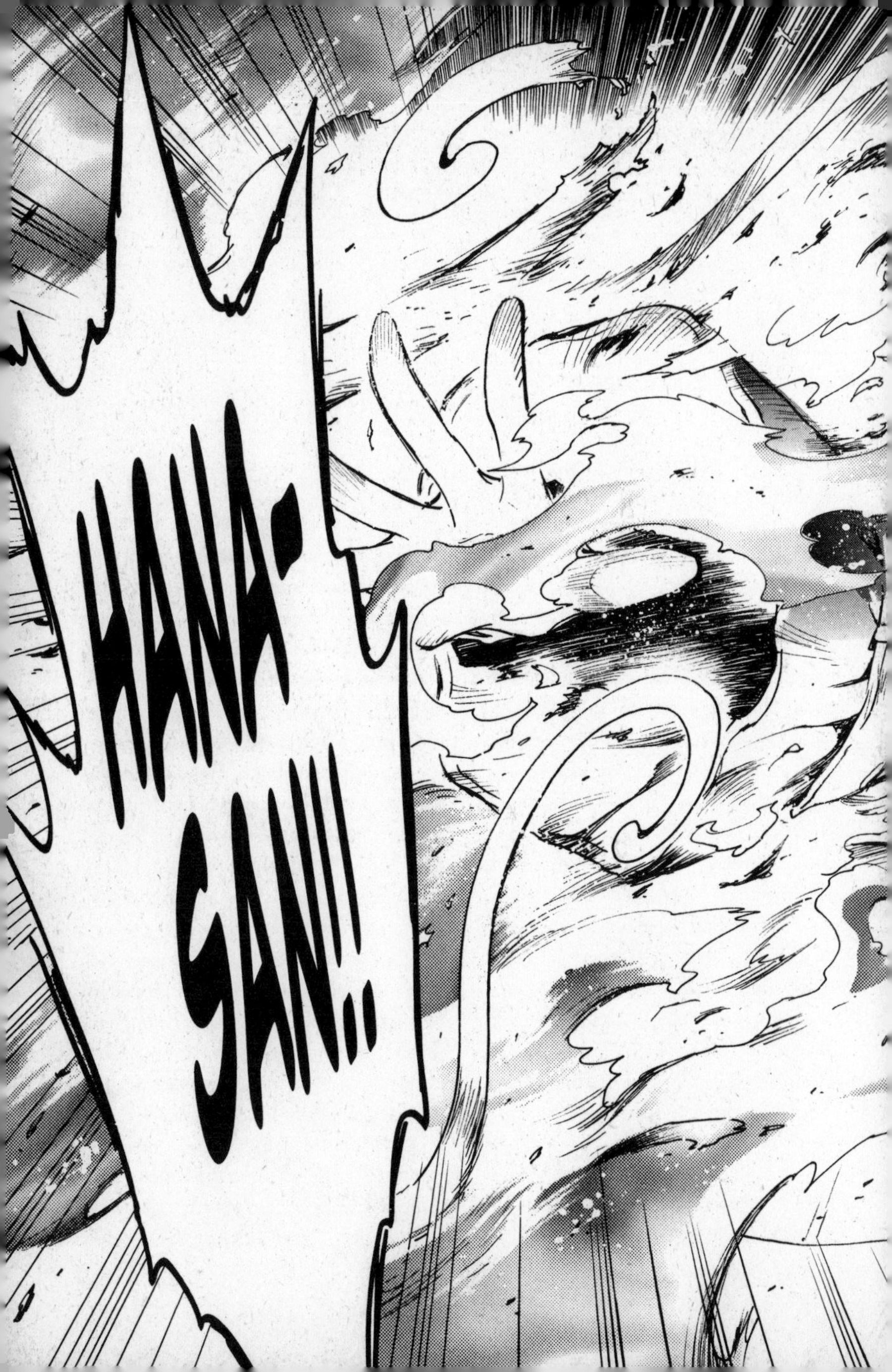
HANA-SAN!!

GATE 7 VOLUME 1 TRANSLATION NOTES

COMPILED BY **WILLIAM FLANAGAN** WITH ADDITIONAL NOTES FROM **CLAMP**

Page 7, general notes on Kyoto: Kyoto was one of the few large Japanese population centers to escape the extremely destructive American firebombing of World War II that burned historical sites in nearly every other Japanese city close to Kyoto's size. The determination not to bomb Kyoto was a conscious decision by American civilian and military leadership in deference to Kyoto's many historical buildings and landmarks. Although some other historical sites in more rural locations—such as Ise or Izumo—were also spared, cities that were formerly rich in history (such as Tokyo, Yokohama, Nagoya, Osaka, and Kobe—not to mention Hiroshima and Nagasaki) have all had to rebuild *replicas* of their ancient historic landmarks. Kyoto is the one large Japanese city where history is still very much in evidence.

Page 8, Kitano Tenmangu Shrine: At the turn of the tenth century, Michizane Sugawara was a man of noble birth and great scholarship. The emperor Uda favored him and gave him a powerful position, but he was slandered by his enemies and forced to die in exile in the year 903. A rash of earthquakes and damaging storms came soon after his death, believed to have been caused by his wrath. At the same time, there were an unusual number of deaths in the houses of the people who slandered him. The imperial throne proclaimed him Karai Tenjin ("god of fire and thunder"). The original shrine on the present site was called Tenman Tenjin, and Sugawara's spirit was enshrined as a god. Because of Sugawara's scholarship, the Tenmangu shrines (there are quite a few in Japan and even one in Hawaii) are a place where students go to pray for good grades. From CLAMP's notes in the original Japanese volume: "There's a fair on the Kitano Tenmangu Shrine grounds every month on the twenty-fifth, and it's always lively, with many people arriving to worship. They call it *Kitano-no-Tenjin-san*! The shrine is also famous for its *ume* (plum) blossoms. Established during the middle of the Heian period in the first year of Emperor Murakami's reign (947), Tenmangu has a deep and abiding history. Address: Bakuro-cho, Kamikyo ward, Kyoto city in Kyoto-fu."

Page 19: *Kuchinawa* is a very old word for "snake" in Japanese. The kanji (Chinese characters) used in the original Japanese volume is the same as the common, present-day word for "snake" (*hebi*), but the ancient pronunciation gives the creatures an old-world feel.

Page 20: *Mizuchi* is also an ancient word. The kanji used is an alternate kanji for "dragon."

Page 22: *Myoho* is a Japanese word that means "arcane," "mystery," or "clever method." *Kamaitachi* literally translates as "weasel scratches," but in this scene it refers to cuts on the skin that one could get from sharp, strong, gale-force winds.

Page 29, *nabe yakiudon*: Normally, *yaki-udon* is a dish made of noodles that are pan or griddle fried together with meats and vegetables. *Nabe yakiudon* is not fried, but rather boiled noodle soup (with meats and vegetables) in an earthenware pot. In many cases, each person eats from his or her own pot.

Page 32, "stringy noodles": When left in hot broth too long, noodles get droopy and stringy. This is called *nobiru* ("stretched") in Japanese, and to many Japanese people this means that the noodle dish is ruined.

Page 34, "the Kyoto dialect": Like most regions, Kyoto has a distinct dialect of its own. The dialect is considered a part of the western dialects (the *Kansai-ben*, which includes Osaka, Kobe, Nara, and others), but it has its own distinct flavor. The Kyoto dialect exudes a sense of old-style, cultured civility.

Page 35, "Tsuji Private School": Fans of *xxxHOLiC* may recognize Cross Private School as the school Kimihiro Watanuki commuted to during the events that took place between volumes 1 and 15 of that series. This private school uses the same kanji as Cross Private School.

Page 36: Kami-shichiken is the name of a district in Kyoto found just east of the Kitano Tenmangu shrine. Its name means "Seven Upper Houses," referring to seven high-class teahouses that employed geisha. It is still one of the *hana machi* ("flower streets") of Japan—one of the official districts for geisha. In this scene, Chikahito uses a simple kanji for "flower," one which refers to the few official geisha districts still found in Japan. The kanji that Tachibana and Sakura use for *hana machi* is a more complicated version. While both the simple kanji and the complicated one have similar meanings (both can mean "flower," "showy," "brilliant," and "gorgeous," among other things), the different kanji spellings make them into two different concepts.

Page 37, Ura-shichiken: *Ura* is usually used to mean "back," as in "back door" or "back rooms"—something that is not seen from the front. *Ura* is also used to mean "ulterior," as in "ulterior motives." In other words, "hidden" or "secret." So Ura-shichiken could mean "Seven Back Houses" or "Seven Secret Houses."

Page 38: The word *inou* is made up of two kanji meaning "unusual" and "mind."

Page 47: Shinshu is the ancient name for an area that encompasses mostly Nagano Prefecture. Chikahito also mentions a "weird time" on this page. Japanese high schools are three-year institutions, and transfer students are rare. A student transferring schools toward the end of his second year of high school is almost unheard of. Even if a student must transfer, the school usually makes arrangements for that student to stay with his class until the end of the school year in March, but Chikahito was transferred in late January or February.

Page 54, from CLAMP's notes in the original Japanese volume: The idea of *nishin* soba noodles was suggested by Yosakichi Matsuno II. Even now, they preserve the legend of its unchanging, ever-delicious taste, a symbol of Kyoto itself.

Page 64: *Ema* are small wooden plaques sold by temples and shrines. Wishes are written on them, then they are hung from a designated area with the hopes that the gods will grant the wishes.

Page 65: The Japanese kanji for "living curse" means "living ghost." In the grudges and curses that Chikahito reads aloud, a "living curse" is something so strong, it can act as a haunting presence even though the person with the grudge is still alive. Sakura comments on "happiness" on this page, too. Buddhist philosophy is largely dismissive of material desires. Shinto is more rooted in the here and now, and shrines such as the Yasui Shrine—which our characters visit—are dedicated to making one's *present* life better.

Page 100, *mentaiko* sauce: *Mentaiko* is the roe (fish eggs) of the Alaska pollock. It has a spicy flavor and was originally a dish brought to Japan through Korea. One of its more popular uses is as a spicy addition to spaghetti.

Page 103, *maiko* and obi: *Maiko* are the geisha in training. Like most Japanese systems of *sempai* and *kōhai* ("mentor" and "protégé"), the established geisha give advice and the *maiko* do all the grunt work while learning their trade. One of these jobs is helping the geisha dress, and one of the final touches is putting on the wide, brilliantly colored cloth sashes called obi, which are tied in an elaborate bow in the back.

Page 105, Tachibana's lecture: In the original Japanese edition, Tachibana says he's

FUUKA: *The name for Hana's* **MYOHO** *technique here is made up of kanji for "wind" and "flower."*

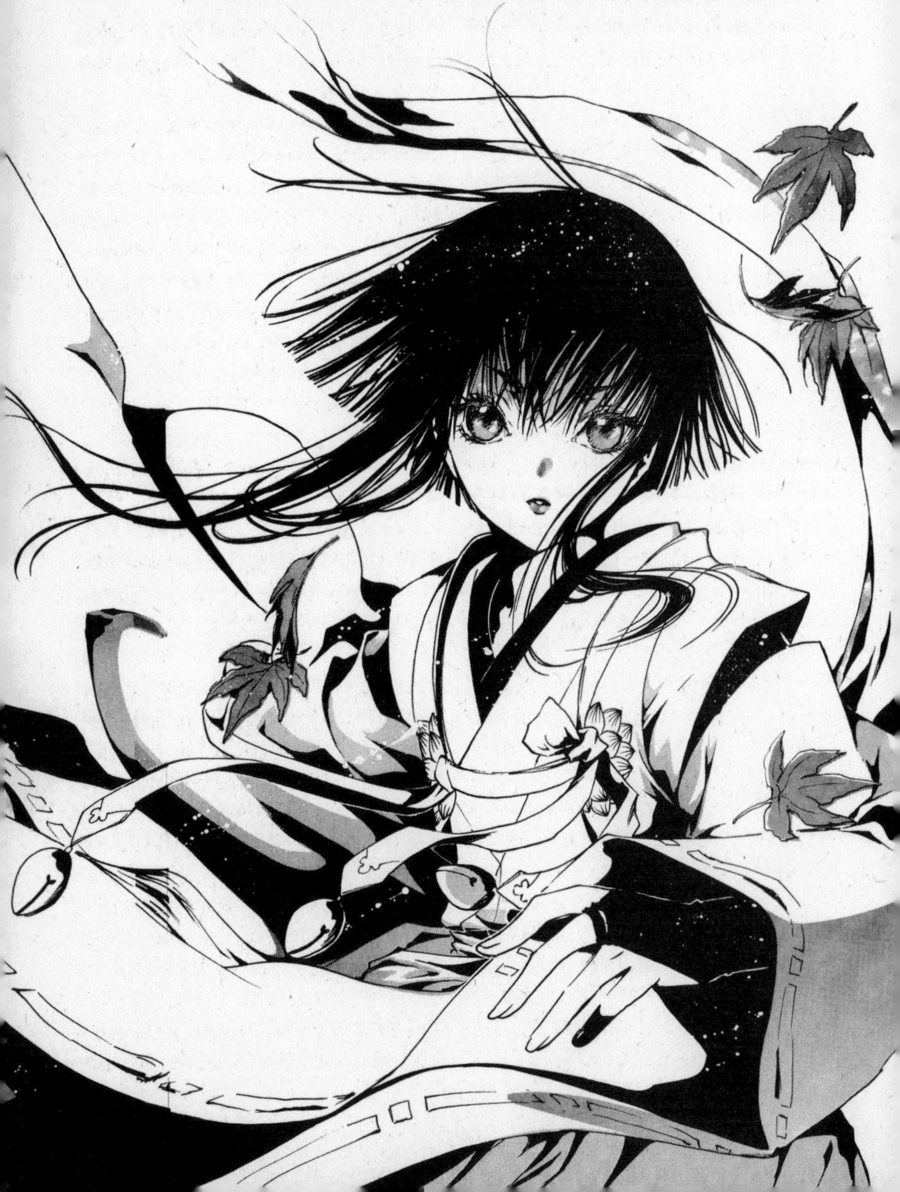

going to a *kōgi*, which means a "lecture." But Chikahito mistakes the word for another meaning of *kōgi*, "complaint." Fortunately in English, "lecture" can mean both "lesson" and "scolding," so this pun was unusually translatable.

Page 116: Ramen can come in all sorts of flavors. *Kogashi* miso is a ramen dish featuring miso that has been charred to make a flavorful, deep-black broth. *Shōyu* is a ramen broth made with a soy-sauce base. *Tonkotsu* is a milky-white ramen broth made from pork marrow bones and fat that has been slow cooked. *Shio* is a light broth flavored with salt. From CLAMP's notes in the original Japanese volume, referring to the restaurant shown in panel 1 on this page: "With branches in places like Tokyo and Hakata in Fukuoka, Gogyo wishes to be a place where one can enjoy a new, fun ramen dining experience. In the back of the shop is a hidden, exclusive bar called Kura that's doing big business. It's an extremely popular restaurant that caters to the needs of every generation."

Page 117: In Japan, an *izakaya* is the equivalent of a good neighborhood bar and grill. Halfway between a bar and a restaurant, it's where people go to relax, eat, and drink.

Page 118, "proper greetings": When one moves into a new place, it is common to go to the landlord and other close or important neighbors with small gifts to pay your respects.

Page 133: *Kotodama* is made of two kanji—one that means "words" and a second meaning "soul." It might translate as "spirit of words." Following on the *kotodama* idea, the *oni*'s name, Mikoto, is made up of the kanji for "gods" and "word."

Page 135: Blythe is an eleven-inch fashion doll with a huge head and eyes that change color. It was originally distributed in 1972 by the now-defunct American toy brand Kenner, but it garnered no popularity and was canceled after only a year. However, in the year 2000, after a series of advertisements using the doll by the Parco department-store chain in Japan, Blythe suddenly became a Japanese sensation. Hasbro, who then held the rights, sold the license to the Japanese toy maker Takara, and Blythe was an instant hit.

Page 144, the noodle shop signs: *Kishimen* is a flat, wide noodle usually served with a soy sauce. *Kishimen* is actually a specialty of the Nagoya area. Ukiya is a chain of soba shops based in Kyoto. Soba is a thin buckwheat noodle that can be served either cold and dipped in a special sauce or hot in a bowl in its own broth like other noodle soups. *Soba-dokoro* is not the name of the restaurant. It is simply an outdoor sign indicating that one can eat soba noodles there. On this page, they are walking down Shinkyogoku, the second-oldest shopping street in Japan (established in 1872), formerly known for live theater and after-movie houses. Ever since the seventies, it has been a destination for Kyoto souvenirs.

KISHIMEN is a flat, wide noodle usually served with a soy sauce. KISHIMEN is actually a specialty of the Nagoya area.

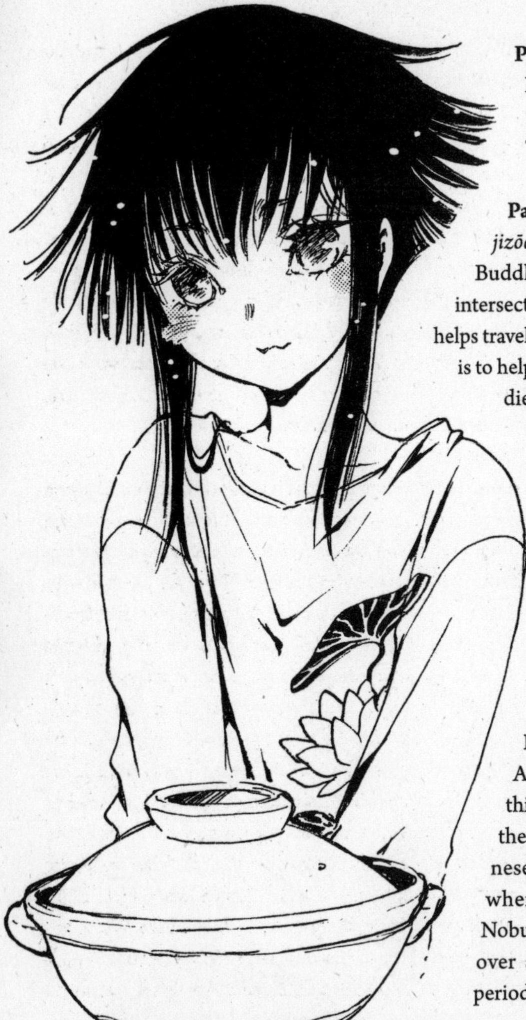

Page 147, *fuuka*: The name for Hana's *myoho* technique here is made up of kanji for "wind" and "flower."

Page 149: The sign in panel 5 says *jizōden*. *Jizō* are small statues of the Buddha that may be set on roads or intersections, because it is Buddha that helps travelers. But another of its functions is to help the souls of children who have died. A *jizōden* is a building that houses *jizō* statues.

Page 150, Sanjō Kawara: This is an area on the banks of the Kamogawa River where it intersects Sanjō Road. It was used for executions during the Japanese middle ages.

Page 157, Momoyama: The Azuchi-Momoyama period is a thirty-year span at the very end of the Warring States period of Japanese history, beginning in 1573, when several victories allowed Nobunaga Oda to consolidate power over an almost-unified Japan. The period carried through the shogunate

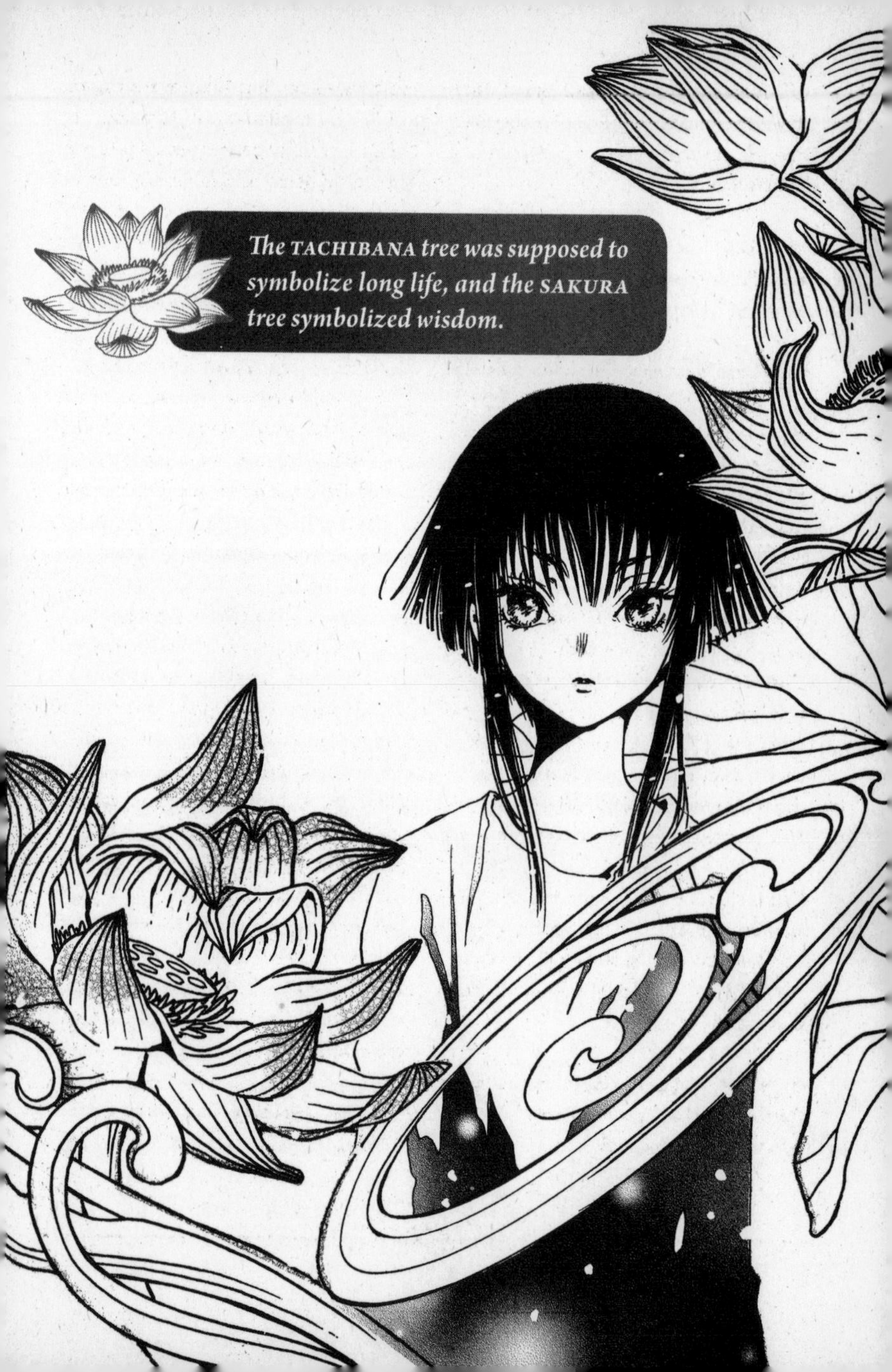
The TACHIBANA tree was supposed to symbolize long life, and the SAKURA tree symbolized wisdom.

of Hideyoshi Toyotomi and ended when Ieyasu Tokunaga founded his shogunate and set the stage for Japan's 265-year-long Edo period.

Page 161, "the origin of the sun": That's what the kanji for "Nihon" (Japan) mean. *Ni* is "sun." *Hon* is "origin."

Page 164: Nobunaga Oda was a powerful warlord who started with a small plot of land in central Japan and quickly expanded his territory with ruthless precision. In 1568, he captured the capital of Kyoto, and from there he fought militant Buddhist sects and rival *daimyo* lords in an effort to unite Japan under his rule. His unification efforts fell slightly short in 1582, when one of his top generals, Mitsuhide Akechi, suddenly turned on him and attacked while he was lightly guarded in Honnouji Temple in Kyoto. Histories tell that Nobunaga committed seppuku (ritual suicide) rather than be captured by his traitorous general, but reportedly, his body was never found.

Page 165: The Dairokutenmaoh is the demon king (*maoh*) of the sixth and highest level of the heavens (*dairokuten*). In Japanese, this being's name is often shortened to Tenma.

Page 169: Mitsuhide Akechi was a general during the Warring States period. He was one of three generals that Nobunaga Oda most relied on, but there were rumors of frequent insults toward Mitsuhide by Nobunaga. Many rumors persist as to why Mitsuhide betrayed Nobunaga, but no reason has ever been confirmed. After Nobunaga's death, Mitsuhide went to the emperor and received the rank of shogun, but only held it thirteen days before he died in battle against fellow general Hideyoshi Toyotomi—who sought revenge for Nobunaga's death. Although most historians agree that Mitsuhide died in battle, there is a rumor that he survived, became a priest named Tenkai, and lived many more years.

Page 170, "your right flank, Tachibana, and your left flank, Sakura": During the Heian period there was a garden where the emperor held important ceremonies and received high-ranking guests. A *tachibana* tree (which produces mandarin oranges) was planted in that garden to the emperor's right and a *sakura* tree (producing cherry blossoms) was planted to his left. The *tachibana* tree was supposed to symbolize long life, and the *sakura* tree symbolized wisdom. He also had troops on the right and left who stood as imperial guards, and they were also referred to as the right *tachibana* and the left *sakura*. Even today, troops on one's flanks are called "right *tachibana*" and "left *sakura*."

Page 172: *Hanakago* is a Japanese word meaning "flower basket."

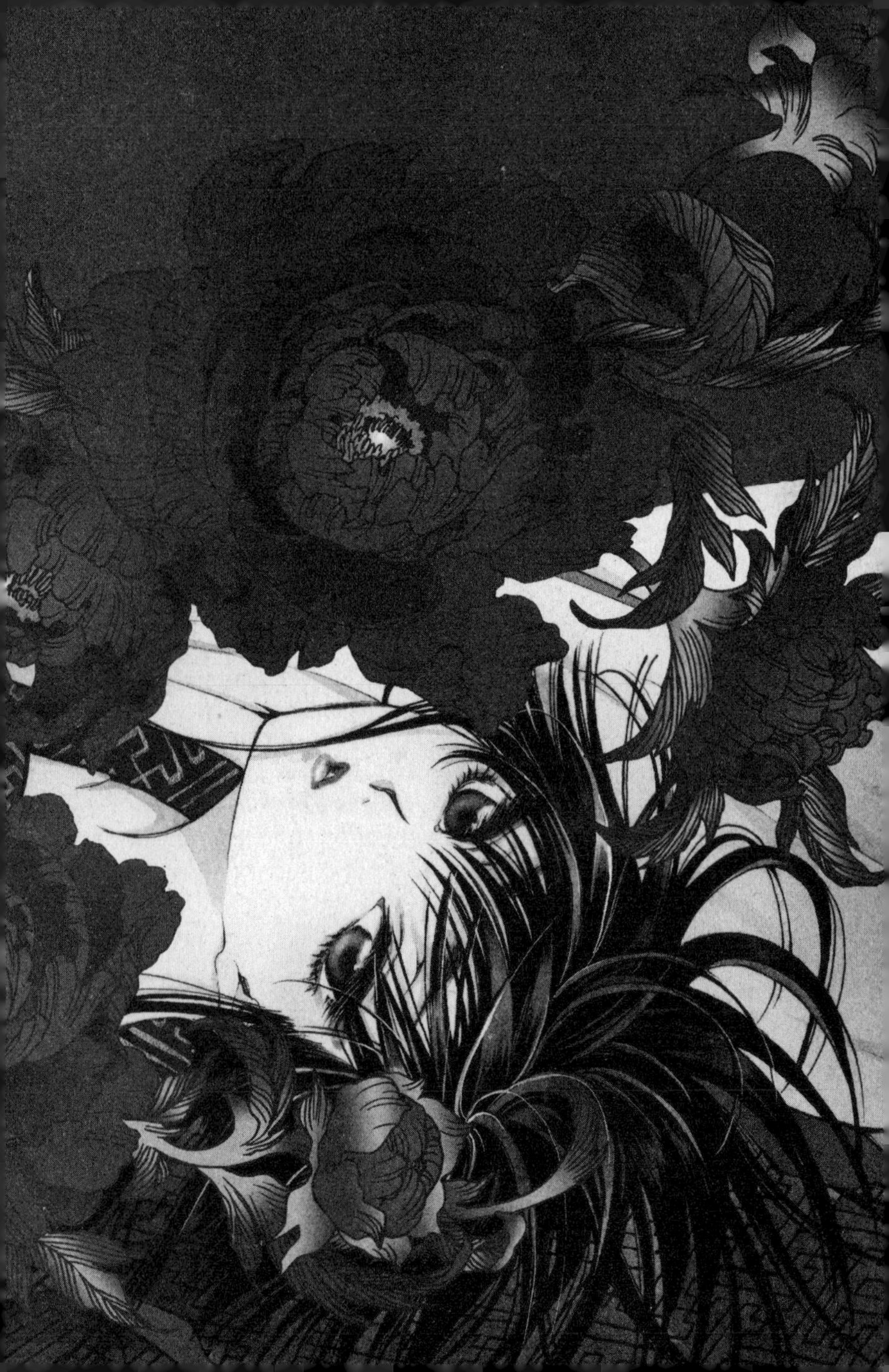

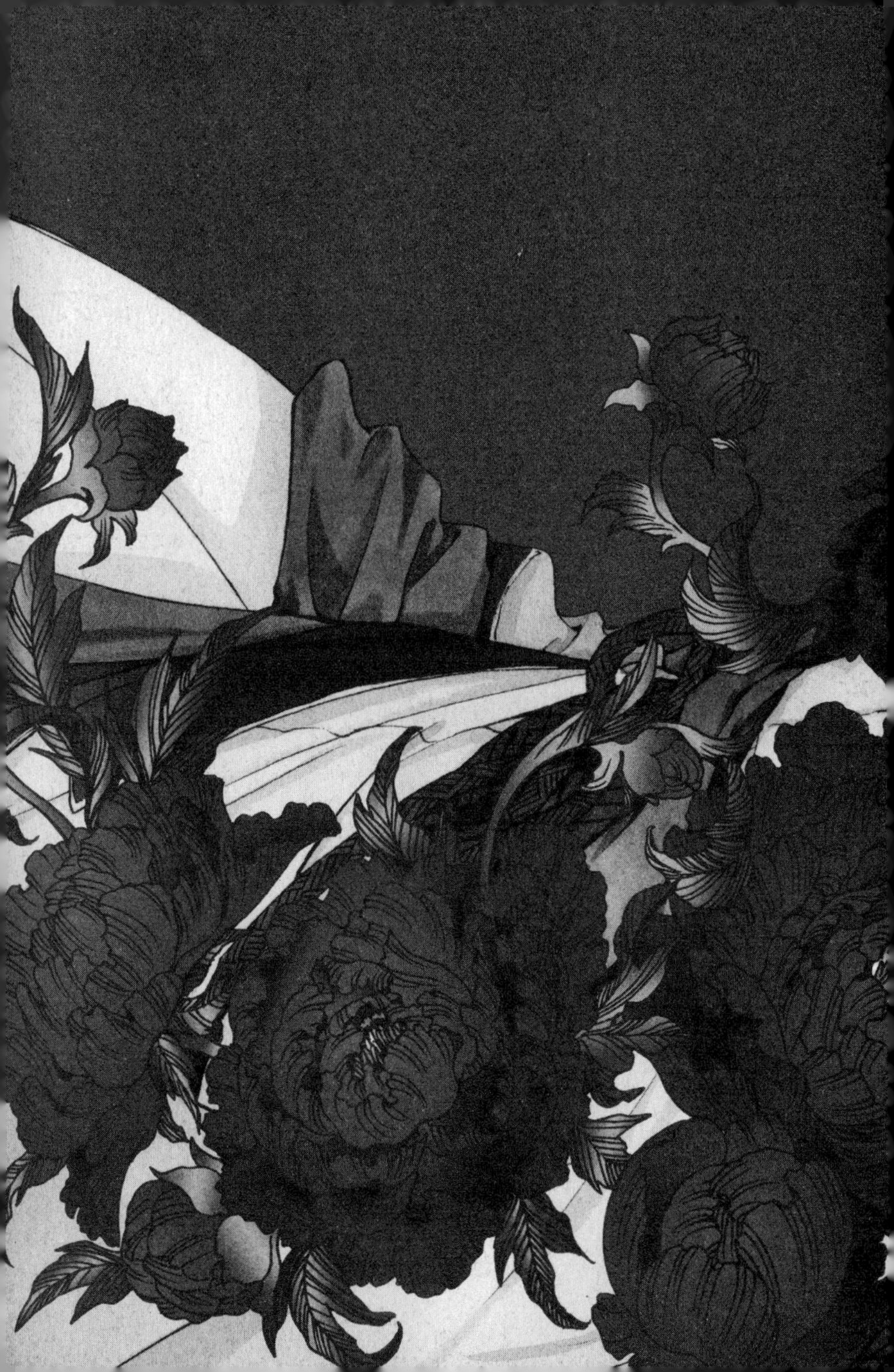

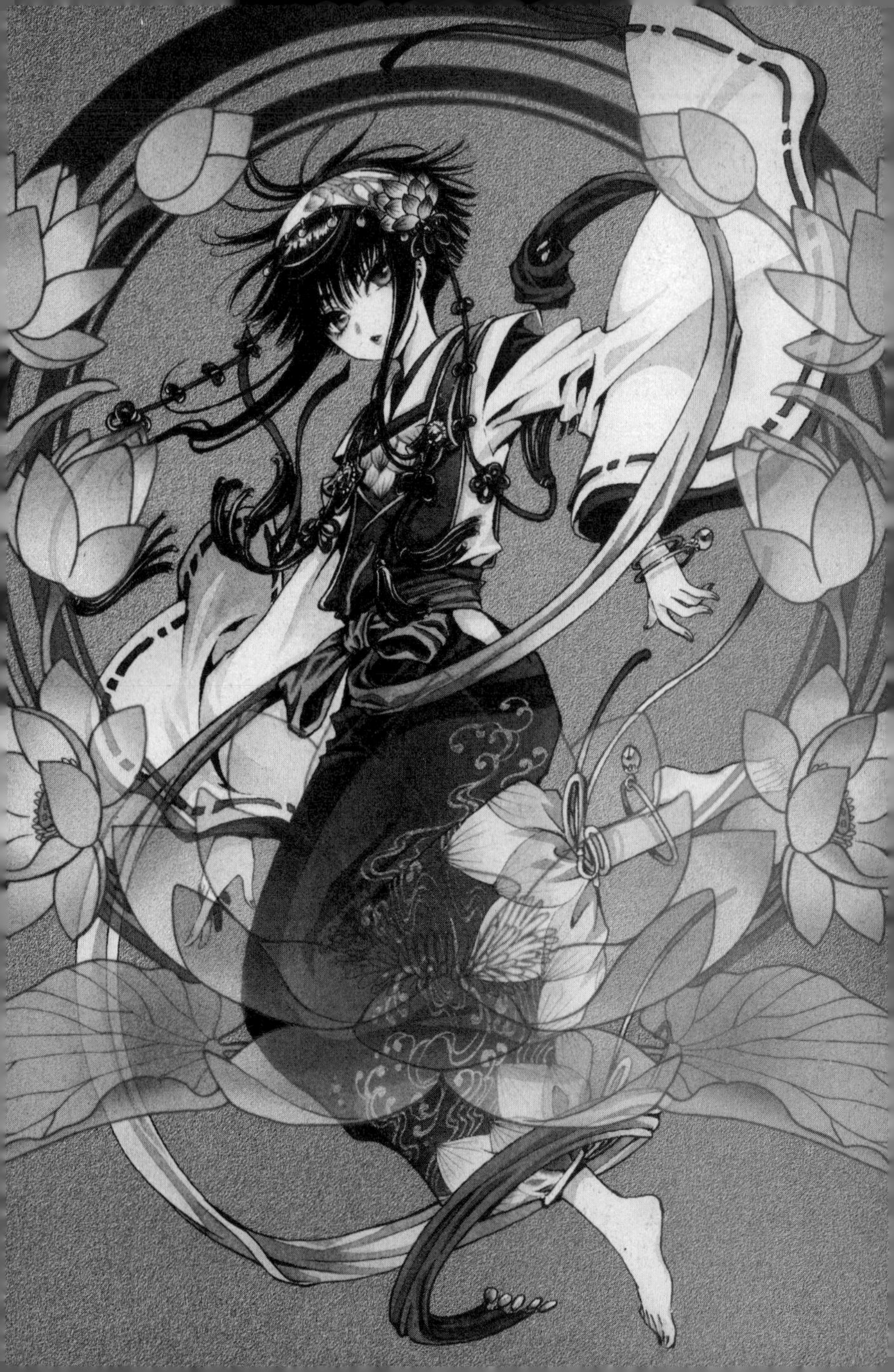

CLAMP オキモノ キモノ
Mokona's OKIMONO KIMONO

CLAMP artist Mokona loves the art of traditional Japanese kimono. In fact, she designs kimono and kimono accessories herself and shares her love in *Okimono Kimono*, a fun and lavishly illustrated book full of drawings and photographs, interviews (including an interview with Onuki Ami of the J-pop duo Puffy AmiYumi), and exclusive short manga stories from the CLAMP artists!

From the creators of such titles as *Clover*, *Chobits*, *Cardcaptor Sakura*, *Magic Knight Rayearth*, and *Tsubasa*, *Okimono Kimono* is now available in English for the first time ever!

ISBN 978-1-59582-456-1

$12.99

CLAMP

Chobits
ちょびっつ

BOOK 1

In near-future Japan, the hottest style for your personal computer, or "persocom," has the appearance of an attractive android! Hideki, a poor student trying to get into a Tokyo university, has neither money nor a girlfriend—then finds a persocom seemingly discarded in an alley. Hideki takes the cute, amnesiac robot home and names her "Chi."

But who is this strange new persocom in his life? Instead of having a digital assistant, Hideki finds himself having to teach Chi how to get along in the everyday world, even while he and his friends try to solve the mystery of her origins. Is she one of the urban-legendary *Chobits*—persocoms built to have the riskiest functions of all: real emotions and free will?

A crossover hit for both female and male readers, CLAMP's best-selling manga ever in America is finally available in omnibus form! Containing sixteen bonus color pages, *Chobits* Volume 1 begins an engaging, touching, exciting story.

ISBN 978-1-59582-451-6

$24.99

DARK
HORSE
MANGA
DarkHorse.com

AVAILABLE AT YOUR LOCAL COMICS SHOP OR BOOKSTORE
To find a comics shop in your area, call 1.888.266.4226. For more information or to order direct: •On the web: DarkHorse.com•E-mail: mailorder@darkhorse.com•Phone: 1.800.862.0052 Mon.–Fri. 9 AM to 5 PM Pacific Time.

Cardcaptor Sakura
カードキャプターさくら

Story and Art by

CLAMP

Fourth grader Sakura Kinomoto has found a strange book in her father's library—a book made by the wizard Clow to store dangerous spirits sealed within a set of magical cards. But when Sakura opens it up, there is nothing left inside but Kero-chan, the book's cute little guardian beast... who informs Sakura that since the Clow cards seem to have escaped while he was asleep, it's now her job to capture them!

With remastered image files straight from CLAMP, Dark Horse is proud to present *Cardcaptor Sakura* in omnibus form! Each book collects three volumes of the original twelve-volume series, and features thirty bonus color pages!

OMNIBUS BOOK ONE
ISBN 978-1-59582-522-3 $19.99

OMNIBUS BOOK TWO
ISBN 978-1-59582-591-9 $19.99

AVAILABLE AT YOUR LOCAL COMICS SHOP OR BOOKSTORE!

To find a comics shop in your area, call 1-888-266-4226

For more information or to order direct: • On the web: DarkHorse.com

E-mail: mailorder@darkhorse.com • Phone: 1-800-862-0052 Mon.–Fri. 9 AM to 5 PM Pacific Time

【 ⊥ ⋔ ⋏ ⋉ ⊑ ⋍ ー ⋂ ⋏ ⊢ 】
translucent

Can you see right through her?

By Kazuhiro Okamoto

Shizuka is an introverted girl dealing with schoolwork, boys, and a medical condition that has begun to turn her invisible! She finds support with Mamoru, a boy who is falling for Shizuka despite her condition, and with Keiko, a woman who suffers from the same illness and has finally turned *completely* invisible! *Translucent's* exploration of what people see, what people think they see, and what people wish to see in themselves and others, makes for an emotionally sensitive manga peppered with moments of surprising humor, heartbreak, and drama.

VOLUME 1
ISBN 978-1-59307-647-4

VOLUME 2
ISBN 978-1-59307-677-1

VOLUME 3
ISBN 978-1-59307-679-5

$9.99 Each!

Previews for *TRANSLUCENT* and other DARK HORSE MANGA titles can be found at darkhorse.com!

AVAILABLE AT YOUR LOCAL COMICS SHOP OR BOOKSTORE
To find a comics shop in your area, call 1-888-266-4226. For more information or to order direct: • On the web: darkhorse.com • E-mail: mailorder@darkhorse.com • Phone: 1-800-862-0052 Mon.–Fri. 9 AM to 5 PM Pacific Time.

DARK HORSE MANGA

BRIDE of the WATER GOD

When Soah's impoverished, desperate village decides to sacrifice her to the Water God Habaek to end a long drought, they believe that drowning one beautiful girl will save their entire community and bring much-needed rain. Not only is Soah surprised to be *rescued* by the Water God instead of killed; she never imagined she'd be a welcomed guest in Habaek's magical kingdom, where an exciting new life awaits her! Most surprising, however, is the Water God himself, and how very different he is from the monster Soah imagined . . .

Created by Mi-Kyung Yun, who received the "Best New Artist" award in 2004 from the esteemed *Dokja-manhwa-daesang* organization, *Bride of the Water God* was the top-selling *shoujo* manhwa in Korea in 2006!

Volume 1
ISBN 978-1-59307-849-2

Volume 2
ISBN 978-1-59307-883-6

Volume 3
ISBN 978-1-59582-305-2

Volume 4
ISBN 978-1-59582-378-6

Volume 5
ISBN 978-1-59582-445-5

Volume 6
ISBN 978-1-59582-605-3

Volume 7
ISBN 978-1-59582-668-8

Volume 8
ISBN 978-1-59582-687-9

Volume 9
ISBN 978-1-59582-688-6

$9.99 each

Previews for BRIDE OF THE WATER GOD and other DARK HORSE MANHWA titles can be found at darkhorse.com!

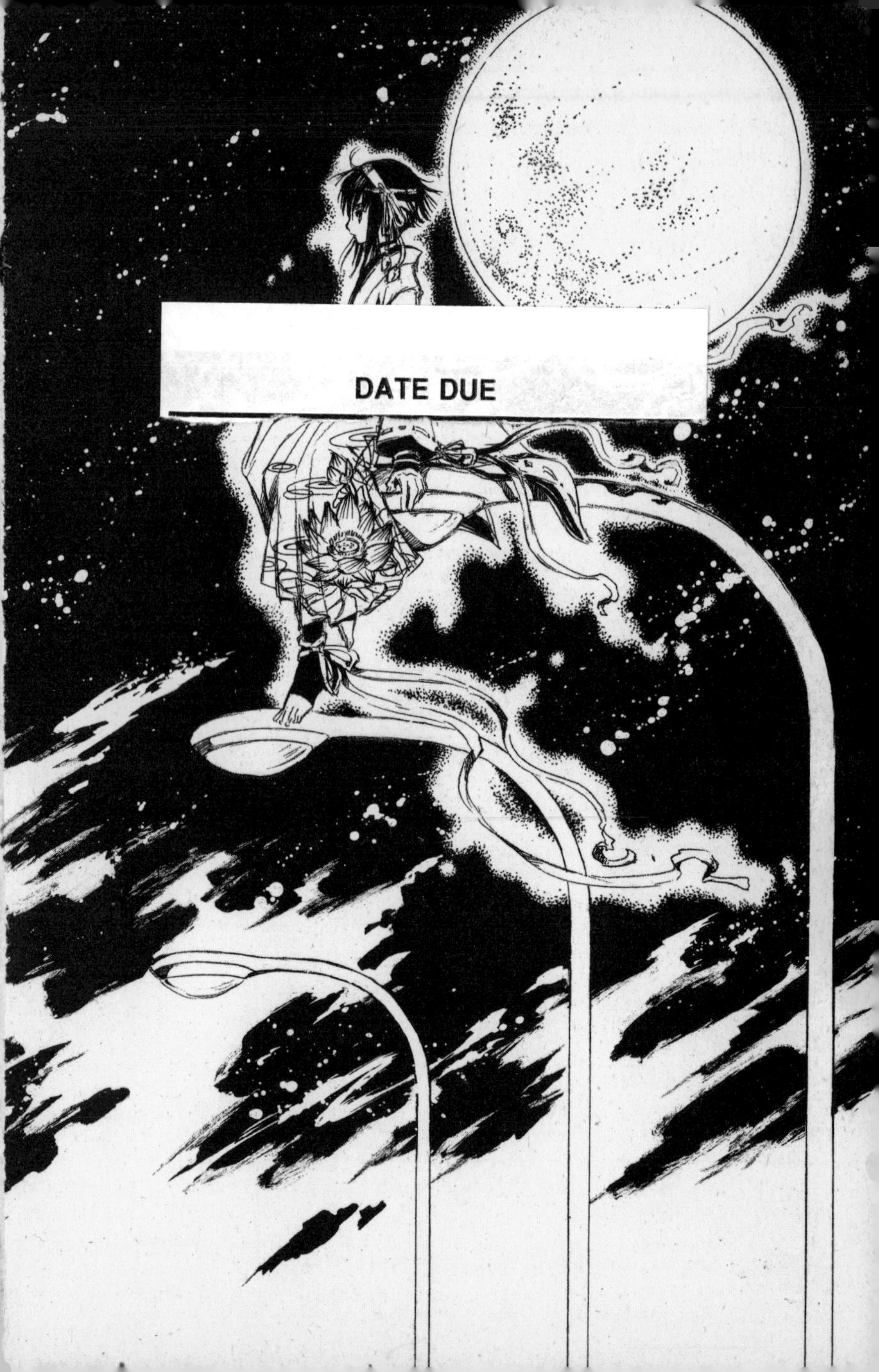